2014 | THE LITTLE DATA BOOK

THE WORLD BANK

Contents

Acknowledgments

The *Little Data Book 2014* was prepared by a team led by William Prince under the management of Neil Fantom and comprising Liu Cui, Federico Escaler, Mahyar Eshragh-Tabary, Juan Feng, Masako Hiraga, Wendy Huang, Bala Bhaskar Naidu Kalimili, Haruna Kashiwase, Buyant Erdene Khaltarkhuu, Elysee Kiti, Ibrahim Levent, Hiroko Maeda, Maurice Nsabimana, Evis Rucaj, Rubena Sukaj, Emi Suzuki, Maryna Taran, and Jomo Tariku working closely with other teams in the Development Data Group of the Development Economics Vice Presidency. The work was carried out under the management of Haishan Fu. Azita Amjadi coordinated all stages of production; Barton Matheson Willse & Worthington typeset the book. Staff from The World Bank's Publishing and Knowledge Division oversaw publication and dissemination of the book.

Foreword

The *Little Data Book 2014* is a pocket edition of *World Development Indicators 2014*. It is intended as a quick reference for users of the *World Development Indicators* database, book, and mobile app. The database, which covers more than 1,300 indicators and spans more than 50 years, is available at data.worldbank.org.

The 214 country tables in *The Little Data Book* present the latest available data for World Bank member countries and other economies with populations of more than 30,000. The 14 summary tables cover regional and income group aggregates.

For more information about these data or other World Bank data publications, visit our data Web site at data.worldbank.org, e-mail us at data@worldbank.org, call our data hotline 800 590 1906 or 202 473 7824, or fax us at 202 522 1498.

To order *World Development Indicators 2014,* visit the publications Web site at www.worldbank.org/publications, call 800 645 7247 or 703 661 1580, or fax 703 661 1501.

Data notes

The data in this book are for 1990, 2000, and 2012 or the most recent year unless otherwise noted in the table or the *Glossary*.

- Growth rates are proportional changes from the previous year unless otherwise noted.

- Regional aggregates include data for low- and middle-income economies only.

- Figures in italics indicate data for years or periods other than those specified.

Symbols used:

..	indicates that data are not available or that aggregates cannot be calculated because of missing data.
0 or 0.0	indicates zero or small enough that the number would round to zero at the displayed number of decimal places.
$	indicates current U.S. dollars.

Lettered notes on some country tables can be found in the *Notes* on page 232.

Data are shown for economies with populations greater than 30,000 or for smaller economies if they are members of the World Bank. The term *country* (used interchangeably with *economy*) does not imply political independence or official recognition by the World Bank but refers to any economy for which the authorities report separate social or economic statistics.

The selection of indicators in these pages includes some of those being used to monitor progress toward the Millennium Development Goals. For more information about the eight goals—halving poverty and increasing well-being by 2015—please see the other books in the *World Development Indicators 2014* family of products.

Regional tables

The country composition of regions is based on the World Bank's analytical regions and may differ from common geographic usage.

East Asia and Pacific
American Samoa, Cambodia, China, Fiji, Indonesia, Kiribati, Democratic People's Republic of Korea, Lao People's Democratic Republic, Malaysia, Marshall Islands, Federated States of Micronesia, Mongolia, Myanmar, Palau, Papua New Guinea, Philippines, Samoa, Solomon Islands, Thailand, Timor-Leste, Tonga, Tuvalu, Vanuatu, Vietnam

Europe and Central Asia
Albania, Armenia, Azerbaijan, Belarus, Bosnia and Herzegovina, Bulgaria, Georgia, Hungary, Kazakhstan, Kosovo, Kyrgyz Republic, Former Yugoslav Republic of Macedonia, Moldova, Montenegro, Romania, Serbia, Tajikistan, Turkey, Turkmenistan, Ukraine, Uzbekistan

Latin America and the Caribbean
Argentina, Belize, Bolivia, Brazil, Colombia, Costa Rica, Cuba, Dominica, Dominican Republic, Ecuador, El Salvador, Grenada, Guatemala, Guyana, Haiti, Honduras, Jamaica, Mexico, Nicaragua, Panama, Paraguay, Peru, St. Lucia, St. Vincent and the Grenadines, Suriname, República Bolivariana de Venezuela

Middle East and North Africa
Algeria, Djibouti, Arab Republic of Egypt, Islamic Republic of Iran, Iraq, Jordan, Lebanon, Libya, Morocco, Syrian Arab Republic, Tunisia, West Bank and Gaza, Republic of Yemen

South Asia
Afghanistan, Bangladesh, Bhutan, India, Maldives, Nepal, Pakistan, Sri Lanka

Sub-Saharan Africa
Angola, Benin, Botswana, Burkina Faso, Burundi, Cabo Verde, Cameroon, Central African Republic, Chad, Comoros, Democratic Republic of the Congo, Republic of Congo, Côte d'Ivoire, Eritrea, Ethiopia, Gabon, The Gambia, Ghana, Guinea, Guinea-Bissau, Kenya, Lesotho, Liberia, Madagascar, Malawi, Mali, Mauritania, Mauritius, Mozambique, Namibia, Niger, Nigeria, Rwanda, São Tomé and Príncipe, Senegal, Seychelles, Sierra Leone, Somalia, South Africa, South Sudan, Sudan, Swaziland, Tanzania, Togo, Uganda, Zambia, Zimbabwe

World

Population (millions)	7,043.9	Population growth (%)	1.1
Surface area (1,000 sq. km)	134,290	Population living below $1.25 a day (%)	..
GNI, Atlas ($ billions)	71,692.4	GNI per capita, Atlas ($)	10,178
GNI, PPP ($ billions)	85,986.8	GNI per capita, PPP ($)	12,207

	1990	2000	2012
People			
Share of poorest 20% in nat'l consumption/income (%)	..	..	..
Life expectancy at birth (years)	66	68	71
Total fertility rate (births per woman)	3.3	2.6	2.5
Adolescent fertility rate (births per 1,000 women 15-19)	65	57	45
Contraceptive prevalence (% of married women 15-49)	58	61	..
Births attended by skilled health staff (% of total)	..	60	65
Under-five mortality rate (per 1,000 live births)	90	75	48
Child malnutrition, underweight (% of under age 5)	24.9	20.6	15.1
Child immunization, measles (% of ages 12-23 mos.)	74	73	84
Primary completion rate, total (% of relevant age group)	81	82	91
Gross secondary enrollment, total (% of relevant age group)	50	60	71
Ratio of girls to boys in primary & secondary school (%)	86	92	97
HIV prevalence rate (% population of ages 15-49)	0.3	0.8	0.8
Environment			
Forests (1,000 sq. km)	41,608	40,761	40,184
Deforestation (avg. annual %, 1990-2000 and 2000-2010)		0.2	0.1
Freshwater use (% of internal resources)	..	8.4	9.2
Access to improved water source (% total pop.)	76	82	89
Access to improved sanitation facilities (% total pop.)	47	56	64
Energy use per capita (kilograms of oil equivalent)	1,665	1,650	1,890
Carbon dioxide emissions per capita (metric tons)	4.2	4.1	4.9
Electricity use per capita (kilowatt-hours)	2,121	2,385	3,044
Economy			
GDP ($ billions)	22,246	32,875	72,496
GDP growth (annual %)	2.9	4.3	2.4
GDP implicit price deflator (annual % growth)	8.0	5.1	3.2
Value added in agriculture (% of GDP)	6	4	3
Value added in industry (% of GDP)	33	29	27
Value added in services (% of GDP)	61	67	70
Exports of goods and services (% of GDP)	20	26	30
Imports of goods and services (% of GDP)	20	26	30
Gross capital formation (% of GDP)	25	23	22
Central government revenue (% of GDP)	..	25.4	23.0
Central government cash surplus/deficit (% of GDP)	..	-1.8	-5.3
States and markets			
Starting a business (days)	..	50	25
Stock market capitalization (% of GDP)	46.8	99.7	75.3
Military expenditures (% of GDP)	4.2	2.2	2.9
Mobile cellular subscriptions (per 100 people)	0.2	12.1	89.3
Individuals using the Internet (% of population)	0.0	6.8	35.5
Paved roads (% of total)	..	49.4	57.0
High-technology exports (% of manufactured exports)	18	24	18
Global links			
Merchandise trade (% of GDP)	32	40	51
Net barter terms of trade index (2000 = 100)	..	..	..
Total external debt stocks ($ millions)	..	..	..
Total debt service (% of exports)	..	..	..
Net migration (thousands)	..	..	..
Personal remittances received ($ billions)	..	..	..
Foreign direct investment, net inflows ($ billions)	196	1,319	1,510
Net official development assistance received ($ billions)	58	50	133

East Asia & Pacific

Population (millions)	1,991.6	Population growth (%)	0.7
Surface area (1,000 sq. km)	16,302	Population living below $1.25 a day (%)	12.5
GNI, Atlas ($ billions)	9,727.7	GNI per capita, Atlas ($)	4,884
GNI, PPP ($ billions)	15,451.5	GNI per capita, PPP ($)	7,758

	1990	2000	2012
People			
Share of poorest 20% in nat'l consumption/income (%)	..	..	..
Life expectancy at birth (years)	68	71	74
Total fertility rate (births per woman)	2.7	1.8	1.9
Adolescent fertility rate (births per 1,000 women 15-19)	25	19	20
Contraceptive prevalence (% of married women 15-49)	75	78	..
Births attended by skilled health staff (% of total)	84	85	91
Under-five mortality rate (per 1,000 live births)	59	42	21
Child malnutrition, underweight (% of under age 5)	20.1	11.2	5.3
Child immunization, measles (% of ages 12-23 mos.)	90	83	94
Primary completion rate, total (% of relevant age group)	100	97	..
Gross secondary enrollment, total (% of relevant age group)	39	60	78
Ratio of girls to boys in primary & secondary school (%)	88	98	102
HIV prevalence rate (% population of ages 15-49)	..	..	..
Environment			
Forests (1,000 sq. km)	4,602	4,524	4,712
Deforestation (avg. annual %, 1990-2000 and 2000-2010)		0.1	-0.4
Freshwater use (% of internal resources)	..	9.5	10.9
Access to improved water source (% total pop.)	68	80	91
Access to improved sanitation facilities (% total pop.)	30	49	67
Energy use per capita (kilograms of oil equivalent)	712	858	1,671
Carbon dioxide emissions per capita (metric tons)	1.9	2.3	4.9
Electricity use per capita (kilowatt-hours)	461	876	2,582
Economy			
GDP ($ billions)	668	1,723	10,330
GDP growth (annual %)	5.6	7.5	7.5
GDP implicit price deflator (annual % growth)	6.7	3.1	1.9
Value added in agriculture (% of GDP)	25	15	11
Value added in industry (% of GDP)	40	45	44
Value added in services (% of GDP)	35	40	45
Exports of goods and services (% of GDP)	21	33	34
Imports of goods and services (% of GDP)	20	29	31
Gross capital formation (% of GDP)	35	32	44
Central government revenue (% of GDP)	..	..	13.1
Central government cash surplus/deficit (% of GDP)	..	..	..
States and markets			
Starting a business (days)	..	53	40
Stock market capitalization (% of GDP)	16.4	46.9	51.5
Military expenditures (% of GDP)	2.3	1.8	1.9
Mobile cellular subscriptions (per 100 people)	0.0	5.7	88.9
Individuals using the Internet (% of population)	0.0	1.9	36.2
Paved roads (% of total)	..	14.4	47.6
High-technology exports (% of manufactured exports)	17	32	26
Global links			
Merchandise trade (% of GDP)	47	59	54
Net barter terms of trade index (2000 = 100)	..	..	..
Total external debt stocks ($ billions)	234	497	1,412
Total debt service (% of exports)	17.7	11.4	4.5
Net migration (thousands)	-2,992	-4,496	-3,061
Personal remittances received ($ billions)	3.1	16.7	78.3
Foreign direct investment, net inflows ($ billions)	10	45	314
Net official development assistance received ($ billions)	7.7	8.6	8.8

Europe & Central Asia

Population (millions)	270.8	Population growth (%)		0.7
Surface area (1,000 sq. km)	6,479	Population living below $1.25 a day (%)		0.7
GNI, Atlas ($ billions)	1,804.4	GNI per capita, Atlas ($)		6,664
GNI, PPP ($ billions)	3,234.8	GNI per capita, PPP ($)		11,946

	1990	2000	2012
People			
Share of poorest 20% in nat'l consumption/income (%)	..	..	..
Life expectancy at birth (years)	68	69	72
Total fertility rate (births per woman)	2.6	1.9	2.0
Adolescent fertility rate (births per 1,000 women 15-19)	56	40	31
Contraceptive prevalence (% of married women 15-49)	..	64	..
Births attended by skilled health staff (% of total)	..	90	96
Under-five mortality rate (per 1,000 live births)	56	40	22
Child malnutrition, underweight (% of under age 5)	12.2	5.2	1.8
Child immunization, measles (% of ages 12-23 mos.)	81	92	94
Primary completion rate, total (% of relevant age group)	95	93	99
Gross secondary enrollment, total (% of relevant age group)	85	84	92
Ratio of girls to boys in primary & secondary school (%)	94	95	97
HIV prevalence rate (% population of ages 15-49)	..	..	..
Environment			
Forests (1,000 sq. km)	612	628	662
Deforestation (avg. annual %, 1990-2000 and 2000-2010)		-0.3	-0.5
Freshwater use (% of internal resources)	..	39.6	34.8
Access to improved water source (% total pop.)	88	92	95
Access to improved sanitation facilities (% total pop.)	87	89	94
Energy use per capita (kilograms of oil equivalent)	2,870	1,812	2,078
Carbon dioxide emissions per capita (metric tons)	6.8	4.6	5.3
Electricity use per capita (kilowatt-hours)	3,178	2,286	2,951
Economy			
GDP ($ billions)	446	478	1,865
GDP growth (annual %)	-0.1	5.9	1.8
GDP implicit price deflator (annual % growth)	13.6	23.1	4.8
Value added in agriculture (% of GDP)	20	12	9
Value added in industry (% of GDP)	37	33	31
Value added in services (% of GDP)	43	55	60
Exports of goods and services (% of GDP)	20	37	36
Imports of goods and services (% of GDP)	24	40	40
Gross capital formation (% of GDP)	26	21	22
Central government revenue (% of GDP)	..	..	34.2
Central government cash surplus/deficit (% of GDP)	..	..	-0.5
States and markets			
Starting a business (days)	..	44	12
Stock market capitalization (% of GDP)	..	19.9	25.6
Military expenditures (% of GDP)	3.6	3.1	2.0
Mobile cellular subscriptions (per 100 people)	0.0	10.0	108.5
Individuals using the Internet (% of population)	0.0	2.2	43.3
Paved roads (% of total)	..	81.2	78.3
High-technology exports (% of manufactured exports)	..	10	8
Global links			
Merchandise trade (% of GDP)	48	56	73
Net barter terms of trade index (2000 = 100)	..	..	..
Total external debt stocks ($ billions)	101	234	1,150
Total debt service (% of exports)	..	26.1	32.9
Net migration (thousands)	-5,578	-2,865	-661
Personal remittances received ($ billions)	3.2	8.2	38.7
Foreign direct investment, net inflows ($ billions)	1.2	9.1	65.2
Net official development assistance received ($ billions)	1.4	4.5	10.0

Latin America & Caribbean

Population (millions)	581.4	Population growth (%)	1.2
Surface area (1,000 sq. km)	19,461	Population living below $1.25 a day (%)	5.5
GNI, Atlas ($ billions)	5,273.2	GNI per capita, Atlas ($)	9,070
GNI, PPP ($ billions)	6,852.9	GNI per capita, PPP ($)	11,787

	1990	2000	2012
People			
Share of poorest 20% in nat'l consumption/income (%)	..	..	..
Life expectancy at birth (years)	68	71	74
Total fertility rate (births per woman)	3.2	2.7	2.2
Adolescent fertility rate (births per 1,000 women 15-19)	85	84	69
Contraceptive prevalence (% of married women 15-49)	59	..	..
Births attended by skilled health staff (% of total)	75	85	..
Under-five mortality rate (per 1,000 live births)	55	33	19
Child malnutrition, underweight (% of under age 5)	7.6	4.9	2.9
Child immunization, measles (% of ages 12-23 mos.)	75	94	95
Primary completion rate, total (% of relevant age group)	83	97	102
Gross secondary enrollment, total (% of relevant age group)	60	83	90
Ratio of girls to boys in primary & secondary school (%)	101	101	102
HIV prevalence rate (% population of ages 15-49)	..	..	..
Environment			
Forests (1,000 sq. km)	10,227	9,727	9,240
Deforestation (avg. annual %, 1990-2000 and 2000-2010)		0.5	0.5
Freshwater use (% of internal resources)	..	2.0	2.0
Access to improved water source (% total pop.)	85	90	94
Access to improved sanitation facilities (% total pop.)	66	74	81
Energy use per capita (kilograms of oil equivalent)	1,041	1,107	1,292
Carbon dioxide emissions per capita (metric tons)	2.2	2.4	2.7
Electricity use per capita (kilowatt-hours)	1,161	1,534	1,985
Economy			
GDP ($ billions)	1,080	2,070	5,344
GDP growth (annual %)	0.5	4.1	2.9
GDP implicit price deflator (annual % growth)	25.1	7.8	4.1
Value added in agriculture (% of GDP)	9	5	5
Value added in industry (% of GDP)	35	32	32
Value added in services (% of GDP)	57	62	63
Exports of goods and services (% of GDP)	17	20	24
Imports of goods and services (% of GDP)	16	20	26
Gross capital formation (% of GDP)	20	20	21
Central government revenue (% of GDP)	18.7	16.3	..
Central government cash surplus/deficit (% of GDP)	-2.7	-1.4	..
States and markets			
Starting a business (days)	..	82	41
Stock market capitalization (% of GDP)	6.5	28.4	43.3
Military expenditures (% of GDP)	3.6	1.2	1.3
Mobile cellular subscriptions (per 100 people)	0.0	11.7	108.1
Individuals using the Internet (% of population)	0.0	3.4	42.7
Paved roads (% of total)	..	26.3	26.0
High-technology exports (% of manufactured exports)	7	17	12
Global links			
Merchandise trade (% of GDP)	22	33	38
Net barter terms of trade index (2000 = 100)	..	..	..
Total external debt stocks ($ billions)	420	714	1,258
Total debt service (% of exports)	24.2	39.5	15.0
Net migration (thousands)	-2,906	-6,019	-3,017
Personal remittances received ($ billions)	5.7	20.1	59.5
Foreign direct investment, net inflows ($ billions)	7	74	150
Net official development assistance received ($ billions)	4.9	4.8	10.1

Middle East & North Africa

Population (millions)	339.6	Population growth (%)	1.7
Surface area (1,000 sq. km)	8,775	Population living below $1.25 a day (%)	2.4
GNI, Atlas ($ billions)	1,112.7	GNI per capita, Atlas ($)	3,450
GNI, PPP ($ billions)	2,277.5	GNI per capita, PPP ($)	7,062

	1990	2000	2012
People			
Share of poorest 20% in nat'l consumption/income (%)	..	..	..
Life expectancy at birth (years)	65	69	71
Total fertility rate (births per woman)	4.8	3.2	2.8
Adolescent fertility rate (births per 1,000 women 15-19)	71	45	37
Contraceptive prevalence (% of married women 15-49)	43	61	..
Births attended by skilled health staff (% of total)	..	78	..
Under-five mortality rate (per 1,000 live births)	68	45	26
Child malnutrition, underweight (% of under age 5)	11.9	8.9	6.2
Child immunization, measles (% of ages 12-23 mos.)	83	90	88
Primary completion rate, total (% of relevant age group)	76	83	91
Gross secondary enrollment, total (% of relevant age group)	56	68	75
Ratio of girls to boys in primary & secondary school (%)	80	89	93
HIV prevalence rate (% population of ages 15-49)	0.1	0.1	0.1
Environment			
Forests (1,000 sq. km)	207	208	211
Deforestation (avg. annual %, 1990-2000 and 2000-2010)		-0.1	-0.1
Freshwater use (% of internal resources)	..	120.3	122.1
Access to improved water source (% total pop.)	87	88	90
Access to improved sanitation facilities (% total pop.)	70	79	88
Energy use per capita (kilograms of oil equivalent)	825	1,027	1,376
Carbon dioxide emissions per capita (metric tons)	2.5	3.2	3.9
Electricity use per capita (kilowatt-hours)	731	1,066	1,696
Economy			
GDP ($ billions)	283	436	1,663
GDP growth (annual %)	7.6	3.8	1.9
GDP implicit price deflator (annual % growth)	17.0	4.1	5.6
Value added in agriculture (% of GDP)	18	13	..
Value added in industry (% of GDP)	33	38	..
Value added in services (% of GDP)	49	49	..
Exports of goods and services (% of GDP)	23	30	..
Imports of goods and services (% of GDP)	33	26	..
Gross capital formation (% of GDP)	29	25	..
Central government revenue (% of GDP)	..	26.2	29.9
Central government cash surplus/deficit (% of GDP)	..	-2.7	-2.5
States and markets			
Starting a business (days)	..	42	21
Stock market capitalization (% of GDP)	..	19.7	28.9
Military expenditures (% of GDP)	2.9	3.5	2.7
Mobile cellular subscriptions (per 100 people)	0.0	2.2	95.1
Individuals using the Internet (% of population)	0.0	0.8	30.7
Paved roads (% of total)	..	73.5	76.7
High-technology exports (% of manufactured exports)	..	3	2
Global links			
Merchandise trade (% of GDP)	42	43	48
Net barter terms of trade index (2000 = 100)	..	..	..
Total external debt stocks ($ billions)	137	144	177
Total debt service (% of exports)	..	14.2	3.9
Net migration (thousands)	-3,091	-1,989	-1,632
Personal remittances received ($ billions)	9.6	11.5	39.0
Foreign direct investment, net inflows ($ billions)	0.7	3.9	22.7
Net official development assistance received ($ billions)	11.7	4.6	13.9

South Asia

Population (millions)	1,649.2	Population growth (%)		1.3
Surface area (1,000 sq. km)	5,131	Population living below $1.25 a day (%)		31.0
GNI, Atlas ($ billions)	2,370.1	GNI per capita, Atlas ($)		1,437
GNI, PPP ($ billions)	5,777.6	GNI per capita, PPP ($)		3,503

	1990	2000	2012
People			
Share of poorest 20% in nat'l consumption/income (%)	..	..	..
Life expectancy at birth (years)	59	63	67
Total fertility rate (births per woman)	4.2	3.3	2.6
Adolescent fertility rate (births per 1,000 women 15-19)	111	81	39
Contraceptive prevalence (% of married women 15-49)	41	45	51
Births attended by skilled health staff (% of total)	..	36	48
Under-five mortality rate (per 1,000 live births)	129	94	60
Child malnutrition, underweight (% of under age 5)	51.9	42.7	32.2
Child immunization, measles (% of ages 12-23 mos.)	56	60	77
Primary completion rate, total (% of relevant age group)	62	67	88
Gross secondary enrollment, total (% of relevant age group)	35	44	59
Ratio of girls to boys in primary & secondary school (%)	68	80	95
HIV prevalence rate (% population of ages 15-49)	0.1	0.3	0.3
Environment			
Forests (1,000 sq. km)	795	794	818
Deforestation (avg. annual %, 1990-2000 and 2000-2010)		0.0	-0.3
Freshwater use (% of internal resources)	42.8	45.9	51.6
Access to improved water source (% total pop.)	71	80	91
Access to improved sanitation facilities (% total pop.)	21	29	40
Energy use per capita (kilograms of oil equivalent)	342	409	555
Carbon dioxide emissions per capita (metric tons)	0.7	1.0	1.4
Electricity use per capita (kilowatt-hours)	243	352	605
Economy			
GDP ($ billions)	411	623	2,303
GDP growth (annual %)	5.4	4.1	4.9
GDP implicit price deflator (annual % growth)	8.6	4.1	6.9
Value added in agriculture (% of GDP)	29	24	18
Value added in industry (% of GDP)	26	26	26
Value added in services (% of GDP)	45	51	56
Exports of goods and services (% of GDP)	8	14	23
Imports of goods and services (% of GDP)	11	15	30
Gross capital formation (% of GDP)	24	23	32
Central government revenue (% of GDP)	13.2	11.9	12.5
Central government cash surplus/deficit (% of GDP)	-3.3	-3.9	-4.3
States and markets			
Starting a business (days)	..	47	16
Stock market capitalization (% of GDP)	10.5	25.5	59.1
Military expenditures (% of GDP)	3.3	3.0	2.4
Mobile cellular subscriptions (per 100 people)	0.0	0.3	68.9
Individuals using the Internet (% of population)	0.0	0.5	11.6
Paved roads (% of total)	..	57.0	45.1
High-technology exports (% of manufactured exports)	3	5	6
Global links			
Merchandise trade (% of GDP)	16	23	42
Net barter terms of trade index (2000 = 100)	..	..	..
Total external debt stocks ($ billions)	126	163	501
Total debt service (% of exports)	31.6	17.5	7.3
Net migration (thousands)	500	-6,243	-7,076
Personal remittances received ($ billions)	6	17	108
Foreign direct investment, net inflows ($ billions)	0.5	4.4	27.4
Net official development assistance received ($ billions)	6.0	4.1	14.2

Sub-Saharan Africa

Population (millions)	911.5	Population growth (%)		2.7
Surface area (1,000 sq. km)	24,262	Population living below $1.25 a day (%)		48.5
GNI, Atlas ($ billions)	1,230.2	GNI per capita, Atlas ($)		1,350
GNI, PPP ($ billions)	2,030.0	GNI per capita, PPP ($)		2,227

	1990	2000	2012
People			
Share of poorest 20% in nat'l consumption/income (%)	..	..	..
Life expectancy at birth (years)	50	50	56
Total fertility rate (births per woman)	6.4	5.8	5.1
Adolescent fertility rate (births per 1,000 women 15–19)	136	127	108
Contraceptive prevalence (% of married women 15–49)	16	22	24
Births attended by skilled health staff (% of total)	..	42	46
Under-five mortality rate (per 1,000 live births)	177	155	98
Child malnutrition, underweight (% of under age 5)	29.6	25.3	20.8
Child immunization, measles (% of ages 12–23 mos.)	57	52	72
Primary completion rate, total (% of relevant age group)	52	54	69
Gross secondary enrollment, total (% of relevant age group)	23	26	41
Ratio of girls to boys in primary & secondary school (%)	81	84	90
HIV prevalence rate (% population of ages 15–49)	2.2	5.8	4.7
Environment			
Forests (1,000 sq. km)	7,406	6,983	6,606
Deforestation (avg. annual %, 1990–2000 and 2000–2010)		0.5	0.5
Freshwater use (% of internal resources)	..	3.2	3.2
Access to improved water source (% total pop.)	48	55	64
Access to improved sanitation facilities (% total pop.)	24	26	30
Energy use per capita (kilograms of oil equivalent)	698	671	681
Carbon dioxide emissions per capita (metric tons)	0.9	0.8	0.8
Electricity use per capita (kilowatt-hours)	537	523	535
Economy			
GDP ($ billions)	303	342	1,290
GDP growth (annual %)	1.3	3.5	4.3
GDP implicit price deflator (annual % growth)	10.6	6.2	5.6
Value added in agriculture (% of GDP)	21	17	16
Value added in industry (% of GDP)	34	34	31
Value added in services (% of GDP)	45	49	53
Exports of goods and services (% of GDP)	26	34	35
Imports of goods and services (% of GDP)	23	29	35
Gross capital formation (% of GDP)	17	16	20
Central government revenue (% of GDP)	..	..	..
Central government cash surplus/deficit (% of GDP)	..	..	..
States and markets			
Starting a business (days)	..	58	27
Stock market capitalization (% of GDP)	52.9	89.5	83.8
Military expenditures (% of GDP)	49.3	2.0	28.9
Mobile cellular subscriptions (per 100 people)	0.0	1.7	59.3
Individuals using the Internet (% of population)	0.0	0.5	14.8
Paved roads (% of total)	..	18.1	15.6
High-technology exports (% of manufactured exports)	..	4	4
Global links			
Merchandise trade (% of GDP)	42	51	62
Net barter terms of trade index (2000 = 100)	..	..	..
Total external debt stocks ($ billions)	176	213	331
Total debt service (% of exports)	..	11.8	4.5
Net migration (thousands)	728	-865	-1,545
Personal remittances received ($ billions)	1.8	4.8	26.7
Foreign direct investment, net inflows ($ billions)	1.2	6.6	37.4
Net official development assistance received ($ billions)	17.8	13.0	46.3

Income group tables

For operational and analytical purposes the World Bank's main criterion for classifying economies is gross national income (GNI) per capita. Each economy in *The Little Data Book* is classified as low income, middle income, or high income. Low- and middle-income economies are sometimes referred to as developing economies. The use of the term is convenient; it is not intended to imply that all economies in the group are experiencing similar development or that other economies have reached a preferred or final stage of development. Classification by income does not necessarily reflect development status. Note: Classifications are fixed during the World Bank's fiscal year (ending on June 30), thus countries remain in the categories in which they are classified irrespective of any revisions to their per capita income data.

Low-income economies are those with a GNI per capita of $1,035 or less in 2012.

Middle-income economies are those with a GNI per capita of more than $1,035 but less than $12,616. Lower-middle-income and upper-middle-income economies are separated at a GNI per capita of $4,085.

High-income economies are those with a GNI per capita of $12,616 or more.

Euro area includes the member states of the Economic and Monetary Union of the European Union that have adopted the euro as their currency: Austria, Belgium, Cyprus, Estonia, Finland, France, Germany, Greece, Ireland, Italy, Latvia, Luxembourg, Malta, Netherlands, Portugal, Slovak Republic, Slovenia, and Spain.

Low income

Population (millions)	846.5	Population growth (%)	2.3
Surface area (1,000 sq. km)	16,198	Population living below $1.25 a day (%)	48.3
GNI, Atlas ($ billions)	499.4	GNI per capita, Atlas ($)	590
GNI, PPP ($ billions)	1,171.1	GNI per capita, PPP ($)	1,383

	1990	2000	2012
People			
Share of poorest 20% in nat'l consumption/income (%)	..	..	..
Life expectancy at birth (years)	53	56	62
Total fertility rate (births per woman)	5.7	4.9	4.1
Adolescent fertility rate (births per 1,000 women 15–19)	126	112	93
Contraceptive prevalence (% of married women 15–49)	24	32	37
Births attended by skilled health staff (% of total)	..	33	47
Under-five mortality rate (per 1,000 live births)	166	134	82
Child malnutrition, underweight (% of under age 5)	39.9	30.9	21.8
Child immunization, measles (% of ages 12–23 mos.)	57	59	80
Primary completion rate, total (% of relevant age group)	46	51	67
Gross secondary enrollment, total (% of relevant age group)	21	31	43
Ratio of girls to boys in primary & secondary school (%)	78	86	93
HIV prevalence rate (% population of ages 15–49)	1.8	3.2	2.3
Environment			
Forests (1,000 sq. km)	4,737	4,424	4,277
Deforestation (avg. annual %, 1990–2000 and 2000–2010)		0.6	0.6
Freshwater use (% of internal resources)	..	3.6	4.4
Access to improved water source (% total pop.)	52	58	69
Access to improved sanitation facilities (% total pop.)	19	30	37
Energy use per capita (kilograms of oil equivalent)	396	332	360
Carbon dioxide emissions per capita (metric tons)	0.7	0.3	0.3
Electricity use per capita (kilowatt-hours)	222	171	233
Economy			
GDP ($ billions)	143	163	506
GDP growth (annual %)	2.7	3.2	6.3
GDP implicit price deflator (annual % growth)	9.3	5.7	6.1
Value added in agriculture (% of GDP)	38	34	28
Value added in industry (% of GDP)	19	21	24
Value added in services (% of GDP)	43	45	48
Exports of goods and services (% of GDP)	13	18	25
Imports of goods and services (% of GDP)	22	26	42
Gross capital formation (% of GDP)	18	19	28
Central government revenue (% of GDP)	..	11.6	14.5
Central government cash surplus/deficit (% of GDP)	..	..	-2.0
States and markets			
Starting a business (days)	..	60	29
Stock market capitalization (% of GDP)	..	..	..
Military expenditures (% of GDP)	2.7	2.2	1.7
Mobile cellular subscriptions (per 100 people)	0.0	0.3	47.2
Individuals using the Internet (% of population)	0.0	0.1	6.2
Paved roads (% of total)	..	14.4	20.6
High-technology exports (% of manufactured exports)	..	4	..
Global links			
Merchandise trade (% of GDP)	28	38	55
Net barter terms of trade index (2000 = 100)	..	..	..
Total external debt stocks ($ billions)	89	110	134
Total debt service (% of exports)	25.4	10.9	4.8
Net migration (thousands)	493	-4,899	-3,647
Personal remittances received ($ billions)	1.4	4.1	30.2
Foreign direct investment, net inflows ($ billions)	0.6	2.4	24.3
Net official development assistance received ($ billions)	14.2	10.4	41.4

Middle income

Population (millions)	4,897.6	Population growth (%)		1.1
Surface area (1,000 sq. km)	64,212	Population living below $1.25 a day (%)		18.0
GNI, Atlas ($ billions)	21,404.7	GNI per capita, Atlas ($)		4,370
GNI, PPP ($ billions)	35,099.0	GNI per capita, PPP ($)		7,167

	1990	2000	2012
People			
Share of poorest 20% in nat'l consumption/income (%)	..	..	..
Life expectancy at birth (years)	65	67	70
Total fertility rate (births per woman)	3.4	2.6	2.4
Adolescent fertility rate (births per 1,000 women 15-19)	64	54	40
Contraceptive prevalence (% of married women 15-49)	60	63	..
Births attended by skilled health staff (% of total)	..	65	69
Under-five mortality rate (per 1,000 live births)	87	71	45
Child malnutrition, underweight (% of under age 5)	26.0	21.4	15.7
Child immunization, measles (% of ages 12-23 mos.)	75	73	84
Primary completion rate, total (% of relevant age group)	83	85	94
Gross secondary enrollment, total (% of relevant age group)	44	57	71
Ratio of girls to boys in primary & secondary school (%)	84	91	98
HIV prevalence rate (% population of ages 15-49)	..	..	..
Environment			
Forests (1,000 sq. km)	19,112	18,441	17,971
Deforestation (avg. annual %, 1990-2000 and 2000-2010)		0.3	0.1
Freshwater use (% of internal resources)	..	10.1	11.3
Access to improved water source (% total pop.)	73	82	90
Access to improved sanitation facilities (% total pop.)	37	49	60
Energy use per capita (kilograms of oil equivalent)	820	849	1,281
Carbon dioxide emissions per capita (metric tons)	2.0	2.2	3.5
Electricity use per capita (kilowatt-hours)	708	921	1,816
Economy			
GDP ($ billions)	3,031	5,511	22,258
GDP growth (annual %)	2.4	5.3	4.9
GDP implicit price deflator (annual % growth)	12.9	8.8	4.3
Value added in agriculture (% of GDP)	19	13	10
Value added in industry (% of GDP)	36	37	36
Value added in services (% of GDP)	44	50	54
Exports of goods and services (% of GDP)	19	28	30
Imports of goods and services (% of GDP)	19	26	31
Gross capital formation (% of GDP)	27	25	32
Central government revenue (% of GDP)	..	..	19.0
Central government cash surplus/deficit (% of GDP)	..	..	..
States and markets			
Starting a business (days)	..	56	28
Stock market capitalization (% of GDP)	21.6	36.1	48.9
Military expenditures (% of GDP)	7.6	2.0	3.3
Mobile cellular subscriptions (per 100 people)	0.0	4.9	87.7
Individuals using the Internet (% of population)	0.0	1.6	29.9
Paved roads (% of total)	..	39.0	53.5
High-technology exports (% of manufactured exports)	10	20	18
Global links			
Merchandise trade (% of GDP)	32	44	51
Net barter terms of trade index (2000 = 100)	..	..	..
Total external debt stocks ($ billions)	1,104	1,856	4,695
Total debt service (% of exports)	21.8	21.3	9.9
Net migration (millions)	-13.8	-17.6	-13.3
Personal remittances received ($ billions)	28	74	320
Foreign direct investment, net inflows ($ billions)	21	141	593
Net official development assistance received ($ billions)	33.0	27.1	53.5

Lower middle income

Population (millions)	2,507.0	Population growth (%)	1.5
Surface area (1,000 sq. km)	20,740	Population living below $1.25 a day (%)	27.1
GNI, Atlas ($ billions)	4,745.3	GNI per capita, Atlas ($)	1,893
GNI, PPP ($ billions)	9,718.6	GNI per capita, PPP ($)	3,877

	1990	2000	2012
People			
Share of poorest 20% in nat'l consumption/income (%)	..	..	..
Life expectancy at birth (years)	60	63	66
Total fertility rate (births per woman)	4.2	3.4	2.9
Adolescent fertility rate (births per 1,000 women 15–19)	95	74	47
Contraceptive prevalence (% of married women 15–49)	40	46	51
Births attended by skilled health staff (% of total)	..	47	57
Under-five mortality rate (per 1,000 live births)	118	93	61
Child malnutrition, underweight (% of under age 5)	38.7	31.6	24.1
Child immunization, measles (% of ages 12–23 mos.)	61	64	75
Primary completion rate, total (% of relevant age group)	70	75	91
Gross secondary enrollment, total (% of relevant age group)	41	47	61
Ratio of girls to boys in primary & secondary school (%)	77	84	95
HIV prevalence rate (% population of ages 15–49)	0.2	0.7	0.6
Environment			
Forests (1,000 sq. km)	6,318	5,905	5,533
Deforestation (avg. annual %, 1990–2000 and 2000–2010)		0.6	0.3
Freshwater use (% of internal resources)	..	17.8	19.6
Access to improved water source (% total pop.)	71	79	88
Access to improved sanitation facilities (% total pop.)	29	39	48
Energy use per capita (kilograms of oil equivalent)	594	573	687
Carbon dioxide emissions per capita (metric tons)	1.1	1.2	1.6
Electricity use per capita (kilowatt-hours)	444	469	734
Economy			
GDP ($ billions)	861	1,239	4,838
GDP growth (annual %)	3.4	4.2	4.7
GDP implicit price deflator (annual % growth)	13.7	6.8	4.6
Value added in agriculture (% of GDP)	26	21	17
Value added in industry (% of GDP)	31	32	32
Value added in services (% of GDP)	43	47	51
Exports of goods and services (% of GDP)	18	27	28
Imports of goods and services (% of GDP)	20	26	33
Gross capital formation (% of GDP)	24	22	29
Central government revenue (% of GDP)	15.5	14.1	15.2
Central government cash surplus/deficit (% of GDP)	-1.6	-3.3	-3.2
States and markets			
Starting a business (days)	..	54	26
Stock market capitalization (% of GDP)	9.5	23.9	50.6
Military expenditures (% of GDP)	19.4	2.8	8.9
Mobile cellular subscriptions (per 100 people)	0.0	1.2	83.1
Individuals using the Internet (% of population)	0.0	0.6	18.7
Paved roads (% of total)	..	29.6	36.0
High-technology exports (% of manufactured exports)	..	16	8
Global links			
Merchandise trade (% of GDP)	30	43	51
Net barter terms of trade index (2000 = 100)	..	..	..
Total external debt stocks ($ billions)	445	592	1,273
Total debt service (% of exports)	25.2	16.7	9.7
Net migration (millions)	-5.8	-12.4	-11.0
Personal remittances received ($ billions)	16	39	200
Foreign direct investment, net inflows ($ billions)	4	11	103
Net official development assistance received ($ billions)	23.1	16.9	35.9

Upper middle income

Population (millions)	2,390.6	Population growth (%)		0.8
Surface area (1,000 sq. km)	43,472	Population living below $1.25 a day (%)		8.4
GNI, Atlas ($ billions)	16,661.1	GNI per capita, Atlas ($)		6,969
GNI, PPP ($ billions)	25,389.9	GNI per capita, PPP ($)		10,621

	1990	2000	2012
People			
Share of poorest 20% in nat'l consumption/income (%)	..	..	..
Life expectancy at birth (years)	69	71	74
Total fertility rate (births per woman)	2.8	1.9	1.9
Adolescent fertility rate (births per 1,000 women 15-19)	38	34	31
Contraceptive prevalence (% of married women 15-49)	76	80	..
Births attended by skilled health staff (% of total)	89	93	96
Under-five mortality rate (per 1,000 live births)	54	38	20
Child malnutrition, underweight (% of under age 5)	12.6	6.5	2.8
Child immunization, measles (% of ages 12-23 mos.)	90	87	96
Primary completion rate, total (% of relevant age group)	97	97	..
Gross secondary enrollment, total (% of relevant age group)	48	70	84
Ratio of girls to boys in primary & secondary school (%)	90	98	102
HIV prevalence rate (% population of ages 15-49)	..	..	..
Environment			
Forests (1,000 sq. km)	12,794	12,536	12,438
Deforestation (avg. annual %, 1990-2000 and 2000-2010)		0.2	0.0
Freshwater use (% of internal resources)	..	6.8	7.4
Access to improved water source (% total pop.)	75	84	93
Access to improved sanitation facilities (% total pop.)	43	59	74
Energy use per capita (kilograms of oil equivalent)	1,021	1,111	1,893
Carbon dioxide emissions per capita (metric tons)	2.7	3.1	5.4
Electricity use per capita (kilowatt-hours)	945	1,350	2,932
Economy			
GDP ($ billions)	2,166	4,272	17,416
GDP growth (annual %)	2.1	5.6	5.0
GDP implicit price deflator (annual % growth)	11.6	9.7	3.8
Value added in agriculture (% of GDP)	17	10	8
Value added in industry (% of GDP)	38	39	38
Value added in services (% of GDP)	45	51	54
Exports of goods and services (% of GDP)	20	28	30
Imports of goods and services (% of GDP)	19	26	30
Gross capital formation (% of GDP)	28	26	33
Central government revenue (% of GDP)	..	..	20.3
Central government cash surplus/deficit (% of GDP)	..	..	..
States and markets			
Starting a business (days)	..	57	30
Stock market capitalization (% of GDP)	24.3	39.4	48.4
Military expenditures (% of GDP)	3.3	1.8	1.8
Mobile cellular subscriptions (per 100 people)	0.0	8.4	92.4
Individuals using the Internet (% of population)	0.0	2.6	41.6
Paved roads (% of total)	..	49.2	67.0
High-technology exports (% of manufactured exports)	11	21	21
Global links			
Merchandise trade (% of GDP)	32	44	50
Net barter terms of trade index (2000 = 100)	..	..	..
Total external debt stocks ($ billions)	660	1,264	3,422
Total debt service (% of exports)	20.5	22.6	10.0
Net migration (thousands)	-8,078	-5,191	-2,314
Personal remittances received ($ billions)	11	35	121
Foreign direct investment, net inflows ($ billions)	16	130	489
Net official development assistance received ($ billions)	9.8	9.5	16.6

Low and middle income

Population (millions)	5,744.1	Population growth (%)		1.3
Surface area (1,000 sq. km)	80,410	Population living below $1.25 a day (%)		20.6
GNI, Atlas ($ billions)	21,916.1	GNI per capita, Atlas ($)		3,815
GNI, PPP ($ billions)	36,250.5	GNI per capita, PPP ($)		6,311

	1990	2000	2012
People			
Share of poorest 20% in nat'l consumption/income (%)	..	..	..
Life expectancy at birth (years)	63	66	69
Total fertility rate (births per woman)	3.7	2.9	2.6
Adolescent fertility rate (births per 1,000 women 15–19)	72	63	49
Contraceptive prevalence (% of married women 15–49)	56	59	..
Births attended by skilled health staff (% of total)	..	59	64
Under-five mortality rate (per 1,000 live births)	99	83	53
Child malnutrition, underweight (% of under age 5)	28.1	23.2	17.0
Child immunization, measles (% of ages 12–23 mos.)	72	71	83
Primary completion rate, total (% of relevant age group)	78	80	89
Gross secondary enrollment, total (% of relevant age group)	41	54	66
Ratio of girls to boys in primary & secondary school (%)	83	90	97
HIV prevalence rate (% population of ages 15–49)	..	..	1.2
Environment			
Forests (1,000 sq. km)	23,849	22,865	22,248
Deforestation (avg. annual %, 1990–2000 and 2000–2010)		0.4	0.2
Freshwater use (% of internal resources)	..	9.2	10.3
Access to improved water source (% total pop.)	70	79	87
Access to improved sanitation facilities (% total pop.)	35	47	57
Energy use per capita (kilograms of oil equivalent)	780	796	1,179
Carbon dioxide emissions per capita (metric tons)	1.8	1.9	3.0
Electricity use per capita (kilowatt-hours)	664	844	1,646
Economy			
GDP ($ billions)	3,167	5,674	22,779
GDP growth (annual %)	2.4	5.2	4.9
GDP implicit price deflator (annual % growth)	11.2	7.3	4.7
Value added in agriculture (% of GDP)	20	13	11
Value added in industry (% of GDP)	36	37	36
Value added in services (% of GDP)	44	50	54
Exports of goods and services (% of GDP)	19	27	30
Imports of goods and services (% of GDP)	19	26	31
Gross capital formation (% of GDP)	27	25	32
Central government revenue (% of GDP)	..	..	18.8
Central government cash surplus/deficit (% of GDP)	..	..	..
States and markets			
Starting a business (days)	..	57	28
Stock market capitalization (% of GDP)	21.3	35.6	48.6
Military expenditures (% of GDP)	7.4	2.0	3.3
Mobile cellular subscriptions (per 100 people)	0.0	4.3	81.7
Individuals using the Internet (% of population)	0.0	1.4	26.5
Paved roads (% of total)	..	30.0	37.9
High-technology exports (% of manufactured exports)	10	20	18
Global links			
Merchandise trade (% of GDP)	32	44	51
Net barter terms of trade index (2000 = 100)	..	..	..
Total external debt stocks ($ billions)	1,194	1,966	4,830
Total debt service (% of exports)	21.9	21.1	9.8
Net migration (millions)	-13.3	-22.5	-17.0
Personal remittances received ($ billions)	29	79	350
Foreign direct investment, net inflows ($ billions)	21	143	617
Net official development assistance received ($ billions)	56	49	133

High income

Population (millions)	1,299.8	Population growth (%)	0.3
Surface area (1,000 sq. km)	53,880	Population living below $1.25 a day (%)	..
GNI, Atlas ($ billions)	49,905.7	GNI per capita, Atlas ($)	38,394
GNI, PPP ($ billions)	50,055.1	GNI per capita, PPP ($)	38,509

	1990	2000	2012
People			
Share of poorest 20% in nat'l consumption/income (%)	..	..	..
Life expectancy at birth (years)	75	76	79
Total fertility rate (births per woman)	1.9	1.6	1.7
Adolescent fertility rate (births per 1,000 women 15–19)	31	25	18
Contraceptive prevalence (% of married women 15–49)	..	..	..
Births attended by skilled health staff (% of total)	..	..	..
Under-five mortality rate (per 1,000 live births)	15	10	6
Child malnutrition, underweight (% of under age 5)	1.4	1.4	1.4
Child immunization, measles (% of ages 12–23 mos.)	84	92	94
Primary completion rate, total (% of relevant age group)	97	97	100
Gross secondary enrollment, total (% of relevant age group)	92	98	100
Ratio of girls to boys in primary & secondary school (%)	100	100	99
HIV prevalence rate (% population of ages 15–49)	..	..	..
Environment			
Forests (1,000 sq. km)	17,759	17,896	17,936
Deforestation (avg. annual %, 1990–2000 and 2000–2010)		-0.1	0.0
Freshwater use (% of internal resources)	..	7.1	7.0
Access to improved water source (% total pop.)	98	98	99
Access to improved sanitation facilities (% total pop.)	95	96	96
Energy use per capita (kilograms of oil equivalent)	4,776	4,985	4,675
Carbon dioxide emissions per capita (metric tons)	11.9	12.1	11.6
Electricity use per capita (kilowatt-hours)	7,226	8,405	8,896
Economy			
GDP ($ billions)	19,068	27,199	49,771
GDP growth (annual %)	2.9	4.1	1.5
GDP implicit price deflator (annual % growth)	5.4	3.3	1.7
Value added in agriculture (% of GDP)	3	2	1
Value added in industry (% of GDP)	32	28	25
Value added in services (% of GDP)	64	70	74
Exports of goods and services (% of GDP)	20	25	30
Imports of goods and services (% of GDP)	20	25	30
Gross capital formation (% of GDP)	24	23	20
Central government revenue (% of GDP)	..	26.2	23.8
Central government cash surplus/deficit (% of GDP)	..	-1.7	-5.6
States and markets			
Starting a business (days)	..	33	17
Stock market capitalization (% of GDP)	50.2	112.0	86.8
Military expenditures (% of GDP)	3.7	2.3	2.7
Mobile cellular subscriptions (per 100 people)	1.0	43.7	122.9
Individuals using the Internet (% of population)	0.2	27.3	75.4
Paved roads (% of total)	..	87.4	83.7
High-technology exports (% of manufactured exports)	19	25	17
Global links			
Merchandise trade (% of GDP)	32	39	51
Net barter terms of trade index (2000 = 100)	..	..	..
Total external debt stocks ($ millions)		..	..
Total debt service (% of exports)	..	..	..
Net migration (millions)	13.5	22.2	16.9
Personal remittances received ($ billions)	39	57	128
Foreign direct investment, net inflows ($ billions)	175	1,176	893
Net official development assistance received ($ millions)	2,816	420	188

Euro area

Population (millions)	331.2	Population growth (%)	-0.6
Surface area (1,000 sq. km)	2,693	Population living below $1.25 a day (%)	..
GNI, Atlas ($ billions)	12,673.5	GNI per capita, Atlas ($)	38,263
GNI, PPP ($ billions)	12,354.0	GNI per capita, PPP ($)	37,299

	1990	2000	2012
People			
Share of poorest 20% in nat'l consumption/income (%)	..	..	..
Life expectancy at birth (years)	76	78	82
Total fertility rate (births per woman)	1.5	1.5	1.5
Adolescent fertility rate (births per 1,000 women 15-19)	14	11	6
Contraceptive prevalence (% of married women 15-49)	..	..	..
Births attended by skilled health staff (% of total)	..	..	..
Under-five mortality rate (per 1,000 live births)	10	6	4
Child malnutrition, underweight (% of under age 5)	..	..	..
Child immunization, measles (% of ages 12-23 mos.)	74	87	93
Primary completion rate, total (% of relevant age group)	98	99	99
Gross secondary enrollment, total (% of relevant age group)	93	103	109
Ratio of girls to boys in primary & secondary school (%)	101	100	99
HIV prevalence rate (% population of ages 15-49)	..	..	..
Environment			
Forests (1,000 sq. km)	891	957	989
Deforestation (avg. annual %, 1990-2000 and 2000-2010)		-0.8	-0.3
Freshwater use (% of internal resources)	..	20.7	19.1
Access to improved water source (% total pop.)	100	100	100
Access to improved sanitation facilities (% total pop.)	100	100	100
Energy use per capita (kilograms of oil equivalent)	3,501	3,711	3,455
Carbon dioxide emissions per capita (metric tons)	8.4	8.3	7.4
Electricity use per capita (kilowatt-hours)	5,318	6,287	6,599
Economy			
GDP ($ billions)	5,697	6,264	12,221
GDP growth (annual %)	3.5	3.8	-0.6
GDP implicit price deflator (annual % growth)	4.4	3.4	1.5
Value added in agriculture (% of GDP)	4	2	2
Value added in industry (% of GDP)	33	28	25
Value added in services (% of GDP)	64	70	73
Exports of goods and services (% of GDP)	27	37	45
Imports of goods and services (% of GDP)	28	36	42
Gross capital formation (% of GDP)	23	22	18
Central government revenue (% of GDP)	..	36.4	35.0
Central government cash surplus/deficit (% of GDP)	..	0.0	-3.2
States and markets			
Starting a business (days)	..	49	13
Stock market capitalization (% of GDP)	21.1	86.8	51.6
Military expenditures (% of GDP)	2.5	1.8	1.5
Mobile cellular subscriptions (per 100 people)	0.4	59.6	120.3
Individuals using the Internet (% of population)	0.1	22.7	75.9
Paved roads (% of total)	..	95.4	93.8
High-technology exports (% of manufactured exports)	13	20	15
Global links			
Merchandise trade (% of GDP)	44	61	72
Net barter terms of trade index (2000 = 100)	..	..	..
Total external debt stocks ($ millions)	..	..	..
Total debt service (% of exports)	..	..	..
Net migration (thousands)	5,030	7,806	3,402
Personal remittances received ($ billions)	27.9	33.4	78.8
Foreign direct investment, net inflows ($ billions)	53	423	201
Net official development assistance received ($ millions)	43.7	82.1	..

Country tables

Cabo Verde

Cabo Verde is the new name for the country previously listed as Cape Verde.

China

Unless otherwise noted, data for China do not include data for Hong Kong SAR, China; Macao SAR, China; or Taiwan, China.

Cyprus

GNI and GDP data and data calculated using GNI and GDP refer to the area controlled by the government of the Republic of Cyprus.

Georgia

GNI, GDP and population data and data calculated using GNI, GDP and population exclude Abkhazia and South Ossetia.

Kosovo, Montenegro, and Serbia

Data for each country are shown separately where available. However, some indicators for Serbia prior to 2006 include data for Montenegro; these data are noted in the tables. Moreover, data for most indicators for Serbia from 1999 onward exclude data for Kosovo, which in 1999 became a territory under international administration pursuant to UN Security Council Resolution 1244 (1999). Kosovo became a member of the World Bank on June 29, 2009, and its data are shown where available.

Moldova

GNI, GDP and population data and data calculated using GNI, GDP and population exclude Transnistria.

Morocco

GNI and GDP data and data calculated using GNI and GDP include Former Spanish Sahara.

South Sudan and Sudan

South Sudan declared its independence on July 9, 2011. Data are shown separately for South Sudan where available. However, data reported for Sudan include South Sudan unless otherwise noted.

Tanzania

GNI and GDP data and data calculated using GNI and GDP refer to mainland Tanzania only.

For more information, see *World Development Indicators 2014* or data .worldbank.org.

Afghanistan

South Asia		Low income
Population (millions)	29.8	Population growth (%)	2.4
Surface area (1,000 sq. km)	652	Population living below $1.25 a day (%)	..
GNI, Atlas ($ billions)	20.4	GNI per capita, Atlas ($)	680
GNI, PPP ($ billions)	46.6	GNI per capita, PPP ($)	1,560

	1990	2000	2012
People			
Share of poorest 20% in nat'l consumption/income (%)	..	..	9.4
Life expectancy at birth (years)	49	55	61
Total fertility rate (births per woman)	7.7	7.7	5.1
Adolescent fertility rate (births per 1,000 women 15–19)	168	158	87
Contraceptive prevalence (% of married women 15–49)	..	5	21
Births attended by skilled health staff (% of total)	..	12	39
Under-five mortality rate (per 1,000 live births)	176	134	99
Child malnutrition, underweight (% of under age 5)	..	32.9	..
Child immunization, measles (% of ages 12–23 mos.)	20	27	68
Primary completion rate, total (% of relevant age group)	29	..	..
Gross secondary enrollment, total (% of relevant age group)	11	13	54
Ratio of girls to boys in primary & secondary school (%)	54	0	67
HIV prevalence rate (% population of ages 15–49)	0.1	0.1	0.1
Environment			
Forests (1,000 sq. km)	14	14	14
Deforestation (avg. annual %, 1990–2000 and 2000–2010)		0.0	0.0
Freshwater use (% of internal resources)	..	43.0	43.0
Access to improved water source (% total pop.)	..	22	64
Access to improved sanitation facilities (% total pop.)	..	23	29
Energy use per capita (kilograms of oil equivalent)	..	..	..
Carbon dioxide emissions per capita (metric tons)	0.23	0.04	0.29
Electricity use per capita (kilowatt-hours)	..	..	..
Economy			
GDP ($ billions)	..	2.5	20.5
GDP growth (annual %)	..	8.4	14.4
GDP implicit price deflator (annual % growth)	..	11.7	8.3
Value added in agriculture (% of GDP)	..	38	25
Value added in industry (% of GDP)	..	24	22
Value added in services (% of GDP)	..	38	54
Exports of goods and services (% of GDP)	..	32	6
Imports of goods and services (% of GDP)	..	65	39
Gross capital formation (% of GDP)	..	12	17
Central government revenue (% of GDP)	..	..	11.4
Central government cash surplus/deficit (% of GDP)	..	..	-0.6
States and markets			
Starting a business (days)	..	..	5
Stock market capitalization (% of GDP)	..	..	..
Military expenditures (% of GDP)	..	2.1	3.6
Mobile cellular subscriptions (per 100 people)	0.0	0.0	60.4
Individuals using the Internet (% of population)	0.0	0.0	5.5
Paved roads (% of total)	..	18.0	36.4
High-technology exports (% of manufactured exports)	..	..	..
Global links			
Merchandise trade (% of GDP)	..	72	32
Net barter terms of trade index (2000 = 100)	..	100	139
Total external debt stocks ($ millions)	..	..	2,709
Total debt service (% of exports)	..	..	0.3
Net migration (thousands)	3,257	137	-400
Personal remittances received ($ millions)	..	..	385
Foreign direct investment, net inflows ($ millions)	-0.3	0.2	94.0
Net official development assistance received ($ millions)	122	136	6,725

Albania

Europe & Central Asia		Upper middle income	
Population (millions)	3.2	Population growth (%)	0.3
Surface area (1,000 sq. km)	29	Population living below $1.25 a day (%)	<2
GNI, Atlas ($ billions)	12.7	GNI per capita, Atlas ($)	4,030
GNI, PPP ($ billions)	29.3	GNI per capita, PPP ($)	9,280

	1990	2000	2012
People			
Share of poorest 20% in nat'l consumption/income (%)	..	9.1	8.1
Life expectancy at birth (years)	72	74	77
Total fertility rate (births per woman)	3.0	2.4	1.8
Adolescent fertility rate (births per 1,000 women 15–19)	42	33	15
Contraceptive prevalence (% of married women 15–49)	..	58	69
Births attended by skilled health staff (% of total)	93	99	99
Under-five mortality rate (per 1,000 live births)	43	29	17
Child malnutrition, underweight (% of under age 5)	..	17.0	6.3
Child immunization, measles (% of ages 12-23 mos.)	88	95	99
Primary completion rate, total (% of relevant age group)	..	94	..
Gross secondary enrollment, total (% of relevant age group)	81	67	..
Ratio of girls to boys in primary & secondary school (%)	93	96	..
HIV prevalence rate (% population of ages 15–49)	..	..	..
Environment			
Forests (1,000 sq. km)	7.9	7.7	7.8
Deforestation (avg. annual %, 1990-2000 and 2000-2010)		0.3	-0.1
Freshwater use (% of internal resources)	4.5	6.8	6.8
Access to improved water source (% total pop.)	..	96	96
Access to improved sanitation facilities (% total pop.)	79	84	91
Energy use per capita (kilograms of oil equivalent)	775	534	689
Carbon dioxide emissions per capita (metric tons)	2.2	0.9	1.4
Electricity use per capita (kilowatt-hours)	498	1,343	2,022
Economy			
GDP ($ billions)	2.1	3.7	12.6
GDP growth (annual %)	-9.6	7.3	1.6
GDP implicit price deflator (annual % growth)	-0.5	4.3	3.0
Value added in agriculture (% of GDP)	36	29	18
Value added in industry (% of GDP)	48	19	16
Value added in services (% of GDP)	16	52	66
Exports of goods and services (% of GDP)	15	19	31
Imports of goods and services (% of GDP)	23	37	49
Gross capital formation (% of GDP)	29	25	25
Central government revenue (% of GDP)	..	19.3	23.7
Central government cash surplus/deficit (% of GDP)	..	-6.5	-3.4
States and markets			
Starting a business (days)	..	41	5
Stock market capitalization (% of GDP)	..	..	..
Military expenditures (% of GDP)	5.9	1.2	1.5
Mobile cellular subscriptions (per 100 people)	0.0	0.9	110.7
Individuals using the Internet (% of population)	0.0	0.1	54.7
Paved roads (% of total)	..	39.0	..
High-technology exports (% of manufactured exports)	..	1	0
Global links			
Merchandise trade (% of GDP)	29	37	54
Net barter terms of trade index (2000 = 100)	..	100	96
Total external debt stocks ($ billions)	0.5	1.1	6.9
Total debt service (% of exports)	4.3	3.7	7.1
Net migration (thousands)	-391	-290	-50
Personal remittances received ($ millions)	152	598	1,027
Foreign direct investment, net inflows ($ millions)	20	143	1,265
Net official development assistance received ($ millions)	11	318	342

Algeria

Middle East & North Africa		Upper middle income	
Population (millions)	38.5	Population growth (%)	1.9
Surface area (1,000 sq. km)	2,382	Population living below $1.25 a day (%)	6.8
GNI, Atlas ($ billions)	193.2	GNI per capita, Atlas ($)	5,020
GNI, PPP ($ billions)	321.6	GNI per capita, PPP ($)	8,360

	1990	2000	2012
People			
Share of poorest 20% in nat'l consumption/income (%)	6.5	..	..
Life expectancy at birth (years)	67	69	71
Total fertility rate (births per woman)	4.8	2.5	2.8
Adolescent fertility rate (births per 1,000 women 15–19)	28	12	10
Contraceptive prevalence (% of married women 15–49)	51	64	61
Births attended by skilled health staff (% of total)	77	93	95
Under-five mortality rate (per 1,000 live births)	50	35	20
Child malnutrition, underweight (% of under age 5)	9.2	5.4	..
Child immunization, measles (% of ages 12–23 mos.)	83	80	95
Primary completion rate, total (% of relevant age group)	77	77	100
Gross secondary enrollment, total (% of relevant age group)	59	62	98
Ratio of girls to boys in primary & secondary school (%)	82	96	100
HIV prevalence rate (% population of ages 15–49)	..	..	..
Environment			
Forests (1,000 sq. km)	17	16	15
Deforestation (avg. annual %, 1990–2000 and 2000–2010)		0.5	0.6
Freshwater use (% of internal resources)	40.0	54.8	54.8
Access to improved water source (% total pop.)	94	89	84
Access to improved sanitation facilities (% total pop.)	89	92	95
Energy use per capita (kilograms of oil equivalent)	846	851	1,108
Carbon dioxide emissions per capita (metric tons)	3.0	2.8	3.3
Electricity use per capita (kilowatt-hours)	522	669	1,091
Economy			
GDP ($ billions)	62	55	206
GDP growth (annual %)	0.8	2.2	3.3
GDP implicit price deflator (annual % growth)	30.3	24.6	5.6
Value added in agriculture (% of GDP)	11	9	9
Value added in industry (% of GDP)	48	59	49
Value added in services (% of GDP)	40	33	42
Exports of goods and services (% of GDP)	23	41	37
Imports of goods and services (% of GDP)	25	21	28
Gross capital formation (% of GDP)	29	25	37
Central government revenue (% of GDP)	..	..	40.6
Central government cash surplus/deficit (% of GDP)	..	..	-0.3
States and markets			
Starting a business (days)	..	25	25
Stock market capitalization (% of GDP)	..	..	..
Military expenditures (% of GDP)	1.5	3.4	4.6
Mobile cellular subscriptions (per 100 people)	0.0	0.3	97.9
Individuals using the Internet (% of population)	0.0	0.5	15.2
Paved roads (% of total)	67.0	69.0	77.1
High-technology exports (% of manufactured exports)	1	4	0
Global links			
Merchandise trade (% of GDP)	37	57	59
Net barter terms of trade index (2000 = 100)	74	100	217
Total external debt stocks ($ billions)	28.2	25.5	5.6
Total debt service (% of exports)	65.1	..	1.1
Net migration (thousands)	-104	-58	-50
Personal remittances received ($ millions)	352	790	213
Foreign direct investment, net inflows ($ millions)	0	280	1,602
Net official development assistance received ($ millions)	332	200	145

American Samoa

Population (thousands)	55	Population growth (%)	-0.3
Surface area (sq. km)	200	Population living below $1.25 a day (%)	..
GNI, Atlas ($ millions)	..	GNI per capita, Atlas ($)	..
GNI, PPP ($ millions)	..	GNI per capita, PPP ($)	..

	1990	2000	2012
People			
Share of poorest 20% in nat'l consumption/income (%)	..	..	..
Life expectancy at birth (years)	..	..	..
Total fertility rate (births per woman)	..	..	..
Adolescent fertility rate (births per 1,000 women 15-19)	..	..	..
Contraceptive prevalence (% of married women 15-49)	..	..	..
Births attended by skilled health staff (% of total)	..	100	..
Under-five mortality rate (per 1,000 live births)	..	..	..
Child malnutrition, underweight (% of under age 5)	..	..	..
Child immunization, measles (% of ages 12-23 mos.)	..	..	..
Primary completion rate, total (% of relevant age group)	..	..	..
Gross secondary enrollment, total (% of relevant age group)	91	..	..
Ratio of girls to boys in primary & secondary school (%)	102	..	..
HIV prevalence rate (% population of ages 15-49)	..	..	..
Environment			
Forests (sq. km)	184	181	177
Deforestation (avg. annual %, 1990-2000 and 2000-2010)		0.2	0.2
Freshwater use (% of internal resources)	..	..	
Access to improved water source (% total pop.)	94	98	100
Access to improved sanitation facilities (% total pop.)	61	62	62
Energy use per capita (kilograms of oil equivalent)	..	..	..
Carbon dioxide emissions per capita (metric tons)	..	..	..
Electricity use per capita (kilowatt-hours)	..	..	..
Economy			
GDP ($ millions)	..	..	..
GDP growth (annual %)	..	..	..
GDP implicit price deflator (annual % growth)	..	..	..
Value added in agriculture (% of GDP)	..	..	..
Value added in industry (% of GDP)	..	..	..
Value added in services (% of GDP)	..	..	..
Exports of goods and services (% of GDP)	..	..	..
Imports of goods and services (% of GDP)	..	..	..
Gross capital formation (% of GDP)	..	..	..
Central government revenue (% of GDP)	..	..	..
Central government cash surplus/deficit (% of GDP)	..	..	..
States and markets			
Starting a business (days)	..	..	..
Stock market capitalization (% of GDP)	..	..	..
Military expenditures (% of GDP)	..	..	..
Mobile cellular subscriptions (per 100 people)	0.0	3.5	..
Individuals using the Internet (% of population)	0.0	..	..
Paved roads (% of total)	..	..	..
High-technology exports (% of manufactured exports)	..	..	..
Global links			
Merchandise trade (% of GDP)	..	..	..
Net barter terms of trade index (2000 = 100)	..	100	129
Total external debt stocks ($ millions)	..	..	..
Total debt service (% of exports)	..	..	..
Net migration (thousands)	..	..	..
Personal remittances received ($ millions)	..	..	..
Foreign direct investment, net inflows ($ millions)	..	..	..
Net official development assistance received ($ millions)	..	..	..

Andorra

High income

Population (thousands)	78	Population growth (%)	0.6
Surface area (sq. km)	470	Population living below $1.25 a day (%)	..
GNI, Atlas ($ billions)	..	GNI per capita, Atlas ($)	..
GNI, PPP ($ millions)	..	GNI per capita, PPP ($)	..

	1990	2000	2012
People			
Share of poorest 20% in nat'l consumption/income (%)	..	..	..
Life expectancy at birth (years)	..	..	..
Total fertility rate (births per woman)	..	..	1.2
Adolescent fertility rate (births per 1,000 women 15–19)	..	..	..
Contraceptive prevalence (% of married women 15–49)	..	..	..
Births attended by skilled health staff (% of total)	..	..	..
Under-five mortality rate (per 1,000 live births)	8	5	3
Child malnutrition, underweight (% of under age 5)	..	..	..
Child immunization, measles (% of ages 12–23 mos.)	..	97	98
Primary completion rate, total (% of relevant age group)	..	..	..
Gross secondary enrollment, total (% of relevant age group)	..	..	..
Ratio of girls to boys in primary & secondary school (%)	..	..	..
HIV prevalence rate (% population of ages 15–49)	..	..	..
Environment			
Forests (sq. km)	160	160	160
Deforestation (avg. annual %, 1990–2000 and 2000–2010)		0.0	0.0
Freshwater use (% of internal resources)	..	..	
Access to improved water source (% total pop.)	100	100	100
Access to improved sanitation facilities (% total pop.)	100	100	100
Energy use per capita (kilograms of oil equivalent)	..	..	
Carbon dioxide emissions per capita (metric tons)	..	8.0	6.6
Electricity use per capita (kilowatt-hours)	..	..	..
Economy			
GDP ($ millions)	1,029	1,134	..
GDP growth (annual %)	3.8	1.2	..
GDP implicit price deflator (annual % growth)	7.3	4.5	..
Value added in agriculture (% of GDP)	..	..	..
Value added in industry (% of GDP)	..	..	..
Value added in services (% of GDP)	..	..	..
Exports of goods and services (% of GDP)	..	..	..
Imports of goods and services (% of GDP)	..	..	..
Gross capital formation (% of GDP)	..	..	..
Central government revenue (% of GDP)	..	..	..
Central government cash surplus/deficit (% of GDP)	..	..	..
States and markets			
Starting a business (days)	..	..	..
Stock market capitalization (% of GDP)	..	..	..
Military expenditures (% of GDP)	..	..	..
Mobile cellular subscriptions (per 100 people)	0.0	36.0	81.5
Individuals using the Internet (% of population)	0.0	10.5	86.4
Paved roads (% of total)	..	..	..
High-technology exports (% of manufactured exports)	..	11	..
Global links			
Merchandise trade (% of GDP)	..	..	..
Net barter terms of trade index (2000 = 100)	..	100	..
Total external debt stocks ($ millions)	..	..	..
Total debt service (% of exports)	..	..	..
Net migration (thousands)	..	..	..
Personal remittances received ($ millions)	..	..	..
Foreign direct investment, net inflows ($ millions)	..	..	..
Net official development assistance received ($ millions)	..	..	..

Angola

Population (millions)	20.8	Population growth (%)	3.1
Surface area (1,000 sq. km)	1,247	Population living below $1.25 a day (%)	43.4
GNI, Atlas ($ billions)	95.4	GNI per capita, Atlas ($)	4,580
GNI, PPP ($ billions)	112.4	GNI per capita, PPP ($)	5,400

	1990	2000	2012
People			
Share of poorest 20% in nat'l consumption/income (%)	..	2.0	5.4
Life expectancy at birth (years)	41	45	51
Total fertility rate (births per woman)	7.2	6.8	6.0
Adolescent fertility rate (births per 1,000 women 15-19)	227	209	170
Contraceptive prevalence (% of married women 15-49)	..	6	..
Births attended by skilled health staff (% of total)	..	45	47
Under-five mortality rate (per 1,000 live births)	213	203	164
Child malnutrition, underweight (% of under age 5)	..	..	15.6
Child immunization, measles (% of ages 12-23 mos.)	38	41	97
Primary completion rate, total (% of relevant age group)	34	..	54
Gross secondary enrollment, total (% of relevant age group)	11	15	32
Ratio of girls to boys in primary & secondary school (%)	..	82	64
HIV prevalence rate (% population of ages 15-49)	0.6	1.7	2.3
Environment			
Forests (1,000 sq. km)	610	597	584
Deforestation (avg. annual %, 1990-2000 and 2000-2010)		0.2	0.2
Freshwater use (% of internal resources)	..	0.4	0.4
Access to improved water source (% total pop.)	42	46	54
Access to improved sanitation facilities (% total pop.)	29	42	60
Energy use per capita (kilograms of oil equivalent)	569	539	673
Carbon dioxide emissions per capita (metric tons)	0.4	0.7	1.6
Electricity use per capita (kilowatt-hours)	61	89	248
Economy			
GDP ($ billions)	10.3	9.1	114.1
GDP growth (annual %)	-0.3	3.0	6.8
GDP implicit price deflator (annual % growth)	10.9	418.2	4.3
Value added in agriculture (% of GDP)	18	6	10
Value added in industry (% of GDP)	41	72	60
Value added in services (% of GDP)	41	22	30
Exports of goods and services (% of GDP)	39	90	60
Imports of goods and services (% of GDP)	21	63	42
Gross capital formation (% of GDP)	12	13	12
Central government revenue (% of GDP)	..	52.8	..
Central government cash surplus/deficit (% of GDP)	..	26.4	..
States and markets			
Starting a business (days)	..	119	66
Stock market capitalization (% of GDP)	..	..	..
Military expenditures (% of GDP)	7.1	6.4	3.6
Mobile cellular subscriptions (per 100 people)	0.0	0.2	47.1
Individuals using the Internet (% of population)	0.0	0.1	16.9
Paved roads (% of total)	..	10.0	..
High-technology exports (% of manufactured exports)	..	..	..
Global links			
Merchandise trade (% of GDP)	53	120	85
Net barter terms of trade index (2000 = 100)	94	100	258
Total external debt stocks ($ billions)	8.6	9.8	22.2
Total debt service (% of exports)	8.1	20.9	5.9
Net migration (thousands)	143	172	66
Personal remittances received ($ millions)	..	..	0.0
Foreign direct investment, net inflows ($ millions)	-335	879	-6,898
Net official development assistance received ($ millions)	266	302	242

Antigua and Barbuda

		High income
Population (thousands)	89	
Population growth (%)		1.0
Surface area (sq. km)	440	
Population living below $1.25 a day (%)		..
GNI, Atlas ($ billions)	1.1	
GNI per capita, Atlas ($)		12,480
GNI, PPP ($ billions)	1.7	
GNI per capita, PPP ($)		18,920

	1990	2000	2012
People			
Share of poorest 20% in nat'l consumption/income (%)	..	..	..
Life expectancy at birth (years)	71	73	76
Total fertility rate (births per woman)	2.1	2.3	2.1
Adolescent fertility rate (births per 1,000 women 15-19)	64	65	49
Contraceptive prevalence (% of married women 15-49)	53	53	..
Births attended by skilled health staff (% of total)	..	100	100
Under-five mortality rate (per 1,000 live births)	24	16	10
Child malnutrition, underweight (% of under age 5)	..	..	..
Child immunization, measles (% of ages 12-23 mos.)	89	95	98
Primary completion rate, total (% of relevant age group)	97	..	100
Gross secondary enrollment, total (% of relevant age group)	120	78	105
Ratio of girls to boys in primary & secondary school (%)	94	..	102
HIV prevalence rate (% population of ages 15-49)	..	..	..
Environment			
Forests (sq. km)	103	100	98
Deforestation (avg. annual %, 1990-2000 and 2000-2010)		0.3	0.2
Freshwater use (% of internal resources)	9.6	9.6	9.6
Access to improved water source (% total pop.)	97	98	98
Access to improved sanitation facilities (% total pop.)	75	85	91
Energy use per capita (kilograms of oil equivalent)	1,596	..	..
Carbon dioxide emissions per capita (metric tons)	4.9	4.4	5.9
Electricity use per capita (kilowatt-hours)	..	..	..
Economy			
GDP ($ millions)	392	788	1,134
GDP growth (annual %)	2.5	5.1	2.8
GDP implicit price deflator (annual % growth)	2.3	15.0	0.7
Value added in agriculture (% of GDP)	4	2	2
Value added in industry (% of GDP)	20	16	20
Value added in services (% of GDP)	76	82	78
Exports of goods and services (% of GDP)	89	63	49
Imports of goods and services (% of GDP)	87	64	54
Gross capital formation (% of GDP)	32	29	32
Central government revenue (% of GDP)	..	15.3	21.1
Central government cash surplus/deficit (% of GDP)	..	-5.3	-1.4
States and markets			
Starting a business (days)	..	..	21
Stock market capitalization (% of GDP)	..	..	..
Military expenditures (% of GDP)	..	..	..
Mobile cellular subscriptions (per 100 people)	0.0	28.3	143.0
Individuals using the Internet (% of population)	0.0	6.5	59.0
Paved roads (% of total)	..	33.0	..
High-technology exports (% of manufactured exports)	..	0	0
Global links			
Merchandise trade (% of GDP)	70	58	52
Net barter terms of trade index (2000 = 100)	..	100	64
Total external debt stocks ($ millions)	..	..	..
Total debt service (% of exports)	..	..	..
Net migration (thousands)	2.6	-0.3	-0.1
Personal remittances received ($ millions)	12.5	20.7	20.6
Foreign direct investment, net inflows ($ millions)	60.6	43.1	70.9
Net official development assistance received ($ millions)	4.6	9.8	2.4

Argentina

Population (millions)	41.1	Population growth (%)		0.9
Surface area (1,000 sq. km)	2,780	Population living below $1.25 a day (%)		<2
GNI, Atlas ($ billions)	..[a]	GNI per capita, Atlas ($)		..[a]
GNI, PPP ($ billions)	..[a]	GNI per capita, PPP ($)		..[a]

	1990	2000	2012
People			
Share of poorest 20% in nat'l consumption/income (%)	5.0	3.2	4.4
Life expectancy at birth (years)	72	74	76
Total fertility rate (births per woman)	3.0	2.5	2.2
Adolescent fertility rate (births per 1,000 women 15-19)	73	64	54
Contraceptive prevalence (% of married women 15-49)	..	65	..
Births attended by skilled health staff (% of total)	96	98	97
Under-five mortality rate (per 1,000 live births)	28	20	14
Child malnutrition, underweight (% of under age 5)	..	..	..
Child immunization, measles (% of ages 12-23 mos.)	93	91	94
Primary completion rate, total (% of relevant age group)	..	99	109
Gross secondary enrollment, total (% of relevant age group)	71	87	92
Ratio of girls to boys in primary & secondary school (%)	107	101	104
HIV prevalence rate (% population of ages 15-49)	0.1	0.4	0.4
Environment			
Forests (1,000 sq. km)	348	319	292
Deforestation (avg. annual %, 1990-2000 and 2000-2010)		0.9	0.8
Freshwater use (% of internal resources)	..	11.8	11.8
Access to improved water source (% total pop.)	94	96	99
Access to improved sanitation facilities (% total pop.)	86	92	97
Energy use per capita (kilograms of oil equivalent)	1,412	1,652	1,967
Carbon dioxide emissions per capita (metric tons)	3.5	3.8	4.5
Electricity use per capita (kilowatt-hours)	1,304	2,087	2,967
Economy			
GDP ($ billions)	141	284	476
GDP growth (annual %)	-2.4	-0.8	1.9[b]
GDP implicit price deflator (annual % growth)	2,076.8	1.0	15.3[b]
Value added in agriculture (% of GDP)	8	5	9
Value added in industry (% of GDP)	36	28	31
Value added in services (% of GDP)	56	67	60
Exports of goods and services (% of GDP)	10	11	20
Imports of goods and services (% of GDP)	5	12	17
Gross capital formation (% of GDP)	14	16	22
Central government revenue (% of GDP)	..	14.1	..
Central government cash surplus/deficit (% of GDP)	..	-5.7	..
States and markets			
Starting a business (days)	..	66	25
Stock market capitalization (% of GDP)	2.3	58.4	7.2
Military expenditures (% of GDP)	1.4	1.1	0.9
Mobile cellular subscriptions (per 100 people)	0.0	17.6	151.9
Individuals using the Internet (% of population)	0.0	7.0	55.8
Paved roads (% of total)	28.5	29.0	32.2
High-technology exports (% of manufactured exports)	8	9	8
Global links			
Merchandise trade (% of GDP)	12	18	31
Net barter terms of trade index (2000 = 100)	64	100	130
Total external debt stocks ($ billions)	63	147	121
Total debt service (% of exports)	37.1	64.0	13.2
Net migration (thousands)	0	-180	-100
Personal remittances received ($ millions)	23	86	573
Foreign direct investment, net inflows ($ billions)	1.8	10.4	12.1
Net official development assistance received ($ millions)	169	52	179

Armenia

Europe & Central Asia		Lower middle income	

Population (millions)	3.0	Population growth (%)	0.2
Surface area (1,000 sq. km)	30	Population living below $1.25 a day (%)	2.5
GNI, Atlas ($ billions)	11.0	GNI per capita, Atlas ($)	3,720
GNI, PPP ($ billions)	20.4	GNI per capita, PPP ($)	6,860

	1990	2000	2012
People			
Share of poorest 20% in nat'l consumption/income (%)	..	7.6	8.8
Life expectancy at birth (years)	68	71	74
Total fertility rate (births per woman)	2.5	1.7	1.7
Adolescent fertility rate (births per 1,000 women 15-19)	74	40	27
Contraceptive prevalence (% of married women 15-49)	56	61	55
Births attended by skilled health staff (% of total)	100	97	100
Under-five mortality rate (per 1,000 live births)	49	30	16
Child malnutrition, underweight (% of under age 5)	..	2.6	5.3
Child immunization, measles (% of ages 12-23 mos.)	93	92	97
Primary completion rate, total (% of relevant age group)	..	94	..
Gross secondary enrollment, total (% of relevant age group)	91	91	96
Ratio of girls to boys in primary & secondary school (%)	..	106	115
HIV prevalence rate (% population of ages 15-49)	0.1	0.1	0.2
Environment			
Forests (1,000 sq. km)	3.5	3.0	2.6
Deforestation (avg. annual %, 1990-2000 and 2000-2010)		1.3	1.5
Freshwater use (% of internal resources)	..	25.3	41.2
Access to improved water source (% total pop.)	..	93	100
Access to improved sanitation facilities (% total pop.)	..	89	91
Energy use per capita (kilograms of oil equivalent)	2,175	655	916
Carbon dioxide emissions per capita (metric tons)	1.2	1.1	1.4
Electricity use per capita (kilowatt-hours)	2,718	1,295	1,755
Economy			
GDP ($ billions)	2.3	1.9	10.0
GDP growth (annual %)	-11.7	5.9	7.2
GDP implicit price deflator (annual % growth)	79.4	-1.4	-1.3
Value added in agriculture (% of GDP)	17	26	22
Value added in industry (% of GDP)	52	39	33
Value added in services (% of GDP)	31	35	45
Exports of goods and services (% of GDP)	35	23	25
Imports of goods and services (% of GDP)	46	51	49
Gross capital formation (% of GDP)	47	19	24
Central government revenue (% of GDP)	..	17.7	24.1
Central government cash surplus/deficit (% of GDP)	..	-0.7	-1.4
States and markets			
Starting a business (days)	..	18	4
Stock market capitalization (% of GDP)	..	0.1	1.3
Military expenditures (% of GDP)	2.1	3.6	3.9
Mobile cellular subscriptions (per 100 people)	0.0	0.6	111.9
Individuals using the Internet (% of population)	0.0	1.3	39.2
Paved roads (% of total)	99.2	96.8	..
High-technology exports (% of manufactured exports)		5	3
Global links			
Merchandise trade (% of GDP)	..	62	57
Net barter terms of trade index (2000 = 100)	..	100	118
Total external debt stocks ($ billions)	0.1	1.0	7.6
Total debt service (% of exports)	1.2	9.2	30.9
Net migration (thousands)	-496	-144	-50
Personal remittances received ($ millions)	..	87	2,123
Foreign direct investment, net inflows ($ millions)	2	104	489
Net official development assistance received ($ millions)	3	216	273

Aruba

High income

Population (thousands)	102	Population growth (%)	0.4
Surface area (sq. km)	180	Population living below $1.25 a day (%)	..
GNI, Atlas ($ millions)	..	GNI per capita, Atlas ($)	..
GNI, PPP ($ millions)	..	GNI per capita, PPP ($)	..

	1990	2000	2012
People			
Share of poorest 20% in nat'l consumption/income (%)	..	..	..
Life expectancy at birth (years)	73	74	75
Total fertility rate (births per woman)	2.2	1.9	1.7
Adolescent fertility rate (births per 1,000 women 15-19)	50	44	27
Contraceptive prevalence (% of married women 15-49)	..	..	..
Births attended by skilled health staff (% of total)	..	96	..
Under-five mortality rate (per 1,000 live births)	..	..	..
Child malnutrition, underweight (% of under age 5)	..	..	..
Child immunization, measles (% of ages 12-23 mos.)	..	..	..
Primary completion rate, total (% of relevant age group)	..	97	95
Gross secondary enrollment, total (% of relevant age group)	..	96	97
Ratio of girls to boys in primary & secondary school (%)	..	99	101
HIV prevalence rate (% population of ages 15-49)	..	..	..
Environment			
Forests (sq. km)	4.0	4.0	4.2
Deforestation (avg. annual %, 1990-2000 and 2000-2010)		0.0	0.0
Freshwater use (% of internal resources)	..	..	..
Access to improved water source (% total pop.)	91	94	98
Access to improved sanitation facilities (% total pop.)	99	98	98
Energy use per capita (kilograms of oil equivalent)	..	..	..
Carbon dioxide emissions per capita (metric tons)	29.6	24.6	22.8
Electricity use per capita (kilowatt-hours)	..	..	..
Economy			
GDP ($ millions)	..	1,873	2,584
GDP growth (annual %)	..	-0.4	-5.7
GDP implicit price deflator (annual % growth)	..	9.1	-5.1
Value added in agriculture (% of GDP)	..	0	1
Value added in industry (% of GDP)	..	17	16
Value added in services (% of GDP)	..	82	83
Exports of goods and services (% of GDP)	..	74	71
Imports of goods and services (% of GDP)	..	71	86
Gross capital formation (% of GDP)	..	25	28
Central government revenue (% of GDP)	..	..	..
Central government cash surplus/deficit (% of GDP)	..	..	..
States and markets			
Starting a business (days)	..	..	..
Stock market capitalization (% of GDP)	..	..	..
Military expenditures (% of GDP)	..	..	..
Mobile cellular subscriptions (per 100 people)	0.0	16.5	131.9
Individuals using the Internet (% of population)	0.0	15.4	74.0
Paved roads (% of total)	..	..	..
High-technology exports (% of manufactured exports)	..	..	10
Global links			
Merchandise trade (% of GDP)	..	54	52
Net barter terms of trade index (2000 = 100)	..	100	122
Total external debt stocks ($ millions)	..	..	..
Total debt service (% of exports)	..	..	..
Net migration (thousands)	14.2	6.3	1.3
Personal remittances received ($ millions)	2.6	7.9	4.9
Foreign direct investment, net inflows ($ millions)	131	-128	-140
Net official development assistance received ($ millions)	30.0	-7.4	..

Australia

High income

Population (millions)	22.7	Population growth (%)		1.7
Surface area (1,000 sq. km)	7,741	Population living below $1.25 a day (%)		..
GNI, Atlas ($ billions)	1,346.6	GNI per capita, Atlas ($)		59,260
GNI, PPP ($ billions)	966.6	GNI per capita, PPP ($)		42,540

	1990	2000	2012
People			
Share of poorest 20% in nat'l consumption/income (%)	..	..	..
Life expectancy at birth (years)	77	79	82
Total fertility rate (births per woman)	1.9	1.8	1.9
Adolescent fertility rate (births per 1,000 women 15-19)	21	18	12
Contraceptive prevalence (% of married women 15-49)	..	71	..
Births attended by skilled health staff (% of total)	100	100	..
Under-five mortality rate (per 1,000 live births)	9	6	5
Child malnutrition, underweight (% of under age 5)	..	..	0.2
Child immunization, measles (% of ages 12-23 mos.)	86	91	94
Primary completion rate, total (% of relevant age group)	..	..	..
Gross secondary enrollment, total (% of relevant age group)	134	161	133
Ratio of girls to boys in primary & secondary school (%)	100	100	97
HIV prevalence rate (% population of ages 15-49)	..	..	..
Environment			
Forests (1,000 sq. km)	1,545	1,549	1,484
Deforestation (avg. annual %, 1990-2000 and 2000-2010)		0.0	0.4
Freshwater use (% of internal resources)	..	4.6	4.6
Access to improved water source (% total pop.)	100	100	100
Access to improved sanitation facilities (% total pop.)	100	100	100
Energy use per capita (kilograms of oil equivalent)	5,053	5,645	5,883
Carbon dioxide emissions per capita (metric tons)	16.8	17.2	16.9
Electricity use per capita (kilowatt-hours)	8,527	10,194	10,712
Economy			
GDP ($ billions)	311	415	1,532
GDP growth (annual %)	3.6	3.8	3.4
GDP implicit price deflator (annual % growth)	5.7	2.6	2.2
Value added in agriculture (% of GDP)	5	3	2
Value added in industry (% of GDP)	31	27	28
Value added in services (% of GDP)	64	70	69
Exports of goods and services (% of GDP)	15	19	21
Imports of goods and services (% of GDP)	17	21	21
Gross capital formation (% of GDP)	29	26	28
Central government revenue (% of GDP)	..	25.9	22.9
Central government cash surplus/deficit (% of GDP)	..	2.0	-3.7
States and markets			
Starting a business (days)	..	3	3
Stock market capitalization (% of GDP)	35.0	89.8	83.9
Military expenditures (% of GDP)	2.1	1.9	1.7
Mobile cellular subscriptions (per 100 people)	1.1	44.5	105.6
Individuals using the Internet (% of population)	0.6	46.8	82.3
Paved roads (% of total)	35.0	40.0	43.3
High-technology exports (% of manufactured exports)	8	15	13
Global links			
Merchandise trade (% of GDP)	26	33	34
Net barter terms of trade index (2000 = 100)	..	100	185
Total external debt stocks ($ millions)	..	..	..
Total debt service (% of exports)	..	..	..
Net migration (thousands)	351	663	750
Personal remittances received ($ billions)	2.4	1.9	1.8
Foreign direct investment, net inflows ($ billions)	8.1	13.6	56.6
Net official development assistance received ($ millions)	..	..	..

Austria

High income

Population (millions)	8.4	Population growth (%)		0.3
Surface area (1,000 sq. km)	84	Population living below $1.25 a day (%)		..
GNI, Atlas ($ billions)	403.4	GNI per capita, Atlas ($)		47,850
GNI, PPP ($ billions)	369.7	GNI per capita, PPP ($)		43,850

	1990	2000	2012
People			
Share of poorest 20% in nat'l consumption/income (%)	..	8.6	..
Life expectancy at birth (years)	76	78	81
Total fertility rate (births per woman)	1.5	1.4	1.4
Adolescent fertility rate (births per 1,000 women 15-19)	21	14	4
Contraceptive prevalence (% of married women 15-49)	..	..	..
Births attended by skilled health staff (% of total)	100	..	..
Under-five mortality rate (per 1,000 live births)	10	6	4
Child malnutrition, underweight (% of under age 5)	..	..	..
Child immunization, measles (% of ages 12-23 mos.)	60	75	76
Primary completion rate, total (% of relevant age group)	..	101	97
Gross secondary enrollment, total (% of relevant age group)	102	98	98
Ratio of girls to boys in primary & secondary school (%)	94	97	97
HIV prevalence rate (% population of ages 15-49)	..	..	..
Environment			
Forests (1,000 sq. km)	38	38	39
Deforestation (avg. annual %, 1990-2000 and 2000-2010)		-0.2	-0.1
Freshwater use (% of internal resources)	6.9	6.6	6.6
Access to improved water source (% total pop.)	100	100	100
Access to improved sanitation facilities (% total pop.)	100	100	100
Energy use per capita (kilograms of oil equivalent)	3,236	3,565	3,902
Carbon dioxide emissions per capita (metric tons)	7.9	8.0	8.0
Electricity use per capita (kilowatt-hours)	6,111	7,076	8,374
Economy			
GDP ($ billions)	165	192	395
GDP growth (annual %)	4.3	3.7	0.9
GDP implicit price deflator (annual % growth)	3.0	0.9	1.7
Value added in agriculture (% of GDP)	4	2	2
Value added in industry (% of GDP)	33	31	29
Value added in services (% of GDP)	64	67	70
Exports of goods and services (% of GDP)	37	46	57
Imports of goods and services (% of GDP)	37	44	54
Gross capital formation (% of GDP)	25	25	23
Central government revenue (% of GDP)	..	37.7	36.3
Central government cash surplus/deficit (% of GDP)	..	-2.0	-2.2
States and markets			
Starting a business (days)	..	25	25
Stock market capitalization (% of GDP)	7.0	15.6	26.9
Military expenditures (% of GDP)	1.2	1.0	0.8
Mobile cellular subscriptions (per 100 people)	1.0	76.3	160.5
Individuals using the Internet (% of population)	0.1	33.7	81.0
Paved roads (% of total)	100.0	100.0	100.0
High-technology exports (% of manufactured exports)	8	15	13
Global links			
Merchandise trade (% of GDP)	55	73	87
Net barter terms of trade index (2000 = 100)	..	100	87
Total external debt stocks ($ millions)	..	..	..
Total debt service (% of exports)	..	..	..
Net migration (thousands)	275	213	150
Personal remittances received ($ billions)	0.6	1.8	2.8
Foreign direct investment, net inflows ($ billions)	0.7	8.5	4.1
Net official development assistance received ($ millions)	..	..	..

Azerbaijan

Europe & Central Asia		Upper middle income
Population (millions)	9.3	
Surface area (1,000 sq. km)	87	
GNI, Atlas ($ billions)	57.9	
GNI, PPP ($ billions)	86.5	

Population growth (%)		1.3
Population living below $1.25 a day (%)		<2
GNI per capita, Atlas ($)		6,220
GNI per capita, PPP ($)		9,310

	1990	2000	2012
People			
Share of poorest 20% in nat'l consumption/income (%)	..	7.5	8.0
Life expectancy at birth (years)	65	67	71
Total fertility rate (births per woman)	2.7	2.0	2.0
Adolescent fertility rate (births per 1,000 women 15–19)	32	37	40
Contraceptive prevalence (% of married women 15–49)	..	55	51
Births attended by skilled health staff (% of total)	97	84	99
Under-five mortality rate (per 1,000 live births)	93	72	35
Child malnutrition, underweight (% of under age 5)	..	14.0	8.4
Child immunization, measles (% of ages 12–23 mos.)	52	67	66
Primary completion rate, total (% of relevant age group)	96	90	92
Gross secondary enrollment, total (% of relevant age group)	89	..	100
Ratio of girls to boys in primary & secondary school (%)	100	..	98
HIV prevalence rate (% population of ages 15–49)	0.1	0.1	0.2
Environment			
Forests (1,000 sq. km)	9.4	9.4	9.4
Deforestation (avg. annual %, 1990–2000 and 2000–2010)		0.0	0.0
Freshwater use (% of internal resources)	..	124.1	150.5
Access to improved water source (% total pop.)	70	74	80
Access to improved sanitation facilities (% total pop.)	..	62	82
Energy use per capita (kilograms of oil equivalent)	3,165	1,403	1,369
Carbon dioxide emissions per capita (metric tons)	7.8	3.7	5.1
Electricity use per capita (kilowatt-hours)	2,576	2,040	1,705
Economy			
GDP ($ billions)	8.9	5.3	66.6
GDP growth (annual %)	-0.7	11.1	2.2
GDP implicit price deflator (annual % growth)	83.5	12.5	1.4
Value added in agriculture (% of GDP)	29	17	5
Value added in industry (% of GDP)	33	45	63
Value added in services (% of GDP)	38	38	31
Exports of goods and services (% of GDP)	44	39	54
Imports of goods and services (% of GDP)	39	38	26
Gross capital formation (% of GDP)	27	21	22
Central government revenue (% of GDP)	..	17.6	41.8
Central government cash surplus/deficit (% of GDP)	..	-4.7	6.1
States and markets			
Starting a business (days)	..	105	7
Stock market capitalization (% of GDP)	..	0.1	..
Military expenditures (% of GDP)	2.1	2.3	4.6
Mobile cellular subscriptions (per 100 people)	0.0	5.2	108.8
Individuals using the Internet (% of population)	0.0	0.1	54.2
Paved roads (% of total)	..	52.0	55.6
High-technology exports (% of manufactured exports)	..	5	7
Global links			
Merchandise trade (% of GDP)	..	55	64
Net barter terms of trade index (2000 = 100)	..	100	200
Total external debt stocks ($ billions)	0.0	1.5	9.7
Total debt service (% of exports)	..	6.4	5.1
Net migration (thousands)	-106	11	0
Personal remittances received ($ millions)	..	57	1,990
Foreign direct investment, net inflows ($ millions)	..	130	5,293
Net official development assistance received ($ millions)	0	139	338

Bahamas, The

Population (thousands)	372	Population growth (%)		1.5
Surface area (1,000 sq. km)	14	Population living below $1.25 a day (%)		..
GNI, Atlas ($ billions)	7.7	GNI per capita, Atlas ($)		20,600
GNI, PPP ($ billions)	10.8	GNI per capita, PPP ($)		29,020

	1990	2000	2012
People			
Share of poorest 20% in nat'l consumption/income (%)	..	..	..
Life expectancy at birth (years)	71	72	75
Total fertility rate (births per woman)	2.6	2.1	1.9
Adolescent fertility rate (births per 1,000 women 15–19)	70	51	28
Contraceptive prevalence (% of married women 15–49)	62	45	..
Births attended by skilled health staff (% of total)	99	99	99
Under-five mortality rate (per 1,000 live births)	23	17	17
Child malnutrition, underweight (% of under age 5)	..	..	..
Child immunization, measles (% of ages 12-23 mos.)	86	93	91
Primary completion rate, total (% of relevant age group)	..	82	93
Gross secondary enrollment, total (% of relevant age group)	86	78	93
Ratio of girls to boys in primary & secondary school (%)	102	97	104
HIV prevalence rate (% population of ages 15–49)	1.9	3.5	3.3
Environment			
Forests (1,000 sq. km)	5.2	5.2	5.2
Deforestation (avg. annual %, 1990–2000 and 2000–2010)		0.0	0.0
Freshwater use (% of internal resources)	..	..	..
Access to improved water source (% total pop.)	..	97	98
Access to improved sanitation facilities (% total pop.)	..	89	92
Energy use per capita (kilograms of oil equivalent)	2,517	..	..
Carbon dioxide emissions per capita (metric tons)	7.6	5.6	6.8
Electricity use per capita (kilowatt-hours)	..	..	..
Economy			
GDP ($ billions)	3.2	6.3	8.1
GDP growth (annual %)	-1.6	4.1	1.8
GDP implicit price deflator (annual % growth)	5.1	0.9	1.6
Value added in agriculture (% of GDP)	3	3	2
Value added in industry (% of GDP)	16	18	18
Value added in services (% of GDP)	81	80	80
Exports of goods and services (% of GDP)	54	44	45
Imports of goods and services (% of GDP)	56	62	63
Gross capital formation (% of GDP)	29	28	33
Central government revenue (% of GDP)	15.7	14.8	17.5
Central government cash surplus/deficit (% of GDP)	-1.9	0.3	-4.1
States and markets			
Starting a business (days)	..	..	24
Stock market capitalization (% of GDP)	..	..	..
Military expenditures (% of GDP)	..	..	..
Mobile cellular subscriptions (per 100 people)	0.7	10.6	80.7
Individuals using the Internet (% of population)	0.0	8.0	71.7
Paved roads (% of total)	52.0	57.0	..
High-technology exports (% of manufactured exports)	..	7	0
Global links			
Merchandise trade (% of GDP)	88	42	55
Net barter terms of trade index (2000 = 100)	..	100	89
Total external debt stocks ($ millions)	..	..	..
Total debt service (% of exports)	..	..	..
Net migration (thousands)	-0.4	15.5	9.7
Personal remittances received ($ millions)	..	..	..
Foreign direct investment, net inflows ($ millions)	-17	250	360
Net official development assistance received ($ millions)	3.2	..	..

Bahrain

High income

Population (millions)	1.3	Population growth (%)	1.9
Surface area (sq. km)	760	Population living below $1.25 a day (%)	..
GNI, Atlas ($ billions)	25.8	GNI per capita, Atlas ($)	19,560
GNI, PPP ($ billions)	27.8	GNI per capita, PPP ($)	22,250

	1990	2000	2012
People			
Share of poorest 20% in nat'l consumption/income (%)	..	..	..
Life expectancy at birth (years)	73	75	77
Total fertility rate (births per woman)	3.7	2.8	2.1
Adolescent fertility rate (births per 1,000 women 15-19)	26	17	14
Contraceptive prevalence (% of married women 15-49)	54	..	..
Births attended by skilled health staff (% of total)	..	..	100
Under-five mortality rate (per 1,000 live births)	23	13	10
Child malnutrition, underweight (% of under age 5)	6.3	..	..
Child immunization, measles (% of ages 12-23 mos.)	87	98	99
Primary completion rate, total (% of relevant age group)	103	99	..
Gross secondary enrollment, total (% of relevant age group)	87	100	96
Ratio of girls to boys in primary & secondary school (%)	103	102	..
HIV prevalence rate (% population of ages 15-49)	..	..	..
Environment			
Forests (sq. km)	2.0	4.0	5.4
Deforestation (avg. annual %, 1990-2000 and 2000-2010)		-5.6	-3.6
Freshwater use (% of internal resources)	5,975.0	5,975.0	8,935.0
Access to improved water source (% total pop.)	95	99	100
Access to improved sanitation facilities (% total pop.)	99	99	99
Energy use per capita (kilograms of oil equivalent)	8,771	8,776	7,353
Carbon dioxide emissions per capita (metric tons)	24.0	27.9	19.3
Electricity use per capita (kilowatt-hours)	6,533	8,590	10,018
Economy			
GDP ($ billions)	4.2	9.1	30.4
GDP growth (annual %)	4.4	5.3	3.4
GDP implicit price deflator (annual % growth)	4.8	30.0	1.1
Value added in agriculture (% of GDP)	1	..	..
Value added in industry (% of GDP)	46	..	..
Value added in services (% of GDP)	53	..	..
Exports of goods and services (% of GDP)	116	79	75
Imports of goods and services (% of GDP)	95	57	48
Gross capital formation (% of GDP)	16	17	20
Central government revenue (% of GDP)	..	..	24.9
Central government cash surplus/deficit (% of GDP)	..	..	-0.5
States and markets			
Starting a business (days)	..	..	9
Stock market capitalization (% of GDP)	..	73.1	52.9
Military expenditures (% of GDP)	5.1	4.0	3.1
Mobile cellular subscriptions (per 100 people)	1.0	30.8	161.2
Individuals using the Internet (% of population)	0.0	6.2	88.0
Paved roads (% of total)	75.4	78.0	83.7
High-technology exports (% of manufactured exports)	..	0	0
Global links			
Merchandise trade (% of GDP)	177	119	117
Net barter terms of trade index (2000 = 100)	..	100	129
Total external debt stocks ($ millions)	..	..	..
Total debt service (% of exports)	..	..	..
Net migration (thousands)	5	143	22
Personal remittances received ($ millions)	..	..	..
Foreign direct investment, net inflows ($ millions)	-183	364	891
Net official development assistance received ($ millions)	138	60	..

Bangladesh

Population (millions)	154.7	Population growth (%)	1.2
Surface area (1,000 sq. km)	144	Population living below $1.25 a day (%)	43.3
GNI, Atlas ($ billions)	129.3	GNI per capita, Atlas ($)	840
GNI, PPP ($ billions)	314.2	GNI per capita, PPP ($)	2,030

	1990	2000	2012
People			
Share of poorest 20% in nat'l consumption/income (%)	9.5	8.7	8.9
Life expectancy at birth (years)	60	65	70
Total fertility rate (births per woman)	4.6	3.1	2.2
Adolescent fertility rate (births per 1,000 women 15–19)	164	117	81
Contraceptive prevalence (% of married women 15–49)	40	54	61
Births attended by skilled health staff (% of total)	..	12	32
Under-five mortality rate (per 1,000 live births)	144	88	41
Child malnutrition, underweight (% of under age 5)	61.5	42.3	36.8
Child immunization, measles (% of ages 12–23 mos.)	65	72	96
Primary completion rate, total (% of relevant age group)	46	..	75
Gross secondary enrollment, total (% of relevant age group)	20	48	51
Ratio of girls to boys in primary & secondary school (%)	76	..	110
HIV prevalence rate (% population of ages 15–49)	0.1	0.1	0.1
Environment			
Forests (1,000 sq. km)	15	15	14
Deforestation (avg. annual %, 1990–2000 and 2000–2010)		0.2	0.2
Freshwater use (% of internal resources)	..	..	34.2
Access to improved water source (% total pop.)	68	76	85
Access to improved sanitation facilities (% total pop.)	33	45	57
Energy use per capita (kilograms of oil equivalent)	119	140	205
Carbon dioxide emissions per capita (metric tons)	0.1	0.2	0.4
Electricity use per capita (kilowatt-hours)	48	101	259
Economy			
GDP ($ billions)	30.5	47.1	116.4
GDP growth (annual %)	5.9	5.9	6.2
GDP implicit price deflator (annual % growth)	6.3	1.9	8.5
Value added in agriculture (% of GDP)	30	26	18
Value added in industry (% of GDP)	21	25	28
Value added in services (% of GDP)	48	49	54
Exports of goods and services (% of GDP)	6	14	23
Imports of goods and services (% of GDP)	14	19	32
Gross capital formation (% of GDP)	17	23	27
Central government revenue (% of GDP)	..	9.8	12.0
Central government cash surplus/deficit (% of GDP)	..	-0.7	-0.9
States and markets			
Starting a business (days)	..	50	11
Stock market capitalization (% of GDP)	1.1	2.5	15.0
Military expenditures (% of GDP)	1.1	1.4	1.3
Mobile cellular subscriptions (per 100 people)	0.0	0.2	62.8
Individuals using the Internet (% of population)	0.0	0.1	6.3
Paved roads (% of total)	7.2	10.0	..
High-technology exports (% of manufactured exports)	0	0	..
Global links			
Merchandise trade (% of GDP)	17	32	51
Net barter terms of trade index (2000 = 100)	117	100	59
Total external debt stocks ($ billions)	12.3	15.6	26.1
Total debt service (% of exports)	34.6	10.5	5.4
Net migration (thousands)	-934	-2,000	-2,041
Personal remittances received ($ billions)	0.8	2.0	14.1
Foreign direct investment, net inflows ($ millions)	3	280	1,178
Net official development assistance received ($ billions)	2.1	1.2	2.2

Barbados

High income

Population (thousands)	283	Population growth (%)	0.5
Surface area (sq. km)	430	Population living below $1.25 a day (%)	..
GNI, Atlas ($ billions)	4.3	GNI per capita, Atlas ($)	15,080
GNI, PPP ($ billions)	7.3	GNI per capita, PPP ($)	25,670

	1990	2000	2012
People			
Share of poorest 20% in nat'l consumption/income (%)	..	..	..
Life expectancy at birth (years)	71	73	75
Total fertility rate (births per woman)	1.7	1.8	1.8
Adolescent fertility rate (births per 1,000 women 15–19)	55	51	48
Contraceptive prevalence (% of married women 15–49)	55	55	..
Births attended by skilled health staff (% of total)	..	98	100
Under-five mortality rate (per 1,000 live births)	18	18	18
Child malnutrition, underweight (% of under age 5)	..	..	..
Child immunization, measles (% of ages 12–23 mos.)	87	94	90
Primary completion rate, total (% of relevant age group)	..	99	104
Gross secondary enrollment, total (% of relevant age group)	86	105	105
Ratio of girls to boys in primary & secondary school (%)	94	108	105
HIV prevalence rate (% population of ages 15–49)	0.2	0.7	0.9
Environment			
Forests (sq. km)	84	84	84
Deforestation (avg. annual %, 1990–2000 and 2000–2010)		0.0	0.0
Freshwater use (% of internal resources)	..	76.1	76.1
Access to improved water source (% total pop.)	95	99	100
Access to improved sanitation facilities (% total pop.)	82	90	..
Energy use per capita (kilograms of oil equivalent)	1,242	..	..
Carbon dioxide emissions per capita (metric tons)	4.1	4.4	5.4
Electricity use per capita (kilowatt-hours)	..	..	..
Economy			
GDP ($ billions)	2.0	3.1	4.2
GDP growth (annual %)	-4.8	2.3	0.0
GDP implicit price deflator (annual % growth)	24.7	0.7	-3.3
Value added in agriculture (% of GDP)	4	2	1
Value added in industry (% of GDP)	21	18	16
Value added in services (% of GDP)	75	80	83
Exports of goods and services (% of GDP)	43	42	42
Imports of goods and services (% of GDP)	43	46	54
Gross capital formation (% of GDP)	14	17	14
Central government revenue (% of GDP)	..	..	27.2
Central government cash surplus/deficit (% of GDP)	..	..	-8.0
States and markets			
Starting a business (days)	..	..	18
Stock market capitalization (% of GDP)	13.9	54.2	106.4
Military expenditures (% of GDP)	..	..	..
Mobile cellular subscriptions (per 100 people)	0.0	10.7	122.5
Individuals using the Internet (% of population)	0.0	4.0	73.3
Paved roads (% of total)	86.8	99.0	..
High-technology exports (% of manufactured exports)	20	23	12
Global links			
Merchandise trade (% of GDP)	45	46	55
Net barter terms of trade index (2000 = 100)	..	100	108
Total external debt stocks ($ millions)	..	..	..
Total debt service (% of exports)	..	..	..
Net migration (thousands)	-3.7	2.0	2.0
Personal remittances received ($ millions)	38	115	82
Foreign direct investment, net inflows ($ millions)	11	19	356
Net official development assistance received ($ millions)	2.6	0.2	16.2

Belarus

Europe & Central Asia		Upper middle income	
Population (millions)	9.5	Population growth (%)	-0.1
Surface area (1,000 sq. km)	208	Population living below $1.25 a day (%)	<2
GNI, Atlas ($ billions)	61.8	GNI per capita, Atlas ($)	6,530
GNI, PPP ($ billions)	141.6	GNI per capita, PPP ($)	14,960

	1990	2000	2012
People			
Share of poorest 20% in nat'l consumption/income (%)	11.1	8.5	9.4
Life expectancy at birth (years)	71	69	72
Total fertility rate (births per woman)	1.9	1.3	1.6
Adolescent fertility rate (births per 1,000 women 15–19)	44	28	21
Contraceptive prevalence (% of married women 15–49)	..	..	63
Births attended by skilled health staff (% of total)	100	100	100
Under-five mortality rate (per 1,000 live births)	17	14	5
Child malnutrition, underweight (% of under age 5)	..	..	..
Child immunization, measles (% of ages 12-23 mos.)	94	98	98
Primary completion rate, total (% of relevant age group)	94	100	103
Gross secondary enrollment, total (% of relevant age group)	97	85	106
Ratio of girls to boys in primary & secondary school (%)	..	101	98
HIV prevalence rate (% population of ages 15–49)	0.1	0.1	0.4
Environment			
Forests (1,000 sq. km)	78	83	87
Deforestation (avg. annual %, 1990-2000 and 2000-2010)		-0.6	-0.4
Freshwater use (% of internal resources)	..	11.7	11.7
Access to improved water source (% total pop.)	100	100	100
Access to improved sanitation facilities (% total pop.)	95	95	94
Energy use per capita (kilograms of oil equivalent)	4,465	2,468	3,114
Carbon dioxide emissions per capita (metric tons)	8.6	5.3	6.6
Electricity use per capita (kilowatt-hours)	4,381	2,989	3,628
Economy			
GDP ($ billions)	17.4	12.7	63.3
GDP growth (annual %)	-1.2	5.8	1.5
GDP implicit price deflator (annual % growth)	103.6	185.3	74.9
Value added in agriculture (% of GDP)	24	14	10
Value added in industry (% of GDP)	47	39	44
Value added in services (% of GDP)	29	47	46
Exports of goods and services (% of GDP)	46	69	82
Imports of goods and services (% of GDP)	44	72	77
Gross capital formation (% of GDP)	27	25	34
Central government revenue (% of GDP)	31.5	28.7	29.0
Central government cash surplus/deficit (% of GDP)	-4.8	0.1	1.7
States and markets			
Starting a business (days)	..	79	9
Stock market capitalization (% of GDP)	..	..	..
Military expenditures (% of GDP)	1.6	1.3	1.2
Mobile cellular subscriptions (per 100 people)	0.0	0.5	113.5
Individuals using the Internet (% of population)	0.0	1.9	46.9
Paved roads (% of total)	95.8	89.0	86.5
High-technology exports (% of manufactured exports)	..	4	3
Global links			
Merchandise trade (% of GDP)	..	125	146
Net barter terms of trade index (2000 = 100)	..	100	101
Total external debt stocks ($ billions)	1.0	2.6	34.2
Total debt service (% of exports)	0.6	4.9	9.5
Net migration (thousands)	-63.1	-6.4	-10.0
Personal remittances received ($ millions)	0	139	1,053
Foreign direct investment, net inflows ($ millions)	7	119	1,464
Net official development assistance received ($ millions)	..	..	103

Belgium

Population (millions)	11.1	Population growth (%)		0.7
Surface area (1,000 sq. km)	31	Population living below $1.25 a day (%)		..
GNI, Atlas ($ billions)	497.6	GNI per capita, Atlas ($)		44,720
GNI, PPP ($ billions)	452.7	GNI per capita, PPP ($)		40,680

	1990	2000	2012
People			
Share of poorest 20% in nat'l consumption/income (%)	..	8.5	..
Life expectancy at birth (years)	76	78	80
Total fertility rate (births per woman)	1.6	1.7	1.8
Adolescent fertility rate (births per 1,000 women 15-19)	11	11	7
Contraceptive prevalence (% of married women 15-49)	78	76	..
Births attended by skilled health staff (% of total)	..	99	..
Under-five mortality rate (per 1,000 live births)	10	6	4
Child malnutrition, underweight (% of under age 5)	..	..	..
Child immunization, measles (% of ages 12-23 mos.)	85	82	96
Primary completion rate, total (% of relevant age group)	79	..	91
Gross secondary enrollment, total (% of relevant age group)	103	145	106
Ratio of girls to boys in primary & secondary school (%)	101	105	98
HIV prevalence rate (% population of ages 15-49)	..	..	..
Environment			
Forests (1,000 sq. km)	6.8	6.7	6.8
Deforestation (avg. annual %, 1990-2000 and 2000-2010)		0.2	-0.2
Freshwater use (% of internal resources)	..	62.8	51.8
Access to improved water source (% total pop.)	100	100	100
Access to improved sanitation facilities (% total pop.)	100	100	100
Energy use per capita (kilograms of oil equivalent)	4,844	5,707	5,148
Carbon dioxide emissions per capita (metric tons)	10.9	11.3	10.0
Electricity use per capita (kilowatt-hours)	6,380	8,248	8,021
Economy			
GDP ($ billions)	203	233	483
GDP growth (annual %)	3.1	3.7	-0.1
GDP implicit price deflator (annual % growth)	2.8	2.0	1.9
Value added in agriculture (% of GDP)	2	1	1
Value added in industry (% of GDP)	31	27	22
Value added in services (% of GDP)	67	72	77
Exports of goods and services (% of GDP)	67	78	86
Imports of goods and services (% of GDP)	65	75	85
Gross capital formation (% of GDP)	23	23	21
Central government revenue (% of GDP)	..	42.8	41.2
Central government cash surplus/deficit (% of GDP)	..	0.0	-3.6
States and markets			
Starting a business (days)	..	56	4
Stock market capitalization (% of GDP)	32.2	78.4	62.1
Military expenditures (% of GDP)	2.3	1.4	1.1
Mobile cellular subscriptions (per 100 people)	0.4	54.8	111.3
Individuals using the Internet (% of population)	0.0	29.4	82.0
Paved roads (% of total)	81.2	78.0	78.2
High-technology exports (% of manufactured exports)	..	11	11
Global links			
Merchandise trade (% of GDP)	117	157	182
Net barter terms of trade index (2000 = 100)	..	100	94
Total external debt stocks ($ millions)	..	..	..
Total debt service (% of exports)	..	..	..
Net migration (thousands)	115	197	150
Personal remittances received ($ billions)	3.6	4.0	10.1
Foreign direct investment, net inflows ($ millions)	..	18,081	-1,917
Net official development assistance received ($ millions)	..	..	..

Belize

Latin America & Caribbean		Upper middle income	
Population (thousands)	324	Population growth (%)	2.4
Surface area (1,000 sq. km)	23	Population living below $1.25 a day (%)	12.2
GNI, Atlas ($ billions)	1.4	GNI per capita, Atlas ($)	4,490
GNI, PPP ($ billions)	2.5	GNI per capita, PPP ($)	7,630

	1990	2000	2012
People			
Share of poorest 20% in nat'l consumption/income (%)	3.0	3.3	..
Life expectancy at birth (years)	71	71	74
Total fertility rate (births per woman)	4.5	3.6	2.7
Adolescent fertility rate (births per 1,000 women 15-19)	126	97	71
Contraceptive prevalence (% of married women 15-49)	47	56	55
Births attended by skilled health staff (% of total)	77	100	96
Under-five mortality rate (per 1,000 live births)	43	25	18
Child malnutrition, underweight (% of under age 5)	5.4	..	6.2
Child immunization, measles (% of ages 12-23 mos.)	86	96	96
Primary completion rate, total (% of relevant age group)	94	101	116
Gross secondary enrollment, total (% of relevant age group)	61	68	84
Ratio of girls to boys in primary & secondary school (%)	98	99	100
HIV prevalence rate (% population of ages 15-49)	0.2	1.7	1.4
Environment			
Forests (1,000 sq. km)	16	15	14
Deforestation (avg. annual %, 1990-2000 and 2000-2010)		0.6	0.7
Freshwater use (% of internal resources)	..	0.9	0.9
Access to improved water source (% total pop.)	73	85	99
Access to improved sanitation facilities (% total pop.)	76	83	91
Energy use per capita (kilograms of oil equivalent)	566	..	..
Carbon dioxide emissions per capita (metric tons)	1.7	2.9	1.4
Electricity use per capita (kilowatt-hours)	..	..	..
Economy			
GDP ($ millions)	413	832	1,493
GDP growth (annual %)	10.6	13.0	5.3
GDP implicit price deflator (annual % growth)	2.8	0.4	0.5
Value added in agriculture (% of GDP)	20	17	13
Value added in industry (% of GDP)	22	21	23
Value added in services (% of GDP)	58	62	64
Exports of goods and services (% of GDP)	62	53	61
Imports of goods and services (% of GDP)	60	74	63
Gross capital formation (% of GDP)	26	29	15
Central government revenue (% of GDP)	25.4	20.4	26.0
Central government cash surplus/deficit (% of GDP)	-0.6	-5.7	-0.2
States and markets			
Starting a business (days)	..	..	44
Stock market capitalization (% of GDP)	..	..	..
Military expenditures (% of GDP)	1.1	0.9	0.9
Mobile cellular subscriptions (per 100 people)	0.0	7.0	53.2
Individuals using the Internet (% of population)	0.0	6.0	25.0
Paved roads (% of total)	..	17.0	..
High-technology exports (% of manufactured exports)	0	0	5
Global links			
Merchandise trade (% of GDP)	83	89	81
Net barter terms of trade index (2000 = 100)	..	100	94
Total external debt stocks ($ millions)	143	528	1,241
Total debt service (% of exports)	7.2	15.3	11.3
Net migration (thousands)	-9.0	4.5	7.6
Personal remittances received ($ millions)	18.5	26.4	75.9
Foreign direct investment, net inflows ($ millions)	17	23	194
Net official development assistance received ($ millions)	30.3	14.7	25.2

Benin

Sub-Saharan Africa		Low income	
Population (millions)	10.1	Population growth (%)	2.7
Surface area (1,000 sq. km)	115	Population living below $1.25 a day (%)	47.3
GNI, Atlas ($ billions)	7.5	GNI per capita, Atlas ($)	750
GNI, PPP ($ billions)	15.6	GNI per capita, PPP ($)	1,550

	1990	2000	2012
People			
Share of poorest 20% in nat'l consumption/income (%)	..	7.0	..
Life expectancy at birth (years)	53	55	59
Total fertility rate (births per woman)	6.7	6.0	4.9
Adolescent fertility rate (births per 1,000 women 15-19)	125	119	90
Contraceptive prevalence (% of married women 15-49)	..	19	13
Births attended by skilled health staff (% of total)	..	66	84
Under-five mortality rate (per 1,000 live births)	181	147	90
Child malnutrition, underweight (% of under age 5)	..	21.5	20.2
Child immunization, measles (% of ages 12-23 mos.)	79	70	72
Primary completion rate, total (% of relevant age group)	19	37	71
Gross secondary enrollment, total (% of relevant age group)	..	22	48
Ratio of girls to boys in primary & secondary school (%)	..	62	79
HIV prevalence rate (% population of ages 15-49)	0.3	1.6	1.1
Environment			
Forests (1,000 sq. km)	58	51	45
Deforestation (avg. annual %, 1990-2000 and 2000-2010)		1.3	1.0
Freshwater use (% of internal resources)	..	1.3	1.3
Access to improved water source (% total pop.)	57	66	76
Access to improved sanitation facilities (% total pop.)	5	9	14
Energy use per capita (kilograms of oil equivalent)	332	285	385
Carbon dioxide emissions per capita (metric tons)	0.1	0.2	0.5
Electricity use per capita (kilowatt-hours)	..	57	..
Economy			
GDP ($ billions)	2.0	2.4	7.6
GDP growth (annual %)	9.0	4.9	5.4
GDP implicit price deflator (annual % growth)	2.2	4.5	6.3
Value added in agriculture (% of GDP)	35	35	32
Value added in industry (% of GDP)	12	13	13
Value added in services (% of GDP)	53	52	54
Exports of goods and services (% of GDP)	19	25	15
Imports of goods and services (% of GDP)	27	30	27
Gross capital formation (% of GDP)	14	19	18
Central government revenue (% of GDP)	..	15.6	17.2
Central government cash surplus/deficit (% of GDP)	..	0.6	-1.4
States and markets			
Starting a business (days)	..	32	15
Stock market capitalization (% of GDP)	..	..	..
Military expenditures (% of GDP)	1.7	0.6	1.0
Mobile cellular subscriptions (per 100 people)	0.0	0.8	83.7
Individuals using the Internet (% of population)	0.0	0.2	3.8
Paved roads (% of total)	20.0	9.5	..
High-technology exports (% of manufactured exports)	..	0	0
Global links			
Merchandise trade (% of GDP)	28	43	48
Net barter terms of trade index (2000 = 100)	107	100	118
Total external debt stocks ($ billions)	1.1	1.4	2.1
Total debt service (% of exports)	9.9	13.6	3.3
Net migration (thousands)	105	99	-10
Personal remittances received ($ millions)	101	87	172
Foreign direct investment, net inflows ($ millions)	62	60	159
Net official development assistance received ($ millions)	267	243	511

Bermuda

High income

Population (thousands)	65	Population growth (%)	0.4
Surface area (sq. km)	50	Population living below $1.25 a day (%)	..
GNI, Atlas ($ billions)	6.8	GNI per capita, Atlas ($)	104,590
GNI, PPP ($ millions)	..	GNI per capita, PPP ($)	..

	1990	2000	2012
People			
Share of poorest 20% in nat'l consumption/income (%)	..	..	..
Life expectancy at birth (years)	74	78	79
Total fertility rate (births per woman)	..	1.7	1.8
Adolescent fertility rate (births per 1,000 women 15-19)	..	..	..
Contraceptive prevalence (% of married women 15-49)	..	..	..
Births attended by skilled health staff (% of total)	..	..	..
Under-five mortality rate (per 1,000 live births)	..	..	..
Child malnutrition, underweight (% of under age 5)	..	..	..
Child immunization, measles (% of ages 12-23 mos.)	..	..	..
Primary completion rate, total (% of relevant age group)	..	97	91
Gross secondary enrollment, total (% of relevant age group)	..	79	77
Ratio of girls to boys in primary & secondary school (%)	..	104	107
HIV prevalence rate (% population of ages 15-49)	..	..	..
Environment			
Forests (sq. km)	10.0	10.0	10.0
Deforestation (avg. annual %, 1990-2000 and 2000-2010)		0.0	0.0
Freshwater use (% of internal resources)	..	..	
Access to improved water source (% total pop.)	..	..	..
Access to improved sanitation facilities (% total pop.)	..	..	..
Energy use per capita (kilograms of oil equivalent)	..	..	..
Carbon dioxide emissions per capita (metric tons)	10.1	8.0	7.3
Electricity use per capita (kilowatt-hours)	..	..	..
Economy			
GDP ($ billions)	1.6	3.5	5.5
GDP growth (annual %)	0.0	9.3	-4.9
GDP implicit price deflator (annual % growth)	6.0	-4.2	3.7
Value added in agriculture (% of GDP)	..	1	1
Value added in industry (% of GDP)	..	12	6
Value added in services (% of GDP)	..	88	93
Exports of goods and services (% of GDP)	..	..	..
Imports of goods and services (% of GDP)	..	..	..
Gross capital formation (% of GDP)	..	..	..
Central government revenue (% of GDP)	..	..	..
Central government cash surplus/deficit (% of GDP)	..	..	..
States and markets			
Starting a business (days)	..	..	..
Stock market capitalization (% of GDP)	..	61.7	27.2
Military expenditures (% of GDP)	..	..	..
Mobile cellular subscriptions (per 100 people)	1.9	20.7	139.5
Individuals using the Internet (% of population)	0.0	42.9	91.3
Paved roads (% of total)	..	..	..
High-technology exports (% of manufactured exports)	..	..	7
Global links			
Merchandise trade (% of GDP)	41	22	17
Net barter terms of trade index (2000 = 100)	..	100	62
Total external debt stocks ($ millions)	..	..	..
Total debt service (% of exports)	..	..	..
Net migration (thousands)	..	..	..
Personal remittances received ($ millions)	..	..	1,191
Foreign direct investment, net inflows ($ millions)	..	67	133
Net official development assistance received ($ millions)	42.2	..	..

Bhutan

South Asia   **Lower middle income**

Population (thousands)	742	Population growth (%)	1.7
Surface area (1,000 sq. km)	38	Population living below $1.25 a day (%)	1.7
GNI, Atlas ($ billions)	1.8	GNI per capita, Atlas ($)	2,420
GNI, PPP ($ billions)	4.6	GNI per capita, PPP ($)	6,200

	1990	2000	2012
People			
Share of poorest 20% in nat'l consumption/income (%)	..	5.4	6.8
Life expectancy at birth (years)	52	60	68
Total fertility rate (births per woman)	5.6	3.6	2.3
Adolescent fertility rate (births per 1,000 women 15–19)	105	78	41
Contraceptive prevalence (% of married women 15–49)	..	31	66
Births attended by skilled health staff (% of total)	..	24	65
Under-five mortality rate (per 1,000 live births)	131	80	45
Child malnutrition, underweight (% of under age 5)	..	14.1	12.8
Child immunization, measles (% of ages 12–23 mos.)	93	78	95
Primary completion rate, total (% of relevant age group)	24	51	101
Gross secondary enrollment, total (% of relevant age group)	..	30	74
Ratio of girls to boys in primary & secondary school (%)	..	85	103
HIV prevalence rate (% population of ages 15–49)	0.1	0.1	0.2
Environment			
Forests (1,000 sq. km)	30	31	33
Deforestation (avg. annual %, 1990–2000 and 2000–2010)		-0.3	-0.3
Freshwater use (% of internal resources)	..	..	0.4
Access to improved water source (% total pop.)	..	86	98
Access to improved sanitation facilities (% total pop.)	..	35	47
Energy use per capita (kilograms of oil equivalent)	104	..	..
Carbon dioxide emissions per capita (metric tons)	0.2	0.7	0.7
Electricity use per capita (kilowatt-hours)	..	..	..
Economy			
GDP ($ millions)	300	439	1,780
GDP growth (annual %)	10.9	6.9	9.4
GDP implicit price deflator (annual % growth)	5.7	2.3	1.5
Value added in agriculture (% of GDP)	35	27	16
Value added in industry (% of GDP)	25	36	44
Value added in services (% of GDP)	40	37	40
Exports of goods and services (% of GDP)	27	29	35
Imports of goods and services (% of GDP)	31	53	53
Gross capital formation (% of GDP)	30	48	56
Central government revenue (% of GDP)	17.0	22.9	22.9
Central government cash surplus/deficit (% of GDP)	-5.8	-2.4	0.5
States and markets			
Starting a business (days)	..	62	32
Stock market capitalization (% of GDP)	..	10.3	..
Military expenditures (% of GDP)	..	..	..
Mobile cellular subscriptions (per 100 people)	0.0	0.0	75.6
Individuals using the Internet (% of population)	0.0	0.4	25.4
Paved roads (% of total)	77.1	62.0	34.2
High-technology exports (% of manufactured exports)	..	0	0
Global links			
Merchandise trade (% of GDP)	50	63	90
Net barter terms of trade index (2000 = 100)	..	100	134
Total external debt stocks ($ millions)	84	212	1,459
Total debt service (% of exports)	..	..	17.8
Net migration (thousands)	-85.9	35.0	10.0
Personal remittances received ($ millions)	..	..	18.1
Foreign direct investment, net inflows ($ millions)	1.6	1.1	9.6
Net official development assistance received ($ millions)	46	53	161

Bolivia

Population (millions)	10.5	Population growth (%)	1.7
Surface area (1,000 sq. km)	1,099	Population living below $1.25 a day (%)	15.6
GNI, Atlas ($ billions)	23.3	GNI per capita, Atlas ($)	2,220
GNI, PPP ($ billions)	51.2	GNI per capita, PPP ($)	4,880

	1990	2000	2012
People			
Share of poorest 20% in nat'l consumption/income (%)	5.6	0.8	2.1
Life expectancy at birth (years)	59	63	67
Total fertility rate (births per woman)	4.9	4.1	3.3
Adolescent fertility rate (births per 1,000 women 15-19)	89	85	72
Contraceptive prevalence (% of married women 15-49)	30	53	61
Births attended by skilled health staff (% of total)	43	69	71
Under-five mortality rate (per 1,000 live births)	123	78	41
Child malnutrition, underweight (% of under age 5)	9.7	5.9	4.5
Child immunization, measles (% of ages 12-23 mos.)	53	84	84
Primary completion rate, total (% of relevant age group)	70	96	92
Gross secondary enrollment, total (% of relevant age group)	..	78	77
Ratio of girls to boys in primary & secondary school (%)	..	97	99
HIV prevalence rate (% population of ages 15-49)	0.1	0.4	0.3
Environment			
Forests (1,000 sq. km)	628	601	569
Deforestation (avg. annual %, 1990-2000 and 2000-2010)		0.4	0.5
Freshwater use (% of internal resources)	..	0.7	0.7
Access to improved water source (% total pop.)	69	79	88
Access to improved sanitation facilities (% total pop.)	28	37	46
Energy use per capita (kilograms of oil equivalent)	384	440	746
Carbon dioxide emissions per capita (metric tons)	0.8	1.2	1.5
Electricity use per capita (kilowatt-hours)	269	412	623
Economy			
GDP ($ billions)	4.9	8.4	27.0
GDP growth (annual %)	4.6	2.5	5.2
GDP implicit price deflator (annual % growth)	16.3	5.2	6.9
Value added in agriculture (% of GDP)	17	15	13
Value added in industry (% of GDP)	35	30	39
Value added in services (% of GDP)	48	55	48
Exports of goods and services (% of GDP)	23	18	47
Imports of goods and services (% of GDP)	24	27	38
Gross capital formation (% of GDP)	13	18	18
Central government revenue (% of GDP)	..	18.4	..
Central government cash surplus/deficit (% of GDP)	..	-8.7	..
States and markets			
Starting a business (days)	..	60	49
Stock market capitalization (% of GDP)	..	20.7	16.4
Military expenditures (% of GDP)	2.8	2.1	1.5
Mobile cellular subscriptions (per 100 people)	0.0	6.9	90.4
Individuals using the Internet (% of population)	0.0	1.4	34.2
Paved roads (% of total)	4.3	7.0	11.6
High-technology exports (% of manufactured exports)	7	40	9
Global links			
Merchandise trade (% of GDP)	33	36	70
Net barter terms of trade index (2000 = 100)	102	100	179
Total external debt stocks ($ billions)	4.4	5.9	6.9
Total debt service (% of exports)	39.4	39.8	5.3
Net migration (thousands)	-100	-131	-125
Personal remittances received ($ millions)	5	127	1,111
Foreign direct investment, net inflows ($ millions)	27	736	1,060
Net official development assistance received ($ millions)	545	482	659

Bosnia and Herzegovina

Europe & Central Asia		Upper middle income
Population (millions)	3.8	Population growth (%)	-0.1
Surface area (1,000 sq. km)	51	Population living below $1.25 a day (%)	<2
GNI, Atlas ($ billions)	18.2	GNI per capita, Atlas ($)	4,750
GNI, PPP ($ billions)	37.0	GNI per capita, PPP ($)	9,650

	1990	2000	2012
People			
Share of poorest 20% in nat'l consumption/income (%)	..	9.1	6.7
Life expectancy at birth (years)	67	75	76
Total fertility rate (births per woman)	1.7	1.4	1.3
Adolescent fertility rate (births per 1,000 women 15–19)	36	21	15
Contraceptive prevalence (% of married women 15–49)	..	48	46
Births attended by skilled health staff (% of total)	97	100	100
Under-five mortality rate (per 1,000 live births)	18	10	7
Child malnutrition, underweight (% of under age 5)	..	4.2	1.5
Child immunization, measles (% of ages 12–23 mos.)	52	80	94
Primary completion rate, total (% of relevant age group)	..	..	..
Gross secondary enrollment, total (% of relevant age group)	..	..	..
Ratio of girls to boys in primary & secondary school (%)	..	..	..
HIV prevalence rate (% population of ages 15–49)	..	..	..
Environment			
Forests (1,000 sq. km)	22	22	22
Deforestation (avg. annual %, 1990-2000 and 2000-2010)		0.1	0.0
Freshwater use (% of internal resources)	..	..	1.0
Access to improved water source (% total pop.)	97	98	100
Access to improved sanitation facilities (% total pop.)	..	95	95
Energy use per capita (kilograms of oil equivalent)	1,550	1,133	1,848
Carbon dioxide emissions per capita (metric tons)	1.0	6.1	8.1
Electricity use per capita (kilowatt-hours)	2,897	1,986	3,189
Economy			
GDP ($ billions)	..	5.5	17.5
GDP growth (annual %)	..	5.5	-0.7
GDP implicit price deflator (annual % growth)	..	28.8	0.6
Value added in agriculture (% of GDP)	..	11	8
Value added in industry (% of GDP)	..	23	25
Value added in services (% of GDP)	..	66	67
Exports of goods and services (% of GDP)	..	29	31
Imports of goods and services (% of GDP)	..	76	55
Gross capital formation (% of GDP)	..	21	22
Central government revenue (% of GDP)	..	37.1	39.7
Central government cash surplus/deficit (% of GDP)	..	0.7	-1.2
States and markets			
Starting a business (days)	..	68	37
Stock market capitalization (% of GDP)	..	..	..
Military expenditures (% of GDP)	..	3.6	1.4
Mobile cellular subscriptions (per 100 people)	0.0	2.4	87.6
Individuals using the Internet (% of population)	0.0	1.1	65.4
Paved roads (% of total)	54.0	52.3	92.1
High-technology exports (% of manufactured exports)	..	2	2
Global links			
Merchandise trade (% of GDP)	..	76	87
Net barter terms of trade index (2000 = 100)	..	100	99
Total external debt stocks ($ billions)	..	2.8	10.6
Total debt service (% of exports)	..	14.2	18.4
Net migration (thousands)	-1,025	38	-5
Personal remittances received ($ billions)	..	1.6	1.8
Foreign direct investment, net inflows ($ millions)	..	146	350
Net official development assistance received ($ millions)	0	738	571

Botswana

Upper middle income

Population (millions)	2.0	Population growth (%)	0.9
Surface area (1,000 sq. km)	582	Population living below $1.25 a day (%)	31.2
GNI, Atlas ($ billions)	15.3	GNI per capita, Atlas ($)	7,650
GNI, PPP ($ billions)	32.2	GNI per capita, PPP ($)	16,060

	1990	2000	2012
People			
Share of poorest 20% in nat'l consumption/income (%)	..	..	..
Life expectancy at birth (years)	63	50	47
Total fertility rate (births per woman)	4.7	3.4	2.7
Adolescent fertility rate (births per 1,000 women 15–19)	103	66	44
Contraceptive prevalence (% of married women 15–49)	33	44	53
Births attended by skilled health staff (% of total)	78	94	95
Under-five mortality rate (per 1,000 live births)	48	85	53
Child malnutrition, underweight (% of under age 5)	..	10.7	11.2
Child immunization, measles (% of ages 12–23 mos.)	87	91	94
Primary completion rate, total (% of relevant age group)	89	89	95
Gross secondary enrollment, total (% of relevant age group)	40	75	..
Ratio of girls to boys in primary & secondary school (%)	108	102	..
HIV prevalence rate (% population of ages 15–49)	4.3	28.2	23.0
Environment			
Forests (1,000 sq. km)	137	125	112
Deforestation (avg. annual %, 1990-2000 and 2000-2010)		0.9	1.0
Freshwater use (% of internal resources)	4.7	8.1	8.1
Access to improved water source (% total pop.)	92	95	97
Access to improved sanitation facilities (% total pop.)	39	52	64
Energy use per capita (kilograms of oil equivalent)	911	1,046	1,115
Carbon dioxide emissions per capita (metric tons)	1.6	2.4	2.7
Electricity use per capita (kilowatt-hours)	715	907	1,603
Economy			
GDP ($ billions)	3.8	5.8	14.5
GDP growth (annual %)	6.8	2.0	4.2
GDP implicit price deflator (annual % growth)	6.3	14.2	1.4
Value added in agriculture (% of GDP)	5	3	3
Value added in industry (% of GDP)	61	51	35
Value added in services (% of GDP)	34	46	62
Exports of goods and services (% of GDP)	55	52	44
Imports of goods and services (% of GDP)	50	40	50
Gross capital formation (% of GDP)	37	30	34
Central government revenue (% of GDP)	50.8	..	35.7
Central government cash surplus/deficit (% of GDP)	19.1	..	-1.9
States and markets			
Starting a business (days)	..	107	60
Stock market capitalization (% of GDP)	6.6	16.9	31.6
Military expenditures (% of GDP)	4.1	3.2	2.3
Mobile cellular subscriptions (per 100 people)	0.0	12.7	153.8
Individuals using the Internet (% of population)	0.0	2.9	11.5
Paved roads (% of total)	32.0	35.3	..
High-technology exports (% of manufactured exports)	..	1	1
Global links			
Merchandise trade (% of GDP)	98	82	96
Net barter terms of trade index (2000 = 100)	98	100	85
Total external debt stocks ($ millions)	553	458	2,488
Total debt service (% of exports)	4.3	2.0	0.8
Net migration (thousands)	17.9	21.3	20.0
Personal remittances received ($ millions)	85.6	26.2	18.2
Foreign direct investment, net inflows ($ millions)	96	57	293
Net official development assistance received ($ millions)	145	31	74

Brazil

Latin America & Caribbean		Upper middle income	
Population (millions)	198.7	Population growth (%)	0.9
Surface area (1,000 sq. km)	8,515	Population living below $1.25 a day (%)	6.1
GNI, Atlas ($ billions)	2,311.1	GNI per capita, Atlas ($)	11,630
GNI, PPP ($ billions)	2,291.0	GNI per capita, PPP ($)	11,530

	1990	2000	2012
People			
Share of poorest 20% in nat'l consumption/income (%)	2.2	2.1	2.9
Life expectancy at birth (years)	67	70	74
Total fertility rate (births per woman)	2.8	2.4	1.8
Adolescent fertility rate (births per 1,000 women 15–19)	82	87	71
Contraceptive prevalence (% of married women 15–49)	59	..	81
Births attended by skilled health staff (% of total)	70	96	97
Under-five mortality rate (per 1,000 live births)	62	33	14
Child malnutrition, underweight (% of under age 5)	5.3	3.7	2.2
Child immunization, measles (% of ages 12–23 mos.)	78	99	99
Primary completion rate, total (% of relevant age group)	92	..	..
Gross secondary enrollment, total (% of relevant age group)	..	..	..
Ratio of girls to boys in primary & secondary school (%)	..	..	..
HIV prevalence rate (% population of ages 15–49)	..	..	..
Environment			
Forests (1,000 sq. km)	5,748	5,459	5,173
Deforestation (avg. annual %, 1990–2000 and 2000–2010)		0.5	0.5
Freshwater use (% of internal resources)	..	1.1	1.1
Access to improved water source (% total pop.)	88	93	98
Access to improved sanitation facilities (% total pop.)	67	75	81
Energy use per capita (kilograms of oil equivalent)	937	1,074	1,371
Carbon dioxide emissions per capita (metric tons)	1.4	1.9	2.2
Electricity use per capita (kilowatt-hours)	1,454	1,900	2,438
Economy			
GDP ($ billions)	462	645	2,253
GDP growth (annual %)	-4.3	4.3	0.9
GDP implicit price deflator (annual % growth)	2,735.5	6.2	5.3
Value added in agriculture (% of GDP)	8	6	5
Value added in industry (% of GDP)	39	28	26
Value added in services (% of GDP)	53	67	68
Exports of goods and services (% of GDP)	8	10	13
Imports of goods and services (% of GDP)	7	12	14
Gross capital formation (% of GDP)	20	18	18
Central government revenue (% of GDP)	22.8	19.9	25.0
Central government cash surplus/deficit (% of GDP)	-3.4	-1.8	-2.6
States and markets			
Starting a business (days)	..	152	108
Stock market capitalization (% of GDP)	3.6	35.1	54.6
Military expenditures (% of GDP)	6.3	1.8	1.5
Mobile cellular subscriptions (per 100 people)	0.0	13.3	125.0
Individuals using the Internet (% of population)	0.0	2.9	49.8
Paved roads (% of total)	9.7	6.0	13.5
High-technology exports (% of manufactured exports)	6	19	10
Global links			
Merchandise trade (% of GDP)	12	18	21
Net barter terms of trade index (2000 = 100)	66	100	129
Total external debt stocks ($ billions)	120	243	440
Total debt service (% of exports)	22.6	85.9	15.5
Net migration (thousands)	-100	-500	-190
Personal remittances received ($ billions)	0.6	1.6	2.6
Foreign direct investment, net inflows ($ billions)	1.0	32.8	76.1
Net official development assistance received ($ millions)	151	231	1,288

Brunei Darussalam

High income

Population (thousands)	412	Population growth (%)	1.4
Surface area (1,000 sq. km)	5.8	Population living below $1.25 a day (%)	..
GNI, Atlas ($ billions)	12.5	GNI per capita, Atlas ($)	31,590
GNI, PPP ($ billions)	19.3	GNI per capita, PPP ($)	49,000

	1990	2000	2012
People			
Share of poorest 20% in nat'l consumption/income (%)	..	..	..
Life expectancy at birth (years)	74	76	78
Total fertility rate (births per woman)	3.5	2.4	2.0
Adolescent fertility rate (births per 1,000 women 15-19)	42	27	23
Contraceptive prevalence (% of married women 15-49)	..	..	..
Births attended by skilled health staff (% of total)	..	99	100
Under-five mortality rate (per 1,000 live births)	12	10	8
Child malnutrition, underweight (% of under age 5)	..	..	..
Child immunization, measles (% of ages 12-23 mos.)	99	99	99
Primary completion rate, total (% of relevant age group)	99	116	102
Gross secondary enrollment, total (% of relevant age group)	75	86	108
Ratio of girls to boys in primary & secondary school (%)	100	100	100
HIV prevalence rate (% population of ages 15-49)	..	..	..
Environment			
Forests (1,000 sq. km)	4.1	4.0	3.8
Deforestation (avg. annual %, 1990-2000 and 2000-2010)		0.4	0.4
Freshwater use (% of internal resources)	0.9	1.1	1.1
Access to improved water source (% total pop.)	..	..	..
Access to improved sanitation facilities (% total pop.)	..	..	..
Energy use per capita (kilograms of oil equivalent)	6,721	7,187	9,427
Carbon dioxide emissions per capita (metric tons)	25.0	19.7	22.9
Electricity use per capita (kilowatt-hours)	4,355	7,577	8,507
Economy			
GDP ($ billions)	3.5	6.0	17.0
GDP growth (annual %)	1.1	2.8	2.2
GDP implicit price deflator (annual % growth)	8.4	29.0	0.8
Value added in agriculture (% of GDP)	1	1	1
Value added in industry (% of GDP)	62	64	71
Value added in services (% of GDP)	37	35	28
Exports of goods and services (% of GDP)	62	67	81
Imports of goods and services (% of GDP)	37	36	31
Gross capital formation (% of GDP)	19	13	14
Central government revenue (% of GDP)	..	..	..
Central government cash surplus/deficit (% of GDP)	..	..	..
States and markets			
Starting a business (days)	..	..	101
Stock market capitalization (% of GDP)	..	..	..
Military expenditures (% of GDP)	6.6	4.1	2.4
Mobile cellular subscriptions (per 100 people)	0.7	28.6	113.9
Individuals using the Internet (% of population)	0.0	9.0	60.3
Paved roads (% of total)	31.4	35.0	82.3
High-technology exports (% of manufactured exports)	..	0	13
Global links			
Merchandise trade (% of GDP)	91	83	100
Net barter terms of trade index (2000 = 100)	..	100	226
Total external debt stocks ($ millions)	..	..	..
Total debt service (% of exports)	..	..	..
Net migration (thousands)	1.1	3.5	1.8
Personal remittances received ($ millions)	..	..	..
Foreign direct investment, net inflows ($ millions)	..	61	850
Net official development assistance received ($ millions)	3.9	..	..

Bulgaria

Population (millions)	7.3	Population growth (%)	-0.6
Surface area (1,000 sq. km)	111	Population living below $1.25 a day (%)	<2
GNI, Atlas ($ billions)	50.0	GNI per capita, Atlas ($)	6,840
GNI, PPP ($ billions)	112.9	GNI per capita, PPP ($)	15,450

	1990	2000	2012
People			
Share of poorest 20% in nat'l consumption/income (%)	10.5	6.5	8.5
Life expectancy at birth (years)	72	72	74
Total fertility rate (births per woman)	1.8	1.3	1.5
Adolescent fertility rate (births per 1,000 women 15–19)	70	44	36
Contraceptive prevalence (% of married women 15–49)	..	63	..
Births attended by skilled health staff (% of total)	99	100	100
Under-five mortality rate (per 1,000 live births)	22	21	12
Child malnutrition, underweight (% of under age 5)	..	1.6	..
Child immunization, measles (% of ages 12–23 mos.)	99	89	94
Primary completion rate, total (% of relevant age group)	99	97	104
Gross secondary enrollment, total (% of relevant age group)	99	93	93
Ratio of girls to boys in primary & secondary school (%)	99	98	97
HIV prevalence rate (% population of ages 15–49)	..	..	..
Environment			
Forests (1,000 sq. km)	33	34	40
Deforestation (avg. annual %, 1990–2000 and 2000–2010)		-0.1	-1.5
Freshwater use (% of internal resources)	35.7	29.2	29.1
Access to improved water source (% total pop.)	100	100	99
Access to improved sanitation facilities (% total pop.)	99	100	100
Energy use per capita (kilograms of oil equivalent)	3,236	2,287	2,615
Carbon dioxide emissions per capita (metric tons)	8.7	5.3	6.0
Electricity use per capita (kilowatt-hours)	4,759	3,674	4,864
Economy			
GDP ($ billions)	20.7	12.9	51.0
GDP growth (annual %)	-9.1	5.7	0.8
GDP implicit price deflator (annual % growth)	26.2	6.6	2.2
Value added in agriculture (% of GDP)	17	13	6
Value added in industry (% of GDP)	49	26	30
Value added in services (% of GDP)	34	61	63
Exports of goods and services (% of GDP)	33	50	67
Imports of goods and services (% of GDP)	37	56	70
Gross capital formation (% of GDP)	26	18	24
Central government revenue (% of GDP)	47.1	32.9	29.4
Central government cash surplus/deficit (% of GDP)	-5.0	-0.4	-2.0
States and markets			
Starting a business (days)	..	32	18
Stock market capitalization (% of GDP)	..	4.8	13.1
Military expenditures (% of GDP)	3.7	2.7	1.5
Mobile cellular subscriptions (per 100 people)	0.0	9.2	148.1
Individuals using the Internet (% of population)	0.0	5.4	55.1
Paved roads (% of total)	91.6	92.1	98.6
High-technology exports (% of manufactured exports)	..	3	8
Global links			
Merchandise trade (% of GDP)	49	88	117
Net barter terms of trade index (2000 = 100)	..	100	107
Total external debt stocks ($ billions)	10.9	12.0	50.8
Total debt service (% of exports)	19.4	18.2	13.0
Net migration (thousands)	-356	-83	-50
Personal remittances received ($ millions)	..	58	1,449
Foreign direct investment, net inflows ($ billions)	0.0	1.0	2.1
Net official development assistance received ($ millions)	..	..	..

Burkina Faso

Sub-Saharan Africa   **Low income**

Population (millions)	16.5	Population growth (%)	2.9
Surface area (1,000 sq. km)	274	Population living below $1.25 a day (%)	44.6
GNI, Atlas ($ billions)	11.0	GNI per capita, Atlas ($)	670
GNI, PPP ($ billions)	24.4	GNI per capita, PPP ($)	1,480

	1990	2000	2012
People			
Share of poorest 20% in nat'l consumption/income (%)	..	7.0	6.7
Life expectancy at birth (years)	49	50	56
Total fertility rate (births per woman)	7.0	6.6	5.7
Adolescent fertility rate (births per 1,000 women 15–19)	147	139	115
Contraceptive prevalence (% of married women 15–49)	8	12	16
Births attended by skilled health staff (% of total)	42	31	66
Under-five mortality rate (per 1,000 live births)	202	186	102
Child malnutrition, underweight (% of under age 5)	29.6	33.7	26.2
Child immunization, measles (% of ages 12–23 mos.)	79	48	87
Primary completion rate, total (% of relevant age group)	19	25	58
Gross secondary enrollment, total (% of relevant age group)	7	10	26
Ratio of girls to boys in primary & secondary school (%)	..	70	91
HIV prevalence rate (% population of ages 15–49)	3.3	2.5	1.0
Environment			
Forests (1,000 sq. km)	68	62	56
Deforestation (avg. annual %, 1990–2000 and 2000–2010)		0.9	1.0
Freshwater use (% of internal resources)	3.0	7.9	7.9
Access to improved water source (% total pop.)	44	60	82
Access to improved sanitation facilities (% total pop.)	8	12	19
Energy use per capita (kilograms of oil equivalent)	..	..	..
Carbon dioxide emissions per capita (metric tons)	0.07	0.09	0.11
Electricity use per capita (kilowatt-hours)	..	..	..
Economy			
GDP ($ billions)	3.1	2.6	10.7
GDP growth (annual %)	-0.6	1.8	9.5
GDP implicit price deflator (annual % growth)	1.8	-1.7	1.9
Value added in agriculture (% of GDP)	29	29	35
Value added in industry (% of GDP)	21	25	26
Value added in services (% of GDP)	50	46	38
Exports of goods and services (% of GDP)	11	9	27
Imports of goods and services (% of GDP)	24	25	34
Gross capital formation (% of GDP)	19	17	28
Central government revenue (% of GDP)	..	11.7	18.2
Central government cash surplus/deficit (% of GDP)	..	-4.6	-3.2
States and markets			
Starting a business (days)	..	40	13
Stock market capitalization (% of GDP)	..	..	..
Military expenditures (% of GDP)	2.3	1.2	1.4
Mobile cellular subscriptions (per 100 people)	0.0	0.2	60.6
Individuals using the Internet (% of population)	0.0	0.1	3.7
Paved roads (% of total)	16.6	13.0	20.6
High-technology exports (% of manufactured exports)	..	3	6
Global links			
Merchandise trade (% of GDP)	22	31	51
Net barter terms of trade index (2000 = 100)	119	100	127
Total external debt stocks ($ billions)	0.8	1.4	2.5
Total debt service (% of exports)	9.4	18.8	2.5
Net migration (thousands)	-150	-125	-125
Personal remittances received ($ millions)	140	67	120
Foreign direct investment, net inflows ($ millions)	0.5	23.2	40.1
Net official development assistance received ($ millions)	327	180	1,159

Burundi

Sub-Saharan Africa		Low income
Population (millions)	9.8	Population growth (%)	3.2
Surface area (1,000 sq. km)	28	Population living below $1.25 a day (%)	81.3
GNI, Atlas ($ billions)	2.4	GNI per capita, Atlas ($)	240
GNI, PPP ($ billions)	5.4	GNI per capita, PPP ($)	550

	1990	2000	2012
People			
Share of poorest 20% in nat'l consumption/income (%)	7.9	5.1	9.0
Life expectancy at birth (years)	47	48	54
Total fertility rate (births per woman)	7.5	7.1	6.1
Adolescent fertility rate (births per 1,000 women 15–19)	49	41	30
Contraceptive prevalence (% of married women 15–49)	..	16	22
Births attended by skilled health staff (% of total)	..	25	60
Under-five mortality rate (per 1,000 live births)	164	150	104
Child malnutrition, underweight (% of under age 5)	..	38.9	29.1
Child immunization, measles (% of ages 12–23 mos.)	74	72	93
Primary completion rate, total (% of relevant age group)	41	24	62
Gross secondary enrollment, total (% of relevant age group)	5	10	28
Ratio of girls to boys in primary & secondary school (%)	79	79	93
HIV prevalence rate (% population of ages 15–49)	1.7	3.3	1.3
Environment			
Forests (1,000 sq. km)	2.9	2.0	1.7
Deforestation (avg. annual %, 1990–2000 and 2000–2010)		3.7	1.4
Freshwater use (% of internal resources)	..	2.9	2.9
Access to improved water source (% total pop.)	69	72	75
Access to improved sanitation facilities (% total pop.)	42	44	47
Energy use per capita (kilograms of oil equivalent)	..	..	..
Carbon dioxide emissions per capita (metric tons)	0.05	0.05	0.03
Electricity use per capita (kilowatt-hours)	..	..	..
Economy			
GDP ($ millions)	1,132	870	2,472
GDP growth (annual %)	3.5	-0.9	4.0
GDP implicit price deflator (annual % growth)	6.0	38.9	15.4
Value added in agriculture (% of GDP)	56	48	41
Value added in industry (% of GDP)	19	17	17
Value added in services (% of GDP)	25	35	43
Exports of goods and services (% of GDP)	8	6	9
Imports of goods and services (% of GDP)	28	16	37
Gross capital formation (% of GDP)	15	3	28
Central government revenue (% of GDP)	18.2	15.8	..
Central government cash surplus/deficit (% of GDP)	-2.3	-2.4	..
States and markets			
Starting a business (days)	..	13	5
Stock market capitalization (% of GDP)	..	..	..
Military expenditures (% of GDP)	3.5	4.9	2.4
Mobile cellular subscriptions (per 100 people)	0.0	0.2	22.8
Individuals using the Internet (% of population)	0.0	0.1	1.2
Paved roads (% of total)	..	7.0	..
High-technology exports (% of manufactured exports)	0	0	3
Global links			
Merchandise trade (% of GDP)	27	23	37
Net barter terms of trade index (2000 = 100)	128	100	149
Total external debt stocks ($ millions)	907	1,126	663
Total debt service (% of exports)	43.4	40.9	8.5
Net migration (thousands)	-250	113	-20
Personal remittances received ($ millions)	..	..	46.4
Foreign direct investment, net inflows ($ millions)	1.3	11.7	0.6
Net official development assistance received ($ millions)	263	93	523

Cabo Verde

Sub-Saharan Africa		Lower middle income	

Population (thousands)	494	Population growth (%)	0.8
Surface area (1,000 sq. km)	4.0	Population living below $1.25 a day (%)	21.0
GNI, Atlas ($ billions)	1.9	GNI per capita, Atlas ($)	3,830
GNI, PPP ($ billions)	2.4	GNI per capita, PPP ($)	4,930

	1990	2000	2012
People			
Share of poorest 20% in nat'l consumption/income (%)	..	4.5	..
Life expectancy at birth (years)	66	70	75
Total fertility rate (births per woman)	5.3	3.7	2.3
Adolescent fertility rate (births per 1,000 women 15–19)	109	99	71
Contraceptive prevalence (% of married women 15–49)	24	53	..
Births attended by skilled health staff (% of total)	..	89	..
Under-five mortality rate (per 1,000 live births)	62	38	22
Child malnutrition, underweight (% of under age 5)	..	..	..
Child immunization, measles (% of ages 12–23 mos.)	79	86	96
Primary completion rate, total (% of relevant age group)	56	106	99
Gross secondary enrollment, total (% of relevant age group)	20	67	93
Ratio of girls to boys in primary & secondary school (%)	99	99	104
HIV prevalence rate (% population of ages 15–49)	0.4	0.6	0.2
Environment			
Forests (sq. km)	578	821	848
Deforestation (avg. annual %, 1990–2000 and 2000–2010)		-3.6	-0.4
Freshwater use (% of internal resources)	..	7.3	7.3
Access to improved water source (% total pop.)	..	83	89
Access to improved sanitation facilities (% total pop.)	..	44	65
Energy use per capita (kilograms of oil equivalent)	83	..	..
Carbon dioxide emissions per capita (metric tons)	0.3	0.4	0.7
Electricity use per capita (kilowatt-hours)	..	..	..
Economy			
GDP ($ millions)	359	605	1,827
GDP growth (annual %)	0.7	14.3	2.5
GDP implicit price deflator (annual % growth)	19.8	-9.4	3.4
Value added in agriculture (% of GDP)	12	11	8
Value added in industry (% of GDP)	26	19	18
Value added in services (% of GDP)	62	69	74
Exports of goods and services (% of GDP)	15	24	32
Imports of goods and services (% of GDP)	59	54	53
Gross capital formation (% of GDP)	..	..	48
Central government revenue (% of GDP)	..	..	22.3
Central government cash surplus/deficit (% of GDP)	..	..	-9.0
States and markets			
Starting a business (days)	..	..	10
Stock market capitalization (% of GDP)	..	..	..
Military expenditures (% of GDP)	0.8	1.1	0.5
Mobile cellular subscriptions (per 100 people)	0.0	4.5	86.0
Individuals using the Internet (% of population)	0.0	1.8	34.7
Paved roads (% of total)	78.0	69.0	..
High-technology exports (% of manufactured exports)	..	1	1
Global links			
Merchandise trade (% of GDP)	40	40	45
Net barter terms of trade index (2000 = 100)	100	100	109
Total external debt stocks ($ millions)	134	320	1,261
Total debt service (% of exports)	9.1	10.7	4.6
Net migration (thousands)	-6.4	-10.9	-17.2
Personal remittances received ($ millions)	59	87	167
Foreign direct investment, net inflows ($ millions)	0.3	33.4	74.1
Net official development assistance received ($ millions)	105	94	246

Cambodia

East Asia & Pacific   **Low income**

Population (millions)	14.9	Population growth (%)	1.8
Surface area (1,000 sq. km)	181	Population living below $1.25 a day (%)	18.6
GNI, Atlas ($ billions)	13.0	GNI per capita, Atlas ($)	880
GNI, PPP ($ billions)	34.6	GNI per capita, PPP ($)	2,330

	1990	2000	2012
People			
Share of poorest 20% in nat'l consumption/income (%)	..	6.9	7.9
Life expectancy at birth (years)	55	62	71
Total fertility rate (births per woman)	5.6	3.8	2.9
Adolescent fertility rate (births per 1,000 women 15-19)	75	49	44
Contraceptive prevalence (% of married women 15-49)	..	24	51
Births attended by skilled health staff (% of total)	..	32	74
Under-five mortality rate (per 1,000 live births)	116	111	40
Child malnutrition, underweight (% of under age 5)	..	39.5	29.0
Child immunization, measles (% of ages 12-23 mos.)	34	65	93
Primary completion rate, total (% of relevant age group)	..	51	98
Gross secondary enrollment, total (% of relevant age group)	28	17	..
Ratio of girls to boys in primary & secondary school (%)	..	82	..
HIV prevalence rate (% population of ages 15-49)	0.1	1.5	0.8
Environment			
Forests (1,000 sq. km)	129	115	100
Deforestation (avg. annual %, 1990–2000 and 2000–2010)		1.1	1.3
Freshwater use (% of internal resources)			1.8
Access to improved water source (% total pop.)	22	42	71
Access to improved sanitation facilities (% total pop.)	3	16	37
Energy use per capita (kilograms of oil equivalent)	..	279	365
Carbon dioxide emissions per capita (metric tons)	0.05	0.16	0.29
Electricity use per capita (kilowatt-hours)	..	33	164
Economy			
GDP ($ billions)	2.5	3.7	14.0
GDP growth (annual %)	..	8.8	7.3
GDP implicit price deflator (annual % growth)	..	-3.2	1.4
Value added in agriculture (% of GDP)	47	38	36
Value added in industry (% of GDP)	13	23	24
Value added in services (% of GDP)	40	39	40
Exports of goods and services (% of GDP)	16	50	54
Imports of goods and services (% of GDP)	33	62	60
Gross capital formation (% of GDP)	12	18	17
Central government revenue (% of GDP)	..	10.3	13.2
Central government cash surplus/deficit (% of GDP)	..	-3.4	-4.4
States and markets			
Starting a business (days)	..	94	104
Stock market capitalization (% of GDP)	..	..	..
Military expenditures (% of GDP)	1.8	2.2	1.5
Mobile cellular subscriptions (per 100 people)	0.0	1.1	128.5
Individuals using the Internet (% of population)	0.0	0.0	4.9
Paved roads (% of total)	7.5	6.3	..
High-technology exports (% of manufactured exports)	..	0	0
Global links			
Merchandise trade (% of GDP)	30	91	137
Net barter terms of trade index (2000 = 100)	..	100	75
Total external debt stocks ($ billions)	1.8	2.6	5.7
Total debt service (% of exports)	4.1	1.7	1.5
Net migration (thousands)	409	-73	-175
Personal remittances received ($ millions)	9	121	256
Foreign direct investment, net inflows ($ millions)	33	149	1,557
Net official development assistance received ($ millions)	41	396	807

Cameroon

Sub-Saharan Africa **Lower middle income**

Population (millions)	21.7	Population growth (%)	2.5
Surface area (1,000 sq. km)	475	Population living below $1.25 a day (%)	9.6
GNI, Atlas ($ billions)	25.3	GNI per capita, Atlas ($)	1,170
GNI, PPP ($ billions)	49.3	GNI per capita, PPP ($)	2,270

	1990	2000	2012
People			
Share of poorest 20% in nat'l consumption/income (%)	..	6.5	6.7
Life expectancy at birth (years)	54	52	55
Total fertility rate (births per woman)	6.4	5.6	4.9
Adolescent fertility rate (births per 1,000 women 15–19)	183	156	116
Contraceptive prevalence (% of married women 15–49)	16	26	23
Births attended by skilled health staff (% of total)	64	60	64
Under-five mortality rate (per 1,000 live births)	135	150	95
Child malnutrition, underweight (% of under age 5)	18.0	15.1	15.1
Child immunization, measles (% of ages 12–23 mos.)	56	49	82
Primary completion rate, total (% of relevant age group)	56	49	73
Gross secondary enrollment, total (% of relevant age group)	25	27	50
Ratio of girls to boys in primary & secondary school (%)	82	85	87
HIV prevalence rate (% population of ages 15–49)	0.5	5.1	4.5
Environment			
Forests (1,000 sq. km)	243	221	197
Deforestation (avg. annual %, 1990-2000 and 2000-2010)		0.9	1.0
Freshwater use (% of internal resources)	0.1	0.4	0.4
Access to improved water source (% total pop.)	51	62	74
Access to improved sanitation facilities (% total pop.)	40	42	45
Energy use per capita (kilograms of oil equivalent)	413	396	318
Carbon dioxide emissions per capita (metric tons)	0.1	0.2	0.4
Electricity use per capita (kilowatt-hours)	194	171	256
Economy			
GDP ($ billions)	11.2	9.3	25.3
GDP growth (annual %)	-6.1	4.2	4.6
GDP implicit price deflator (annual % growth)	1.6	2.8	2.8
Value added in agriculture (% of GDP)	25	22	..
Value added in industry (% of GDP)	29	36	..
Value added in services (% of GDP)	46	42	..
Exports of goods and services (% of GDP)	20	29	29
Imports of goods and services (% of GDP)	17	25	32
Gross capital formation (% of GDP)	18	17	19
Central government revenue (% of GDP)	14.3	14.1	..
Central government cash surplus/deficit (% of GDP)	-5.6	0.1	..
States and markets			
Starting a business (days)	..	45	15
Stock market capitalization (% of GDP)	..	..	..
Military expenditures (% of GDP)	1.5	1.3	1.4
Mobile cellular subscriptions (per 100 people)	0.0	0.6	60.4
Individuals using the Internet (% of population)	0.0	0.3	5.7
Paved roads (% of total)	10.5	8.0	10.1
High-technology exports (% of manufactured exports)	3	1	4
Global links			
Merchandise trade (% of GDP)	31	36	46
Net barter terms of trade index (2000 = 100)	81	100	157
Total external debt stocks ($ billions)	6.6	10.6	3.7
Total debt service (% of exports)	20.5	20.8	3.1
Net migration (thousands)	-80.0	-80.0	-50.0
Personal remittances received ($ millions)	23	30	210
Foreign direct investment, net inflows ($ millions)	-113	159	526
Net official development assistance received ($ millions)	444	377	596

Canada

Population (millions)	34.8	Population growth (%)	1.2
Surface area (1,000 sq. km)	9,985	Population living below $1.25 a day (%)	..
GNI, Atlas ($ billions)	1,792.3	GNI per capita, Atlas ($)	51,570
GNI, PPP ($ billions)	1,469.0	GNI per capita, PPP ($)	42,270

	1990	2000	2012
People			
Share of poorest 20% in nat'l consumption/income (%)	..	7.2	..
Life expectancy at birth (years)	77	79	81
Total fertility rate (births per woman)	1.8	1.5	1.6
Adolescent fertility rate (births per 1,000 women 15-19)	24	17	14
Contraceptive prevalence (% of married women 15-49)	..	74	..
Births attended by skilled health staff (% of total)	..	98	100
Under-five mortality rate (per 1,000 live births)	8	6	5
Child malnutrition, underweight (% of under age 5)	..	..	..
Child immunization, measles (% of ages 12-23 mos.)	89	96	98
Primary completion rate, total (% of relevant age group)	..	97	..
Gross secondary enrollment, total (% of relevant age group)	99	102	102
Ratio of girls to boys in primary & secondary school (%)	100	101	99
HIV prevalence rate (% population of ages 15-49)	..	..	..
Environment			
Forests (1,000 sq. km)	3,101	3,101	3,101
Deforestation (avg. annual %, 1990-2000 and 2000-2010)		0.0	0.0
Freshwater use (% of internal resources)	..	1.6	1.6
Access to improved water source (% total pop.)	100	100	100
Access to improved sanitation facilities (% total pop.)	100	100	100
Energy use per capita (kilograms of oil equivalent)	7,505	8,172	7,270
Carbon dioxide emissions per capita (metric tons)	16.2	17.4	14.7
Electricity use per capita (kilowatt-hours)	16,109	16,991	16,473
Economy			
GDP ($ billions)	583	725	1,780
GDP growth (annual %)	0.2	5.2	1.7
GDP implicit price deflator (annual % growth)	3.2	4.1	1.7
Value added in agriculture (% of GDP)	3	2	..
Value added in industry (% of GDP)	31	33	..
Value added in services (% of GDP)	66	65	..
Exports of goods and services (% of GDP)	26	46	30
Imports of goods and services (% of GDP)	26	40	32
Gross capital formation (% of GDP)	21	20	23
Central government revenue (% of GDP)	20.9	21.4	17.2
Central government cash surplus/deficit (% of GDP)	-5.1	2.3	-1.3
States and markets			
Starting a business (days)	..	3	5
Stock market capitalization (% of GDP)	41.5	116.1	113.3
Military expenditures (% of GDP)	2.0	1.1	1.3
Mobile cellular subscriptions (per 100 people)	2.1	28.4	80.1
Individuals using the Internet (% of population)	0.4	51.3	86.8
Paved roads (% of total)	35.0	39.9	..
High-technology exports (% of manufactured exports)	14	19	12
Global links			
Merchandise trade (% of GDP)	43	72	52
Net barter terms of trade index (2000 = 100)	..	100	119
Total external debt stocks ($ millions)	..	..	..
Total debt service (% of exports)	..	..	..
Net migration (thousands)	699	1,029	1,100
Personal remittances received ($ millions)	..	..	1,206
Foreign direct investment, net inflows ($ billions)	7.6	66.1	43.1
Net official development assistance received ($ millions)	..	..	..

Cayman Islands

High income

Population (thousands)	58	Population growth (%)		1.7
Surface area (sq. km)	264	Population living below $1.25 a day (%)		..
GNI, Atlas ($ millions)	..	GNI per capita, Atlas ($)		..
GNI, PPP ($ millions)	..	GNI per capita, PPP ($)		..

	1990	2000	2012
People			
Share of poorest 20% in nat'l consumption/income (%)	..	..	..
Life expectancy at birth (years)	..	..	..
Total fertility rate (births per woman)	..	..	..
Adolescent fertility rate (births per 1,000 women 15-19)	..	..	..
Contraceptive prevalence (% of married women 15-49)	..	..	..
Births attended by skilled health staff (% of total)	..	..	..
Under-five mortality rate (per 1,000 live births)	..	..	..
Child malnutrition, underweight (% of under age 5)	..	..	..
Child immunization, measles (% of ages 12-23 mos.)	..	..	..
Primary completion rate, total (% of relevant age group)	..	104	..
Gross secondary enrollment, total (% of relevant age group)	..	95	..
Ratio of girls to boys in primary & secondary school (%)	..	92	..
HIV prevalence rate (% population of ages 15-49)	..	..	..
Environment			
Forests (sq. km)	124	124	127
Deforestation (avg. annual %, 1990-2000 and 2000-2010)		0.0	0.0
Freshwater use (% of internal resources)	..	..	..
Access to improved water source (% total pop.)	..	93	96
Access to improved sanitation facilities (% total pop.)	96	96	96
Energy use per capita (kilograms of oil equivalent)	..	..	..
Carbon dioxide emissions per capita (metric tons)	10.1	10.9	10.6
Electricity use per capita (kilowatt-hours)	..	..	..
Economy			
GDP ($ millions)	..	..	..
GDP growth (annual %)	..	..	..
GDP implicit price deflator (annual % growth)	..	..	..
Value added in agriculture (% of GDP)	..	..	..
Value added in industry (% of GDP)	..	..	..
Value added in services (% of GDP)	..	..	..
Exports of goods and services (% of GDP)	..	..	..
Imports of goods and services (% of GDP)	..	..	..
Gross capital formation (% of GDP)	..	..	..
Central government revenue (% of GDP)	..	..	..
Central government cash surplus/deficit (% of GDP)	..	..	..
States and markets			
Starting a business (days)	..	..	..
Stock market capitalization (% of GDP)	..	..	..
Military expenditures (% of GDP)	..	..	..
Mobile cellular subscriptions (per 100 people)	0.0	25.7	171.7
Individuals using the Internet (% of population)	0.0	..	74.1
Paved roads (% of total)	..	..	97.9
High-technology exports (% of manufactured exports)	..	..	..
Global links			
Merchandise trade (% of GDP)	..	..	..
Net barter terms of trade index (2000 = 100)	..	100	83
Total external debt stocks ($ millions)	..	..	..
Total debt service (% of exports)	..	..	..
Net migration (thousands)	..	..	..
Personal remittances received ($ millions)	..	..	..
Foreign direct investment, net inflows ($ billions)	0.0	7.6	4.2
Net official development assistance received ($ millions)	3.0	..	..

Central African Republic

Sub-Saharan Africa | **Low income**

Population (millions)	4.5	Population growth (%)	2.0
Surface area (1,000 sq. km)	623	Population living below $1.25 a day (%)	62.8
GNI, Atlas ($ billions)	2.3	GNI per capita, Atlas ($)	510
GNI, PPP ($ billions)	4.9	GNI per capita, PPP ($)	1,080

	1990	2000	2012
People			
Share of poorest 20% in nat'l consumption/income (%)	2.0	5.2	3.4
Life expectancy at birth (years)	46	44	49
Total fertility rate (births per woman)	5.8	5.4	4.5
Adolescent fertility rate (births per 1,000 women 15-19)	149	127	98
Contraceptive prevalence (% of married women 15-49)	..	28	15
Births attended by skilled health staff (% of total)	..	44	54
Under-five mortality rate (per 1,000 live births)	171	164	129
Child malnutrition, underweight (% of under age 5)	..	21.8	28.0
Child immunization, measles (% of ages 12-23 mos.)	82	36	49
Primary completion rate, total (% of relevant age group)	30	..	45
Gross secondary enrollment, total (% of relevant age group)	11	12	18
Ratio of girls to boys in primary & secondary school (%)	59	..	70
HIV prevalence rate (% population of ages 15-49)	..	..	..
Environment			
Forests (1,000 sq. km)	232	229	226
Deforestation (avg. annual %, 1990-2000 and 2000-2010)		0.1	0.1
Freshwater use (% of internal resources)	..	0.0	0.0
Access to improved water source (% total pop.)	59	62	68
Access to improved sanitation facilities (% total pop.)	15	17	22
Energy use per capita (kilograms of oil equivalent)	..	..	..
Carbon dioxide emissions per capita (metric tons)	0.07	0.07	0.06
Electricity use per capita (kilowatt-hours)	..	..	..
Economy			
GDP ($ millions)	1,441	915	2,184
GDP growth (annual %)	-2.1	-2.5	6.9
GDP implicit price deflator (annual % growth)	1.8	8.5	-0.1
Value added in agriculture (% of GDP)	49	52	54
Value added in industry (% of GDP)	20	15	14
Value added in services (% of GDP)	30	33	32
Exports of goods and services (% of GDP)	17	20	12
Imports of goods and services (% of GDP)	26	25	22
Gross capital formation (% of GDP)	13	11	15
Central government revenue (% of GDP)	..	..	11.0
Central government cash surplus/deficit (% of GDP)	..	..	0.7
States and markets			
Starting a business (days)	..	22	22
Stock market capitalization (% of GDP)	..	..	..
Military expenditures (% of GDP)	1.6	1.1	2.6
Mobile cellular subscriptions (per 100 people)	0.0	0.1	25.3
Individuals using the Internet (% of population)	0.0	0.1	3.0
Paved roads (% of total)	..	2.7	6.8
High-technology exports (% of manufactured exports)	1	0	0
Global links			
Merchandise trade (% of GDP)	19	30	24
Net barter terms of trade index (2000 = 100)	238	100	69
Total external debt stocks ($ millions)	699	872	552
Total debt service (% of exports)	13.2	..	..
Net migration (thousands)	37.4	-45.0	10.0
Personal remittances received ($ millions)	0.1	..	..
Foreign direct investment, net inflows ($ millions)	0.7	0.9	71.2
Net official development assistance received ($ millions)	249	75	227

Chad

Population (millions)	12.4	Population growth (%)	3.0
Surface area (1,000 sq. km)	1,284	Population living below $1.25 a day (%)	*61.9*
GNI, Atlas ($ billions)	9.6	GNI per capita, Atlas ($)	770
GNI, PPP ($ billions)	20.1	GNI per capita, PPP ($)	1,620

	1990	2000	2012
People			
Share of poorest 20% in nat'l consumption/income (%)	..	*6.3*	..
Life expectancy at birth (years)	46	47	51
Total fertility rate (births per woman)	7.3	7.4	6.4
Adolescent fertility rate (births per 1,000 women 15-19)	218	212	152
Contraceptive prevalence (% of married women 15-49)	..	8	5
Births attended by skilled health staff (% of total)	..	16	*23*
Under-five mortality rate (per 1,000 live births)	209	189	150
Child malnutrition, underweight (% of under age 5)	..	29.4	..
Child immunization, measles (% of ages 12-23 mos.)	32	28	64
Primary completion rate, total (% of relevant age group)	17	22	35
Gross secondary enrollment, total (% of relevant age group)	7	11	23
Ratio of girls to boys in primary & secondary school (%)	42	56	70
HIV prevalence rate (% population of ages 15-49)	1.7	3.8	2.7
Environment			
Forests (1,000 sq. km)	131	123	*114*
Deforestation (avg. annual %, 1990-2000 and 2000-2010)		0.6	0.7
Freshwater use (% of internal resources)	..	2.4	2.4
Access to improved water source (% total pop.)	40	45	51
Access to improved sanitation facilities (% total pop.)	8	10	12
Energy use per capita (kilograms of oil equivalent)	..	..	..
Carbon dioxide emissions per capita (metric tons)	0.02	0.02	*0.04*
Electricity use per capita (kilowatt-hours)	..	..	..
Economy			
GDP ($ billions)	1.7	1.4	12.9
GDP growth (annual %)	-4.2	-0.9	8.9
GDP implicit price deflator (annual % growth)	8.0	5.3	5.3
Value added in agriculture (% of GDP)	29	42	56
Value added in industry (% of GDP)	18	11	13
Value added in services (% of GDP)	53	46	31
Exports of goods and services (% of GDP)	13	17	29
Imports of goods and services (% of GDP)	28	35	39
Gross capital formation (% of GDP)	7	23	27
Central government revenue (% of GDP)	..	..	..
Central government cash surplus/deficit (% of GDP)	..	..	..
States and markets			
Starting a business (days)	..	64	62
Stock market capitalization (% of GDP)	..	..	..
Military expenditures (% of GDP)	3.3	1.9	*2.0*
Mobile cellular subscriptions (per 100 people)	0.0	0.1	35.4
Individuals using the Internet (% of population)	0.0	0.0	2.1
Paved roads (% of total)	0.8	1.0	..
High-technology exports (% of manufactured exports)	..	..	..
Global links			
Merchandise trade (% of GDP)	27	36	50
Net barter terms of trade index (2000 = 100)	112	100	221
Total external debt stocks ($ billions)	0.5	1.1	1.8
Total debt service (% of exports)	4.3	..	..
Net migration (thousands)	-10	*219*	-120
Personal remittances received ($ millions)	0.8	..	..
Foreign direct investment, net inflows ($ millions)	9	115	323
Net official development assistance received ($ millions)	311	131	479

Channel Islands

High income

Population (thousands)	161	Population growth (%)	0.5
Surface area (sq. km)	190	Population living below $1.25 a day (%)	..
GNI, Atlas ($ billions)	..	GNI per capita, Atlas ($)	..
GNI, PPP ($ millions)	..	GNI per capita, PPP ($)	..

	1990	2000	2012
People			
Share of poorest 20% in nat'l consumption/income (%)	..	..	..
Life expectancy at birth (years)	75	78	80
Total fertility rate (births per woman)	1.5	1.4	1.5
Adolescent fertility rate (births per 1,000 women 15-19)	17	13	8
Contraceptive prevalence (% of married women 15-49)	..	..	..
Births attended by skilled health staff (% of total)	..	..	..
Under-five mortality rate (per 1,000 live births)	..	..	..
Child malnutrition, underweight (% of under age 5)	..	..	..
Child immunization, measles (% of ages 12-23 mos.)	..	..	..
Primary completion rate, total (% of relevant age group)	..	..	..
Gross secondary enrollment, total (% of relevant age group)	..	..	..
Ratio of girls to boys in primary & secondary school (%)	..	..	..
HIV prevalence rate (% population of ages 15-49)	..	..	..
Environment			
Forests (sq. km)	8.0	8.0	8.0
Deforestation (avg. annual %, 1990-2000 and 2000-2010)		..	
Freshwater use (% of internal resources)	..	..	
Access to improved water source (% total pop.)	..	..	..
Access to improved sanitation facilities (% total pop.)	..	..	..
Energy use per capita (kilograms of oil equivalent)	..	..	..
Carbon dioxide emissions per capita (metric tons)	..	..	..
Electricity use per capita (kilowatt-hours)	..	..	..
Economy			
GDP ($ billions)	..	6.4	..
GDP growth (annual %)	..	5.8	..
GDP implicit price deflator (annual % growth)	..	3.9	..
Value added in agriculture (% of GDP)	..	..	..
Value added in industry (% of GDP)	..	..	..
Value added in services (% of GDP)	..	..	..
Exports of goods and services (% of GDP)	..	..	..
Imports of goods and services (% of GDP)	..	..	..
Gross capital formation (% of GDP)	..	..	..
Central government revenue (% of GDP)	..	..	..
Central government cash surplus/deficit (% of GDP)	..	..	..
States and markets			
Starting a business (days)	..	..	..
Stock market capitalization (% of GDP)	..	..	..
Military expenditures (% of GDP)	..	..	..
Mobile cellular subscriptions (per 100 people)	..	..	..
Individuals using the Internet (% of population)	..	..	..
Paved roads (% of total)	..	..	..
High-technology exports (% of manufactured exports)	..	..	..
Global links			
Merchandise trade (% of GDP)	..	..	..
Net barter terms of trade index (2000 = 100)	..	..	..
Total external debt stocks ($ millions)	..	..	..
Total debt service (% of exports)	..	..	..
Net migration (thousands)	2.1	4.6	3.7
Personal remittances received ($ millions)	..	..	..
Foreign direct investment, net inflows ($ millions)	..	..	..
Net official development assistance received ($ millions)	..	..	..

Chile

High income

Population (millions)	17.5	Population growth (%)	0.9
Surface area (1,000 sq. km)	756	Population living below $1.25 a day (%)	<2
GNI, Atlas ($ billions)	249.9	GNI per capita, Atlas ($)	14,310
GNI, PPP ($ billions)	357.2	GNI per capita, PPP ($)	20,450

	1990	2000	2012
People			
Share of poorest 20% in nat'l consumption/income (%)	3.6	3.7	4.3
Life expectancy at birth (years)	74	77	80
Total fertility rate (births per woman)	2.6	2.1	1.8
Adolescent fertility rate (births per 1,000 women 15–19)	66	64	55
Contraceptive prevalence (% of married women 15–49)	56	61	58
Births attended by skilled health staff (% of total)	99	100	100
Under-five mortality rate (per 1,000 live births)	19	11	9
Child malnutrition, underweight (% of under age 5)	..	0.7	0.5
Child immunization, measles (% of ages 12-23 mos.)	97	97	90
Primary completion rate, total (% of relevant age group)	..	98	97
Gross secondary enrollment, total (% of relevant age group)	78	82	89
Ratio of girls to boys in primary & secondary school (%)	101	100	100
HIV prevalence rate (% population of ages 15–49)	0.1	0.4	0.4
Environment			
Forests (1,000 sq. km)	153	158	163
Deforestation (avg. annual %, 1990–2000 and 2000–2010)		-0.4	-0.2
Freshwater use (% of internal resources)	2.3	1.3	1.3
Access to improved water source (% total pop.)	90	95	99
Access to improved sanitation facilities (% total pop.)	85	92	99
Energy use per capita (kilograms of oil equivalent)	1,060	1,629	1,874
Carbon dioxide emissions per capita (metric tons)	2.6	3.8	4.2
Electricity use per capita (kilowatt-hours)	1,243	2,481	3,568
Economy			
GDP ($ billions)	32	79	270
GDP growth (annual %)	3.7	4.5	5.6
GDP implicit price deflator (annual % growth)	22.5	10.3	1.8
Value added in agriculture (% of GDP)	9	6	4
Value added in industry (% of GDP)	41	32	36
Value added in services (% of GDP)	50	62	61
Exports of goods and services (% of GDP)	34	29	34
Imports of goods and services (% of GDP)	31	29	34
Gross capital formation (% of GDP)	25	23	25
Central government revenue (% of GDP)	..	20.5	22.7
Central government cash surplus/deficit (% of GDP)	..	-0.6	1.3
States and markets			
Starting a business (days)	..	27	6
Stock market capitalization (% of GDP)	43.1	76.1	116.1
Military expenditures (% of GDP)	3.3	2.7	2.0
Mobile cellular subscriptions (per 100 people)	0.1	22.0	138.2
Individuals using the Internet (% of population)	0.0	16.6	61.4
Paved roads (% of total)	13.8	19.0	23.8
High-technology exports (% of manufactured exports)	5	3	5
Global links			
Merchandise trade (% of GDP)	51	48	59
Net barter terms of trade index (2000 = 100)	114	100	182
Total external debt stocks ($ millions)	..	..	..
Total debt service (% of exports)	..	..	..
Net migration (thousands)	90.0	30.0	30.0
Personal remittances received ($ millions)	0.4	13.3	4.4
Foreign direct investment, net inflows ($ billions)	0.7	4.9	30.3
Net official development assistance received ($ millions)	104	49	126

China

Population (millions)	1,350.7	Population growth (%)	0.5
Surface area (1,000 sq. km)	9,600	Population living below $1.25 a day (%)	11.8
GNI, Atlas ($ billions)	7,731.3	GNI per capita, Atlas ($)	5,720
GNI, PPP ($ billions)	12,205.8	GNI per capita, PPP ($)	9,040

	1990	2000	2012
People			
Share of poorest 20% in nat'l consumption/income (%)	8.0	6.4	4.7
Life expectancy at birth (years)[c]	69	72	75
Total fertility rate (births per woman)	2.5	1.5	1.7
Adolescent fertility rate (births per 1,000 women 15-19)	13	7	9
Contraceptive prevalence (% of married women 15-49)	85	84	88
Births attended by skilled health staff (% of total)	94	97	100
Under-five mortality rate (per 1,000 live births)	54	37	14
Child malnutrition, underweight (% of under age 5)	12.6	7.4	3.4
Child immunization, measles (% of ages 12-23 mos.)	98	84	99
Primary completion rate, total (% of relevant age group)	106	..	..
Gross secondary enrollment, total (% of relevant age group)	38	58	89
Ratio of girls to boys in primary & secondary school (%)	85	98	101
HIV prevalence rate (% population of ages 15-49)	..	..	..
Environment			
Forests (1,000 sq. km)	1,571	1,770	2,096
Deforestation (avg. annual %, 1990-2000 and 2000-2010)		-1.2	-1.6
Freshwater use (% of internal resources)	17.8	18.7	19.7
Access to improved water source (% total pop.)	67	80	92
Access to improved sanitation facilities (% total pop.)	24	45	65
Energy use per capita (kilograms of oil equivalent)	767	920	2,029
Carbon dioxide emissions per capita (metric tons)	2.2	2.7	6.2
Electricity use per capita (kilowatt-hours)	511	993	3,298
Economy			
GDP ($ billions)	357	1,198	8,227
GDP growth (annual %)	3.8	8.4	7.8
GDP implicit price deflator (annual % growth)	5.8	2.1	1.8
Value added in agriculture (% of GDP)	27	15	10
Value added in industry (% of GDP)	41	46	45
Value added in services (% of GDP)	32	39	45
Exports of goods and services (% of GDP)	16	23	27
Imports of goods and services (% of GDP)	13	21	25
Gross capital formation (% of GDP)	36	35	49
Central government revenue (% of GDP)	..	..	11.6
Central government cash surplus/deficit (% of GDP)	..	..	..
States and markets			
Starting a business (days)	..	48	33
Stock market capitalization (% of GDP)	0.5	48.5	44.9
Military expenditures (% of GDP)	2.6	1.9[d]	2.0[d]
Mobile cellular subscriptions (per 100 people)	0.0	6.7	80.8
Individuals using the Internet (% of population)	0.0	1.8	42.3
Paved roads (% of total)	..	43.5	63.7
High-technology exports (% of manufactured exports)	6	19	26
Global links			
Merchandise trade (% of GDP)	32	40	47
Net barter terms of trade index (2000 = 100)	102	100	72
Total external debt stocks ($ billions)	55	146	754
Total debt service (% of exports)	11.7	9.1	3.3
Net migration (thousands)	-824	-2,298	-1,500
Personal remittances received ($ billions)	0.2	4.8	39.2
Foreign direct investment, net inflows ($ billions)	3	38	253
Net official development assistance received ($ billions)	2.0	1.7	-0.2

Colombia

Latin America & Caribbean   **Upper middle income**

Population (millions)	47.7	Population growth (%)		1.3
Surface area (1,000 sq. km)	1,142	Population living below $1.25 a day (%)		8.2
GNI, Atlas ($ billions)	334.8	GNI per capita, Atlas ($)		7,020
GNI, PPP ($ billions)	476.4	GNI per capita, PPP ($)		9,990

	1990	2000	2012
People			
Share of poorest 20% in nat'l consumption/income (%)	3.6	1.9	3.0
Life expectancy at birth (years)	68	71	74
Total fertility rate (births per woman)	3.1	2.6	2.3
Adolescent fertility rate (births per 1,000 women 15-19)	83	94	69
Contraceptive prevalence (% of married women 15-49)	66	77	79
Births attended by skilled health staff (% of total)	94	86	99
Under-five mortality rate (per 1,000 live births)	35	25	18
Child malnutrition, underweight (% of under age 5)	8.8	4.9	3.4
Child immunization, measles (% of ages 12-23 mos.)	82	88	94
Primary completion rate, total (% of relevant age group)	74	95	105
Gross secondary enrollment, total (% of relevant age group)	52	72	93
Ratio of girls to boys in primary & secondary school (%)	108	104	103
HIV prevalence rate (% population of ages 15-49)	0.1	0.6	0.5
Environment			
Forests (1,000 sq. km)	625	615	604
Deforestation (avg. annual %, 1990-2000 and 2000-2010)		0.2	0.2
Freshwater use (% of internal resources)	..	0.6	0.6
Access to improved water source (% total pop.)	88	90	91
Access to improved sanitation facilities (% total pop.)	69	75	80
Energy use per capita (kilograms of oil equivalent)	727	647	671
Carbon dioxide emissions per capita (metric tons)	1.7	1.5	1.6
Electricity use per capita (kilowatt-hours)	866	840	1,123
Economy			
GDP ($ billions)	40	100	370
GDP growth (annual %)	6.0	4.4	4.2
GDP implicit price deflator (annual % growth)	26.1	31.8	2.6
Value added in agriculture (% of GDP)	17	9	7
Value added in industry (% of GDP)	38	29	38
Value added in services (% of GDP)	45	62	56
Exports of goods and services (% of GDP)	21	16	18
Imports of goods and services (% of GDP)	15	17	20
Gross capital formation (% of GDP)	19	15	23
Central government revenue (% of GDP)	..	22.8	23.4
Central government cash surplus/deficit (% of GDP)	..	-5.0	-1.1
States and markets			
Starting a business (days)	..	60	15
Stock market capitalization (% of GDP)	3.5	9.6	70.9
Military expenditures (% of GDP)	2.2	3.0	3.3
Mobile cellular subscriptions (per 100 people)	0.0	5.7	102.9
Individuals using the Internet (% of population)	0.0	2.2	49.0
Paved roads (% of total)	11.9	14.4	..
High-technology exports (% of manufactured exports)	5	8	5
Global links			
Merchandise trade (% of GDP)	31	25	32
Net barter terms of trade index (2000 = 100)	81	100	151
Total external debt stocks ($ billions)	17.4	33.2	79.1
Total debt service (% of exports)	43.3	29.7	22.0
Net migration (thousands)	-250	-120	-120
Personal remittances received ($ billions)	0.5	1.6	4.0
Foreign direct investment, net inflows ($ billions)	0.5	2.4	15.6
Net official development assistance received ($ millions)	89	186	764

Comoros

Population (thousands)	718	Population growth (%)	2.4
Surface area (1,000 sq. km)	1.9	Population living below $1.25 a day (%)	46.1
GNI, Atlas ($ millions)	605.2	GNI per capita, Atlas ($)	840
GNI, PPP ($ millions)	867.2	GNI per capita, PPP ($)	1,210

	1990	2000	2012
People			
Share of poorest 20% in nat'l consumption/income (%)	..	2.6	..
Life expectancy at birth (years)	56	58	61
Total fertility rate (births per woman)	5.6	5.3	4.8
Adolescent fertility rate (births per 1,000 women 15-19)	73	65	51
Contraceptive prevalence (% of married women 15-49)	..	26	19
Births attended by skilled health staff (% of total)	..	62	82
Under-five mortality rate (per 1,000 live births)	124	99	78
Child malnutrition, underweight (% of under age 5)	16.2	25.0	..
Child immunization, measles (% of ages 12-23 mos.)	87	70	85
Primary completion rate, total (% of relevant age group)	44	53	..
Gross secondary enrollment, total (% of relevant age group)	24	32	73
Ratio of girls to boys in primary & secondary school (%)	..	84	93
HIV prevalence rate (% population of ages 15-49)	0.1	0.1	2.1
Environment			
Forests (sq. km)	120	80	26
Deforestation (avg. annual %, 1990-2000 and 2000-2010)		4.0	9.3
Freshwater use (% of internal resources)	..	0.8	0.8
Access to improved water source (% total pop.)	87	92	95
Access to improved sanitation facilities (% total pop.)	18	28	35
Energy use per capita (kilograms of oil equivalent)	43	..	..
Carbon dioxide emissions per capita (metric tons)	0.2	0.2	0.2
Electricity use per capita (kilowatt-hours)	..	..	..
Economy			
GDP ($ millions)	250	202	596
GDP growth (annual %)	5.1	1.4	3.0
GDP implicit price deflator (annual % growth)	2.2	3.4	2.6
Value added in agriculture (% of GDP)	41	49	46
Value added in industry (% of GDP)	8	12	12
Value added in services (% of GDP)	50	40	42
Exports of goods and services (% of GDP)	14	17	15
Imports of goods and services (% of GDP)	37	33	52
Gross capital formation (% of GDP)	20	10	12
Central government revenue (% of GDP)	..	..	..
Central government cash surplus/deficit (% of GDP)	..	..	..
States and markets			
Starting a business (days)	..	..	15
Stock market capitalization (% of GDP)	..	..	..
Military expenditures (% of GDP)	..	..	..
Mobile cellular subscriptions (per 100 people)	0.0	0.0	39.5
Individuals using the Internet (% of population)	0.0	0.3	6.0
Paved roads (% of total)	69.3	77.0	..
High-technology exports (% of manufactured exports)	..	0	7
Global links			
Merchandise trade (% of GDP)	28	28	55
Net barter terms of trade index (2000 = 100)	86	100	80
Total external debt stocks ($ millions)	185	227	251
Total debt service (% of exports)	2.9	4.8	3.8
Net migration (thousands)	-3.0	-10.0	-10.0
Personal remittances received ($ millions)	9.9	..	..
Foreign direct investment, net inflows ($ millions)	0.4	0.1	17.0
Net official development assistance received ($ millions)	44.9	18.7	68.7

Congo, Dem. Rep.

Sub-Saharan Africa			Low income
Population (millions)	65.7	Population growth (%)	2.7
Surface area (1,000 sq. km)	2,345	Population living below $1.25 a day (%)	87.7
GNI, Atlas ($ billions)	15.4	GNI per capita, Atlas ($)	230
GNI, PPP ($ billions)	25.5	GNI per capita, PPP ($)	390

	1990	2000	2012
People			
Share of poorest 20% in nat'l consumption/income (%)	..	..	5.5
Life expectancy at birth (years)	47	46	50
Total fertility rate (births per woman)	7.1	7.1	6.0
Adolescent fertility rate (births per 1,000 women 15-19)	137	131	135
Contraceptive prevalence (% of married women 15-49)	8	31	17
Births attended by skilled health staff (% of total)	..	61	80
Under-five mortality rate (per 1,000 live births)	171	171	146
Child malnutrition, underweight (% of under age 5)	..	33.6	24.2
Child immunization, measles (% of ages 12-23 mos.)	38	46	73
Primary completion rate, total (% of relevant age group)	52	35	73
Gross secondary enrollment, total (% of relevant age group)	23	..	43
Ratio of girls to boys in primary & secondary school (%)	70	..	80
HIV prevalence rate (% population of ages 15-49)	1.3	1.5	1.1
Environment			
Forests (1,000 sq. km)	1,604	1,572	1,538
Deforestation (avg. annual %, 1990-2000 and 2000-2010)		0.2	0.2
Freshwater use (% of internal resources)	..	0.1	0.1
Access to improved water source (% total pop.)	43	44	46
Access to improved sanitation facilities (% total pop.)	17	23	31
Energy use per capita (kilograms of oil equivalent)	338	355	383
Carbon dioxide emissions per capita (metric tons)	0.12	0.04	0.05
Electricity use per capita (kilowatt-hours)	130	97	105
Economy			
GDP ($ billions)	9.3	4.3	17.2
GDP growth (annual %)	-6.6	-6.9	7.2
GDP implicit price deflator (annual % growth)	109.0	515.8	2.3
Value added in agriculture (% of GDP)	31	50	45
Value added in industry (% of GDP)	29	20	22
Value added in services (% of GDP)	40	30	33
Exports of goods and services (% of GDP)	30	22	55
Imports of goods and services (% of GDP)	29	21	67
Gross capital formation (% of GDP)	9	1	27
Central government revenue (% of GDP)	10.1	3.7	23.4
Central government cash surplus/deficit (% of GDP)	-6.5	-4.2	3.8
States and markets			
Starting a business (days)	..	166	31
Stock market capitalization (% of GDP)	..	..	..
Military expenditures (% of GDP)	..	1.0	1.8
Mobile cellular subscriptions (per 100 people)	0.0	0.0	30.6
Individuals using the Internet (% of population)	0.0	0.0	1.7
Paved roads (% of total)	..	1.8	..
High-technology exports (% of manufactured exports)	..	..	..
Global links			
Merchandise trade (% of GDP)	43	35	72
Net barter terms of trade index (2000 = 100)	86	100	143
Total external debt stocks ($ billions)	10.3	11.8	5.7
Total debt service (% of exports)	..	..	3.2
Net migration (thousands)	1,202	-242	-75
Personal remittances received ($ millions)	..	..	12.2
Foreign direct investment, net inflows ($ millions)	-14	72	2,892
Net official development assistance received ($ millions)	896	177	2,859

Congo, Rep.

Sub-Saharan Africa		**Lower middle income**
Population (millions)	4.3	Population growth (%)	2.6
Surface area (1,000 sq. km)	342	Population living below $1.25 a day (%)	*54.1*
GNI, Atlas ($ billions)	11.1	GNI per capita, Atlas ($)	2,550
GNI, PPP ($ billions)	15.0	GNI per capita, PPP ($)	3,450

	1990	2000	2012
People			
Share of poorest 20% in nat'l consumption/income (%)	..	..	..
Life expectancy at birth (years)	55	52	58
Total fertility rate (births per woman)	5.3	5.1	5.0
Adolescent fertility rate (births per 1,000 women 15-19)	132	136	127
Contraceptive prevalence (% of married women 15-49)	..	..	45
Births attended by skilled health staff (% of total)	..	..	94
Under-five mortality rate (per 1,000 live births)	100	118	96
Child malnutrition, underweight (% of under age 5)	..	..	..
Child immunization, measles (% of ages 12-23 mos.)	75	34	80
Primary completion rate, total (% of relevant age group)	61	*57*	*73*
Gross secondary enrollment, total (% of relevant age group)	49	36	54
Ratio of girls to boys in primary & secondary school (%)	89	85	100
HIV prevalence rate (% population of ages 15-49)	4.4	4.9	2.8
Environment			
Forests (1,000 sq. km)	227	226	224
Deforestation (avg. annual %, 1990-2000 and 2000-2010)		0.1	*0.1*
Freshwater use (% of internal resources)	..	0.0	*0.0*
Access to improved water source (% total pop.)	..	69	75
Access to improved sanitation facilities (% total pop.)	..	13	15
Energy use per capita (kilograms of oil equivalent)	325	260	*393*
Carbon dioxide emissions per capita (metric tons)	0.5	0.3	*0.5*
Electricity use per capita (kilowatt-hours)	172	96	*172*
Economy			
GDP ($ billions)	2.8	3.2	13.7
GDP growth (annual %)	1.0	7.6	3.8
GDP implicit price deflator (annual % growth)	-1.0	47.0	-1.2
Value added in agriculture (% of GDP)	13	5	3
Value added in industry (% of GDP)	41	72	77
Value added in services (% of GDP)	46	23	20
Exports of goods and services (% of GDP)	52	80	*87*
Imports of goods and services (% of GDP)	19	44	*35*
Gross capital formation (% of GDP)	16	23	*25*
Central government revenue (% of GDP)	..	32.3	..
Central government cash surplus/deficit (% of GDP)	..	-1.3	..
States and markets			
Starting a business (days)	..	37	101
Stock market capitalization (% of GDP)	..	..	..
Military expenditures (% of GDP)	..	1.4	*1.1*
Mobile cellular subscriptions (per 100 people)	0.0	2.2	98.8
Individuals using the Internet (% of population)	0.0	0.0	6.1
Paved roads (% of total)	9.7	10.0	*7.1*
High-technology exports (% of manufactured exports)	5	..	4
Global links			
Merchandise trade (% of GDP)	57	92	118
Net barter terms of trade index (2000 = 100)	63	100	221
Total external debt stocks ($ billions)	4.9	4.9	2.8
Total debt service (% of exports)	34.6	1.7	..
Net migration (thousands)	15.5	-13.3	-45.4
Personal remittances received ($ millions)	4.4	10.4	..
Foreign direct investment, net inflows ($ millions)	23	166	2,758
Net official development assistance received ($ millions)	217	32	139

Costa Rica

Latin America & Caribbean   **Upper middle income**

Population (millions)	4.8	Population growth (%)	1.4
Surface area (1,000 sq. km)	51	Population living below $1.25 a day (%)	3.1
GNI, Atlas ($ billions)	42.4	GNI per capita, Atlas ($)	8,820
GNI, PPP ($ billions)	60.1	GNI per capita, PPP ($)	12,500

	1990	2000	2012
People			
Share of poorest 20% in nat'l consumption/income (%)	3.8	4.0	3.9
Life expectancy at birth (years)	76	78	80
Total fertility rate (births per woman)	3.2	2.4	1.8
Adolescent fertility rate (births per 1,000 women 15–19)	96	81	61
Contraceptive prevalence (% of married women 15–49)	75	80	82
Births attended by skilled health staff (% of total)	98	98	99
Under-five mortality rate (per 1,000 live births)	17	13	10
Child malnutrition, underweight (% of under age 5)	2.5	..	1.1
Child immunization, measles (% of ages 12-23 mos.)	90	82	90
Primary completion rate, total (% of relevant age group)	75	87	95
Gross secondary enrollment, total (% of relevant age group)	43	61	104
Ratio of girls to boys in primary & secondary school (%)	100	101	102
HIV prevalence rate (% population of ages 15-49)	0.1	0.2	0.3
Environment			
Forests (1,000 sq. km)	26	24	26
Deforestation (avg. annual %, 1990-2000 and 2000-2010)		0.8	-0.9
Freshwater use (% of internal resources)	..	2.4	2.4
Access to improved water source (% total pop.)	93	95	97
Access to improved sanitation facilities (% total pop.)	88	91	94
Energy use per capita (kilograms of oil equivalent)	545	731	983
Carbon dioxide emissions per capita (metric tons)	1.0	1.4	1.7
Electricity use per capita (kilowatt-hours)	1,086	1,519	1,844
Economy			
GDP ($ billions)	7.4	15.9	45.1
GDP growth (annual %)	3.9	1.8	5.1
GDP implicit price deflator (annual % growth)	17.1	7.0	4.0
Value added in agriculture (% of GDP)	12	9	6
Value added in industry (% of GDP)	30	32	25
Value added in services (% of GDP)	58	58	69
Exports of goods and services (% of GDP)	30	49	38
Imports of goods and services (% of GDP)	36	46	42
Gross capital formation (% of GDP)	18	17	21
Central government revenue (% of GDP)	..	..	24.3
Central government cash surplus/deficit (% of GDP)	..	..	-3.5
States and markets			
Starting a business (days)	..	77	24
Stock market capitalization (% of GDP)	5.5	18.3	4.5
Military expenditures (% of GDP)	..	..	..
Mobile cellular subscriptions (per 100 people)	0.0	5.4	111.9
Individuals using the Internet (% of population)	0.0	5.8	47.5
Paved roads (% of total)	15.3	22.0	26.0
High-technology exports (% of manufactured exports)	..	52	40
Global links			
Merchandise trade (% of GDP)	46	77	64
Net barter terms of trade index (2000 = 100)	75	100	78
Total external debt stocks ($ billions)	3.8	4.7	14.5
Total debt service (% of exports)	24.5	8.2	17.6
Net migration (thousands)	62.4	84.0	64.3
Personal remittances received ($ millions)	12	136	562
Foreign direct investment, net inflows ($ millions)	163	409	2,636
Net official development assistance received ($ millions)	227	10	33

Côte d'Ivoire

Sub-Saharan Africa		Lower middle income	
Population (millions)	19.8	Population growth (%)	2.3
Surface area (1,000 sq. km)	322	Population living below $1.25 a day (%)	23.8
GNI, Atlas ($ billions)	24.2	GNI per capita, Atlas ($)	1,220
GNI, PPP ($ billions)	38.2	GNI per capita, PPP ($)	1,920

	1990	2000	2012
People			
Share of poorest 20% in nat'l consumption/income (%)	7.1	5.0	5.6
Life expectancy at birth (years)	53	46	50
Total fertility rate (births per woman)	6.4	5.4	4.9
Adolescent fertility rate (births per 1,000 women 15-19)	149	126	130
Contraceptive prevalence (% of married women 15-49)	..	15	18
Births attended by skilled health staff (% of total)	..	63	59
Under-five mortality rate (per 1,000 live births)	152	145	108
Child malnutrition, underweight (% of under age 5)	..	18.2	29.4
Child immunization, measles (% of ages 12-23 mos.)	56	68	85
Primary completion rate, total (% of relevant age group)	42	45	61
Gross secondary enrollment, total (% of relevant age group)	..	24	..
Ratio of girls to boys in primary & secondary school (%)	..	69	..
HIV prevalence rate (% population of ages 15-49)	2.3	6.6	3.2
Environment			
Forests (1,000 sq. km)	102	103	104
Deforestation (avg. annual %, 1990–2000 and 2000–2010)		-0.1	-0.2
Freshwater use (% of internal resources)	1.4	1.8	1.8
Access to improved water source (% total pop.)	76	78	80
Access to improved sanitation facilities (% total pop.)	15	18	22
Energy use per capita (kilograms of oil equivalent)	357	417	579
Carbon dioxide emissions per capita (metric tons)	0.5	0.4	0.3
Electricity use per capita (kilowatt-hours)	158	177	212
Economy			
GDP ($ billions)	10.8	10.4	24.7
GDP growth (annual %)	-1.1	-3.7	9.5
GDP implicit price deflator (annual % growth)	-4.5	-0.4	1.3
Value added in agriculture (% of GDP)	32	24	..
Value added in industry (% of GDP)	23	25	..
Value added in services (% of GDP)	44	51	..
Exports of goods and services (% of GDP)	32	40	..
Imports of goods and services (% of GDP)	27	33	..
Gross capital formation (% of GDP)	7	11	..
Central government revenue (% of GDP)	..	15.6	17.8
Central government cash surplus/deficit (% of GDP)	..	-2.4	-3.1
States and markets			
Starting a business (days)	..	62	8
Stock market capitalization (% of GDP)	5.1	11.4	31.7
Military expenditures (% of GDP)	1.3	1.6	1.7
Mobile cellular subscriptions (per 100 people)	0.0	2.9	91.2
Individuals using the Internet (% of population)	0.0	0.2	2.4
Paved roads (% of total)	8.7	10.0	7.9
High-technology exports (% of manufactured exports)	..	3	15
Global links			
Merchandise trade (% of GDP)	48	61	90
Net barter terms of trade index (2000 = 100)	143	100	144
Total external debt stocks ($ billions)	17.3	12.2	9.9
Total debt service (% of exports)	35.4	22.7	5.9
Net migration (thousands)	375	-420	50
Personal remittances received ($ millions)	44	119	373
Foreign direct investment, net inflows ($ millions)	48	235	478
Net official development assistance received ($ millions)	686	351	2,636

Croatia

High income

Population (millions)	4.3	Population growth (%)		-0.3
Surface area (1,000 sq. km)	57	Population living below $1.25 a day (%)		<2
GNI, Atlas ($ billions)	57.6	GNI per capita, Atlas ($)		13,490
GNI, PPP ($ billions)	86.2	GNI per capita, PPP ($)		20,200

	1990	2000	2012
People			
Share of poorest 20% in nat'l consumption/income (%)	10.3	8.3	8.1
Life expectancy at birth (years)	72	73	77
Total fertility rate (births per woman)	1.6	1.4	1.5
Adolescent fertility rate (births per 1,000 women 15–19)	19	16	13
Contraceptive prevalence (% of married women 15–49)	..	69	..
Births attended by skilled health staff (% of total)	100	100	100
Under-five mortality rate (per 1,000 live births)	13	8	5
Child malnutrition, underweight (% of under age 5)	..	..	..
Child immunization, measles (% of ages 12-23 mos.)	90	93	95
Primary completion rate, total (% of relevant age group)	..	93	94
Gross secondary enrollment, total (% of relevant age group)	79	86	98
Ratio of girls to boys in primary & secondary school (%)	102	101	103
HIV prevalence rate (% population of ages 15–49)	..	..	..
Environment			
Forests (1,000 sq. km)	19	19	19
Deforestation (avg. annual %, 1990-2000 and 2000-2010)		-0.2	-0.2
Freshwater use (% of internal resources)	..	..	1.7
Access to improved water source (% total pop.)	98	98	99
Access to improved sanitation facilities (% total pop.)	98	98	98
Energy use per capita (kilograms of oil equivalent)	1,888	1,760	1,971
Carbon dioxide emissions per capita (metric tons)	3.8	4.4	4.7
Electricity use per capita (kilowatt-hours)	2,965	2,856	3,901
Economy			
GDP ($ billions)	24.8	21.5	59.2
GDP growth (annual %)	..	3.8	-2.0
GDP implicit price deflator (annual % growth)		4.6	2.0
Value added in agriculture (% of GDP)	11	6	5
Value added in industry (% of GDP)	36	29	26
Value added in services (% of GDP)	53	65	69
Exports of goods and services (% of GDP)	78	42	43
Imports of goods and services (% of GDP)	86	45	43
Gross capital formation (% of GDP)	12	19	19
Central government revenue (% of GDP)	33.0	35.7	33.2
Central government cash surplus/deficit (% of GDP)	-4.6	-5.3	-4.7
States and markets			
Starting a business (days)	..	29	8
Stock market capitalization (% of GDP)	..	12.7	36.4
Military expenditures (% of GDP)	7.6	3.1	1.7
Mobile cellular subscriptions (per 100 people)	0.0	23.1	115.4
Individuals using the Internet (% of population)	0.0	6.6	63.0
Paved roads (% of total)	..	84.6	91.1
High-technology exports (% of manufactured exports)	6	9	10
Global links			
Merchandise trade (% of GDP)	88	57	56
Net barter terms of trade index (2000 = 100)	..	100	98
Total external debt stocks ($ millions)	..	..	..
Total debt service (% of exports)	..	..	..
Net migration (thousands)	-93.4	-30.0	-20.0
Personal remittances received ($ millions)	230	641	1,437
Foreign direct investment, net inflows ($ billions)	0.0	1.1	1.4
Net official development assistance received ($ millions)	0	66	151

Cuba

Latin America & Caribbean		**Upper middle income**	
Population (millions)	11.3	Population growth (%)	0.0
Surface area (1,000 sq. km)	110	Population living below $1.25 a day (%)	..
GNI, Atlas ($ billions)	66.4	GNI per capita, Atlas ($)	5,890
GNI, PPP ($ millions)	..	GNI per capita, PPP ($)	..

	1990	2000	2012
People			
Share of poorest 20% in nat'l consumption/income (%)	..	..	..
Life expectancy at birth (years)	75	77	79
Total fertility rate (births per woman)	1.8	1.6	1.5
Adolescent fertility rate (births per 1,000 women 15-19)	76	57	43
Contraceptive prevalence (% of married women 15-49)	..	73	74
Births attended by skilled health staff (% of total)	100	100	100
Under-five mortality rate (per 1,000 live births)	13	8	6
Child malnutrition, underweight (% of under age 5)	..	3.4	..
Child immunization, measles (% of ages 12-23 mos.)	94	94	99
Primary completion rate, total (% of relevant age group)	94	96	96
Gross secondary enrollment, total (% of relevant age group)	89	82	90
Ratio of girls to boys in primary & secondary school (%)	105	100	100
HIV prevalence rate (% population of ages 15-49)	0.1	0.1	0.1
Environment			
Forests (1,000 sq. km)	21	24	29
Deforestation (avg. annual %, 1990-2000 and 2000-2010)		-1.7	-1.7
Freshwater use (% of internal resources)	..	19.8	19.8
Access to improved water source (% total pop.)	..	91	94
Access to improved sanitation facilities (% total pop.)	81	87	93
Energy use per capita (kilograms of oil equivalent)	1,669	1,154	992
Carbon dioxide emissions per capita (metric tons)	3.1	2.3	3.4
Electricity use per capita (kilowatt-hours)	1,212	1,137	1,327
Economy			
GDP ($ billions)	28.6	30.6	68.2
GDP growth (annual %)	-2.9	5.9	2.7
GDP implicit price deflator (annual % growth)	5.3	1.7	3.3
Value added in agriculture (% of GDP)	14	8	5
Value added in industry (% of GDP)	19	28	21
Value added in services (% of GDP)	67	64	74
Exports of goods and services (% of GDP)	30	14	20
Imports of goods and services (% of GDP)	41	17	19
Gross capital formation (% of GDP)	25	13	12
Central government revenue (% of GDP)	..	..	..
Central government cash surplus/deficit (% of GDP)	..	..	..
States and markets			
Starting a business (days)	..	..	..
Stock market capitalization (% of GDP)	..	..	..
Military expenditures (% of GDP)	6.4	3.5	3.3
Mobile cellular subscriptions (per 100 people)	0.0	0.1	14.9
Individuals using the Internet (% of population)	0.0	0.5	25.6
Paved roads (% of total)	50.5	49.0	..
High-technology exports (% of manufactured exports)	..	21	..
Global links			
Merchandise trade (% of GDP)	34	21	30
Net barter terms of trade index (2000 = 100)	..	100	145
Total external debt stocks ($ millions)	..	..	..
Total debt service (% of exports)	..	..	..
Net migration (thousands)	-114	-143	-140
Personal remittances received ($ millions)	..	..	..
Foreign direct investment, net inflows ($ millions)	..	..	..
Net official development assistance received ($ millions)	51.8	44.0	87.9

Curaçao

High income

Population (thousands)	152	Population growth (%)	1.0
Surface area (sq. km)	444	Population living below $1.25 a day (%)	..
GNI, Atlas ($ millions)	..	GNI per capita, Atlas ($)	..
GNI, PPP ($ millions)	..	GNI per capita, PPP ($)	..

	1990	2000	2012
People			
Share of poorest 20% in nat'l consumption/income (%)	..	..	..
Life expectancy at birth (years)	..	..	77
Total fertility rate (births per woman)	..	..	2.2
Adolescent fertility rate (births per 1,000 women 15-19)	52	39	28
Contraceptive prevalence (% of married women 15-49)	..	..	..
Births attended by skilled health staff (% of total)	..	..	..
Under-five mortality rate (per 1,000 live births)	..	..	..
Child malnutrition, underweight (% of under age 5)	..	..	..
Child immunization, measles (% of ages 12-23 mos.)	..	..	..
Primary completion rate, total (% of relevant age group)	..	..	..
Gross secondary enrollment, total (% of relevant age group)	..	..	..
Ratio of girls to boys in primary & secondary school (%)	..	..	..
HIV prevalence rate (% population of ages 15-49)	..	..	..
Environment			
Forests (sq. km)	..	..	..
Deforestation (avg. annual %, 1990-2000 and 2000-2010)		..	..
Freshwater use (% of internal resources)	..	..	..
Access to improved water source (% total pop.)	..	..	..
Access to improved sanitation facilities (% total pop.)	..	..	..
Energy use per capita (kilograms of oil equivalent)	..	..	..
Carbon dioxide emissions per capita (metric tons)	..	..	..
Electricity use per capita (kilowatt-hours)	..	..	..
Economy			
GDP ($ millions)	..	..	..
GDP growth (annual %)	..	..	..
GDP implicit price deflator (annual % growth)	..	..	..
Value added in agriculture (% of GDP)	..	..	..
Value added in industry (% of GDP)	..	..	..
Value added in services (% of GDP)	..	..	..
Exports of goods and services (% of GDP)	..	..	..
Imports of goods and services (% of GDP)	..	..	..
Gross capital formation (% of GDP)	..	..	..
Central government revenue (% of GDP)	..	..	..
Central government cash surplus/deficit (% of GDP)	..	..	..
States and markets			
Starting a business (days)	..	..	..
Stock market capitalization (% of GDP)	..	..	..
Military expenditures (% of GDP)	..	..	..
Mobile cellular subscriptions (per 100 people)	..	..	..
Individuals using the Internet (% of population)	..	..	..
Paved roads (% of total)	..	..	..
High-technology exports (% of manufactured exports)	..	..	..
Global links			
Merchandise trade (% of GDP)	..	..	..
Net barter terms of trade index (2000 = 100)	..	..	100
Total external debt stocks ($ millions)	..	..	..
Total debt service (% of exports)	..	..	..
Net migration (thousands)	-11.5	-6.1	14.1
Personal remittances received ($ millions)	..	..	30.4
Foreign direct investment, net inflows ($ millions)	..	..	56.9
Net official development assistance received ($ millions)	..	..	..

Cyprus

Population (millions)	1.1	Population growth (%)	1.1
Surface area (1,000 sq. km)	9.3	Population living below $1.25 a day (%)	..
GNI, Atlas ($ billions)	22.8	GNI per capita, Atlas ($)	26,110
GNI, PPP ($ billions)	26.1	GNI per capita, PPP ($)	29,840

	1990	2000	2012
People			
Share of poorest 20% in nat'l consumption/income (%)	..	..	..
Life expectancy at birth (years)	77	78	80
Total fertility rate (births per woman)	2.4	1.7	1.5
Adolescent fertility rate (births per 1,000 women 15-19)	28	10	5
Contraceptive prevalence (% of married women 15-49)	..	..	..
Births attended by skilled health staff (% of total)	..	99	..
Under-five mortality rate (per 1,000 live births)	11	7	3
Child malnutrition, underweight (% of under age 5)	..	..	..
Child immunization, measles (% of ages 12-23 mos.)	77	86	86
Primary completion rate, total (% of relevant age group)	79	98	102
Gross secondary enrollment, total (% of relevant age group)	64	93	93
Ratio of girls to boys in primary & secondary school (%)	101	101	100
HIV prevalence rate (% population of ages 15-49)	..	..	..
Environment			
Forests (1,000 sq. km)	1.6	1.7	1.7
Deforestation (avg. annual %, 1990-2000 and 2000-2010)		-0.6	-0.1
Freshwater use (% of internal resources)	29.0	24.9	23.6
Access to improved water source (% total pop.)	100	100	100
Access to improved sanitation facilities (% total pop.)	100	100	100
Energy use per capita (kilograms of oil equivalent)	1,781	2,265	2,121
Carbon dioxide emissions per capita (metric tons)	6.1	7.3	7.0
Electricity use per capita (kilowatt-hours)	2,430	3,373	4,271
Economy			
GDP ($ billions)	5.6	9.3	22.8
GDP growth (annual %)	7.4	5.0	-2.4
GDP implicit price deflator (annual % growth)	5.4	3.8	1.6
Value added in agriculture (% of GDP)	7	4	..
Value added in industry (% of GDP)	26	19	..
Value added in services (% of GDP)	67	77	..
Exports of goods and services (% of GDP)	52	55	40
Imports of goods and services (% of GDP)	57	55	47
Gross capital formation (% of GDP)	27	18	18
Central government revenue (% of GDP)	..	..	39.1
Central government cash surplus/deficit (% of GDP)	..	..	-6.3
States and markets			
Starting a business (days)	..	..	8
Stock market capitalization (% of GDP)	22.4	46.7	8.8
Military expenditures (% of GDP)	7.4	3.0	2.1
Mobile cellular subscriptions (per 100 people)	0.4	23.1	98.4
Individuals using the Internet (% of population)	0.0	15.3	61.0
Paved roads (% of total)	59.6	61.0	65.8
High-technology exports (% of manufactured exports)	4	2	13
Global links			
Merchandise trade (% of GDP)	63	51	40
Net barter terms of trade index (2000 = 100)	..	100	94
Total external debt stocks ($ millions)	..	..	..
Total debt service (% of exports)	..	..	..
Net migration (thousands)	43.2	61.8	35.0
Personal remittances received ($ millions)	79	64	112
Foreign direct investment, net inflows ($ millions)	127	855	1,247
Net official development assistance received ($ millions)	38.4	..	..

Czech Republic

High income

Population (millions)	10.5	Population growth (%)	0.1
Surface area (1,000 sq. km)	79	Population living below $1.25 a day (%)	<2
GNI, Atlas ($ billions)	190.5	GNI per capita, Atlas ($)	18,130
GNI, PPP ($ billions)	267.9	GNI per capita, PPP ($)	25,480

	1990	2000	2012
People			
Share of poorest 20% in nat'l consumption/income (%)	10.4	..	..
Life expectancy at birth (years)	71	75	78
Total fertility rate (births per woman)	1.9	1.2	1.5
Adolescent fertility rate (births per 1,000 women 15-19)	45	13	5
Contraceptive prevalence (% of married women 15-49)	78	..	..
Births attended by skilled health staff (% of total)	100	100	100
Under-five mortality rate (per 1,000 live births)	15	7	4
Child malnutrition, underweight (% of under age 5)	0.9	2.1	..
Child immunization, measles (% of ages 12-23 mos.)	98	98	98
Primary completion rate, total (% of relevant age group)	98	99	102
Gross secondary enrollment, total (% of relevant age group)	91	89	97
Ratio of girls to boys in primary & secondary school (%)	94	101	100
HIV prevalence rate (% population of ages 15-49)	..	..	..
Environment			
Forests (1,000 sq. km)	26	26	27
Deforestation (avg. annual %, 1990-2000 and 2000-2010)		0.0	-0.1
Freshwater use (% of internal resources)	..	13.3	12.9
Access to improved water source (% total pop.)	100	100	100
Access to improved sanitation facilities (% total pop.)	100	100	100
Energy use per capita (kilograms of oil equivalent)	4,797	3,997	4,074
Carbon dioxide emissions per capita (metric tons)	13.5	12.2	10.7
Electricity use per capita (kilowatt-hours)	5,600	5,704	6,289
Economy			
GDP ($ billions)	39.1	58.8	196.4
GDP growth (annual %)	-11.6	4.2	-1.0
GDP implicit price deflator (annual % growth)	36.2	1.4	1.6
Value added in agriculture (% of GDP)	8	4	2
Value added in industry (% of GDP)	40	38	37
Value added in services (% of GDP)	52	59	60
Exports of goods and services (% of GDP)	39	61	78
Imports of goods and services (% of GDP)	37	63	72
Gross capital formation (% of GDP)	23	30	23
Central government revenue (% of GDP)	33.6	29.4	29.2
Central government cash surplus/deficit (% of GDP)	0.1	-3.5	-4.4
States and markets			
Starting a business (days)	..	40	20
Stock market capitalization (% of GDP)	..	18.7	18.9
Military expenditures (% of GDP)	2.1	2.0	1.1
Mobile cellular subscriptions (per 100 people)	0.0	42.4	126.8
Individuals using the Internet (% of population)	0.0	9.8	75.0
Paved roads (% of total)	100.0	100.0	..
High-technology exports (% of manufactured exports)	4	8	16
Global links			
Merchandise trade (% of GDP)	75	104	151
Net barter terms of trade index (2000 = 100)	..	100	101
Total external debt stocks ($ millions)	..	..	..
Total debt service (% of exports)	..	..	..
Net migration (thousands)	30	67	200
Personal remittances received ($ millions)	138	297	2,026
Foreign direct investment, net inflows ($ billions)	0.7	5.0	10.6
Net official development assistance received ($ millions)	..	..	..

Denmark

High income

Population (millions)	5.6	Population growth (%)			0.4
Surface area (1,000 sq. km)	43	Population living below $1.25 a day (%)			..
GNI, Atlas ($ billions)	334.8	GNI per capita, Atlas ($)			59,870
GNI, PPP ($ billions)	246.4	GNI per capita, PPP ($)			44,070

	1990	2000	2012
People			
Share of poorest 20% in nat'l consumption/income (%)	..	..	..
Life expectancy at birth (years)	75	77	80
Total fertility rate (births per woman)	1.7	1.8	1.7
Adolescent fertility rate (births per 1,000 women 15-19)	9	7	5
Contraceptive prevalence (% of married women 15-49)	78	..	..
Births attended by skilled health staff (% of total)	..	..	..
Under-five mortality rate (per 1,000 live births)	9	6	4
Child malnutrition, underweight (% of under age 5)	..	..	..
Child immunization, measles (% of ages 12-23 mos.)	84	99	90
Primary completion rate, total (% of relevant age group)	95	100	99
Gross secondary enrollment, total (% of relevant age group)	110	127	120
Ratio of girls to boys in primary & secondary school (%)	101	102	101
HIV prevalence rate (% population of ages 15-49)	..	..	..
Environment			
Forests (1,000 sq. km)	4.5	4.9	5.5
Deforestation (avg. annual %, 1990-2000 and 2000-2010)		-0.9	-1.1
Freshwater use (% of internal resources)	18.9	11.4	11.0
Access to improved water source (% total pop.)	100	100	100
Access to improved sanitation facilities (% total pop.)	100	100	100
Energy use per capita (kilograms of oil equivalent)	3,377	3,490	3,048
Carbon dioxide emissions per capita (metric tons)	9.7	8.9	8.3
Electricity use per capita (kilowatt-hours)	5,945	6,482	6,122
Economy			
GDP ($ billions)	136	160	315
GDP growth (annual %)	1.6	3.5	-0.4
GDP implicit price deflator (annual % growth)	2.8	3.0	2.3
Value added in agriculture (% of GDP)	4	3	1
Value added in industry (% of GDP)	26	27	22
Value added in services (% of GDP)	71	71	77
Exports of goods and services (% of GDP)	37	47	55
Imports of goods and services (% of GDP)	33	40	50
Gross capital formation (% of GDP)	20	21	17
Central government revenue (% of GDP)	..	35.3	40.5
Central government cash surplus/deficit (% of GDP)	..	1.6	-2.0
States and markets			
Starting a business (days)	..	7	6
Stock market capitalization (% of GDP)	28.8	67.3	71.3
Military expenditures (% of GDP)	2.0	1.5	1.4
Mobile cellular subscriptions (per 100 people)	2.9	63.0	117.6
Individuals using the Internet (% of population)	0.1	39.2	93.0
Paved roads (% of total)	100.0	100.0	100.0
High-technology exports (% of manufactured exports)	16	21	14
Global links			
Merchandise trade (% of GDP)	52	60	63
Net barter terms of trade index (2000 = 100)	..	100	100
Total external debt stocks ($ millions)	..	..	..
Total debt service (% of exports)	..	..	..
Net migration (thousands)	65.5	46.3	75.0
Personal remittances received ($ millions)	464	667	1,257
Foreign direct investment, net inflows ($ billions)	1.1	36.0	1.3
Net official development assistance received ($ millions)	..	..	..

Djibouti

Middle East & North Africa		Lower middle income	

Population (thousands)	860	Population growth (%)	1.5
Surface area (1,000 sq. km)	23	Population living below $1.25 a day (%)	18.8
GNI, Atlas ($ millions)	..	GNI per capita, Atlas ($)	..
GNI, PPP ($ millions)	..	GNI per capita, PPP ($)	..

	1990	2000	2012
People			
Share of poorest 20% in nat'l consumption/income (%)	..	6.0	..
Life expectancy at birth (years)	57	57	61
Total fertility rate (births per woman)	6.1	4.5	3.5
Adolescent fertility rate (births per 1,000 women 15-19)	68	28	19
Contraceptive prevalence (% of married women 15-49)	..	9	23
Births attended by skilled health staff (% of total)	..	61	93
Under-five mortality rate (per 1,000 live births)	119	108	81
Child malnutrition, underweight (% of under age 5)	20.2	25.4	29.8
Child immunization, measles (% of ages 12-23 mos.)	85	50	83
Primary completion rate, total (% of relevant age group)	28	26	52
Gross secondary enrollment, total (% of relevant age group)	10	14	46
Ratio of girls to boys in primary & secondary school (%)	72	71	83
HIV prevalence rate (% population of ages 15-49)	0.1	2.1	1.2
Environment			
Forests (sq. km)	56	56	56
Deforestation (avg. annual %, 1990-2000 and 2000-2010)		0.0	0.0
Freshwater use (% of internal resources)	..	6.3	6.3
Access to improved water source (% total pop.)	77	82	92
Access to improved sanitation facilities (% total pop.)	62	62	61
Energy use per capita (kilograms of oil equivalent)	220	..	..
Carbon dioxide emissions per capita (metric tons)	0.7	0.6	0.6
Electricity use per capita (kilowatt-hours)	..	..	..
Economy			
GDP ($ millions)	452	551	..
GDP growth (annual %)	-4.3	0.4	..
GDP implicit price deflator (annual % growth)	6.8	2.4	..
Value added in agriculture (% of GDP)	3	4	..
Value added in industry (% of GDP)	22	15	..
Value added in services (% of GDP)	75	81	..
Exports of goods and services (% of GDP)	54	35	..
Imports of goods and services (% of GDP)	78	50	..
Gross capital formation (% of GDP)	14	9	..
Central government revenue (% of GDP)	..	..	..
Central government cash surplus/deficit (% of GDP)	..	..	..
States and markets			
Starting a business (days)	..	..	17
Stock market capitalization (% of GDP)	..	..	..
Military expenditures (% of GDP)	6.9	4.7	..
Mobile cellular subscriptions (per 100 people)	0.0	0.0	24.7
Individuals using the Internet (% of population)	0.0	0.2	8.3
Paved roads (% of total)	..	45.0	..
High-technology exports (% of manufactured exports)	..	..	0
Global links			
Merchandise trade (% of GDP)	53	43	..
Net barter terms of trade index (2000 = 100)	..	100	82
Total external debt stocks ($ millions)	155	299	808
Total debt service (% of exports)	4.7	6.9	8.8
Net migration (thousands)	-15.0	-18.2	-16.0
Personal remittances received ($ millions)	13.1	12.3	33.3
Foreign direct investment, net inflows ($ millions)	2	3	110
Net official development assistance received ($ millions)	207	72	147

Dominica

Latin America & Caribbean		Upper middle income	
Population (thousands)	72	Population growth (%)	0.4
Surface area (sq. km)	750	Population living below $1.25 a day (%)	..
GNI, Atlas ($ millions)	461.6	GNI per capita, Atlas ($)	6,440
GNI, PPP ($ millions)	859.0	GNI per capita, PPP ($)	11,980

	1990	2000	2012
People			
Share of poorest 20% in nat'l consumption/income (%)	..	..	..
Life expectancy at birth (years)	74	77	..
Total fertility rate (births per woman)	2.5	1.9	..
Adolescent fertility rate (births per 1,000 women 15-19)	..	..	..
Contraceptive prevalence (% of married women 15-49)	..	50	..
Births attended by skilled health staff (% of total)	..	100	100
Under-five mortality rate (per 1,000 live births)	17	16	13
Child malnutrition, underweight (% of under age 5)	..	..	..
Child immunization, measles (% of ages 12-23 mos.)	88	99	99
Primary completion rate, total (% of relevant age group)	101	119	104
Gross secondary enrollment, total (% of relevant age group)	70	106	97
Ratio of girls to boys in primary & secondary school (%)	102	106	103
HIV prevalence rate (% population of ages 15-49)	..	..	..
Environment			
Forests (sq. km)	500	473	444
Deforestation (avg. annual %, 1990-2000 and 2000-2010)		0.6	0.6
Freshwater use (% of internal resources)	..	..	..
Access to improved water source (% total pop.)	..	94	..
Access to improved sanitation facilities (% total pop.)	..	81	..
Energy use per capita (kilograms of oil equivalent)	298	..	..
Carbon dioxide emissions per capita (metric tons)	0.8	1.5	1.9
Electricity use per capita (kilowatt-hours)	..	..	..
Economy			
GDP ($ millions)	166	324	480
GDP growth (annual %)	5.3	-5.6	-1.7
GDP implicit price deflator (annual % growth)	3.0	28.4	0.8
Value added in agriculture (% of GDP)	25	14	15
Value added in industry (% of GDP)	19	19	16
Value added in services (% of GDP)	56	67	69
Exports of goods and services (% of GDP)	55	45	40
Imports of goods and services (% of GDP)	81	56	51
Gross capital formation (% of GDP)	41	21	22
Central government revenue (% of GDP)	..	24.4	27.0
Central government cash surplus/deficit (% of GDP)	..	-5.4	-11.9
States and markets			
Starting a business (days)	..	..	12
Stock market capitalization (% of GDP)	..	..	..
Military expenditures (% of GDP)	..	..	..
Mobile cellular subscriptions (per 100 people)	0.0	1.7	152.5
Individuals using the Internet (% of population)	0.0	8.8	55.2
Paved roads (% of total)	45.6	50.0	81.9
High-technology exports (% of manufactured exports)	2	7	9
Global links			
Merchandise trade (% of GDP)	104	62	49
Net barter terms of trade index (2000 = 100)	..	100	103
Total external debt stocks ($ millions)	91	183	284
Total debt service (% of exports)	6.6	7.4	10.0
Net migration (thousands)	..	..	..
Personal remittances received ($ millions)	13.9	16.3	23.2
Foreign direct investment, net inflows ($ millions)	12.9	17.6	19.6
Net official development assistance received ($ millions)	19.6	15.2	25.7

Dominican Republic

Latin America & Caribbean		Upper middle income	
Population (millions)	10.3	Population growth (%)	1.3
Surface area (1,000 sq. km)	49	Population living below $1.25 a day (%)	2.2
GNI, Atlas ($ billions)	56.3	GNI per capita, Atlas ($)	5,470
GNI, PPP ($ billions)	99.3	GNI per capita, PPP ($)	9,660

	1990	2000	2012
People			
Share of poorest 20% in nat'l consumption/income (%)	4.2	3.7	4.7
Life expectancy at birth (years)	68	71	73
Total fertility rate (births per woman)	3.5	2.9	2.5
Adolescent fertility rate (births per 1,000 women 15-19)	113	110	100
Contraceptive prevalence (% of married women 15-49)	56	65	73
Births attended by skilled health staff (% of total)	92	98	98
Under-five mortality rate (per 1,000 live births)	60	40	27
Child malnutrition, underweight (% of under age 5)	8.4	3.5	3.4
Child immunization, measles (% of ages 12-23 mos.)	70	85	79
Primary completion rate, total (% of relevant age group)	..	77	90
Gross secondary enrollment, total (% of relevant age group)	..	59	76
Ratio of girls to boys in primary & secondary school (%)	..	104	99
HIV prevalence rate (% population of ages 15-49)	0.5	1.3	0.7
Environment			
Forests (1,000 sq. km)	20	20	20
Deforestation (avg. annual %, 1990-2000 and 2000-2010)		0.0	0.0
Freshwater use (% of internal resources)	..	16.6	16.6
Access to improved water source (% total pop.)	89	86	81
Access to improved sanitation facilities (% total pop.)	73	77	82
Energy use per capita (kilograms of oil equivalent)	563	866	727
Carbon dioxide emissions per capita (metric tons)	1.3	2.3	2.1
Electricity use per capita (kilowatt-hours)	385	722	893
Economy			
GDP ($ billions)	7.1	24.0	59.0
GDP growth (annual %)	-5.5	5.7	3.9
GDP implicit price deflator (annual % growth)	50.5	6.9	5.2
Value added in agriculture (% of GDP)	15	7	6
Value added in industry (% of GDP)	34	36	32
Value added in services (% of GDP)	60	57	62
Exports of goods and services (% of GDP)	34	37	25
Imports of goods and services (% of GDP)	44	46	34
Gross capital formation (% of GDP)	25	23	16
Central government revenue (% of GDP)	..	..	14.4
Central government cash surplus/deficit (% of GDP)	..	..	-2.9
States and markets			
Starting a business (days)	..	77	19
Stock market capitalization (% of GDP)	..	..	..
Military expenditures (% of GDP)	0.7	1.0	0.6
Mobile cellular subscriptions (per 100 people)	0.0	8.1	86.9
Individuals using the Internet (% of population)	0.0	3.7	45.0
Paved roads (% of total)	44.7	49.0	..
High-technology exports (% of manufactured exports)	..	1	3
Global links			
Merchandise trade (% of GDP)	73	63	45
Net barter terms of trade index (2000 = 100)	96	100	91
Total external debt stocks ($ billions)	4.5	4.7	16.9
Total debt service (% of exports)	12.5	5.7	14.0
Net migration (thousands)	-129	-148	-140
Personal remittances received ($ billions)	0.3	1.8	3.6
Foreign direct investment, net inflows ($ millions)	133	953	3,857
Net official development assistance received ($ millions)	102	56	261

Ecuador

Latin America & Caribbean		Upper middle income	
Population (millions)	15.5	Population growth (%)	1.6
Surface area (1,000 sq. km)	256	Population living below $1.25 a day (%)	4.6
GNI, Atlas ($ billions)	80.1	GNI per capita, Atlas ($)	5,170
GNI, PPP ($ billions)	147.0	GNI per capita, PPP ($)	9,490

	1990	2000	2012
People			
Share of poorest 20% in nat'l consumption/income (%)	..	3.0	4.3
Life expectancy at birth (years)	69	73	76
Total fertility rate (births per woman)	3.8	3.1	2.6
Adolescent fertility rate (births per 1,000 women 15–19)	87	85	77
Contraceptive prevalence (% of married women 15–49)	53	66	..
Births attended by skilled health staff (% of total)	..	99	..
Under-five mortality rate (per 1,000 live births)	56	34	23
Child malnutrition, underweight (% of under age 5)	..	6.2	..
Child immunization, measles (% of ages 12–23 mos.)	60	99	94
Primary completion rate, total (% of relevant age group)	96	98	111
Gross secondary enrollment, total (% of relevant age group)	59	59	87
Ratio of girls to boys in primary & secondary school (%)	100	100	101
HIV prevalence rate (% population of ages 15–49)	0.2	0.6	0.6
Environment			
Forests (1,000 sq. km)	138	118	97
Deforestation (avg. annual %, 1990–2000 and 2000–2010)		1.5	1.8
Freshwater use (% of internal resources)	..	3.5	3.5
Access to improved water source (% total pop.)	74	80	86
Access to improved sanitation facilities (% total pop.)	57	70	83
Energy use per capita (kilograms of oil equivalent)	577	624	849
Carbon dioxide emissions per capita (metric tons)	1.7	1.7	2.2
Electricity use per capita (kilowatt-hours)	486	642	1,192
Economy			
GDP ($ billions)	15.2	18.3	84.0
GDP growth (annual %)	3.7	1.1	5.1
GDP implicit price deflator (annual % growth)	5.8	-4.7	4.1
Value added in agriculture (% of GDP)	21	16	10
Value added in industry (% of GDP)	30	36	37
Value added in services (% of GDP)	49	48	53
Exports of goods and services (% of GDP)	23	32	31
Imports of goods and services (% of GDP)	22	27	33
Gross capital formation (% of GDP)	24	21	28
Central government revenue (% of GDP)	9.8	..	..
Central government cash surplus/deficit (% of GDP)	2.0	..	..
States and markets			
Starting a business (days)	..	92	56
Stock market capitalization (% of GDP)	0.4	3.8	7.0
Military expenditures (% of GDP)	1.3	1.5	2.8
Mobile cellular subscriptions (per 100 people)	0.0	3.8	106.2
Individuals using the Internet (% of population)	0.0	1.5	35.1
Paved roads (% of total)	13.4	19.0	14.8
High-technology exports (% of manufactured exports)	0	6	2
Global links			
Merchandise trade (% of GDP)	30	47	58
Net barter terms of trade index (2000 = 100)	114	100	135
Total external debt stocks ($ billions)	12.2	13.3	16.9
Total debt service (% of exports)	33.2	30.6	9.8
Net migration (thousands)	-17.7	-43.5	-30.0
Personal remittances received ($ billions)	0.1	1.3	2.5
Foreign direct investment, net inflows ($ millions)	126	-23	591
Net official development assistance received ($ millions)	159	146	149

Egypt, Arab Rep.

Middle East & North Africa		Lower middle income	
Population (millions)	80.7	Population growth (%)	1.7
Surface area (1,000 sq. km)	1,001	Population living below $1.25 a day (%)	<2
GNI, Atlas ($ billions)	240.3	GNI per capita, Atlas ($)	2,980
GNI, PPP ($ billions)	520.7	GNI per capita, PPP ($)	6,450

	1990	2000	2012
People			
Share of poorest 20% in nat'l consumption/income (%)	8.7	9.0	9.2
Life expectancy at birth (years)	65	69	71
Total fertility rate (births per woman)	4.4	3.3	2.8
Adolescent fertility rate (births per 1,000 women 15–19)	77	55	43
Contraceptive prevalence (% of married women 15–49)	48	56	60
Births attended by skilled health staff (% of total)	37	61	79
Under-five mortality rate (per 1,000 live births)	86	45	21
Child malnutrition, underweight (% of under age 5)	10.5	4.3	6.8
Child immunization, measles (% of ages 12–23 mos.)	86	98	93
Primary completion rate, total (% of relevant age group)	..	97	107
Gross secondary enrollment, total (% of relevant age group)	73	86	86
Ratio of girls to boys in primary & secondary school (%)	81	92	97
HIV prevalence rate (% population of ages 15–49)	0.1	0.1	0.1
Environment			
Forests (sq. km)	440	590	706
Deforestation (avg. annual %, 1990–2000 and 2000–2010)		-3.0	-1.7
Freshwater use (% of internal resources)	..	3,794.4	3,794.4
Access to improved water source (% total pop.)	93	96	99
Access to improved sanitation facilities (% total pop.)	72	86	96
Energy use per capita (kilograms of oil equivalent)	574	615	978
Carbon dioxide emissions per capita (metric tons)	1.3	2.1	2.6
Electricity use per capita (kilowatt-hours)	675	1,017	1,743
Economy			
GDP ($ billions)	43	100	263
GDP growth (annual %)	5.7	5.4	2.2
GDP implicit price deflator (annual % growth)	18.4	4.9	12.4
Value added in agriculture (% of GDP)	19	17	14
Value added in industry (% of GDP)	29	33	39
Value added in services (% of GDP)	52	50	46
Exports of goods and services (% of GDP)	20	16	17
Imports of goods and services (% of GDP)	33	23	26
Gross capital formation (% of GDP)	29	20	16
Central government revenue (% of GDP)	23.0	24.3	21.5
Central government cash surplus/deficit (% of GDP)	-2.0	-6.7	-10.6
States and markets			
Starting a business (days)	..	37	8
Stock market capitalization (% of GDP)	4.1	28.8	22.1
Military expenditures (% of GDP)	4.7	3.2	1.7
Mobile cellular subscriptions (per 100 people)	0.0	2.1	119.9
Individuals using the Internet (% of population)	0.0	0.6	44.1
Paved roads (% of total)	72.0	78.0	92.2
High-technology exports (% of manufactured exports)	..	0	1
Global links			
Merchandise trade (% of GDP)	37	20	38
Net barter terms of trade index (2000 = 100)	101	100	156
Total external debt stocks ($ billions)	33.0	29.2	40.0
Total debt service (% of exports)	28.6	9.8	6.6
Net migration (thousands)	-1,109	-371	-216
Personal remittances received ($ billions)	4.3	2.9	19.2
Foreign direct investment, net inflows ($ billions)	0.7	1.2	2.8
Net official development assistance received ($ billions)	6.1	1.4	1.8

El Salvador

Latin America & Caribbean		Lower middle income
Population (millions)	6.3	Population growth (%)	0.7
Surface area (1,000 sq. km)	21	Population living below $1.25 a day (%)	9.0
GNI, Atlas ($ billions)	22.6	GNI per capita, Atlas ($)	3,590
GNI, PPP ($ billions)	42.3	GNI per capita, PPP ($)	6,720

	1990	2000	2012
People			
Share of poorest 20% in nat'l consumption/income (%)	2.6	2.3	3.7
Life expectancy at birth (years)	66	70	72
Total fertility rate (births per woman)	4.0	2.9	2.2
Adolescent fertility rate (births per 1,000 women 15-19)	122	100	76
Contraceptive prevalence (% of married women 15-49)	53	67	73
Births attended by skilled health staff (% of total)	87	92	96
Under-five mortality rate (per 1,000 live births)	59	32	16
Child malnutrition, underweight (% of under age 5)	7.2	6.1	6.6
Child immunization, measles (% of ages 12-23 mos.)	98	97	93
Primary completion rate, total (% of relevant age group)	63	83	101
Gross secondary enrollment, total (% of relevant age group)	38	54	69
Ratio of girls to boys in primary & secondary school (%)	102	97	97
HIV prevalence rate (% population of ages 15-49)	0.3	0.8	0.6
Environment			
Forests (1,000 sq. km)	3.8	3.3	2.8
Deforestation (avg. annual %, 1990-2000 and 2000-2010)		1.3	1.5
Freshwater use (% of internal resources)	4.1	7.8	7.8
Access to improved water source (% total pop.)	75	84	90
Access to improved sanitation facilities (% total pop.)	50	61	70
Energy use per capita (kilograms of oil equivalent)	462	666	690
Carbon dioxide emissions per capita (metric tons)	0.5	1.0	1.0
Electricity use per capita (kilowatt-hours)	347	608	830
Economy			
GDP ($ billions)	4.8	13.1	23.9
GDP growth (annual %)	4.8	2.2	1.9
GDP implicit price deflator (annual % growth)	4.7	3.1	1.2
Value added in agriculture (% of GDP)	17	10	12
Value added in industry (% of GDP)	27	31	27
Value added in services (% of GDP)	55	58	61
Exports of goods and services (% of GDP)	19	27	28
Imports of goods and services (% of GDP)	31	42	46
Gross capital formation (% of GDP)	14	17	14
Central government revenue (% of GDP)	..	16.0	20.4
Central government cash surplus/deficit (% of GDP)	..	-4.7	-2.2
States and markets			
Starting a business (days)	..	115	17
Stock market capitalization (% of GDP)	..	15.5	45.0
Military expenditures (% of GDP)	4.2	1.3	1.0
Mobile cellular subscriptions (per 100 people)	0.0	12.5	137.3
Individuals using the Internet (% of population)	0.0	1.2	25.5
Paved roads (% of total)	14.4	19.8	53.1
High-technology exports (% of manufactured exports)	..	3	5
Global links			
Merchandise trade (% of GDP)	38	60	65
Net barter terms of trade index (2000 = 100)	84	100	90
Total external debt stocks ($ billions)	2.2	4.5	13.3
Total debt service (% of exports)	21.7	9.9	18.7
Net migration (thousands)	-255	-356	-225
Personal remittances received ($ billions)	0.4	1.8	3.9
Foreign direct investment, net inflows ($ millions)	2	173	467
Net official development assistance received ($ millions)	347	180	230

Equatorial Guinea

High income

Population (thousands)	736	Population growth (%)		2.8
Surface area (1,000 sq. km)	28	Population living below $1.25 a day (%)		..
GNI, Atlas ($ billions)	10.0	GNI per capita, Atlas ($)		13,560
GNI, PPP ($ billions)	13.7	GNI per capita, PPP ($)		18,570

	1990	2000	2012
People			
Share of poorest 20% in nat'l consumption/income (%)	..	..	..
Life expectancy at birth (years)	47	48	53
Total fertility rate (births per woman)	5.9	5.8	4.9
Adolescent fertility rate (births per 1,000 women 15-19)	134	131	113
Contraceptive prevalence (% of married women 15-49)	..	10	..
Births attended by skilled health staff (% of total)	..	65	..
Under-five mortality rate (per 1,000 live births)	182	143	100
Child malnutrition, underweight (% of under age 5)	..	15.7	..
Child immunization, measles (% of ages 12-23 mos.)	88	51	51
Primary completion rate, total (% of relevant age group)	..	48	55
Gross secondary enrollment, total (% of relevant age group)	42	31	..
Ratio of girls to boys in primary & secondary school (%)	82	72	..
HIV prevalence rate (% population of ages 15-49)	0.8	3.3	6.2
Environment			
Forests (1,000 sq. km)	19	17	16
Deforestation (avg. annual %, 1990-2000 and 2000-2010)		0.7	0.7
Freshwater use (% of internal resources)	..	0.1	0.1
Access to improved water source (% total pop.)	..	51	..
Access to improved sanitation facilities (% total pop.)	..	89	..
Energy use per capita (kilograms of oil equivalent)	..	..	..
Carbon dioxide emissions per capita (metric tons)	0.3	0.9	6.7
Electricity use per capita (kilowatt-hours)	..	..	..
Economy			
GDP ($ billions)	0.1	1.2	17.7
GDP growth (annual %)	3.3	12.5	2.5
GDP implicit price deflator (annual % growth)	-2.5	46.6	11.1
Value added in agriculture (% of GDP)	62	10	..
Value added in industry (% of GDP)	11	87	..
Value added in services (% of GDP)	28	3	..
Exports of goods and services (% of GDP)	32	99	84
Imports of goods and services (% of GDP)	70	86	61
Gross capital formation (% of GDP)	17	72	51
Central government revenue (% of GDP)	..	..	48.4
Central government cash surplus/deficit (% of GDP)	..	..	-9.4
States and markets			
Starting a business (days)	..	..	135
Stock market capitalization (% of GDP)	..	..	..
Military expenditures (% of GDP)	..	..	3.6
Mobile cellular subscriptions (per 100 people)	0.0	1.0	68.1
Individuals using the Internet (% of population)	0.0	0.1	13.9
Paved roads (% of total)	..	..	..
High-technology exports (% of manufactured exports)	..	..	..
Global links			
Merchandise trade (% of GDP)	95	125	121
Net barter terms of trade index (2000 = 100)	38	100	245
Total external debt stocks ($ millions)	..	..	..
Total debt service (% of exports)	..	..	..
Net migration (thousands)	15.0	25.0	20.0
Personal remittances received ($ millions)	1.3	..	..
Foreign direct investment, net inflows ($ millions)	11	154	2,115
Net official development assistance received ($ millions)	60.2	21.3	14.2

Eritrea

Sub-Saharan Africa			Low income
Population (millions)	6.1	Population growth (%)	3.3
Surface area (1,000 sq. km)	118	Population living below $1.25 a day (%)	..
GNI, Atlas ($ billions)	2.8	GNI per capita, Atlas ($)	450
GNI, PPP ($ billions)	3.4	GNI per capita, PPP ($)	550

	1990	2000	2012
People			
Share of poorest 20% in nat'l consumption/income (%)	..	..	..
Life expectancy at birth (years)	48	56	62
Total fertility rate (births per woman)	6.5	5.9	4.8
Adolescent fertility rate (births per 1,000 women 15–19)	119	98	65
Contraceptive prevalence (% of married women 15–49)	..	8	..
Births attended by skilled health staff (% of total)	..	28	..
Under-five mortality rate (per 1,000 live births)	150	89	52
Child malnutrition, underweight (% of under age 5)	36.9	34.5	..
Child immunization, measles (% of ages 12–23 mos.)	34	76	99
Primary completion rate, total (% of relevant age group)	..	32	31
Gross secondary enrollment, total (% of relevant age group)	13	22	30
Ratio of girls to boys in primary & secondary school (%)	82	79	82
HIV prevalence rate (% population of ages 15–49)	1.2	2.2	0.7
Environment			
Forests (1,000 sq. km)	16	16	15
Deforestation (avg. annual %, 1990–2000 and 2000–2010)		0.3	0.3
Freshwater use (% of internal resources)	..	14.8	20.8
Access to improved water source (% total pop.)	43	54	..
Access to improved sanitation facilities (% total pop.)	9	11	..
Energy use per capita (kilograms of oil equivalent)	263	180	129
Carbon dioxide emissions per capita (metric tons)	..	0.15	0.09
Electricity use per capita (kilowatt-hours)	37	44	49
Economy			
GDP ($ millions)	477	706	3,092
GDP growth (annual %)	13.5	-3.1	7.0
GDP implicit price deflator (annual % growth)	-1.4	25.0	10.8
Value added in agriculture (% of GDP)	31	13	15
Value added in industry (% of GDP)	12	20	22
Value added in services (% of GDP)	57	66	63
Exports of goods and services (% of GDP)	11	10	14
Imports of goods and services (% of GDP)	45	58	23
Gross capital formation (% of GDP)	8	22	10
Central government revenue (% of GDP)	..	..	..
Central government cash surplus/deficit (% of GDP)	..	..	..
States and markets			
Starting a business (days)	..	..	84
Stock market capitalization (% of GDP)	..	..	..
Military expenditures (% of GDP)	22.0	32.7	..
Mobile cellular subscriptions (per 100 people)	0.0	0.0	5.0
Individuals using the Internet (% of population)	0.0	0.1	0.8
Paved roads (% of total)	19.4	22.0	..
High-technology exports (% of manufactured exports)	..	0	..
Global links			
Merchandise trade (% of GDP)	77	72	46
Net barter terms of trade index (2000 = 100)	99	100	99
Total external debt stocks ($ millions)	..	330	994
Total debt service (% of exports)	..	4.3	..
Net migration (thousands)	-359	229	55
Personal remittances received ($ millions)	..	3.3	..
Foreign direct investment, net inflows ($ millions)	..	27.9	73.7
Net official development assistance received ($ millions)	5	177	134

Estonia

High income

Population (millions)	1.3	Population growth (%)		-0.4
Surface area (1,000 sq. km)	45	Population living below $1.25 a day (%)		<2
GNI, Atlas ($ billions)	21.6	GNI per capita, Atlas ($)		16,270
GNI, PPP ($ billions)	31.0	GNI per capita, PPP ($)		23,280

	1990	2000	2012
People			
Share of poorest 20% in nat'l consumption/income (%)	6.4	6.6	..
Life expectancy at birth (years)	69	70	76
Total fertility rate (births per woman)	2.1	1.4	1.6
Adolescent fertility rate (births per 1,000 women 15-19)	46	25	17
Contraceptive prevalence (% of married women 15-49)	..	..	..
Births attended by skilled health staff (% of total)	99	100	100
Under-five mortality rate (per 1,000 live births)	20	11	4
Child malnutrition, underweight (% of under age 5)	..	..	..
Child immunization, measles (% of ages 12-23 mos.)	0	93	94
Primary completion rate, total (% of relevant age group)	..	94	96
Gross secondary enrollment, total (% of relevant age group)	105	93	109
Ratio of girls to boys in primary & secondary school (%)	103	100	100
HIV prevalence rate (% population of ages 15-49)	..	..	..
Environment			
Forests (1,000 sq. km)	21	22	22
Deforestation (avg. annual %, 1990-2000 and 2000-2010)		-0.7	0.1
Freshwater use (% of internal resources)	..	11.5	14.1
Access to improved water source (% total pop.)	99	99	99
Access to improved sanitation facilities (% total pop.)	95	95	95
Energy use per capita (kilograms of oil equivalent)	6,316	3,418	4,304
Carbon dioxide emissions per capita (metric tons)	15.0	11.0	13.7
Electricity use per capita (kilowatt-hours)	5,890	4,596	6,279
Economy			
GDP ($ billions)	1.7	5.7	22.4
GDP growth (annual %)	..	9.7	3.9
GDP implicit price deflator (annual % growth)	..	4.8	3.3
Value added in agriculture (% of GDP)	..	5	4
Value added in industry (% of GDP)	..	28	29
Value added in services (% of GDP)	..	68	67
Exports of goods and services (% of GDP)	66	85	91
Imports of goods and services (% of GDP)	70	88	90
Gross capital formation (% of GDP)	28	28	28
Central government revenue (% of GDP)	..	29.4	32.9
Central government cash surplus/deficit (% of GDP)	..	0.2	1.0
States and markets			
Starting a business (days)	..	72	7
Stock market capitalization (% of GDP)	..	32.5	10.4
Military expenditures (% of GDP)	0.8	1.4	1.9
Mobile cellular subscriptions (per 100 people)	0.0	40.8	160.4
Individuals using the Internet (% of population)	0.0	28.6	79.0
Paved roads (% of total)	51.8	20.0	18.2
High-technology exports (% of manufactured exports)	..	30	11
Global links			
Merchandise trade (% of GDP)	..	157	151
Net barter terms of trade index (2000 = 100)	..	100	94
Total external debt stocks ($ millions)	..	..	..
Total debt service (% of exports)	..	..	..
Net migration (thousands)	-112	-14	0
Personal remittances received ($ millions)	..	4	401
Foreign direct investment, net inflows ($ millions)	82	387	1,648
Net official development assistance received ($ millions)	..	..	..

Ethiopia

Sub-Saharan Africa			**Low income**
Population (millions)	91.7	Population growth (%)	2.6
Surface area (1,000 sq. km)	1,104	Population living below $1.25 a day (%)	30.7
GNI, Atlas ($ billions)	34.7	GNI per capita, Atlas ($)	380
GNI, PPP ($ billions)	101.5	GNI per capita, PPP ($)	1,110

	1990	2000	2012
People			
Share of poorest 20% in nat'l consumption/income (%)	..	9.2	8.0
Life expectancy at birth (years)	47	52	63
Total fertility rate (births per woman)	7.2	6.5	4.6
Adolescent fertility rate (births per 1,000 women 15-19)	118	110	78
Contraceptive prevalence (% of married women 15-49)	5	8	29
Births attended by skilled health staff (% of total)	..	6	10
Under-five mortality rate (per 1,000 live births)	204	146	68
Child malnutrition, underweight (% of under age 5)	43.3	42.0	29.2
Child immunization, measles (% of ages 12-23 mos.)	38	33	66
Primary completion rate, total (% of relevant age group)	23	22	..
Gross secondary enrollment, total (% of relevant age group)	14	14	..
Ratio of girls to boys in primary & secondary school (%)	69	65	..
HIV prevalence rate (% population of ages 15-49)	1.3	3.7	1.3
Environment			
Forests (1,000 sq. km)	167	137	122
Deforestation (avg. annual %, 1990-2000 and 2000-2010)		1.0	1.1
Freshwater use (% of internal resources)	..	4.6	4.6
Access to improved water source (% total pop.)	13	29	52
Access to improved sanitation facilities (% total pop.)	2	8	24
Energy use per capita (kilograms of oil equivalent)	411	382	381
Carbon dioxide emissions per capita (metric tons)	0.06	0.09	0.07
Electricity use per capita (kilowatt-hours)	23	23	52
Economy			
GDP ($ billions)	12.1	8.1	41.6
GDP growth (annual %)	2.7	6.1	8.5
GDP implicit price deflator (annual % growth)	3.3	5.8	34.2
Value added in agriculture (% of GDP)	54	49	49
Value added in industry (% of GDP)	11	12	10
Value added in services (% of GDP)	35	39	41
Exports of goods and services (% of GDP)	6	12	14
Imports of goods and services (% of GDP)	9	24	32
Gross capital formation (% of GDP)	13	23	35
Central government revenue (% of GDP)	12.4	12.0	11.1
Central government cash surplus/deficit (% of GDP)	-6.6	-4.3	-1.4
States and markets			
Starting a business (days)	..	46	15
Stock market capitalization (% of GDP)	..	..	..
Military expenditures (% of GDP)	6.5	7.7	0.9
Mobile cellular subscriptions (per 100 people)	0.0	0.0	22.4
Individuals using the Internet (% of population)	0.0	0.0	1.5
Paved roads (% of total)	15.0	12.0	13.7
High-technology exports (% of manufactured exports)	..	0	2
Global links			
Merchandise trade (% of GDP)	11	22	36
Net barter terms of trade index (2000 = 100)	125	100	131
Total external debt stocks ($ billions)	8.6	5.5	10.5
Total debt service (% of exports)	39.0	13.7	7.2
Net migration (thousands)	1,295	-83	-60
Personal remittances received ($ millions)	5	53	624
Foreign direct investment, net inflows ($ millions)	0	135	279
Net official development assistance received ($ billions)	1.0	0.7	3.3

Faeroe Islands

High income

Population (thousands)	50	Population growth (%)		-0.1
Surface area (1,000 sq. km)	1.4	Population living below $1.25 a day (%)		..
GNI, Atlas ($ millions)	..	GNI per capita, Atlas ($)		..
GNI, PPP ($ millions)	..	GNI per capita, PPP ($)		..

	1990	2000	2012
People			
Share of poorest 20% in nat'l consumption/income (%)	..	..	..
Life expectancy at birth (years)	77	79	82
Total fertility rate (births per woman)	..	..	..
Adolescent fertility rate (births per 1,000 women 15-19)	..	..	..
Contraceptive prevalence (% of married women 15-49)	..	..	..
Births attended by skilled health staff (% of total)	..	..	..
Under-five mortality rate (per 1,000 live births)	..	..	..
Child malnutrition, underweight (% of under age 5)	..	..	..
Child immunization, measles (% of ages 12-23 mos.)	..	..	..
Primary completion rate, total (% of relevant age group)	..	..	..
Gross secondary enrollment, total (% of relevant age group)	..	..	..
Ratio of girls to boys in primary & secondary school (%)	..	..	..
HIV prevalence rate (% population of ages 15-49)	..	..	..
Environment			
Forests (sq. km)	1.0	1.0	1.0
Deforestation (avg. annual %, 1990-2000 and 2000-2010)		0.0	0.0
Freshwater use (% of internal resources)	..	..	
Access to improved water source (% total pop.)	..	..	
Access to improved sanitation facilities (% total pop.)	..	..	
Energy use per capita (kilograms of oil equivalent)	..	..	..
Carbon dioxide emissions per capita (metric tons)	13.0	15.3	14.3
Electricity use per capita (kilowatt-hours)	..	..	..
Economy			
GDP ($ millions)	..	1,062	2,198
GDP growth (annual %)	..	..	..
GDP implicit price deflator (annual % growth)	..	..	..
Value added in agriculture (% of GDP)	..	..	..
Value added in industry (% of GDP)	..	..	..
Value added in services (% of GDP)	..	..	..
Exports of goods and services (% of GDP)	..	..	..
Imports of goods and services (% of GDP)	..	..	..
Gross capital formation (% of GDP)	..	..	..
Central government revenue (% of GDP)	..	..	..
Central government cash surplus/deficit (% of GDP)	..	..	..
States and markets			
Starting a business (days)	..	..	..
Stock market capitalization (% of GDP)	..	..	..
Military expenditures (% of GDP)	..	..	..
Mobile cellular subscriptions (per 100 people)	0.0	36.5	118.6
Individuals using the Internet (% of population)	0.0	32.9	85.3
Paved roads (% of total)	..	..	
High-technology exports (% of manufactured exports)	0	0	1
Global links			
Merchandise trade (% of GDP)	..	95	70
Net barter terms of trade index (2000 = 100)	..	100	104
Total external debt stocks ($ millions)	..	..	..
Total debt service (% of exports)	..	..	..
Net migration (thousands)	..	..	..
Personal remittances received ($ millions)	..	43	158
Foreign direct investment, net inflows ($ millions)	..	..	..
Net official development assistance received ($ millions)	..	..	..

Fiji

East Asia & Pacific		**Upper middle income**
Population (thousands)	875	Population growth (%)	0.8
Surface area (1,000 sq. km)	18	Population living below $1.25 a day (%)	5.9
GNI, Atlas ($ billions)	3.6	GNI per capita, Atlas ($)	4,110
GNI, PPP ($ billions)	4.1	GNI per capita, PPP ($)	4,690

	1990	2000	2012
People			
Share of poorest 20% in nat'l consumption/income (%)	..	4.1	6.2
Life expectancy at birth (years)	66	68	70
Total fertility rate (births per woman)	3.4	3.1	2.6
Adolescent fertility rate (births per 1,000 women 15-19)	63	43	43
Contraceptive prevalence (% of married women 15-49)	..	44	32
Births attended by skilled health staff (% of total)	..	99	100
Under-five mortality rate (per 1,000 live births)	31	24	22
Child malnutrition, underweight (% of under age 5)	6.9	5.3	..
Child immunization, measles (% of ages 12-23 mos.)	84	81	99
Primary completion rate, total (% of relevant age group)	105	95	103
Gross secondary enrollment, total (% of relevant age group)	77	78	90
Ratio of girls to boys in primary & secondary school (%)	98	103	104
HIV prevalence rate (% population of ages 15-49)	0.1	0.1	0.2
Environment			
Forests (1,000 sq. km)	10	10	10
Deforestation (avg. annual %, 1990-2000 and 2000-2010)		-0.3	-0.3
Freshwater use (% of internal resources)	..	0.3	0.3
Access to improved water source (% total pop.)	85	91	96
Access to improved sanitation facilities (% total pop.)	57	74	87
Energy use per capita (kilograms of oil equivalent)	392	..	..
Carbon dioxide emissions per capita (metric tons)	1.1	1.1	1.5
Electricity use per capita (kilowatt-hours)	..	..	..
Economy			
GDP ($ millions)	1,337	1,684	3,908
GDP growth (annual %)	5.8	-1.7	2.3
GDP implicit price deflator (annual % growth)	6.7	-4.7	1.6
Value added in agriculture (% of GDP)	20	17	13
Value added in industry (% of GDP)	24	22	19
Value added in services (% of GDP)	56	61	68
Exports of goods and services (% of GDP)	62	65	62
Imports of goods and services (% of GDP)	67	70	65
Gross capital formation (% of GDP)	14	17	..
Central government revenue (% of GDP)	26.8	..	..
Central government cash surplus/deficit (% of GDP)	0.9	..	..
States and markets			
Starting a business (days)	..	45	59
Stock market capitalization (% of GDP)	..	14.5	11.6
Military expenditures (% of GDP)	2.3	1.9	1.5
Mobile cellular subscriptions (per 100 people)	0.0	6.8	98.2
Individuals using the Internet (% of population)	0.0	1.5	33.7
Paved roads (% of total)	44.5	49.0	..
High-technology exports (% of manufactured exports)	12	0	2
Global links			
Merchandise trade (% of GDP)	94	84	87
Net barter terms of trade index (2000 = 100)	142	100	108
Total external debt stocks ($ millions)	308	182	732
Total debt service (% of exports)	9.1	2.4	1.3
Net migration (thousands)	-35.8	-61.8	-28.7
Personal remittances received ($ millions)	22	44	191
Foreign direct investment, net inflows ($ millions)	92	1	267
Net official development assistance received ($ millions)	50	29	107

Finland

Population (millions)	5.4	Population growth (%)	0.5
Surface area (1,000 sq. km)	338	Population living below $1.25 a day (%)	..
GNI, Atlas ($ billions)	251.7	GNI per capita, Atlas ($)	46,490
GNI, PPP ($ billions)	212.0	GNI per capita, PPP ($)	39,150

	1990	2000	2012
People			
Share of poorest 20% in nat'l consumption/income (%)	..	9.6	..
Life expectancy at birth (years)	75	77	81
Total fertility rate (births per woman)	1.8	1.7	1.8
Adolescent fertility rate (births per 1,000 women 15-19)	12	10	9
Contraceptive prevalence (% of married women 15-49)	77	..	..
Births attended by skilled health staff (% of total)	100	100	..
Under-five mortality rate (per 1,000 live births)	7	4	3
Child malnutrition, underweight (% of under age 5)	..	..	..
Child immunization, measles (% of ages 12-23 mos.)	97	96	97
Primary completion rate, total (% of relevant age group)	102	96	97
Gross secondary enrollment, total (% of relevant age group)	115	125	107
Ratio of girls to boys in primary & secondary school (%)	109	105	102
HIV prevalence rate (% population of ages 15-49)	..	..	..
Environment			
Forests (1,000 sq. km)	219	225	222
Deforestation (avg. annual %, 1990-2000 and 2000-2010)		-0.3	0.1
Freshwater use (% of internal resources)	2.2	2.1	1.5
Access to improved water source (% total pop.)	100	100	100
Access to improved sanitation facilities (% total pop.)	100	100	100
Energy use per capita (kilograms of oil equivalent)	5,692	6,227	6,183
Carbon dioxide emissions per capita (metric tons)	10.4	10.1	11.5
Electricity use per capita (kilowatt-hours)	12,486	15,304	15,738
Economy			
GDP ($ billions)	139	122	248
GDP growth (annual %)	0.5	5.3	-0.8
GDP implicit price deflator (annual % growth)	5.4	2.6	2.9
Value added in agriculture (% of GDP)	6	3	3
Value added in industry (% of GDP)	33	34	26
Value added in services (% of GDP)	61	62	71
Exports of goods and services (% of GDP)	23	44	41
Imports of goods and services (% of GDP)	24	34	41
Gross capital formation (% of GDP)	28	21	20
Central government revenue (% of GDP)	..	41.1	38.4
Central government cash surplus/deficit (% of GDP)	..	6.8	-0.5
States and markets			
Starting a business (days)	..	31	14
Stock market capitalization (% of GDP)	16.3	241.1	64.1
Military expenditures (% of GDP)	1.5	1.3	1.5
Mobile cellular subscriptions (per 100 people)	5.2	72.0	172.3
Individuals using the Internet (% of population)	0.4	37.2	91.0
Paved roads (% of total)	61.0	62.0	65.8
High-technology exports (% of manufactured exports)	8	27	9
Global links			
Merchandise trade (% of GDP)	39	66	60
Net barter terms of trade index (2000 = 100)	..	100	87
Total external debt stocks ($ millions)	..	..	..
Total debt service (% of exports)	..	..	..
Net migration (thousands)	47.2	31.9	50.0
Personal remittances received ($ millions)	63	473	866
Foreign direct investment, net inflows ($ billions)	0.8	9.1	4.3
Net official development assistance received ($ millions)	..	..	..

France

			High income
Population (millions)	65.7	Population growth (%)	0.5
Surface area (1,000 sq. km)	549	Population living below $1.25 a day (%)	..
GNI, Atlas ($ billions)	2,742.9	GNI per capita, Atlas ($)	41,750
GNI, PPP ($ billions)	2,458.1	GNI per capita, PPP ($)	37,420

	1990	2000	2012
People			
Share of poorest 20% in nat'l consumption/income (%)	..	..	..
Life expectancy at birth (years)	77	79	83
Total fertility rate (births per woman)	1.8	1.9	2.0
Adolescent fertility rate (births per 1,000 women 15-19)	12	10	6
Contraceptive prevalence (% of married women 15-49)	81	82	..
Births attended by skilled health staff (% of total)	99	..	..
Under-five mortality rate (per 1,000 live births)	9	5	4
Child malnutrition, underweight (% of under age 5)	..	..	..
Child immunization, measles (% of ages 12-23 mos.)	71	84	89
Primary completion rate, total (% of relevant age group)	111	97	..
Gross secondary enrollment, total (% of relevant age group)	96	106	110
Ratio of girls to boys in primary & secondary school (%)	103	100	100
HIV prevalence rate (% population of ages 15-49)	..	..	..
Environment			
Forests (1,000 sq. km)	145	154	160
Deforestation (avg. annual %, 1990-2000 and 2000-2010)		-0.6	-0.4
Freshwater use (% of internal resources)	18.8	16.4	15.8
Access to improved water source (% total pop.)	100	100	100
Access to improved sanitation facilities (% total pop.)	100	100	100
Energy use per capita (kilograms of oil equivalent)	3,835	4,137	3,831
Carbon dioxide emissions per capita (metric tons)	6.8	6.0	5.6
Electricity use per capita (kilowatt-hours)	5,951	7,238	7,289
Economy			
GDP ($ billions)	1,244	1,326	2,613
GDP growth (annual %)	2.6	3.7	0.0
GDP implicit price deflator (annual % growth)	2.8	1.6	1.5
Value added in agriculture (% of GDP)	4	2	2
Value added in industry (% of GDP)	27	23	19
Value added in services (% of GDP)	69	75	79
Exports of goods and services (% of GDP)	21	29	27
Imports of goods and services (% of GDP)	22	28	30
Gross capital formation (% of GDP)	22	20	20
Central government revenue (% of GDP)	..	43.2	42.7
Central government cash surplus/deficit (% of GDP)	..	-1.6	-5.1
States and markets			
Starting a business (days)	..	41	7
Stock market capitalization (% of GDP)	25.2	109.1	69.8
Military expenditures (% of GDP)	3.4	2.5	2.3
Mobile cellular subscriptions (per 100 people)	0.5	49.1	97.4
Individuals using the Internet (% of population)	0.1	14.3	83.0
Paved roads (% of total)	..	100.0	100.0
High-technology exports (% of manufactured exports)	17	25	25
Global links			
Merchandise trade (% of GDP)	36	50	48
Net barter terms of trade index (2000 = 100)	..	100	89
Total external debt stocks ($ millions)	..	..	..
Total debt service (% of exports)	..	..	..
Net migration (thousands)	138	1,078	650
Personal remittances received ($ billions)	4.0	8.6	21.7
Foreign direct investment, net inflows ($ billions)	13.2	42.4	28.1
Net official development assistance received ($ millions)	..	..	..

French Polynesia

Population (thousands)	274	Population growth (%)	1.1
Surface area (1,000 sq. km)	4.0	Population living below $1.25 a day (%)	..
GNI, Atlas ($ billions)	..	GNI per capita, Atlas ($)	..
GNI, PPP ($ millions)	..	GNI per capita, PPP ($)	..

	1990	2000	2012
People			
Share of poorest 20% in nat'l consumption/income (%)	..	..	..
Life expectancy at birth (years)	69	72	76
Total fertility rate (births per woman)	3.4	2.5	2.1
Adolescent fertility rate (births per 1,000 women 15–19)	63	47	38
Contraceptive prevalence (% of married women 15–49)	..	..	..
Births attended by skilled health staff (% of total)	..	99	..
Under-five mortality rate (per 1,000 live births)	..	..	..
Child malnutrition, underweight (% of under age 5)	..	..	..
Child immunization, measles (% of ages 12-23 mos.)	..	..	..
Primary completion rate, total (% of relevant age group)	..	..	..
Gross secondary enrollment, total (% of relevant age group)	67	..	..
Ratio of girls to boys in primary & secondary school (%)	111	..	..
HIV prevalence rate (% population of ages 15–49)	..	..	..
Environment			
Forests (1,000 sq. km)	0.6	1.1	1.6
Deforestation (avg. annual %, 1990-2000 and 2000-2010)		-6.7	-4.0
Freshwater use (% of internal resources)	..	..	..
Access to improved water source (% total pop.)	100	100	100
Access to improved sanitation facilities (% total pop.)	99	98	97
Energy use per capita (kilograms of oil equivalent)	..	..	..
Carbon dioxide emissions per capita (metric tons)	3.2	2.7	3.3
Electricity use per capita (kilowatt-hours)	..	..	..
Economy			
GDP ($ billions)	3.2	3.4	..
GDP growth (annual %)	2.2	4.0	..
GDP implicit price deflator (annual % growth)	0.8	1.0	..
Value added in agriculture (% of GDP)	1	5	..
Value added in industry (% of GDP)	..	..	..
Value added in services (% of GDP)	..	..	..
Exports of goods and services (% of GDP)	1	5	..
Imports of goods and services (% of GDP)	28	24	..
Gross capital formation (% of GDP)	..	..	..
Central government revenue (% of GDP)	..	..	..
Central government cash surplus/deficit (% of GDP)	..	..	..
States and markets			
Starting a business (days)	..	..	..
Stock market capitalization (% of GDP)	..	..	..
Military expenditures (% of GDP)	..	..	..
Mobile cellular subscriptions (per 100 people)	0.0	16.8	82.5
Individuals using the Internet (% of population)	0.0	6.4	52.9
Paved roads (% of total)	..	..	..
High-technology exports (% of manufactured exports)	..	8	2
Global links			
Merchandise trade (% of GDP)	33	35	..
Net barter terms of trade index (2000 = 100)	..	100	79
Total external debt stocks ($ millions)	..	..	..
Total debt service (% of exports)	..	..	..
Net migration (thousands)	-4.3	0.1	-0.5
Personal remittances received ($ millions)	..	408	755
Foreign direct investment, net inflows ($ millions)	..	10.9	87.4
Net official development assistance received ($ millions)	260	352	..

Gabon

Sub-Saharan Africa		Upper middle income	
Population (millions)	1.6	Population growth (%)	2.4
Surface area (1,000 sq. km)	268	Population living below $1.25 a day (%)	4.8
GNI, Atlas ($ billions)	16.4	GNI per capita, Atlas ($)	10,040
GNI, PPP ($ billions)	23.0	GNI per capita, PPP ($)	14,090

	1990	2000	2012
People			
Share of poorest 20% in nat'l consumption/income (%)	..	..	..
Life expectancy at birth (years)	61	60	63
Total fertility rate (births per woman)	5.4	4.6	4.1
Adolescent fertility rate (births per 1,000 women 15-19)	160	133	103
Contraceptive prevalence (% of married women 15-49)	..	33	31
Births attended by skilled health staff (% of total)	..	86	89
Under-five mortality rate (per 1,000 live births)	92	86	62
Child malnutrition, underweight (% of under age 5)	..	8.8	6.5
Child immunization, measles (% of ages 12-23 mos.)	76	55	71
Primary completion rate, total (% of relevant age group)	67	74	..
Gross secondary enrollment, total (% of relevant age group)	37	53	..
Ratio of girls to boys in primary & secondary school (%)	97	97	..
HIV prevalence rate (% population of ages 15-49)	1.0	5.8	4.0
Environment			
Forests (1,000 sq. km)	220	220	220
Deforestation (avg. annual %, 1990-2000 and 2000-2010)		0.0	0.0
Freshwater use (% of internal resources)	..	0.1	0.1
Access to improved water source (% total pop.)	..	84	92
Access to improved sanitation facilities (% total pop.)	..	39	41
Energy use per capita (kilograms of oil equivalent)	1,248	1,194	1,253
Carbon dioxide emissions per capita (metric tons)	5.1	0.9	1.7
Electricity use per capita (kilowatt-hours)	922	882	907
Economy			
GDP ($ billions)	6.0	5.1	18.4
GDP growth (annual %)	5.2	-1.9	5.6
GDP implicit price deflator (annual % growth)	15.4	28.1	0.4
Value added in agriculture (% of GDP)	7	6	4
Value added in industry (% of GDP)	43	56	62
Value added in services (% of GDP)	50	38	34
Exports of goods and services (% of GDP)	46	69	57
Imports of goods and services (% of GDP)	31	33	31
Gross capital formation (% of GDP)	22	22	31
Central government revenue (% of GDP)	..	..	..
Central government cash surplus/deficit (% of GDP)	..	..	..
States and markets			
Starting a business (days)	..	..	50
Stock market capitalization (% of GDP)	..	..	..
Military expenditures (% of GDP)	..	1.8	1.4
Mobile cellular subscriptions (per 100 people)	0.0	9.8	179.5
Individuals using the Internet (% of population)	0.0	1.2	8.6
Paved roads (% of total)	8.2	10.0	12.0
High-technology exports (% of manufactured exports)	45	5	3
Global links			
Merchandise trade (% of GDP)	52	70	87
Net barter terms of trade index (2000 = 100)	157	100	226
Total external debt stocks ($ billions)	4.0	3.9	2.9
Total debt service (% of exports)	6.4	9.9	..
Net migration (thousands)	5.0	9.6	5.0
Personal remittances received ($ millions)	0.9	6.1	..
Foreign direct investment, net inflows ($ millions)	73	-43	702
Net official development assistance received ($ millions)	131	12	73

Gambia, The

Population (millions)	1.8	Population growth (%)	3.2
Surface area (1,000 sq. km)	11	Population living below $1.25 a day (%)	33.6
GNI, Atlas ($ millions)	912.3	GNI per capita, Atlas ($)	510
GNI, PPP ($ millions)	3,277.9	GNI per capita, PPP ($)	1,830

	1990	2000	2012
People			
Share of poorest 20% in nat'l consumption/income (%)	..	4.8	..
Life expectancy at birth (years)	52	55	59
Total fertility rate (births per woman)	6.1	5.9	5.8
Adolescent fertility rate (births per 1,000 women 15-19)	164	124	116
Contraceptive prevalence (% of married women 15-49)	12	10	13
Births attended by skilled health staff (% of total)	44	55	57
Under-five mortality rate (per 1,000 live births)	170	116	73
Child malnutrition, underweight (% of under age 5)	..	15.4	15.8
Child immunization, measles (% of ages 12-23 mos.)	86	89	95
Primary completion rate, total (% of relevant age group)	44	72	70
Gross secondary enrollment, total (% of relevant age group)	17	..	57
Ratio of girls to boys in primary & secondary school (%)	58	..	100
HIV prevalence rate (% population of ages 15-49)	0.1	0.9	1.3
Environment			
Forests (1,000 sq. km)	4.4	4.6	4.8
Deforestation (avg. annual %, 1990-2000 and 2000-2010)		-0.4	-0.4
Freshwater use (% of internal resources)	..	2.4	2.4
Access to improved water source (% total pop.)	76	83	90
Access to improved sanitation facilities (% total pop.)	..	61	60
Energy use per capita (kilograms of oil equivalent)	67	..	..
Carbon dioxide emissions per capita (metric tons)	0.2	0.2	0.3
Electricity use per capita (kilowatt-hours)	..	..	..
Economy			
GDP ($ millions)	317	783	907
GDP growth (annual %)	3.6	5.5	5.3
GDP implicit price deflator (annual % growth)	12.0	2.2	4.5
Value added in agriculture (% of GDP)	24	25	20
Value added in industry (% of GDP)	11	15	13
Value added in services (% of GDP)	65	61	67
Exports of goods and services (% of GDP)	60	26	29
Imports of goods and services (% of GDP)	72	31	51
Gross capital formation (% of GDP)	22	5	23
Central government revenue (% of GDP)	19.4	..	..
Central government cash surplus/deficit (% of GDP)	0.1	..	..
States and markets			
Starting a business (days)	..	..	27
Stock market capitalization (% of GDP)	..	..	..
Military expenditures (% of GDP)	1.1	0.4	..
Mobile cellular subscriptions (per 100 people)	0.0	0.5	85.2
Individuals using the Internet (% of population)	0.0	0.9	12.4
Paved roads (% of total)	..	35.0	..
High-technology exports (% of manufactured exports)	..	3	3
Global links			
Merchandise trade (% of GDP)	69	26	53
Net barter terms of trade index (2000 = 100)	100	100	92
Total external debt stocks ($ millions)	369	490	513
Total debt service (% of exports)	22.2	14.8	7.1
Net migration (thousands)	-14.8	-13.7	-13.5
Personal remittances received ($ millions)	..	56	141
Foreign direct investment, net inflows ($ millions)	14.1	18.3	33.5
Net official development assistance received ($ millions)	97	50	139

Georgia

Europe & Central Asia		Lower middle income	
Population (millions)	4.5	Population growth (%)	0.2
Surface area (1,000 sq. km)	70	Population living below $1.25 a day (%)	18.0
GNI, Atlas ($ billions)	14.8	GNI per capita, Atlas ($)	3,290
GNI, PPP ($ billions)	26.0	GNI per capita, PPP ($)	5,790

	1990	2000	2012
People			
Share of poorest 20% in nat'l consumption/income (%)	..	5.3	5.0
Life expectancy at birth (years)	70	72	74
Total fertility rate (births per woman)	2.2	1.6	1.8
Adolescent fertility rate (births per 1,000 women 15–19)	72	53	47
Contraceptive prevalence (% of married women 15–49)	..	41	53
Births attended by skilled health staff (% of total)	97	96	100
Under-five mortality rate (per 1,000 live births)	35	34	20
Child malnutrition, underweight (% of under age 5)	..	2.7	1.1
Child immunization, measles (% of ages 12–23 mos.)	16	73	93
Primary completion rate, total (% of relevant age group)	..	98	108
Gross secondary enrollment, total (% of relevant age group)	95	79	87
Ratio of girls to boys in primary & secondary school (%)	98	98	..
HIV prevalence rate (% population of ages 15–49)	0.1	0.1	0.3
Environment			
Forests (1,000 sq. km)	28	28	27
Deforestation (avg. annual %, 1990–2000 and 2000–2010)		0.0	0.1
Freshwater use (% of internal resources)	..	..	3.1
Access to improved water source (% total pop.)	85	89	99
Access to improved sanitation facilities (% total pop.)	96	95	93
Energy use per capita (kilograms of oil equivalent)	2,586	649	790
Carbon dioxide emissions per capita (metric tons)	3.1	1.0	1.4
Electricity use per capita (kilowatt-hours)	3,039	1,453	1,918
Economy			
GDP ($ billions)	7.7	3.1	15.7
GDP growth (annual %)	-14.8	1.8	6.0
GDP implicit price deflator (annual % growth)	22.4	4.7	1.3
Value added in agriculture (% of GDP)	32	22	9
Value added in industry (% of GDP)	33	22	23
Value added in services (% of GDP)	35	56	68
Exports of goods and services (% of GDP)	40	23	38
Imports of goods and services (% of GDP)	46	40	58
Gross capital formation (% of GDP)	31	27	29
Central government revenue (% of GDP)	..	10.4	25.8
Central government cash surplus/deficit (% of GDP)	..	-1.6	-0.5
States and markets			
Starting a business (days)	..	25	2
Stock market capitalization (% of GDP)	..	0.8	6.0
Military expenditures (% of GDP)	..	0.6	2.9
Mobile cellular subscriptions (per 100 people)	0.0	4.1	107.8
Individuals using the Internet (% of population)	0.0	0.5	45.5
Paved roads (% of total)	93.8	93.4	36.4
High-technology exports (% of manufactured exports)	..	11	2
Global links			
Merchandise trade (% of GDP)	..	34	65
Net barter terms of trade index (2000 = 100)	..	100	134
Total external debt stocks ($ billions)	0.1	1.8	13.4
Total debt service (% of exports)	..	12.5	23.3
Net migration (thousands)	-544	-309	-125
Personal remittances received ($ millions)	..	274	1,770
Foreign direct investment, net inflows ($ millions)	..	131	831
Net official development assistance received ($ millions)	0	169	662

Germany

High income

Population (millions)	80.4	Population growth (%)	-1.7
Surface area (1,000 sq. km)	357	Population living below $1.25 a day (%)	..
GNI, Atlas ($ billions)	3,624.6	GNI per capita, Atlas ($)	45,070
GNI, PPP ($ billions)	3,516.2	GNI per capita, PPP ($)	43,720

	1990	2000	2012
People			
Share of poorest 20% in nat'l consumption/income (%)	..	8.5	..
Life expectancy at birth (years)	75	78	81
Total fertility rate (births per woman)	1.5	1.4	1.4
Adolescent fertility rate (births per 1,000 women 15-19)	16	13	4
Contraceptive prevalence (% of married women 15-49)	70	..	..
Births attended by skilled health staff (% of total)	..	..	100
Under-five mortality rate (per 1,000 live births)	9	5	4
Child malnutrition, underweight (% of under age 5)	..	..	..
Child immunization, measles (% of ages 12-23 mos.)	75	92	97
Primary completion rate, total (% of relevant age group)	96	102	100
Gross secondary enrollment, total (% of relevant age group)	98	96	102
Ratio of girls to boys in primary & secondary school (%)	99	99	96
HIV prevalence rate (% population of ages 15-49)	..	..	..
Environment			
Forests (1,000 sq. km)	107	111	111
Deforestation (avg. annual %, 1990-2000 and 2000-2010)		-0.3	0.0
Freshwater use (% of internal resources)	..	36.6	30.2
Access to improved water source (% total pop.)	100	100	100
Access to improved sanitation facilities (% total pop.)	100	100	100
Energy use per capita (kilograms of oil equivalent)	4,421	4,094	3,822
Carbon dioxide emissions per capita (metric tons)	11.6	10.1	9.1
Electricity use per capita (kilowatt-hours)	6,640	6,635	7,081
Economy			
GDP ($ billions)	1,714	1,886	3,428
GDP growth (annual %)	5.3	3.1	0.7
GDP implicit price deflator (annual % growth)	3.4	-0.7	1.5
Value added in agriculture (% of GDP)	1	1	1
Value added in industry (% of GDP)	37	31	31
Value added in services (% of GDP)	61	68	69
Exports of goods and services (% of GDP)	25	33	52
Imports of goods and services (% of GDP)	25	33	46
Gross capital formation (% of GDP)	23	22	17
Central government revenue (% of GDP)	..	30.3	28.9
Central government cash surplus/deficit (% of GDP)		1.4	-0.4
States and markets			
Starting a business (days)	..	45	15
Stock market capitalization (% of GDP)	20.7	67.3	43.4
Military expenditures (% of GDP)	2.5	1.5	1.3
Mobile cellular subscriptions (per 100 people)	0.3	57.7	111.6
Individuals using the Internet (% of population)	0.1	30.2	84.0
Paved roads (% of total)	99.0	..	..
High-technology exports (% of manufactured exports)	12	19	16
Global links			
Merchandise trade (% of GDP)	45	56	75
Net barter terms of trade index (2000 = 100)	..	100	95
Total external debt stocks ($ millions)	..	..	..
Total debt service (% of exports)	..	..	..
Net migration (thousands)	3,233	937	550
Personal remittances received ($ billions)	4.9	3.6	14.0
Foreign direct investment, net inflows ($ billions)	3	210	27
Net official development assistance received ($ millions)	..	..	..

Ghana

Sub-Saharan Africa			Lower middle income	
Population (millions)	25.4		Population growth (%)	2.2
Surface area (1,000 sq. km)	239		Population living below $1.25 a day (%)	28.6
GNI, Atlas ($ billions)	39.4		GNI per capita, Atlas ($)	1,550
GNI, PPP ($ billions)	48.4		GNI per capita, PPP ($)	1,910

	1990	2000	2012
People			
Share of poorest 20% in nat'l consumption/income (%)	7.0	5.6	5.2
Life expectancy at birth (years)	57	57	61
Total fertility rate (births per woman)	5.6	4.7	3.9
Adolescent fertility rate (births per 1,000 women 15-19)	110	81	58
Contraceptive prevalence (% of married women 15-49)	17	22	34
Births attended by skilled health staff (% of total)	44	47	68
Under-five mortality rate (per 1,000 live births)	128	103	72
Child malnutrition, underweight (% of under age 5)	25.1	20.3	14.3
Child immunization, measles (% of ages 12-23 mos.)	61	90	88
Primary completion rate, total (% of relevant age group)	66	72	98
Gross secondary enrollment, total (% of relevant age group)	36	41	61
Ratio of girls to boys in primary & secondary school (%)	78	90	96
HIV prevalence rate (% population of ages 15-49)	0.7	2.3	1.4
Environment			
Forests (1,000 sq. km)	74	61	48
Deforestation (avg. annual %, 1990-2000 and 2000-2010)		2.0	2.1
Freshwater use (% of internal resources)	..	3.2	3.2
Access to improved water source (% total pop.)	54	71	87
Access to improved sanitation facilities (% total pop.)	7	10	14
Energy use per capita (kilograms of oil equivalent)	362	411	425
Carbon dioxide emissions per capita (metric tons)	0.3	0.3	0.4
Electricity use per capita (kilowatt-hours)	327	346	344
Economy			
GDP ($ billions)	5.9	5.0	40.7
GDP growth (annual %)	3.3	3.7	7.9
GDP implicit price deflator (annual % growth)	31.2	27.2	13.3
Value added in agriculture (% of GDP)	45	39	23
Value added in industry (% of GDP)	17	28	27
Value added in services (% of GDP)	38	32	50
Exports of goods and services (% of GDP)	17	49	46
Imports of goods and services (% of GDP)	26	67	56
Gross capital formation (% of GDP)	14	24	31
Central government revenue (% of GDP)	12.5	18.1	19.4
Central government cash surplus/deficit (% of GDP)	..	-6.5	-3.9
States and markets			
Starting a business (days)	..	22	14
Stock market capitalization (% of GDP)	1.2	10.1	8.5
Military expenditures (% of GDP)	0.5	1.0	0.3
Mobile cellular subscriptions (per 100 people)	0.0	0.7	101.0
Individuals using the Internet (% of population)	0.0	0.2	17.1
Paved roads (% of total)	19.6	30.0	12.6
High-technology exports (% of manufactured exports)	2	2	7
Global links			
Merchandise trade (% of GDP)	36	93	74
Net barter terms of trade index (2000 = 100)	100	100	172
Total external debt stocks ($ billions)	3.7	6.3	12.4
Total debt service (% of exports)	38.4	16.0	4.2
Net migration (thousands)	-16	166	-100
Personal remittances received ($ millions)	6	32	138
Foreign direct investment, net inflows ($ millions)	15	166	3,295
Net official development assistance received ($ millions)	560	598	1,808

Greece

Population (millions)	11.1	Population growth (%)	-0.3
Surface area (1,000 sq. km)	132	Population living below $1.25 a day (%)	..
GNI, Atlas ($ billions)	262.4	GNI per capita, Atlas ($)	23,660
GNI, PPP ($ billions)	290.3	GNI per capita, PPP ($)	26,170

	1990	2000	2012
People			
Share of poorest 20% in nat'l consumption/income (%)	..	6.7	..
Life expectancy at birth (years)	77	78	81
Total fertility rate (births per woman)	1.4	1.3	1.3
Adolescent fertility rate (births per 1,000 women 15-19)	22	11	12
Contraceptive prevalence (% of married women 15-49)	..	76	..
Births attended by skilled health staff (% of total)	..	..	..
Under-five mortality rate (per 1,000 live births)	13	8	5
Child malnutrition, underweight (% of under age 5)	..	..	..
Child immunization, measles (% of ages 12-23 mos.)	76	89	99
Primary completion rate, total (% of relevant age group)	98	..	100
Gross secondary enrollment, total (% of relevant age group)	94	89	111
Ratio of girls to boys in primary & secondary school (%)	99	103	98
HIV prevalence rate (% population of ages 15-49)	..	..	..
Environment			
Forests (1,000 sq. km)	33	36	39
Deforestation (avg. annual %, 1990-2000 and 2000-2010)		-0.9	-0.8
Freshwater use (% of internal resources)	12.1	17.1	16.3
Access to improved water source (% total pop.)	96	99	100
Access to improved sanitation facilities (% total pop.)	97	98	99
Energy use per capita (kilograms of oil equivalent)	2,111	2,481	2,343
Carbon dioxide emissions per capita (metric tons)	7.2	8.4	7.7
Electricity use per capita (kilowatt-hours)	3,234	4,539	5,380
Economy			
GDP ($ billions)	93	124	249
GDP growth (annual %)	0.0	4.5	-6.4
GDP implicit price deflator (annual % growth)	20.7	3.4	-0.8
Value added in agriculture (% of GDP)	..	..	3
Value added in industry (% of GDP)	..	..	16
Value added in services (% of GDP)	..	..	80
Exports of goods and services (% of GDP)	18	26	27
Imports of goods and services (% of GDP)	31	40	32
Gross capital formation (% of GDP)	25	25	14
Central government revenue (% of GDP)	..	41.9	41.0
Central government cash surplus/deficit (% of GDP)	..	-3.8	-9.8
States and markets			
Starting a business (days)	..	38	14
Stock market capitalization (% of GDP)	16.3	89.1	17.9
Military expenditures (% of GDP)	3.4	3.6	2.6
Mobile cellular subscriptions (per 100 people)	0.0	54.0	120.0
Individuals using the Internet (% of population)	0.0	9.1	56.0
Paved roads (% of total)	91.7	92.0	..
High-technology exports (% of manufactured exports)	2	14	9
Global links			
Merchandise trade (% of GDP)	30	36	38
Net barter terms of trade index (2000 = 100)	..	100	87
Total external debt stocks ($ millions)	..	..	..
Total debt service (% of exports)	..	..	..
Net migration (thousands)	465	54	50
Personal remittances received ($ billions)	1.8	2.2	0.7
Foreign direct investment, net inflows ($ billions)	1.0	1.1	1.7
Net official development assistance received ($ millions)			

Greenland

Population (thousands)	57	Population growth (%)	-0.1
Surface area (1,000 sq. km)	410e	Population living below $1.25 a day (%)	..
GNI, Atlas ($ billions)	1.5	GNI per capita, Atlas ($)	26,020
GNI, PPP ($ millions)	..	GNI per capita, PPP ($)	..

	1990	2000	2012
People			
Share of poorest 20% in nat'l consumption/income (%)	..	..	..
Life expectancy at birth (years)	65	67	71
Total fertility rate (births per woman)	2.4	2.3	2.0
Adolescent fertility rate (births per 1,000 women 15-19)	..	..	..
Contraceptive prevalence (% of married women 15-49)	..	..	..
Births attended by skilled health staff (% of total)	..	..	..
Under-five mortality rate (per 1,000 live births)	..	..	..
Child malnutrition, underweight (% of under age 5)	..	..	..
Child immunization, measles (% of ages 12-23 mos.)	..	..	..
Primary completion rate, total (% of relevant age group)	..	..	..
Gross secondary enrollment, total (% of relevant age group)	..	..	..
Ratio of girls to boys in primary & secondary school (%)	..	..	..
HIV prevalence rate (% population of ages 15-49)	..	..	..
Environment			
Forests (sq. km)	2.0	2.0	2.2
Deforestation (avg. annual %, 1990-2000 and 2000-2010)		0.0	0.0
Freshwater use (% of internal resources)	..	..	..
Access to improved water source (% total pop.)	100	100	100
Access to improved sanitation facilities (% total pop.)	100	100	100
Energy use per capita (kilograms of oil equivalent)	..	..	..
Carbon dioxide emissions per capita (metric tons)	10.0	9.5	11.1
Electricity use per capita (kilowatt-hours)	..	..	..
Economy			
GDP ($ millions)	1,019	1,068	1,268
GDP growth (annual %)	-11.7	7.1	-5.4
GDP implicit price deflator (annual % growth)	5.1	2.1	-19.0
Value added in agriculture (% of GDP)	..	..	..
Value added in industry (% of GDP)	..	..	..
Value added in services (% of GDP)	..	..	..
Exports of goods and services (% of GDP)	..	..	..
Imports of goods and services (% of GDP)	..	..	..
Gross capital formation (% of GDP)	..	..	..
Central government revenue (% of GDP)	..	..	..
Central government cash surplus/deficit (% of GDP)	..	..	..
States and markets			
Starting a business (days)	..	..	..
Stock market capitalization (% of GDP)	..	..	..
Military expenditures (% of GDP)	..	..	..
Mobile cellular subscriptions (per 100 people)	0.0	26.9	104.7
Individuals using the Internet (% of population)	0.0	31.7	64.9
Paved roads (% of total)	..	..	..
High-technology exports (% of manufactured exports)	10	37	2
Global links			
Merchandise trade (% of GDP)	88	60	87
Net barter terms of trade index (2000 = 100)	..	100	79
Total external debt stocks ($ millions)	..	..	..
Total debt service (% of exports)	..	..	..
Net migration (thousands)	..	..	..
Personal remittances received ($ millions)	..	..	..
Foreign direct investment, net inflows ($ millions)	..	..	..
Net official development assistance received ($ millions)	..	..	..

Grenada

Latin America & Caribbean   **Upper middle income**

Population (thousands)	105	Population growth (%)	0.4
Surface area (sq. km)	340	Population living below $1.25 a day (%)	..
GNI, Atlas ($ millions)	761.5	GNI per capita, Atlas ($)	7,220
GNI, PPP ($ millions)	1,091.7	GNI per capita, PPP ($)	10,350

	1990	2000	2012
People			
Share of poorest 20% in nat'l consumption/income (%)	..	..	..
Life expectancy at birth (years)	68	70	73
Total fertility rate (births per woman)	3.8	2.6	2.2
Adolescent fertility rate (births per 1,000 women 15–19)	90	55	35
Contraceptive prevalence (% of married women 15–49)	54	54	54
Births attended by skilled health staff (% of total)	..	100	99
Under-five mortality rate (per 1,000 live births)	22	16	14
Child malnutrition, underweight (% of under age 5)	..	..	..
Child immunization, measles (% of ages 12–23 mos.)	85	92	94
Primary completion rate, total (% of relevant age group)	..	93	112
Gross secondary enrollment, total (% of relevant age group)	91	108	108
Ratio of girls to boys in primary & secondary school (%)	104	103	99
HIV prevalence rate (% population of ages 15–49)	..	..	..
Environment			
Forests (sq. km)	170	170	170
Deforestation (avg. annual %, 1990–2000 and 2000–2010)		0.0	0.0
Freshwater use (% of internal resources)	..	..	..
Access to improved water source (% total pop.)	97	97	97
Access to improved sanitation facilities (% total pop.)	98	98	98
Energy use per capita (kilograms of oil equivalent)	441	..	..
Carbon dioxide emissions per capita (metric tons)	1.1	1.9	2.5
Electricity use per capita (kilowatt-hours)	..	..	..
Economy			
GDP ($ millions)	221	523	767
GDP growth (annual %)	5.2	2.5	0.6
GDP implicit price deflator (annual % growth)	-1.4	34.5	-6.6
Value added in agriculture (% of GDP)	13	6	6
Value added in industry (% of GDP)	18	21	12
Value added in services (% of GDP)	69	73	83
Exports of goods and services (% of GDP)	42	45	25
Imports of goods and services (% of GDP)	63	59	51
Gross capital formation (% of GDP)	38	38	18
Central government revenue (% of GDP)	..	21.4	20.6
Central government cash surplus/deficit (% of GDP)	..	-2.1	-5.8
States and markets			
Starting a business (days)	..	..	15
Stock market capitalization (% of GDP)	..	..	..
Military expenditures (% of GDP)	..	..	..
Mobile cellular subscriptions (per 100 people)	0.2	4.2	121.3
Individuals using the Internet (% of population)	0.0	4.1	42.1
Paved roads (% of total)	55.4	61.0	..
High-technology exports (% of manufactured exports)	4	30	..
Global links			
Merchandise trade (% of GDP)	60	55	48
Net barter terms of trade index (2000 = 100)	..	100	91
Total external debt stocks ($ millions)	112	203	591
Total debt service (% of exports)	4.3	6.0	7.7
Net migration (thousands)	-3.9	-4.1	-4.3
Personal remittances received ($ millions)	18.0	46.4	29.4
Foreign direct investment, net inflows ($ millions)	12.9	37.4	30.2
Net official development assistance received ($ millions)	13.8	16.5	7.7

Guam

			High income
Population (thousands)	163	Population growth (%)	1.2
Surface area (sq. km)	540	Population living below $1.25 a day (%)	..
GNI, Atlas ($ millions)	..	GNI per capita, Atlas ($)	..
GNI, PPP ($ millions)	..	GNI per capita, PPP ($)	..

	1990	2000	2012
People			
Share of poorest 20% in nat'l consumption/income (%)	..	..	..
Life expectancy at birth (years)	72	75	79
Total fertility rate (births per woman)	3.0	2.8	2.4
Adolescent fertility rate (births per 1,000 women 15-19)	80	62	50
Contraceptive prevalence (% of married women 15-49)	..	67	..
Births attended by skilled health staff (% of total)	..	99	..
Under-five mortality rate (per 1,000 live births)	..	..	..
Child malnutrition, underweight (% of under age 5)	..	..	..
Child immunization, measles (% of ages 12-23 mos.)	..	..	..
Primary completion rate, total (% of relevant age group)	..	..	..
Gross secondary enrollment, total (% of relevant age group)	..	..	..
Ratio of girls to boys in primary & secondary school (%)	..	..	..
HIV prevalence rate (% population of ages 15-49)	..	..	..
Environment			
Forests (sq. km)	259	259	259
Deforestation (avg. annual %, 1990-2000 and 2000-2010)		0.0	0.0
Freshwater use (% of internal resources)	..	..	..
Access to improved water source (% total pop.)	100	100	100
Access to improved sanitation facilities (% total pop.)	89	89	90
Energy use per capita (kilograms of oil equivalent)	..	..	..
Carbon dioxide emissions per capita (metric tons)	..	..	..
Electricity use per capita (kilowatt-hours)	..	..	..
Economy			
GDP ($ millions)	..	..	..
GDP growth (annual %)	..	..	..
GDP implicit price deflator (annual % growth)	..	..	..
Value added in agriculture (% of GDP)	..	..	..
Value added in industry (% of GDP)	..	..	..
Value added in services (% of GDP)	..	..	..
Exports of goods and services (% of GDP)	..	..	..
Imports of goods and services (% of GDP)	..	..	..
Gross capital formation (% of GDP)	..	..	..
Central government revenue (% of GDP)	..	..	..
Central government cash surplus/deficit (% of GDP)	..	..	..
States and markets			
Starting a business (days)	..	..	..
Stock market capitalization (% of GDP)	..	..	..
Military expenditures (% of GDP)	..	..	..
Mobile cellular subscriptions (per 100 people)	0.0	17.5	..
Individuals using the Internet (% of population)	0.0	16.1	61.5
Paved roads (% of total)	..	..	..
High-technology exports (% of manufactured exports)	..	..	..
Global links			
Merchandise trade (% of GDP)	..	..	..
Net barter terms of trade index (2000 = 100)	..	100	81
Total external debt stocks ($ millions)	..	..	..
Total debt service (% of exports)	..	..	..
Net migration (thousands)	1.7	-9.6	0.0
Personal remittances received ($ millions)	..	..	..
Foreign direct investment, net inflows ($ millions)	..	..	..
Net official development assistance received ($ millions)	..	..	..

Guatemala

Latin America & Caribbean		Lower middle income

Population (millions)	15.1	Population growth (%)	2.5
Surface area (1,000 sq. km)	109	Population living below $1.25 a day (%)	13.5
GNI, Atlas ($ billions)	47.1	GNI per capita, Atlas ($)	3,120
GNI, PPP ($ billions)	73.6	GNI per capita, PPP ($)	4,880

	1990	2000	2012
People			
Share of poorest 20% in nat'l consumption/income (%)	2.2	3.5	3.1
Life expectancy at birth (years)	62	68	72
Total fertility rate (births per woman)	5.6	4.8	3.8
Adolescent fertility rate (births per 1,000 women 15-19)	129	118	97
Contraceptive prevalence (% of married women 15-49)	..	38	54
Births attended by skilled health staff (% of total)	..	41	52
Under-five mortality rate (per 1,000 live births)	80	51	32
Child malnutrition, underweight (% of under age 5)	..	19.6	13.0
Child immunization, measles (% of ages 12-23 mos.)	68	86	93
Primary completion rate, total (% of relevant age group)	..	58	88
Gross secondary enrollment, total (% of relevant age group)	23	38	65
Ratio of girls to boys in primary & secondary school (%)	87	89	95
HIV prevalence rate (% population of ages 15-49)	0.1	0.8	0.7
Environment			
Forests (1,000 sq. km)	47	42	36
Deforestation (avg. annual %, 1990-2000 and 2000-2010)		1.2	1.4
Freshwater use (% of internal resources)	..	2.7	2.7
Access to improved water source (% total pop.)	81	87	94
Access to improved sanitation facilities (% total pop.)	62	71	80
Energy use per capita (kilograms of oil equivalent)	496	628	691
Carbon dioxide emissions per capita (metric tons)	0.6	0.9	0.8
Electricity use per capita (kilowatt-hours)	209	344	539
Economy			
GDP ($ billions)	7.7	19.3	50.2
GDP growth (annual %)	3.1	3.6	3.0
GDP implicit price deflator (annual % growth)	40.5	6.8	2.9
Value added in agriculture (% of GDP)	..	15	12
Value added in industry (% of GDP)	..	29	29
Value added in services (% of GDP)	..	56	59
Exports of goods and services (% of GDP)	21	20	25
Imports of goods and services (% of GDP)	25	29	36
Gross capital formation (% of GDP)	14	18	14
Central government revenue (% of GDP)	7.9	10.2	11.5
Central government cash surplus/deficit (% of GDP)	-1.9	-1.8	-2.3
States and markets			
Starting a business (days)	..	39	20
Stock market capitalization (% of GDP)	..	0.9	..
Military expenditures (% of GDP)	1.5	0.8	0.4
Mobile cellular subscriptions (per 100 people)	0.0	7.6	137.8
Individuals using the Internet (% of population)	0.0	0.7	16.0
Paved roads (% of total)	24.9	34.5	44.8
High-technology exports (% of manufactured exports)	6	8	5
Global links			
Merchandise trade (% of GDP)	37	39	54
Net barter terms of trade index (2000 = 100)	115	100	88
Total external debt stocks ($ billions)	2.9	3.9	15.0
Total debt service (% of exports)	15.4	9.7	10.9
Net migration (thousands)	-360	-300	-75
Personal remittances received ($ millions)	119	596	5,035
Foreign direct investment, net inflows ($ millions)	48	230	1,150
Net official development assistance received ($ millions)	201	263	299

Guinea

Sub-Saharan Africa			Low income
Population (millions)	11.5	Population growth (%)	2.6
Surface area (1,000 sq. km)	246	Population living below $1.25 a day (%)	43.3
GNI, Atlas ($ billions)	5.0	GNI per capita, Atlas ($)	440
GNI, PPP ($ billions)	11.1	GNI per capita, PPP ($)	970

	1990	2000	2012
People			
Share of poorest 20% in nat'l consumption/income (%)	3.1	6.4	6.4
Life expectancy at birth (years)	50	51	56
Total fertility rate (births per woman)	6.6	5.9	5.0
Adolescent fertility rate (births per 1,000 women 15–19)	181	168	131
Contraceptive prevalence (% of married women 15–49)	2	6	6
Births attended by skilled health staff (% of total)	31	35	45
Under-five mortality rate (per 1,000 live births)	241	171	101
Child malnutrition, underweight (% of under age 5)	..	29.1	16.3
Child immunization, measles (% of ages 12-23 mos.)	35	42	58
Primary completion rate, total (% of relevant age group)	20	31	61
Gross secondary enrollment, total (% of relevant age group)	11	18	38
Ratio of girls to boys in primary & secondary school (%)	42	62	78
HIV prevalence rate (% population of ages 15–49)	0.2	1.2	1.7
Environment			
Forests (1,000 sq. km)	73	69	65
Deforestation (avg. annual %, 1990-2000 and 2000-2010)		0.5	0.5
Freshwater use (% of internal resources)	..	0.7	0.7
Access to improved water source (% total pop.)	52	63	75
Access to improved sanitation facilities (% total pop.)	8	13	19
Energy use per capita (kilograms of oil equivalent)	..	..	..
Carbon dioxide emissions per capita (metric tons)	0.2	0.1	0.1
Electricity use per capita (kilowatt-hours)	..	..	..
Economy			
GDP ($ billions)	2.7	3.0	5.6
GDP growth (annual %)	4.3	2.5	3.9
GDP implicit price deflator (annual % growth)	17.3	6.3	12.9
Value added in agriculture (% of GDP)	24	22	21
Value added in industry (% of GDP)	33	33	45
Value added in services (% of GDP)	43	44	33
Exports of goods and services (% of GDP)	31	25	30
Imports of goods and services (% of GDP)	33	29	62
Gross capital formation (% of GDP)	25	20	18
Central government revenue (% of GDP)	..	12.0	..
Central government cash surplus/deficit (% of GDP)	..	-2.4	..
States and markets			
Starting a business (days)	..	40	16
Stock market capitalization (% of GDP)	..	..	..
Military expenditures (% of GDP)	2.4	1.5	..
Mobile cellular subscriptions (per 100 people)	0.0	0.5	41.8
Individuals using the Internet (% of population)	0.0	0.1	1.5
Paved roads (% of total)	15.2	17.0	..
High-technology exports (% of manufactured exports)	..	0	..
Global links			
Merchandise trade (% of GDP)	52	43	66
Net barter terms of trade index (2000 = 100)	122	100	104
Total external debt stocks ($ billions)	2.5	3.1	1.1
Total debt service (% of exports)	20.1	20.7	7.0
Net migration (thousands)	800	-368	-10
Personal remittances received ($ millions)	18.0	1.2	66.3
Foreign direct investment, net inflows ($ millions)	18	10	605
Net official development assistance received ($ millions)	292	153	340

Guinea-Bissau

Sub-Saharan Africa   **Low income**

Population (millions)	1.7	Population growth (%)	2.4
Surface area (1,000 sq. km)	36	Population living below $1.25 a day (%)	48.9
GNI, Atlas ($ millions)	855.6	GNI per capita, Atlas ($)	510
GNI, PPP ($ millions)	1,830.1	GNI per capita, PPP ($)	1,100

	1990	2000	2012
People			
Share of poorest 20% in nat'l consumption/income (%)	2.1	7.3	..
Life expectancy at birth (years)	49	51	54
Total fertility rate (births per woman)	6.6	5.8	5.0
Adolescent fertility rate (births per 1,000 women 15-19)	136	131	99
Contraceptive prevalence (% of married women 15-49)	..	8	14
Births attended by skilled health staff (% of total)	..	35	43
Under-five mortality rate (per 1,000 live births)	206	174	129
Child malnutrition, underweight (% of under age 5)	..	21.9	16.6
Child immunization, measles (% of ages 12-23 mos.)	53	71	69
Primary completion rate, total (% of relevant age group)	5	29	64
Gross secondary enrollment, total (% of relevant age group)	5	18	..
Ratio of girls to boys in primary & secondary school (%)	55	65	..
HIV prevalence rate (% population of ages 15-49)	0.2	2.4	3.9
Environment			
Forests (1,000 sq. km)	22	21	20
Deforestation (avg. annual %, 1990-2000 and 2000-2010)		0.4	0.5
Freshwater use (% of internal resources)	0.1	1.1	1.1
Access to improved water source (% total pop.)	36	52	74
Access to improved sanitation facilities (% total pop.)	..	12	20
Energy use per capita (kilograms of oil equivalent)	73	..	..
Carbon dioxide emissions per capita (metric tons)	0.2	0.1	0.2
Electricity use per capita (kilowatt-hours)	..	..	..
Economy			
GDP ($ millions)	244	362	822
GDP growth (annual %)	6.1	3.6	-6.7
GDP implicit price deflator (annual % growth)	30.2	79.9	-1.5
Value added in agriculture (% of GDP)	61	59	..
Value added in industry (% of GDP)	19	13	..
Value added in services (% of GDP)	21	28	..
Exports of goods and services (% of GDP)	10	19	17
Imports of goods and services (% of GDP)	37	31	32
Gross capital formation (% of GDP)	30	7	7
Central government revenue (% of GDP)	..	..	..
Central government cash surplus/deficit (% of GDP)	..	..	..
States and markets			
Starting a business (days)	..	..	9
Stock market capitalization (% of GDP)	..	..	..
Military expenditures (% of GDP)	2.1	2.6	2.0
Mobile cellular subscriptions (per 100 people)	0.0	0.0	63.1
Individuals using the Internet (% of population)	0.0	0.2	2.9
Paved roads (% of total)	8.3	27.9	..
High-technology exports (% of manufactured exports)	..	..	..
Global links			
Merchandise trade (% of GDP)	43	33	46
Net barter terms of trade index (2000 = 100)	146	100	82
Total external debt stocks ($ millions)	695	948	279
Total debt service (% of exports)	32.3	7.1	9.5
Net migration (thousands)	-30.0	-30.0	-10.0
Personal remittances received ($ millions)	1.0	8.0	45.9
Foreign direct investment, net inflows ($ millions)	2.0	0.7	16.2
Net official development assistance received ($ millions)	126	81	79

Guyana

Latin America & Caribbean		Lower middle income	
Population (thousands)	795	Population growth (%)	0.6
Surface area (1,000 sq. km)	215	Population living below $1.25 a day (%)	8.7
GNI, Atlas ($ billions)	2.7	GNI per capita, Atlas ($)	3,410
GNI, PPP ($ billions)	2.7	GNI per capita, PPP ($)	3,340

	1990	2000	2012
People			
Share of poorest 20% in nat'l consumption/income (%)	4.3	4.5	..
Life expectancy at birth (years)	62	63	66
Total fertility rate (births per woman)	2.5	2.6	2.6
Adolescent fertility rate (births per 1,000 women 15-19)	68	85	88
Contraceptive prevalence (% of married women 15-49)	38	37	43
Births attended by skilled health staff (% of total)	..	86	92
Under-five mortality rate (per 1,000 live births)	60	46	35
Child malnutrition, underweight (% of under age 5)	16.1	11.9	11.1
Child immunization, measles (% of ages 12-23 mos.)	73	86	99
Primary completion rate, total (% of relevant age group)	97	102	85
Gross secondary enrollment, total (% of relevant age group)	..	97	101
Ratio of girls to boys in primary & secondary school (%)	..	98	114
HIV prevalence rate (% population of ages 15-49)	0.1	0.6	1.3
Environment			
Forests (1,000 sq. km)	152	152	152
Deforestation (avg. annual %, 1990-2000 and 2000-2010)		0.0	0.0
Freshwater use (% of internal resources)	0.6	0.7	0.7
Access to improved water source (% total pop.)	77	86	98
Access to improved sanitation facilities (% total pop.)	76	79	84
Energy use per capita (kilograms of oil equivalent)	527	..	..
Carbon dioxide emissions per capita (metric tons)	1.6	2.2	2.2
Electricity use per capita (kilowatt-hours)	..	..	..
Economy			
GDP ($ millions)	397	713	2,851
GDP growth (annual %)	-3.0	-1.4	4.8
GDP implicit price deflator (annual % growth)	56.4	6.6	5.7
Value added in agriculture (% of GDP)	38	31	21
Value added in industry (% of GDP)	25	29	34
Value added in services (% of GDP)	37	40	45
Exports of goods and services (% of GDP)	63	96	..
Imports of goods and services (% of GDP)	80	111	..
Gross capital formation (% of GDP)	31	24	25
Central government revenue (% of GDP)	..	..	..
Central government cash surplus/deficit (% of GDP)	..	..	..
States and markets			
Starting a business (days)	..	..	20
Stock market capitalization (% of GDP)	..	12.7	21.4
Military expenditures (% of GDP)	0.9	1.5	1.1
Mobile cellular subscriptions (per 100 people)	0.0	5.4	68.8
Individuals using the Internet (% of population)	0.0	6.6	33.0
Paved roads (% of total)	6.6	7.0	..
High-technology exports (% of manufactured exports)	..	2	0
Global links			
Merchandise trade (% of GDP)	143	150	112
Net barter terms of trade index (2000 = 100)	..	100	128
Total external debt stocks ($ billions)	2.0	1.4	2.0
Total debt service (% of exports)	18.7	10.2	8.7
Net migration (thousands)	-46.5	-32.8	-32.8
Personal remittances received ($ millions)	1	27	469
Foreign direct investment, net inflows ($ millions)	8	67	276
Net official development assistance received ($ millions)	168	116	114

Haiti

Latin America & Caribbean		**Low income**
Population (millions)	10.2	Population growth (%)	1.4
Surface area (1,000 sq. km)	28	Population living below $1.25 a day (%)	61.7
GNI, Atlas ($ billions)	7.7	GNI per capita, Atlas ($)	760
GNI, PPP ($ billions)	12.4	GNI per capita, PPP ($)	1,220

	1990	2000	2012
People			
Share of poorest 20% in nat'l consumption/income (%)	..	2.4	..
Life expectancy at birth (years)	54	57	63
Total fertility rate (births per woman)	5.4	4.3	3.2
Adolescent fertility rate (births per 1,000 women 15-19)	73	56	42
Contraceptive prevalence (% of married women 15-49)	10	28	35
Births attended by skilled health staff (% of total)	23	24	37
Under-five mortality rate (per 1,000 live births)	144	105	76
Child malnutrition, underweight (% of under age 5)	23.7	13.9	18.9
Child immunization, measles (% of ages 12-23 mos.)	31	55	58
Primary completion rate, total (% of relevant age group)	..	..	..
Gross secondary enrollment, total (% of relevant age group)	..	..	..
Ratio of girls to boys in primary & secondary school (%)	..	..	..
HIV prevalence rate (% population of ages 15-49)	3.8	3.0	2.1
Environment			
Forests (1,000 sq. km)	1.2	1.1	1.0
Deforestation (avg. annual %, 1990-2000 and 2000-2010)		0.6	0.8
Freshwater use (% of internal resources)	7.5	9.2	9.2
Access to improved water source (% total pop.)	61	61	62
Access to improved sanitation facilities (% total pop.)	19	21	24
Energy use per capita (kilograms of oil equivalent)	219	234	320
Carbon dioxide emissions per capita (metric tons)	0.1	0.2	0.2
Electricity use per capita (kilowatt-hours)	58	35	32
Economy			
GDP ($ billions)	3.5	3.7	7.8
GDP growth (annual %)	..	0.9	2.8
GDP implicit price deflator (annual % growth)	..	11.1	7.5
Value added in agriculture (% of GDP)	..	..	..
Value added in industry (% of GDP)	..	..	..
Value added in services (% of GDP)	..	..	..
Exports of goods and services (% of GDP)	10	13	13
Imports of goods and services (% of GDP)	29	33	48
Gross capital formation (% of GDP)	24	27	29
Central government revenue (% of GDP)	..	..	..
Central government cash surplus/deficit (% of GDP)	..	..	..
States and markets			
Starting a business (days)	..	202	97
Stock market capitalization (% of GDP)	..	..	..
Military expenditures (% of GDP)	0.1	..	..
Mobile cellular subscriptions (per 100 people)	0.0	0.6	59.9
Individuals using the Internet (% of population)	0.0	0.2	9.8
Paved roads (% of total)	21.9	24.0	..
High-technology exports (% of manufactured exports)	14	..	..
Global links			
Merchandise trade (% of GDP)	16	37	46
Net barter terms of trade index (2000 = 100)	132	100	68
Total external debt stocks ($ billions)	0.9	1.2	1.2
Total debt service (% of exports)	11.9	9.2	0.3
Net migration (thousands)	-133	-170	-175
Personal remittances received ($ millions)	123	578	1,612
Foreign direct investment, net inflows ($ millions)	8	13	179
Net official development assistance received ($ millions)	167	208	1,275

Honduras

Latin America & Caribbean		Lower middle income	
Population (millions)	7.9	Population growth (%)	2.0
Surface area (1,000 sq. km)	112	Population living below $1.25 a day (%)	17.9
GNI, Atlas ($ billions)	16.8	GNI per capita, Atlas ($)	2,120
GNI, PPP ($ billions)	30.8	GNI per capita, PPP ($)	3,880

	1990	2000	2012
People			
Share of poorest 20% in nat'l consumption/income (%)	2.8	2.7	2.0
Life expectancy at birth (years)	67	70	73
Total fertility rate (births per woman)	5.1	4.0	3.1
Adolescent fertility rate (births per 1,000 women 15-19)	129	107	84
Contraceptive prevalence (% of married women 15-49)	47	62	73
Births attended by skilled health staff (% of total)	47	56	83
Under-five mortality rate (per 1,000 live births)	59	38	23
Child malnutrition, underweight (% of under age 5)	15.8	12.5	8.6
Child immunization, measles (% of ages 12-23 mos.)	90	98	93
Primary completion rate, total (% of relevant age group)	64	80	100
Gross secondary enrollment, total (% of relevant age group)	33	..	73
Ratio of girls to boys in primary & secondary school (%)	104	..	107
HIV prevalence rate (% population of ages 15-49)	0.8	1.3	0.5
Environment			
Forests (1,000 sq. km)	81	64	51
Deforestation (avg. annual %, 1990-2000 and 2000-2010)		2.4	2.1
Freshwater use (% of internal resources)	..	1.2	1.2
Access to improved water source (% total pop.)	73	81	90
Access to improved sanitation facilities (% total pop.)	48	63	80
Energy use per capita (kilograms of oil equivalent)	485	479	609
Carbon dioxide emissions per capita (metric tons)	0.5	0.8	1.1
Electricity use per capita (kilowatt-hours)	372	515	708
Economy			
GDP ($ billions)	3.0	7.1	18.4
GDP growth (annual %)	0.1	5.7	3.9
GDP implicit price deflator (annual % growth)	21.2	30.8	4.0
Value added in agriculture (% of GDP)	22	16	15
Value added in industry (% of GDP)	26	32	28
Value added in services (% of GDP)	51	52	57
Exports of goods and services (% of GDP)	37	54	50
Imports of goods and services (% of GDP)	40	66	70
Gross capital formation (% of GDP)	23	28	26
Central government revenue (% of GDP)	..	20.0	21.1
Central government cash surplus/deficit (% of GDP)	..	-3.0	-3.2
States and markets			
Starting a business (days)	..	62	14
Stock market capitalization (% of GDP)	1.3	8.8	..
Military expenditures (% of GDP)	..	0.7	1.1
Mobile cellular subscriptions (per 100 people)	0.0	2.5	92.9
Individuals using the Internet (% of population)	0.0	1.2	18.1
Paved roads (% of total)	21.1	20.0	..
High-technology exports (% of manufactured exports)	1	0	1
Global links			
Merchandise trade (% of GDP)	61	103	104
Net barter terms of trade index (2000 = 100)	78	100	84
Total external debt stocks ($ billions)	3.8	5.5	5.0
Total debt service (% of exports)	38.3	9.9	13.8
Net migration (thousands)	-120	-150	-50
Personal remittances received ($ millions)	63	484	2,909
Foreign direct investment, net inflows ($ millions)	44	382	1,068
Net official development assistance received ($ millions)	448	448	572

Hong Kong SAR, China

High income

Population (millions)	7.2	Population growth (%)	1.2
Surface area (1,000 sq. km)	1.1	Population living below $1.25 a day (%)	..
GNI, Atlas ($ billions)	261.6	GNI per capita, Atlas ($)	36,560
GNI, PPP ($ billions)	373.4	GNI per capita, PPP ($)	52,190

	1990	2000	2012
People			
Share of poorest 20% in nat'l consumption/income (%)	..	..	..
Life expectancy at birth (years)	77	81	83
Total fertility rate (births per woman)	1.3	1.0	1.3
Adolescent fertility rate (births per 1,000 women 15-19)	7	4	3
Contraceptive prevalence (% of married women 15-49)	86	86	80
Births attended by skilled health staff (% of total)	..	..	..
Under-five mortality rate (per 1,000 live births)	..	..	..
Child malnutrition, underweight (% of under age 5)	..	..	..
Child immunization, measles (% of ages 12-23 mos.)	..	..	..
Primary completion rate, total (% of relevant age group)	102	95	98
Gross secondary enrollment, total (% of relevant age group)	76	76	106
Ratio of girls to boys in primary & secondary school (%)	102	98	99
HIV prevalence rate (% population of ages 15-49)	..	..	..
Environment			
Forests (sq. km)	..	..	..
Deforestation (avg. annual %, 1990-2000 and 2000-2010)		..	..
Freshwater use (% of internal resources)		..	..
Access to improved water source (% total pop.)	..	..	..
Access to improved sanitation facilities (% total pop.)	..	..	..
Energy use per capita (kilograms of oil equivalent)	1,518	2,009	2,106
Carbon dioxide emissions per capita (metric tons)	4.8	6.1	5.2
Electricity use per capita (kilowatt-hours)	4,178	5,447	5,949
Economy			
GDP ($ billions)	77	172	263
GDP growth (annual %)	3.8	7.7	1.5
GDP implicit price deflator (annual % growth)	7.6	-3.4	3.9
Value added in agriculture (% of GDP)	..	0	0
Value added in industry (% of GDP)	..	12	7
Value added in services (% of GDP)	..	88	93
Exports of goods and services (% of GDP)	131	142	225
Imports of goods and services (% of GDP)	122	137	224
Gross capital formation (% of GDP)	27	28	26
Central government revenue (% of GDP)	..	14.7	23.8
Central government cash surplus/deficit (% of GDP)	..	-6.7	3.8
States and markets			
Starting a business (days)	..	11	3
Stock market capitalization (% of GDP)	108.4	363.1	420.9
Military expenditures (% of GDP)	..	..	..
Mobile cellular subscriptions (per 100 people)	2.3	79.7	229.2
Individuals using the Internet (% of population)	0.0	27.8	72.8
Paved roads (% of total)	100.0	100.0	100.0
High-technology exports (% of manufactured exports)	17	23	16
Global links			
Merchandise trade (% of GDP)	217	243	398
Net barter terms of trade index (2000 = 100)	100	100	96
Total external debt stocks ($ millions)	..	..	..
Total debt service (% of exports)	..	..	..
Net migration (thousands)	156	-41	150
Personal remittances received ($ millions)	..	136	368
Foreign direct investment, net inflows ($ billions)	..	61.9	74.6
Net official development assistance received ($ millions)	38.2	..	..

Hungary

Population (millions)	9.9	Population growth (%)	-0.5
Surface area (1,000 sq. km)	93	Population living below $1.25 a day (%)	<2
GNI, Atlas ($ billions)	123.1	GNI per capita, Atlas ($)	12,410
GNI, PPP ($ billions)	211.8	GNI per capita, PPP ($)	21,350

	1990	2000	2012
People			
Share of poorest 20% in nat'l consumption/income (%)	10.4	9.6	8.4
Life expectancy at birth (years)	69	71	75
Total fertility rate (births per woman)	1.9	1.3	1.3
Adolescent fertility rate (births per 1,000 women 15-19)	41	23	12
Contraceptive prevalence (% of married women 15-49)	81	..	..
Births attended by skilled health staff (% of total)	99	100	99
Under-five mortality rate (per 1,000 live births)	19	11	6
Child malnutrition, underweight (% of under age 5)	..	..	..
Child immunization, measles (% of ages 12-23 mos.)	99	99	99
Primary completion rate, total (% of relevant age group)	82	96	99
Gross secondary enrollment, total (% of relevant age group)	87	96	101
Ratio of girls to boys in primary & secondary school (%)	100	100	98
HIV prevalence rate (% population of ages 15-49)	..	..	..
Environment			
Forests (1,000 sq. km)	18	19	20
Deforestation (avg. annual %, 1990–2000 and 2000–2010)		-0.6	-0.6
Freshwater use (% of internal resources)	..	97.3	93.2
Access to improved water source (% total pop.)	96	99	100
Access to improved sanitation facilities (% total pop.)	100	100	100
Energy use per capita (kilograms of oil equivalent)	2,772	2,448	2,369
Carbon dioxide emissions per capita (metric tons)	6.1	5.6	5.1
Electricity use per capita (kilowatt-hours)	3,427	3,309	3,895
Economy			
GDP ($ billions)	33.1	46.4	124.6
GDP growth (annual %)	-3.5	4.2	-1.7
GDP implicit price deflator (annual % growth)	25.7	9.7	3.2
Value added in agriculture (% of GDP)	15	6	4
Value added in industry (% of GDP)	39	32	31
Value added in services (% of GDP)	46	62	65
Exports of goods and services (% of GDP)	31	75	94
Imports of goods and services (% of GDP)	29	78	87
Gross capital formation (% of GDP)	25	27	19
Central government revenue (% of GDP)	..	38.5	48.2
Central government cash surplus/deficit (% of GDP)	..	-2.8	3.7
States and markets			
Starting a business (days)	..	52	5
Stock market capitalization (% of GDP)	1.5	25.9	16.9
Military expenditures (% of GDP)	2.8	1.7	0.8
Mobile cellular subscriptions (per 100 people)	0.0	30.1	116.1
Individuals using the Internet (% of population)	0.0	7.0	72.0
Paved roads (% of total)	44.1	39.2	37.9
High-technology exports (% of manufactured exports)	4	27	18
Global links			
Merchandise trade (% of GDP)	62	130	160
Net barter terms of trade index (2000 = 100)	..	100	93
Total external debt stocks ($ billions)	21	31	204
Total debt service (% of exports)	..		84.6
Net migration (thousands)	96.8	66.2	75.0
Personal remittances received ($ millions)	..	281	2,144
Foreign direct investment, net inflows ($ billions)	0.6	2.8	9.4
Net official development assistance received ($ millions)	..	..	..

Iceland

Population (thousands)	321	Population growth (%)	0.5
Surface area (1,000 sq. km)	103	Population living below $1.25 a day (%)	..
GNI, Atlas ($ billions)	12.3	GNI per capita, Atlas ($)	38,270
GNI, PPP ($ billions)	11.2	GNI per capita, PPP ($)	34,770

	1990	2000	2012
People			
Share of poorest 20% in nat'l consumption/income (%)	..	..	..
Life expectancy at birth (years)	78	80	83
Total fertility rate (births per woman)	2.3	2.1	2.0
Adolescent fertility rate (births per 1,000 women 15-19)	28	20	11
Contraceptive prevalence (% of married women 15-49)	..	..	..
Births attended by skilled health staff (% of total)	..	..	..
Under-five mortality rate (per 1,000 live births)	6	4	2
Child malnutrition, underweight (% of under age 5)	..	..	..
Child immunization, measles (% of ages 12-23 mos.)	99	91	90
Primary completion rate, total (% of relevant age group)	..	98	99
Gross secondary enrollment, total (% of relevant age group)	98	107	109
Ratio of girls to boys in primary & secondary school (%)	98	102	101
HIV prevalence rate (% population of ages 15-49)	..	..	..
Environment			
Forests (sq. km)	87	184	308
Deforestation (avg. annual %, 1990-2000 and 2000-2010)		-7.8	-5.0
Freshwater use (% of internal resources)	0.1	0.1	0.1
Access to improved water source (% total pop.)	100	100	100
Access to improved sanitation facilities (% total pop.)	100	100	100
Energy use per capita (kilograms of oil equivalent)	8,196	11,023	18,775
Carbon dioxide emissions per capita (metric tons)	7.8	7.7	6.2
Electricity use per capita (kilowatt-hours)	16,148	26,202	52,374
Economy			
GDP ($ billions)	6.4	8.7	13.6
GDP growth (annual %)	1.2	4.3	1.4
GDP implicit price deflator (annual % growth)	15.2	3.6	2.8
Value added in agriculture (% of GDP)	12	8	7
Value added in industry (% of GDP)	31	26	24
Value added in services (% of GDP)	57	65	69
Exports of goods and services (% of GDP)	34	34	59
Imports of goods and services (% of GDP)	32	41	53
Gross capital formation (% of GDP)	19	23	15
Central government revenue (% of GDP)	..	33.3	30.0
Central government cash surplus/deficit (% of GDP)	..	2.7	-5.3
States and markets			
Starting a business (days)	..	..	5
Stock market capitalization (% of GDP)	..	51.0	20.8
Military expenditures (% of GDP)	..	..	0.1
Mobile cellular subscriptions (per 100 people)	3.9	76.4	108.1
Individuals using the Internet (% of population)	0.0	44.5	96.2
Paved roads (% of total)	19.9	30.0	40.7
High-technology exports (% of manufactured exports)	10	13	14
Global links			
Merchandise trade (% of GDP)	51	52	72
Net barter terms of trade index (2000 = 100)	..	100	87
Total external debt stocks ($ millions)	..	..	..
Total debt service (% of exports)	..	..	..
Net migration (thousands)	-1.1	3.9	5.4
Personal remittances received ($ millions)	62.3	87.6	19.2
Foreign direct investment, net inflows ($ millions)	22	155	1,086
Net official development assistance received ($ millions)	..	..	..

India

South Asia			Lower middle income

Population (millions)	1,236.7	Population growth (%)	1.3
Surface area (1,000 sq. km)	3,287	Population living below $1.25 a day (%)	32.7
GNI, Atlas ($ billions)	1,913.2	GNI per capita, Atlas ($)	1,550
GNI, PPP ($ billions)	4,730.3	GNI per capita, PPP ($)	3,820

	1990	2000	2012
People			
Share of poorest 20% in nat'l consumption/income (%)	8.8	..	8.5
Life expectancy at birth (years)	59	62	66
Total fertility rate (births per woman)	3.9	3.1	2.5
Adolescent fertility rate (births per 1,000 women 15–19)	108	79	33
Contraceptive prevalence (% of married women 15–49)	41	47	55
Births attended by skilled health staff (% of total)	34	43	52
Under-five mortality rate (per 1,000 live births)	126	92	56
Child malnutrition, underweight (% of under age 5)	59.5	44.4	43.5
Child immunization, measles (% of ages 12–23 mos.)	56	59	74
Primary completion rate, total (% of relevant age group)	64	73	96
Gross secondary enrollment, total (% of relevant age group)	37	46	69
Ratio of girls to boys in primary & secondary school (%)	67	79	98
HIV prevalence rate (% population of ages 15–49)	0.1	0.4	0.3
Environment			
Forests (1,000 sq. km)	639	654	686
Deforestation (avg. annual %, 1990–2000 and 2000–2010)		-0.2	-0.5
Freshwater use (% of internal resources)	34.6	42.2	52.6
Access to improved water source (% total pop.)	70	81	93
Access to improved sanitation facilities (% total pop.)	18	25	36
Energy use per capita (kilograms of oil equivalent)	365	439	614
Carbon dioxide emissions per capita (metric tons)	0.8	1.1	1.7
Electricity use per capita (kilowatt-hours)	270	391	684
Economy			
GDP ($ billions)	327	477	1,859
GDP growth (annual %)	5.5	3.8	4.7
GDP implicit price deflator (annual % growth)	10.7	3.6	7.2
Value added in agriculture (% of GDP)	29	23	18
Value added in industry (% of GDP)	26	26	26
Value added in services (% of GDP)	44	51	56
Exports of goods and services (% of GDP)	7	13	24
Imports of goods and services (% of GDP)	8	14	31
Gross capital formation (% of GDP)	25	24	35
Central government revenue (% of GDP)	12.2	11.5	12.4
Central government cash surplus/deficit (% of GDP)	-3.3	-3.7	-3.8
States and markets			
Starting a business (days)	..	89	27
Stock market capitalization (% of GDP)	11.8	31.1	68.0
Military expenditures (% of GDP)	3.1	2.9	2.4
Mobile cellular subscriptions (per 100 people)	0.0	0.3	69.9
Individuals using the Internet (% of population)	0.0	0.5	12.6
Paved roads (% of total)	47.3	47.0	53.8
High-technology exports (% of manufactured exports)	4	6	7
Global links			
Merchandise trade (% of GDP)	13	20	42
Net barter terms of trade index (2000 = 100)	86	100	127
Total external debt stocks ($ billions)	86	101	379
Total debt service (% of exports)	34.9	17.5	6.8
Net migration (thousands)	-127	-1,923	-2,294
Personal remittances received ($ billions)	2.4	12.9	68.8
Foreign direct investment, net inflows ($ billions)	0.2	3.6	24.0
Net official development assistance received ($ billions)	1.4	1.4	1.7

Indonesia

East Asia & Pacific		**Lower middle income**	
Population (millions)	246.9	Population growth (%)	1.2
Surface area (1,000 sq. km)	1,905	Population living below $1.25 a day (%)	16.2
GNI, Atlas ($ billions)	844.0	GNI per capita, Atlas ($)	3,420
GNI, PPP ($ billions)	1,168.7	GNI per capita, PPP ($)	4,730

	1990	2000	2012
People			
Share of poorest 20% in nat'l consumption/income (%)	9.4	9.6	7.3
Life expectancy at birth (years)	63	67	71
Total fertility rate (births per woman)	3.1	2.5	2.4
Adolescent fertility rate (births per 1,000 women 15-19)	67	50	48
Contraceptive prevalence (% of married women 15-49)	50	55	62
Births attended by skilled health staff (% of total)	41	67	83
Under-five mortality rate (per 1,000 live births)	84	52	31
Child malnutrition, underweight (% of under age 5)	31.0	24.8	18.6
Child immunization, measles (% of ages 12-23 mos.)	58	76	80
Primary completion rate, total (% of relevant age group)	95	95	100
Gross secondary enrollment, total (% of relevant age group)	47	56	81
Ratio of girls to boys in primary & secondary school (%)	92	98	103
HIV prevalence rate (% population of ages 15-49)	0.1	0.1	0.4
Environment			
Forests (1,000 sq. km)	1,185	994	937
Deforestation (avg. annual %, 1990-2000 and 2000-2010)		1.8	0.5
Freshwater use (% of internal resources)	3.7	5.6	5.6
Access to improved water source (% total pop.)	70	78	85
Access to improved sanitation facilities (% total pop.)	35	47	59
Energy use per capita (kilograms of oil equivalent)	552	741	857
Carbon dioxide emissions per capita (metric tons)	0.8	1.3	1.8
Electricity use per capita (kilowatt-hours)	165	395	680
Economy			
GDP ($ billions)	114	165	878
GDP growth (annual %)	9.0	4.9	6.2
GDP implicit price deflator (annual % growth)	7.7	20.4	4.5
Value added in agriculture (% of GDP)	19	16	14
Value added in industry (% of GDP)	39	46	47
Value added in services (% of GDP)	41	38	39
Exports of goods and services (% of GDP)	25	41	24
Imports of goods and services (% of GDP)	24	30	26
Gross capital formation (% of GDP)	31	22	36
Central government revenue (% of GDP)	16.6	18.3	16.2
Central government cash surplus/deficit (% of GDP)	0.7	-3.7	-1.1
States and markets			
Starting a business (days)	..	168	48
Stock market capitalization (% of GDP)	7.1	16.3	45.2
Military expenditures (% of GDP)	0.9	0.5	0.8
Mobile cellular subscriptions (per 100 people)	0.0	1.8	114.2
Individuals using the Internet (% of population)	0.0	0.9	15.4
Paved roads (% of total)	45.1	58.0	57.0
High-technology exports (% of manufactured exports)	2	16	7
Global links			
Merchandise trade (% of GDP)	42	66	43
Net barter terms of trade index (2000 = 100)	95	100	129
Total external debt stocks ($ billions)	70	144	255
Total debt service (% of exports)	33.5	22.8	17.1
Net migration (thousands)	-347	-526	-700
Personal remittances received ($ billions)	0.2	1.2	7.2
Foreign direct investment, net inflows ($ billions)	1.1	-4.6	19.6
Net official development assistance received ($ billions)	1.7	1.7	0.1

Iran, Islamic Rep.

Middle East & North Africa		Upper middle income	
Population (millions)	76.4	Population growth (%)	1.3
Surface area (1,000 sq. km)	1,745	Population living below $1.25 a day (%)	<2
GNI, Atlas ($ billions)	318.3	GNI per capita, Atlas ($)	4,330
GNI, PPP ($ billions)	756.6	GNI per capita, PPP ($)	10,290

	1990	2000	2012
People			
Share of poorest 20% in nat'l consumption/income (%)	5.2	5.2	..
Life expectancy at birth (years)	63	70	74
Total fertility rate (births per woman)	4.8	2.2	1.9
Adolescent fertility rate (births per 1,000 women 15–19)	90	39	32
Contraceptive prevalence (% of married women 15–49)	49	74	77
Births attended by skilled health staff (% of total)	..	90	96
Under-five mortality rate (per 1,000 live births)	56	35	18
Child malnutrition, underweight (% of under age 5)	..	4.6	..
Child immunization, measles (% of ages 12–23 mos.)	85	99	98
Primary completion rate, total (% of relevant age group)	85	93	102
Gross secondary enrollment, total (% of relevant age group)	53	79	86
Ratio of girls to boys in primary & secondary school (%)	82	94	96
HIV prevalence rate (% population of ages 15–49)	0.1	0.1	0.2
Environment			
Forests (1,000 sq. km)	111	111	111
Deforestation (avg. annual %, 1990–2000 and 2000–2010)		0.0	0.0
Freshwater use (% of internal resources)	..	69.8	72.6
Access to improved water source (% total pop.)	92	94	96
Access to improved sanitation facilities (% total pop.)	71	79	89
Energy use per capita (kilograms of oil equivalent)	1,230	1,866	2,813
Carbon dioxide emissions per capita (metric tons)	3.7	5.7	7.7
Electricity use per capita (kilowatt-hours)	941	1,540	2,649
Economy			
GDP ($ billions)	116	101	552
GDP growth (annual %)	13.7	5.1	-1.9
GDP implicit price deflator (annual % growth)	20.6	26.4	22.2
Value added in agriculture (% of GDP)	19	14	..
Value added in industry (% of GDP)	29	37	..
Value added in services (% of GDP)	52	50	..
Exports of goods and services (% of GDP)	15	23	..
Imports of goods and services (% of GDP)	23	17	..
Gross capital formation (% of GDP)	37	33	..
Central government revenue (% of GDP)	18.7	23.4	29.1
Central government cash surplus/deficit (% of GDP)	-1.9	1.8	0.5
States and markets			
Starting a business (days)	..	29	16
Stock market capitalization (% of GDP)	2.2	7.3	25.5
Military expenditures (% of GDP)	2.1	3.8	2.2
Mobile cellular subscriptions (per 100 people)	0.0	1.5	76.1
Individuals using the Internet (% of population)	0.0	0.9	26.0
Paved roads (% of total)	..	63.0	74.3
High-technology exports (% of manufactured exports)	..	1	4
Global links			
Merchandise trade (% of GDP)	34	42	28
Net barter terms of trade index (2000 = 100)	..	100	194
Total external debt stocks ($ billions)	9.0	8.0	11.5
Total debt service (% of exports)	3.2	9.7	..
Net migration (thousands)	-2,276	-70	-300
Personal remittances received ($ millions)	1,200	536	1,330
Foreign direct investment, net inflows ($ millions)	-362	39	4,870
Net official development assistance received ($ millions)	106	130	149

Iraq

Middle East & North Africa   **Upper middle income**

Population (millions)	32.6	Population growth (%)	2.5
Surface area (1,000 sq. km)	435	Population living below $1.25 a day (%)	2.8
GNI, Atlas ($ billions)	199.8	GNI per capita, Atlas ($)	6,130
GNI, PPP ($ billions)	242.9	GNI per capita, PPP ($)	7,460

	1990	2000	2012
People			
Share of poorest 20% in nat'l consumption/income (%)	..	..	8.7
Life expectancy at birth (years)	68	71	69
Total fertility rate (births per woman)	5.9	5.0	4.1
Adolescent fertility rate (births per 1,000 women 15–19)	70	66	69
Contraceptive prevalence (% of married women 15–49)	14	44	53
Births attended by skilled health staff (% of total)	54	72	91
Under-five mortality rate (per 1,000 live births)	53	45	34
Child malnutrition, underweight (% of under age 5)	10.4	12.9	7.1
Child immunization, measles (% of ages 12–23 mos.)	75	86	69
Primary completion rate, total (% of relevant age group)	59	56	..
Gross secondary enrollment, total (% of relevant age group)	47	37	..
Ratio of girls to boys in primary & secondary school (%)	77	77	..
HIV prevalence rate (% population of ages 15–49)	..	..	..
Environment			
Forests (1,000 sq. km)	8.0	8.2	8.3
Deforestation (avg. annual %, 1990–2000 and 2000–2010)		-0.2	-0.1
Freshwater use (% of internal resources)	121.6	187.5	187.5
Access to improved water source (% total pop.)	78	80	85
Access to improved sanitation facilities (% total pop.)	..	75	85
Energy use per capita (kilograms of oil equivalent)	1,125	1,090	1,266
Carbon dioxide emissions per capita (metric tons)	3.0	3.0	3.7
Electricity use per capita (kilowatt-hours)	1,302	1,225	1,343
Economy			
GDP ($ billions)	..	..	216
GDP growth (annual %)	..	2.3	9.3
GDP implicit price deflator (annual % growth)	..	-19.6	2.9
Value added in agriculture (% of GDP)	..	..	..
Value added in industry (% of GDP)	..	..	..
Value added in services (% of GDP)	..	..	..
Exports of goods and services (% of GDP)	..	76	45
Imports of goods and services (% of GDP)	..	50	36
Gross capital formation (% of GDP)	..	29	18
Central government revenue (% of GDP)	..	..	..
Central government cash surplus/deficit (% of GDP)	..	..	..
States and markets			
Starting a business (days)	..	..	29
Stock market capitalization (% of GDP)	..	..	..
Military expenditures (% of GDP)	..	..	2.8
Mobile cellular subscriptions (per 100 people)	0.0	0.0	81.6
Individuals using the Internet (% of population)	0.0	0.1	7.1
Paved roads (% of total)	77.9	84.3	..
High-technology exports (% of manufactured exports)	..	..	..
Global links			
Merchandise trade (% of GDP)	..	..	70
Net barter terms of trade index (2000 = 100)	..	100	227
Total external debt stocks ($ millions)	..	..	..
Total debt service (% of exports)	..	..	..
Net migration (thousands)	-154	-266	450
Personal remittances received ($ millions)	..	..	271
Foreign direct investment, net inflows ($ millions)	0	-3	3,400
Net official development assistance received ($ millions)	63	102	1,301

Ireland

Population (millions)	4.6	Population growth (%)	0.2
Surface area (1,000 sq. km)	70	Population living below $1.25 a day (%)	..
GNI, Atlas ($ billions)	179.0	GNI per capita, Atlas ($)	39,020
GNI, PPP ($ billions)	164.2	GNI per capita, PPP ($)	35,790

	1990	2000	2012
People			
Share of poorest 20% in nat'l consumption/income (%)	..	7.4	..
Life expectancy at birth (years)	75	77	81
Total fertility rate (births per woman)	2.1	1.9	2.0
Adolescent fertility rate (births per 1,000 women 15-19)	16	19	8
Contraceptive prevalence (% of married women 15-49)	..	75	..
Births attended by skilled health staff (% of total)	..	100	..
Under-five mortality rate (per 1,000 live births)	9	7	4
Child malnutrition, underweight (% of under age 5)	..	..	..
Child immunization, measles (% of ages 12-23 mos.)	78	79	92
Primary completion rate, total (% of relevant age group)	103	95	..
Gross secondary enrollment, total (% of relevant age group)	99	105	118
Ratio of girls to boys in primary & secondary school (%)	105	103	101
HIV prevalence rate (% population of ages 15-49)	..	..	..
Environment			
Forests (1,000 sq. km)	4.7	6.4	7.5
Deforestation (avg. annual %, 1990-2000 and 2000-2010)		-3.2	-1.5
Freshwater use (% of internal resources)	..	1.6	1.6
Access to improved water source (% total pop.)	100	100	100
Access to improved sanitation facilities (% total pop.)	99	99	99
Energy use per capita (kilograms of oil equivalent)	2,809	3,567	2,910
Carbon dioxide emissions per capita (metric tons)	8.9	10.9	8.8
Electricity use per capita (kilowatt-hours)	3,768	5,796	5,701
Economy			
GDP ($ billions)	48	97	211
GDP growth (annual %)	8.5	10.6	0.2
GDP implicit price deflator (annual % growth)	-0.7	5.3	0.7
Value added in agriculture (% of GDP)	9	4	2
Value added in industry (% of GDP)	34	35	28
Value added in services (% of GDP)	57	61	71
Exports of goods and services (% of GDP)	56	98	108
Imports of goods and services (% of GDP)	51	84	84
Gross capital formation (% of GDP)	21	24	11
Central government revenue (% of GDP)	..	33.1	31.6
Central government cash surplus/deficit (% of GDP)	..	4.9	-13.0
States and markets			
Starting a business (days)	..	18	10
Stock market capitalization (% of GDP)	..	84.1	51.7
Military expenditures (% of GDP)	1.2	0.7	0.6
Mobile cellular subscriptions (per 100 people)	0.7	64.7	107.2
Individuals using the Internet (% of population)	0.0	17.9	79.0
Paved roads (% of total)	94.0	100.0	100.0
High-technology exports (% of manufactured exports)	41	48	23
Global links			
Merchandise trade (% of GDP)	92	132	85
Net barter terms of trade index (2000 = 100)	..	100	93
Total external debt stocks ($ millions)	..	..	..
Total debt service (% of exports)	..	..	..
Net migration (thousands)	-11	200	50
Personal remittances received ($ millions)	286	252	700
Foreign direct investment, net inflows ($ billions)	0.6	25.5	41.0
Net official development assistance received ($ millions)	..	..	..

Isle of Man

High income

Population (thousands)	85	Population growth (%)		0.7
Surface area (sq. km)	570	Population living below $1.25 a day (%)		..
GNI, Atlas ($ billions)	..	GNI per capita, Atlas ($)		..
GNI, PPP ($ millions)	..	GNI per capita, PPP ($)		..

	1990	2000	2012
People			
Share of poorest 20% in nat'l consumption/income (%)	..	..	
Life expectancy at birth (years)	..	78	..
Total fertility rate (births per woman)	..	1.7	..
Adolescent fertility rate (births per 1,000 women 15-19)	..	..	..
Contraceptive prevalence (% of married women 15-49)	..	..	..
Births attended by skilled health staff (% of total)	..	..	..
Under-five mortality rate (per 1,000 live births)	..	..	..
Child malnutrition, underweight (% of under age 5)	..	..	..
Child immunization, measles (% of ages 12-23 mos.)	..	..	..
Primary completion rate, total (% of relevant age group)	..	..	..
Gross secondary enrollment, total (% of relevant age group)	..	..	..
Ratio of girls to boys in primary & secondary school (%)	..	..	..
HIV prevalence rate (% population of ages 15-49)	..	..	..
Environment			
Forests (sq. km)	35	35	35
Deforestation (avg. annual %, 1990-2000 and 2000-2010)		0.0	0.0
Freshwater use (% of internal resources)	..	..	
Access to improved water source (% total pop.)	..	..	..
Access to improved sanitation facilities (% total pop.)	..	..	..
Energy use per capita (kilograms of oil equivalent)	..	..	..
Carbon dioxide emissions per capita (metric tons)	..	..	..
Electricity use per capita (kilowatt-hours)	..	..	..
Economy			
GDP ($ millions)	..	1,564	..
GDP growth (annual %)	4.2	5.3	..
GDP implicit price deflator (annual % growth)	9.0	3.3	..
Value added in agriculture (% of GDP)	..	..	..
Value added in industry (% of GDP)	..	..	..
Value added in services (% of GDP)	..	..	..
Exports of goods and services (% of GDP)	..	..	..
Imports of goods and services (% of GDP)	..	..	..
Gross capital formation (% of GDP)	..	..	..
Central government revenue (% of GDP)	..	..	..
Central government cash surplus/deficit (% of GDP)	..	..	..
States and markets			
Starting a business (days)	..	..	..
Stock market capitalization (% of GDP)	..	..	..
Military expenditures (% of GDP)	..	..	..
Mobile cellular subscriptions (per 100 people)	..	..	..
Individuals using the Internet (% of population)	..	..	..
Paved roads (% of total)	..	..	..
High-technology exports (% of manufactured exports)	..	..	..
Global links			
Merchandise trade (% of GDP)	..	..	..
Net barter terms of trade index (2000 = 100)	..	..	..
Total external debt stocks ($ millions)	..	..	..
Total debt service (% of exports)	..	..	..
Net migration (thousands)	..	..	..
Personal remittances received ($ millions)	..	..	..
Foreign direct investment, net inflows ($ millions)	..	..	..
Net official development assistance received ($ millions)	..	..	..

Israel

Population (millions)	7.9	Population growth (%)	1.8
Surface area (1,000 sq. km)	22	Population living below $1.25 a day (%)	..
GNI, Atlas ($ billions)	253.4	GNI per capita, Atlas ($)	32,030
GNI, PPP ($ billions)	240.2	GNI per capita, PPP ($)	30,370

	1990	2000	2012
People			
Share of poorest 20% in nat'l consumption/income (%)	..	5.7	..
Life expectancy at birth (years)	77	79	82
Total fertility rate (births per woman)	2.8	3.0	3.0
Adolescent fertility rate (births per 1,000 women 15–19)	20	17	8
Contraceptive prevalence (% of married women 15–49)	68	..	..
Births attended by skilled health staff (% of total)	..	..	..
Under-five mortality rate (per 1,000 live births)	12	7	4
Child malnutrition, underweight (% of under age 5)	..	..	..
Child immunization, measles (% of ages 12-23 mos.)	91	97	96
Primary completion rate, total (% of relevant age group)	..	104	102
Gross secondary enrollment, total (% of relevant age group)	89	103	102
Ratio of girls to boys in primary & secondary school (%)	104	100	101
HIV prevalence rate (% population of ages 15–49)	..	..	..
Environment			
Forests (1,000 sq. km)	1.3	1.5	1.5
Deforestation (avg. annual %, 1990-2000 and 2000-2010)		-1.5	-0.1
Freshwater use (% of internal resources)	240.5	244.1	260.5
Access to improved water source (% total pop.)	100	100	100
Access to improved sanitation facilities (% total pop.)	100	100	100
Energy use per capita (kilograms of oil equivalent)	2,460	2,899	3,044
Carbon dioxide emissions per capita (metric tons)	7.2	10.0	9.3
Electricity use per capita (kilowatt-hours)	4,176	6,323	6,926
Economy			
GDP ($ billions)	52	125	258
GDP growth (annual %)	6.8	9.3	3.4
GDP implicit price deflator (annual % growth)	15.9	1.6	4.0
Value added in agriculture (% of GDP)	..	..	..
Value added in industry (% of GDP)	..	..	..
Value added in services (% of GDP)	..	..	..
Exports of goods and services (% of GDP)	35	37	36
Imports of goods and services (% of GDP)	45	37	36
Gross capital formation (% of GDP)	25	20	21
Central government revenue (% of GDP)	..	40.6	31.7
Central government cash surplus/deficit (% of GDP)	..	-3.6	-5.4
States and markets			
Starting a business (days)	..	20	14
Stock market capitalization (% of GDP)	6.3	51.3	57.6
Military expenditures (% of GDP)	14.5	8.0	5.7
Mobile cellular subscriptions (per 100 people)	0.3	73.2	120.7
Individuals using the Internet (% of population)	0.1	20.9	73.4
Paved roads (% of total)	100.0	100.0	100.0
High-technology exports (% of manufactured exports)	11	19	16
Global links			
Merchandise trade (% of GDP)	55	55	54
Net barter terms of trade index (2000 = 100)	..	100	98
Total external debt stocks ($ millions)	..	..	..
Total debt service (% of exports)	..	..	..
Net migration (thousands)	457	103	-76
Personal remittances received ($ millions)	812	400	685
Foreign direct investment, net inflows ($ billions)	0.2	8.0	9.5
Net official development assistance received ($ billions)	1.4	..	..

Italy

High income

Population (millions)	59.5	Population growth (%)	-2.0
Surface area (1,000 sq. km)	301	Population living below $1.25 a day (%)	..
GNI, Atlas ($ billions)	2,062.5	GNI per capita, Atlas ($)	34,640
GNI, PPP ($ billions)	2,065.9	GNI per capita, PPP ($)	34,700

	1990	2000	2012
People			
Share of poorest 20% in nat'l consumption/income (%)	..	6.5	..
Life expectancy at birth (years)	77	80	83
Total fertility rate (births per woman)	1.3	1.3	1.4
Adolescent fertility rate (births per 1,000 women 15–19)	9	7	4
Contraceptive prevalence (% of married women 15–49)	..	..	..
Births attended by skilled health staff (% of total)	..	99	..
Under-five mortality rate (per 1,000 live births)	10	6	4
Child malnutrition, underweight (% of under age 5)	..	..	..
Child immunization, measles (% of ages 12-23 mos.)	43	74	90
Primary completion rate, total (% of relevant age group)	100	102	103
Gross secondary enrollment, total (% of relevant age group)	79	93	101
Ratio of girls to boys in primary & secondary school (%)	100	98	99
HIV prevalence rate (% population of ages 15–49)	..	..	..
Environment			
Forests (1,000 sq. km)	76	84	92
Deforestation (avg. annual %, 1990–2000 and 2000–2010)		-1.0	-0.9
Freshwater use (% of internal resources)	..	24.9	24.9
Access to improved water source (% total pop.)	100	100	100
Access to improved sanitation facilities (% total pop.)	..	..	..
Energy use per capita (kilograms of oil equivalent)	2,584	3,012	2,664
Carbon dioxide emissions per capita (metric tons)	7.4	7.9	6.7
Electricity use per capita (kilowatt-hours)	4,145	5,300	5,393
Economy			
GDP ($ billions)	1,138	1,104	2,015
GDP growth (annual %)	2.0	3.7	-2.5
GDP implicit price deflator (annual % growth)	8.9	1.9	1.7
Value added in agriculture (% of GDP)	4	3	2
Value added in industry (% of GDP)	31	28	24
Value added in services (% of GDP)	65	69	74
Exports of goods and services (% of GDP)	19	27	30
Imports of goods and services (% of GDP)	19	26	29
Gross capital formation (% of GDP)	23	21	18
Central government revenue (% of GDP)	..	36.9	37.6
Central government cash surplus/deficit (% of GDP)	..	-0.8	-3.5
States and markets			
Starting a business (days)	..	23	6
Stock market capitalization (% of GDP)	13.1	69.6	23.8
Military expenditures (% of GDP)	2.1	2.0	1.7
Mobile cellular subscriptions (per 100 people)	0.5	74.1	159.8
Individuals using the Internet (% of population)	0.0	23.1	58.0
Paved roads (% of total)	100.0	100.0	..
High-technology exports (% of manufactured exports)	8	9	7
Global links			
Merchandise trade (% of GDP)	31	43	49
Net barter terms of trade index (2000 = 100)	..	100	95
Total external debt stocks ($ millions)	..	..	..
Total debt service (% of exports)	..	..	..
Net migration (thousands)	153	1,853	900
Personal remittances received ($ billions)	5.1	1.9	7.3
Foreign direct investment, net inflows ($ billions)	6.4	13.2	6.7
Net official development assistance received ($ millions)	..	..	..

Jamaica

Latin America & Caribbean		Upper middle income	
Population (millions)	2.7	Population growth (%)	0.3
Surface area (1,000 sq. km)	11	Population living below $1.25 a day (%)	<2
GNI, Atlas ($ billions)	13.9	GNI per capita, Atlas ($)	5,130
GNI, PPP ($ billions)	..	GNI per capita, PPP ($)	..

	1990	2000	2012
People			
Share of poorest 20% in nat'l consumption/income (%)	5.9	0.0	..
Life expectancy at birth (years)	71	70	73
Total fertility rate (births per woman)	2.9	2.6	2.3
Adolescent fertility rate (births per 1,000 women 15-19)	107	89	70
Contraceptive prevalence (% of married women 15-49)	55	69	72
Births attended by skilled health staff (% of total)	92	96	98
Under-five mortality rate (per 1,000 live births)	30	23	17
Child malnutrition, underweight (% of under age 5)	4.0	3.8	3.2
Child immunization, measles (% of ages 12-23 mos.)	74	88	93
Primary completion rate, total (% of relevant age group)	97	88	..
Gross secondary enrollment, total (% of relevant age group)	70	87	85
Ratio of girls to boys in primary & secondary school (%)	102	100	..
HIV prevalence rate (% population of ages 15-49)	1.6	2.4	1.7
Environment			
Forests (1,000 sq. km)	3.4	3.4	3.4
Deforestation (avg. annual %, 1990-2000 and 2000-2010)		0.1	0.1
Freshwater use (% of internal resources)	..	6.2	6.2
Access to improved water source (% total pop.)	93	93	93
Access to improved sanitation facilities (% total pop.)	79	80	80
Energy use per capita (kilograms of oil equivalent)	1,165	1,479	1,135
Carbon dioxide emissions per capita (metric tons)	3.3	4.0	2.7
Electricity use per capita (kilowatt-hours)	879	2,334	1,553
Economy			
GDP ($ billions)	4.6	9.0	14.8
GDP growth (annual %)	4.2	0.9	-0.5
GDP implicit price deflator (annual % growth)	25.1	10.6	6.4
Value added in agriculture (% of GDP)	8	7	7
Value added in industry (% of GDP)	37	26	21
Value added in services (% of GDP)	55	67	72
Exports of goods and services (% of GDP)	48	33	30
Imports of goods and services (% of GDP)	52	49	53
Gross capital formation (% of GDP)	26	27	20
Central government revenue (% of GDP)	..	31.8	31.6
Central government cash surplus/deficit (% of GDP)	..	-2.4	-4.2
States and markets			
Starting a business (days)	..	31	6
Stock market capitalization (% of GDP)	19.8	39.8	43.3
Military expenditures (% of GDP)	0.6	0.5	0.9
Mobile cellular subscriptions (per 100 people)	0.0	14.2	96.3
Individuals using the Internet (% of population)	0.0	3.1	46.5
Paved roads (% of total)	64.0	70.1	..
High-technology exports (% of manufactured exports)	0	0	1
Global links			
Merchandise trade (% of GDP)	67	51	56
Net barter terms of trade index (2000 = 100)	..	100	87
Total external debt stocks ($ billions)	4.7	4.7	14.3
Total debt service (% of exports)	27.9	18.6	38.2
Net migration (thousands)	-112	-76	-80
Personal remittances received ($ millions)	229	892	2,145
Foreign direct investment, net inflows ($ millions)	138	468	229
Net official development assistance received ($ millions)	271	9	21

Japan

Population (millions)	127.6	Population growth (%)	-0.2
Surface area (1,000 sq. km)	378	Population living below $1.25 a day (%)	..
GNI, Atlas ($ billions)	6,106.7	GNI per capita, Atlas ($)	47,870
GNI, PPP ($ billions)	4,687.6	GNI per capita, PPP ($)	36,750

	1990	2000	2012
People			
Share of poorest 20% in nat'l consumption/income (%)	10.6	..	..
Life expectancy at birth (years)	79	81	83
Total fertility rate (births per woman)	1.5	1.4	1.4
Adolescent fertility rate (births per 1,000 women 15-19)	4	5	5
Contraceptive prevalence (% of married women 15-49)	58	56	..
Births attended by skilled health staff (% of total)	100	100	..
Under-five mortality rate (per 1,000 live births)	6	5	3
Child malnutrition, underweight (% of under age 5)	..	..	..
Child immunization, measles (% of ages 12-23 mos.)	73	96	96
Primary completion rate, total (% of relevant age group)	103	103	102
Gross secondary enrollment, total (% of relevant age group)	96	102	102
Ratio of girls to boys in primary & secondary school (%)	101	101	100
HIV prevalence rate (% population of ages 15-49)	..	..	..
Environment			
Forests (1,000 sq. km)	250	249	250
Deforestation (avg. annual %, 1990-2000 and 2000-2010)		0.0	0.0
Freshwater use (% of internal resources)	21.3	20.9	20.9
Access to improved water source (% total pop.)	100	100	100
Access to improved sanitation facilities (% total pop.)	100	100	100
Energy use per capita (kilograms of oil equivalent)	3,556	4,091	3,539
Carbon dioxide emissions per capita (metric tons)	8.9	9.6	9.2
Electricity use per capita (kilowatt-hours)	6,486	7,974	7,848
Economy			
GDP ($ billions)	3,104	4,731	5,961
GDP growth (annual %)	5.6	2.3	2.0
GDP implicit price deflator (annual % growth)	2.3	-1.2	-0.9
Value added in agriculture (% of GDP)	2	2	1
Value added in industry (% of GDP)	38	31	26
Value added in services (% of GDP)	60	67	73
Exports of goods and services (% of GDP)	10	11	15
Imports of goods and services (% of GDP)	9	9	17
Gross capital formation (% of GDP)	32	25	21
Central government revenue (% of GDP)	..	..	11.4
Central government cash surplus/deficit (% of GDP)	..	..	-8.3
States and markets			
Starting a business (days)	..	31	22
Stock market capitalization (% of GDP)	94.1	66.7	61.8
Military expenditures (% of GDP)	0.8	1.0	1.0
Mobile cellular subscriptions (per 100 people)	0.7	53.1	110.9
Individuals using the Internet (% of population)	0.0	30.0	79.1
Paved roads (% of total)	69.2	76.1	..
High-technology exports (% of manufactured exports)	24	29	17
Global links			
Merchandise trade (% of GDP)	17	18	28
Net barter terms of trade index (2000 = 100)	..	100	60
Total external debt stocks ($ millions)	..	..	..
Total debt service (% of exports)	..	..	..
Net migration (thousands)	451	622	350
Personal remittances received ($ billions)	0.5	1.4	2.5
Foreign direct investment, net inflows ($ billions)	1.8	8.2	2.5
Net official development assistance received ($ millions)	..	..	..

Jordan

Middle East & North Africa		Upper middle income	
Population (millions)	6.3	Population growth (%)	2.2
Surface area (1,000 sq. km)	89	Population living below $1.25 a day (%)	<2
GNI, Atlas ($ billions)	29.5	GNI per capita, Atlas ($)	4,670
GNI, PPP ($ billions)	37.8	GNI per capita, PPP ($)	5,980

	1990	2000	2012
People			
Share of poorest 20% in nat'l consumption/income (%)	6.0	6.7	7.7
Life expectancy at birth (years)	70	72	74
Total fertility rate (births per woman)	5.5	4.1	3.3
Adolescent fertility rate (births per 1,000 women 15–19)	52	36	26
Contraceptive prevalence (% of married women 15–49)	40	56	61
Births attended by skilled health staff (% of total)	87	100	100
Under-five mortality rate (per 1,000 live births)	37	28	19
Child malnutrition, underweight (% of under age 5)	4.8	3.6	1.9
Child immunization, measles (% of ages 12–23 mos.)	87	94	98
Primary completion rate, total (% of relevant age group)	96	101	93
Gross secondary enrollment, total (% of relevant age group)	76	86	89
Ratio of girls to boys in primary & secondary school (%)	102	103	101
HIV prevalence rate (% population of ages 15–49)	..	..	..
Environment			
Forests (sq. km)	975	975	975
Deforestation (avg. annual %, 1990–2000 and 2000–2010)		0.0	0.0
Freshwater use (% of internal resources)	144.3	144.3	138.0
Access to improved water source (% total pop.)	97	97	96
Access to improved sanitation facilities (% total pop.)	97	98	98
Energy use per capita (kilograms of oil equivalent)	1,033	1,014	1,143
Carbon dioxide emissions per capita (metric tons)	3.3	3.2	3.4
Electricity use per capita (kilowatt-hours)	1,050	1,377	2,289
Economy			
GDP ($ billions)	4.2	8.5	31.0
GDP growth (annual %)	1.0	4.2	2.7
GDP implicit price deflator (annual % growth)	12.7	-0.4	4.5
Value added in agriculture (% of GDP)	8	2	3
Value added in industry (% of GDP)	26	26	30
Value added in services (% of GDP)	66	72	67
Exports of goods and services (% of GDP)	60	42	44
Imports of goods and services (% of GDP)	90	69	74
Gross capital formation (% of GDP)	31	22	27
Central government revenue (% of GDP)	25.3	25.1	21.5
Central government cash surplus/deficit (% of GDP)	-3.4	-2.0	-8.3
States and markets			
Starting a business (days)	..	79	12
Stock market capitalization (% of GDP)	48.1	58.4	87.0
Military expenditures (% of GDP)	7.8	6.3	4.7
Mobile cellular subscriptions (per 100 people)	0.0	8.2	128.2
Individuals using the Internet (% of population)	0.0	2.6	41.0
Paved roads (% of total)	100.0	100.0	100.0
High-technology exports (% of manufactured exports)	2	8	3
Global links			
Merchandise trade (% of GDP)	88	77	92
Net barter terms of trade index (2000 = 100)	94	100	84
Total external debt stocks ($ billions)	8.3	11.1	18.6
Total debt service (% of exports)	24.4	20.1	6.9
Net migration (thousands)	401	-184	400
Personal remittances received ($ billions)	0.5	1.8	3.6
Foreign direct investment, net inflows ($ millions)	38	913	1,497
Net official development assistance received ($ millions)	952	553	1,417

Kazakhstan

Europe & Central Asia		Upper middle income

Population (millions)	16.8	Population growth (%)	1.4
Surface area (1,000 sq. km)	2,725	Population living below $1.25 a day (%)	<2
GNI, Atlas ($ billions)	164.3	GNI per capita, Atlas ($)	9,780
GNI, PPP ($ billions)	197.9	GNI per capita, PPP ($)	11,790

	1990	2000	2012
People			
Share of poorest 20% in nat'l consumption/income (%)	7.5	5.5	9.1
Life expectancy at birth (years)	68	66	69
Total fertility rate (births per woman)	2.7	1.8	2.6
Adolescent fertility rate (births per 1,000 women 15-19)	51	34	30
Contraceptive prevalence (% of married women 15-49)	..	66	51
Births attended by skilled health staff (% of total)	99	98	100
Under-five mortality rate (per 1,000 live births)	54	44	19
Child malnutrition, underweight (% of under age 5)	..	3.8	3.7
Child immunization, measles (% of ages 12-23 mos.)	89	99	96
Primary completion rate, total (% of relevant age group)	..	95	102
Gross secondary enrollment, total (% of relevant age group)	102	96	98
Ratio of girls to boys in primary & secondary school (%)	104	102	98
HIV prevalence rate (% population of ages 15-49)	..	..	..
Environment			
Forests (1,000 sq. km)	34	34	33
Deforestation (avg. annual %, 1990-2000 and 2000-2010)		0.2	0.2
Freshwater use (% of internal resources)	..	30.6	32.9
Access to improved water source (% total pop.)	94	94	93
Access to improved sanitation facilities (% total pop.)	96	97	97
Energy use per capita (kilograms of oil equivalent)	4,493	2,397	4,717
Carbon dioxide emissions per capita (metric tons)	15.9	8.6	15.2
Electricity use per capita (kilowatt-hours)	5,905	3,170	4,893
Economy			
GDP ($ billions)	27	18	204
GDP growth (annual %)	-11.0	9.8	5.0
GDP implicit price deflator (annual % growth)	96.4	17.4	4.8
Value added in agriculture (% of GDP)	27	9	5
Value added in industry (% of GDP)	45	40	39
Value added in services (% of GDP)	29	51	56
Exports of goods and services (% of GDP)	74	57	48
Imports of goods and services (% of GDP)	75	49	30
Gross capital formation (% of GDP)	32	18	23
Central government revenue (% of GDP)	..	11.3	23.9
Central government cash surplus/deficit (% of GDP)	..	0.1	7.7
States and markets			
Starting a business (days)	..	26	12
Stock market capitalization (% of GDP)	..	7.3	11.5
Military expenditures (% of GDP)	1.0	0.8	1.2
Mobile cellular subscriptions (per 100 people)	0.0	1.4	185.8
Individuals using the Internet (% of population)	0.0	0.7	53.3
Paved roads (% of total)	55.1	94.0	88.7
High-technology exports (% of manufactured exports)	..	4	30
Global links			
Merchandise trade (% of GDP)	..	76	67
Net barter terms of trade index (2000 = 100)	..	100	231
Total external debt stocks ($ billions)	0	13	137
Total debt service (% of exports)	..	32.4	23.5
Net migration (thousands)	-1,512	45	0
Personal remittances received ($ millions)	..	122	171
Foreign direct investment, net inflows ($ billions)	0.1	1.3	15.1
Net official development assistance received ($ millions)	112	189	130

Kenya

Population (millions)	43.2	Population growth (%)	2.7
Surface area (1,000 sq. km)	580	Population living below $1.25 a day (%)	43.4
GNI, Atlas ($ billions)	37.2	GNI per capita, Atlas ($)	860
GNI, PPP ($ billions)	74.7	GNI per capita, PPP ($)	1,730

	1990	2000	2012
People			
Share of poorest 20% in nat'l consumption/income (%)	3.4	..	..
Life expectancy at birth (years)	59	53	61
Total fertility rate (births per woman)	6.0	5.0	4.5
Adolescent fertility rate (births per 1,000 women 15–19)	127	105	94
Contraceptive prevalence (% of married women 15–49)	27	39	46
Births attended by skilled health staff (% of total)	50	42	44
Under-five mortality rate (per 1,000 live births)	98	110	73
Child malnutrition, underweight (% of under age 5)	20.1	17.5	16.4
Child immunization, measles (% of ages 12–23 mos.)	78	78	93
Primary completion rate, total (% of relevant age group)	..	..	..
Gross secondary enrollment, total (% of relevant age group)	40	39	60
Ratio of girls to boys in primary & secondary school (%)	92	98	95
HIV prevalence rate (% population of ages 15–49)	2.5	8.9	6.1
Environment			
Forests (1,000 sq. km)	37	36	35
Deforestation (avg. annual %, 1990–2000 and 2000–2010)		0.4	0.3
Freshwater use (% of internal resources)	9.9	9.9	13.2
Access to improved water source (% total pop.)	43	52	62
Access to improved sanitation facilities (% total pop.)	25	27	30
Energy use per capita (kilograms of oil equivalent)	455	449	480
Carbon dioxide emissions per capita (metric tons)	0.2	0.3	0.3
Electricity use per capita (kilowatt-hours)	125	113	155
Economy			
GDP ($ billions)	8.6	12.7	40.7
GDP growth (annual %)	4.2	0.6	4.6
GDP implicit price deflator (annual % growth)	10.6	6.1	10.1
Value added in agriculture (% of GDP)	30	32	30
Value added in industry (% of GDP)	19	17	17
Value added in services (% of GDP)	51	51	53
Exports of goods and services (% of GDP)	26	22	27
Imports of goods and services (% of GDP)	31	32	44
Gross capital formation (% of GDP)	24	17	20
Central government revenue (% of GDP)	19.5	19.7	21.8
Central government cash surplus/deficit (% of GDP)	-2.8	2.0	-4.8
States and markets			
Starting a business (days)	..	60	32
Stock market capitalization (% of GDP)	5.3	10.1	36.3
Military expenditures (% of GDP)	2.9	1.3	2.0
Mobile cellular subscriptions (per 100 people)	0.0	0.4	71.2
Individuals using the Internet (% of population)	0.0	0.3	32.1
Paved roads (% of total)	12.8	12.0	7.0
High-technology exports (% of manufactured exports)	4	4	6
Global links			
Merchandise trade (% of GDP)	38	38	55
Net barter terms of trade index (2000 = 100)	70	100	90
Total external debt stocks ($ billions)	7.1	6.2	11.6
Total debt service (% of exports)	35.4	21.0	5.1
Net migration (thousands)	222	25	-50
Personal remittances received ($ millions)	139	538	1,214
Foreign direct investment, net inflows ($ millions)	57	111	259
Net official development assistance received ($ billions)	1.2	0.5	2.7

Kiribati

East Asia & Pacific		Lower middle income

Population (thousands)	101	Population growth (%)	1.5
Surface area (sq. km)	810	Population living below $1.25 a day (%)	..
GNI, Atlas ($ millions)	254.2	GNI per capita, Atlas ($)	2,520
GNI, PPP ($ millions)	389.5	GNI per capita, PPP ($)	3,870

	1990	2000	2012
People			
Share of poorest 20% in nat'l consumption/income (%)	..	..	..
Life expectancy at birth (years)	61	65	69
Total fertility rate (births per woman)	4.6	3.9	3.0
Adolescent fertility rate (births per 1,000 women 15–19)	47	35	17
Contraceptive prevalence (% of married women 15–49)	..	36	22
Births attended by skilled health staff (% of total)	..	89	80
Under-five mortality rate (per 1,000 live births)	94	71	60
Child malnutrition, underweight (% of under age 5)	..	..	..
Child immunization, measles (% of ages 12–23 mos.)	75	80	91
Primary completion rate, total (% of relevant age group)	103	102	..
Gross secondary enrollment, total (% of relevant age group)	38	67	..
Ratio of girls to boys in primary & secondary school (%)	100	106	..
HIV prevalence rate (% population of ages 15–49)	..	..	..
Environment			
Forests (sq. km)	122	122	122
Deforestation (avg. annual %, 1990–2000 and 2000–2010)		0.0	0.0
Freshwater use (% of internal resources)	..	..	..
Access to improved water source (% total pop.)	50	59	67
Access to improved sanitation facilities (% total pop.)	28	34	40
Energy use per capita (kilograms of oil equivalent)	100	..	..
Carbon dioxide emissions per capita (metric tons)	0.3	0.4	0.6
Electricity use per capita (kilowatt-hours)	..	..	..
Economy			
GDP ($ millions)	28.4	67.5	175.0
GDP growth (annual %)	2.1	9.5	2.8
GDP implicit price deflator (annual % growth)	-4.7	-2.8	-1.6
Value added in agriculture (% of GDP)	19	22	25
Value added in industry (% of GDP)	8	12	8
Value added in services (% of GDP)	74	66	67
Exports of goods and services (% of GDP)	12	13	11
Imports of goods and services (% of GDP)	147	93	106
Gross capital formation (% of GDP)	93	..	..
Central government revenue (% of GDP)	..	..	50.9
Central government cash surplus/deficit (% of GDP)	..	..	-7.2
States and markets			
Starting a business (days)	..	21	31
Stock market capitalization (% of GDP)	..	..	..
Military expenditures (% of GDP)	..	..	..
Mobile cellular subscriptions (per 100 people)	0.0	0.4	15.9
Individuals using the Internet (% of population)	0.0	1.8	10.7
Paved roads (% of total)	..	..	..
High-technology exports (% of manufactured exports)	..	..	38
Global links			
Merchandise trade (% of GDP)	105	65	63
Net barter terms of trade index (2000 = 100)	..	100	97
Total external debt stocks ($ millions)	..	..	..
Total debt service (% of exports)	..	..	..
Net migration (thousands)	-4.3	-0.9	-1.0
Personal remittances received ($ millions)	5.1	..	..
Foreign direct investment, net inflows ($ millions)	0.3	0.7	-1.7
Net official development assistance received ($ millions)	20.2	17.9	64.7

Korea, Dem. People's Rep.

East Asia & Pacific   **Low income**

Population (millions)	24.8	Population growth (%)	0.5
Surface area (1,000 sq. km)	121	Population living below $1.25 a day (%)	..
GNI, Atlas ($ millions)	..	GNI per capita, Atlas ($)	..
GNI, PPP ($ millions)	..	GNI per capita, PPP ($)	..

	1990	2000	2012
People			
Share of poorest 20% in nat'l consumption/income (%)	..	..	..
Life expectancy at birth (years)	69	65	70
Total fertility rate (births per woman)	2.3	2.0	2.0
Adolescent fertility rate (births per 1,000 women 15–19)	2	1	1
Contraceptive prevalence (% of married women 15–49)	62	69	..
Births attended by skilled health staff (% of total)	..	97	100
Under-five mortality rate (per 1,000 live births)	44	60	29
Child malnutrition, underweight (% of under age 5)	..	24.7	18.8
Child immunization, measles (% of ages 12–23 mos.)	98	78	99
Primary completion rate, total (% of relevant age group)	..	..	..
Gross secondary enrollment, total (% of relevant age group)	..	..	..
Ratio of girls to boys in primary & secondary school (%)	..	..	..
HIV prevalence rate (% population of ages 15–49)	..	..	..
Environment			
Forests (1,000 sq. km)	82	69	55
Deforestation (avg. annual %, 1990–2000 and 2000–2010)		1.7	2.0
Freshwater use (% of internal resources)	..		12.9
Access to improved water source (% total pop.)	100	100	98
Access to improved sanitation facilities (% total pop.)	..	61	82
Energy use per capita (kilograms of oil equivalent)	1,645	863	773
Carbon dioxide emissions per capita (metric tons)	12.1	3.4	2.9
Electricity use per capita (kilowatt-hours)	1,243	715	739
Economy			
GDP ($ millions)	..	..	..
GDP growth (annual %)	..	..	..
GDP implicit price deflator (annual % growth)	..	..	..
Value added in agriculture (% of GDP)	..	..	..
Value added in industry (% of GDP)	..	..	..
Value added in services (% of GDP)	..	..	..
Exports of goods and services (% of GDP)	..	..	..
Imports of goods and services (% of GDP)	..	..	..
Gross capital formation (% of GDP)	..	..	..
Central government revenue (% of GDP)	..	..	..
Central government cash surplus/deficit (% of GDP)	..	..	..
States and markets			
Starting a business (days)	..	..	..
Stock market capitalization (% of GDP)	..	..	..
Military expenditures (% of GDP)	..	..	..
Mobile cellular subscriptions (per 100 people)	0.0	0.0	6.9
Individuals using the Internet (% of population)	0.0	0.0	0.0
Paved roads (% of total)	5.7	6.0	..
High-technology exports (% of manufactured exports)	..	..	..
Global links			
Merchandise trade (% of GDP)	..	..	..
Net barter terms of trade index (2000 = 100)	..	100	86
Total external debt stocks ($ millions)	..	..	..
Total debt service (% of exports)	..	..	..
Net migration (thousands)	0.0	0.0	0.0
Personal remittances received ($ millions)	..	..	..
Foreign direct investment, net inflows ($ millions)	-60.8	3.4	79.0
Net official development assistance received ($ millions)	7.7	73.3	98.1

Korea, Rep.

Population (millions)	50.0	Population growth (%)	0.5
Surface area (1,000 sq. km)	100	Population living below $1.25 a day (%)	..
GNI, Atlas ($ billions)	1,133.8	GNI per capita, Atlas ($)	22,670
GNI, PPP ($ billions)	1,509.0	GNI per capita, PPP ($)	30,180

	1990	2000	2012
People			
Share of poorest 20% in nat'l consumption/income (%)	..	7.9	..
Life expectancy at birth (years)	71	76	81
Total fertility rate (births per woman)	1.6	1.5	1.3
Adolescent fertility rate (births per 1,000 women 15-19)	5	3	2
Contraceptive prevalence (% of married women 15-49)	79	79	80
Births attended by skilled health staff (% of total)	..	100	..
Under-five mortality rate (per 1,000 live births)	7	6	4
Child malnutrition, underweight (% of under age 5)	..	0.9	..
Child immunization, measles (% of ages 12-23 mos.)	93	95	99
Primary completion rate, total (% of relevant age group)	99	104	103
Gross secondary enrollment, total (% of relevant age group)	93	99	97
Ratio of girls to boys in primary & secondary school (%)	98	100	99
HIV prevalence rate (% population of ages 15-49)	..	..	..
Environment			
Forests (1,000 sq. km)	64	63	62
Deforestation (avg. annual %, 1990-2000 and 2000-2010)		0.1	0.1
Freshwater use (% of internal resources)	..	39.3	39.3
Access to improved water source (% total pop.)	..	93	98
Access to improved sanitation facilities (% total pop.)	100	100	100
Energy use per capita (kilograms of oil equivalent)	2,171	4,003	5,260
Carbon dioxide emissions per capita (metric tons)	5.8	9.5	11.5
Electricity use per capita (kilowatt-hours)	2,373	5,907	10,162
Economy			
GDP ($ billions)	264	533	1,130
GDP growth (annual %)	9.2	8.5	2.0
GDP implicit price deflator (annual % growth)	10.5	5.0	1.0
Value added in agriculture (% of GDP)	9	5	3
Value added in industry (% of GDP)	42	38	39
Value added in services (% of GDP)	49	57	58
Exports of goods and services (% of GDP)	28	39	57
Imports of goods and services (% of GDP)	29	36	53
Gross capital formation (% of GDP)	38	31	28
Central government revenue (% of GDP)	16.8	22.3	23.3
Central government cash surplus/deficit (% of GDP)	1.7	4.4	1.8
States and markets			
Starting a business (days)	..	17	6
Stock market capitalization (% of GDP)	42.1	32.2	104.5
Military expenditures (% of GDP)	3.8	2.6	2.8
Mobile cellular subscriptions (per 100 people)	0.2	58.3	109.4
Individuals using the Internet (% of population)	0.0	44.7	84.1
Paved roads (% of total)	71.5	76.0	80.4
High-technology exports (% of manufactured exports)	18	35	26
Global links			
Merchandise trade (% of GDP)	51	62	94
Net barter terms of trade index (2000 = 100)	133	100	62
Total external debt stocks ($ millions)	..	..	..
Total debt service (% of exports)	..	..	..
Net migration (thousands)	-633	-98	300
Personal remittances received ($ billions)	2.4	4.9	8.5
Foreign direct investment, net inflows ($ billions)	0.8	9.3	5.0
Net official development assistance received ($ millions)	52.0	-55.1	..

Kosovo

Population (millions)	1.8	Population growth (%)		0.9
Surface area (1,000 sq. km)	11	Population living below $1.25 a day (%)		..
GNI, Atlas ($ billions)	6.5	GNI per capita, Atlas ($)		3,600
GNI, PPP ($ millions)	..	GNI per capita, PPP ($)		..

	1990	2000	2012
People			
Share of poorest 20% in nat'l consumption/income (%)	..	..	..
Life expectancy at birth (years)	68	68	70
Total fertility rate (births per woman)	3.9	3.0	2.2
Adolescent fertility rate (births per 1,000 women 15-19)	..	..	..
Contraceptive prevalence (% of married women 15-49)	..	..	..
Births attended by skilled health staff (% of total)	..	..	..
Under-five mortality rate (per 1,000 live births)	..	..	..
Child malnutrition, underweight (% of under age 5)	..	..	..
Child immunization, measles (% of ages 12-23 mos.)	..	..	..
Primary completion rate, total (% of relevant age group)	..	..	..
Gross secondary enrollment, total (% of relevant age group)	..	..	..
Ratio of girls to boys in primary & secondary school (%)	..	..	..
HIV prevalence rate (% population of ages 15-49)	..	..	..
Environment			
Forests (sq. km)	..	..	..
Deforestation (avg. annual %, 1990-2000 and 2000-2010)			..
Freshwater use (% of internal resources)	..	..	..
Access to improved water source (% total pop.)	..	..	..
Access to improved sanitation facilities (% total pop.)	..	..	..
Energy use per capita (kilograms of oil equivalent)	..	909	1,411
Carbon dioxide emissions per capita (metric tons)	..	..	..
Electricity use per capita (kilowatt-hours)	..	1,557	2,947
Economy			
GDP ($ millions)	..	1,849	6,445
GDP growth (annual %)	..	27.0	2.7
GDP implicit price deflator (annual % growth)	..	11.4	2.4
Value added in agriculture (% of GDP)	..	..	14
Value added in industry (% of GDP)	..	..	20
Value added in services (% of GDP)	..	..	67
Exports of goods and services (% of GDP)	..	..	18
Imports of goods and services (% of GDP)	..	..	53
Gross capital formation (% of GDP)	..	..	30
Central government revenue (% of GDP)	..	..	..
Central government cash surplus/deficit (% of GDP)	..	..	..
States and markets			
Starting a business (days)	..	..	30
Stock market capitalization (% of GDP)	..	..	..
Military expenditures (% of GDP)	..	..	..
Mobile cellular subscriptions (per 100 people)	..	..	..
Individuals using the Internet (% of population)	..	..	..
Paved roads (% of total)	..	..	26.0
High-technology exports (% of manufactured exports)	..	..	..
Global links			
Merchandise trade (% of GDP)	..	..	..
Net barter terms of trade index (2000 = 100)	..	..	..
Total external debt stocks ($ millions)	0	72	2,002
Total debt service (% of exports)	..	..	8.8
Net migration (thousands)	..	..	..
Personal remittances received ($ millions)	..	..	1,059
Foreign direct investment, net inflows ($ millions)	..	..	293
Net official development assistance received ($ millions)	..	..	568

Kuwait

High income

Population (millions)	3.3	Population growth (%)		3.9
Surface area (1,000 sq. km)	18	Population living below $1.25 a day (%)		..
GNI, Atlas ($ billions)	140.2	GNI per capita, Atlas ($)		44,880
GNI, PPP ($ billions)	149.2	GNI per capita, PPP ($)		47,750

	1990	2000	2012
People			
Share of poorest 20% in nat'l consumption/income (%)	..	..	..
Life expectancy at birth (years)	72	73	74
Total fertility rate (births per woman)	2.4	2.9	2.6
Adolescent fertility rate (births per 1,000 women 15-19)	24	22	14
Contraceptive prevalence (% of married women 15-49)	..	52	..
Births attended by skilled health staff (% of total)	..	100	100
Under-five mortality rate (per 1,000 live births)	16	13	11
Child malnutrition, underweight (% of under age 5)	..	2.2	2.2
Child immunization, measles (% of ages 12-23 mos.)	66	99	99
Primary completion rate, total (% of relevant age group)	57	115	..
Gross secondary enrollment, total (% of relevant age group)	77	114	..
Ratio of girls to boys in primary & secondary school (%)	93	100	..
HIV prevalence rate (% population of ages 15-49)	..	..	..
Environment			
Forests (sq. km)	35	49	64
Deforestation (avg. annual %, 1990-2000 and 2000-2010)		-3.5	-2.6
Freshwater use (% of internal resources)	..		..
Access to improved water source (% total pop.)	99	99	99
Access to improved sanitation facilities (% total pop.)	100	100	100
Energy use per capita (kilograms of oil equivalent)	4,423	9,865	10,408
Carbon dioxide emissions per capita (metric tons)	23.5	28.9	31.3
Electricity use per capita (kilowatt-hours)	8,365	15,091	16,122
Economy			
GDP ($ billions)	18.4	37.7	183.2
GDP growth (annual %)	25.9	4.7	6.2
GDP implicit price deflator (annual % growth)	-1.7	20.5	9.0
Value added in agriculture (% of GDP)	1	0	..
Value added in industry (% of GDP)	52	59	..
Value added in services (% of GDP)	47	40	..
Exports of goods and services (% of GDP)	45	56	71
Imports of goods and services (% of GDP)	58	30	23
Gross capital formation (% of GDP)	18	11	15
Central government revenue (% of GDP)	58.7	48.3	61.7
Central government cash surplus/deficit (% of GDP)	6.1	4.9	27.9
States and markets			
Starting a business (days)	..	35	32
Stock market capitalization (% of GDP)	40.8	55.1	53.0
Military expenditures (% of GDP)	48.7	7.1	3.3
Mobile cellular subscriptions (per 100 people)	1.0	25.0	156.9
Individuals using the Internet (% of population)	0.0	6.7	79.2
Paved roads (% of total)	72.9	80.6	..
High-technology exports (% of manufactured exports)	3	0	1
Global links			
Merchandise trade (% of GDP)	60	71	80
Net barter terms of trade index (2000 = 100)	..	100	228
Total external debt stocks ($ millions)	..	..	..
Total debt service (% of exports)	..	..	..
Net migration (thousands)	-602	200	300
Personal remittances received ($ millions)	..	..	8.3
Foreign direct investment, net inflows ($ millions)	6	16	1,851
Net official development assistance received ($ millions)	12.9		

Kyrgyz Republic

Europe & Central Asia			Low income
Population (millions)	5.6	Population growth (%)	1.7
Surface area (1,000 sq. km)	200	Population living below $1.25 a day (%)	5.0
GNI, Atlas ($ billions)	5.5	GNI per capita, Atlas ($)	990
GNI, PPP ($ billions)	12.4	GNI per capita, PPP ($)	2,220

	1990	2000	2012
People			
Share of poorest 20% in nat'l consumption/income (%)	2.5	8.4	7.7
Life expectancy at birth (years)	68	69	70
Total fertility rate (births per woman)	3.7	2.4	3.1
Adolescent fertility rate (births per 1,000 women 15–19)	61	46	29
Contraceptive prevalence (% of married women 15–49)	..	..	36
Births attended by skilled health staff (% of total)	99	99	99
Under-five mortality rate (per 1,000 live births)	71	50	27
Child malnutrition, underweight (% of under age 5)	..	..	2.7
Child immunization, measles (% of ages 12–23 mos.)	94	98	98
Primary completion rate, total (% of relevant age group)	..	93	98
Gross secondary enrollment, total (% of relevant age group)	102	84	88
Ratio of girls to boys in primary & secondary school (%)	100	101	99
HIV prevalence rate (% population of ages 15–49)	0.1	0.1	0.3
Environment			
Forests (1,000 sq. km)	8.4	8.6	9.7
Deforestation (avg. annual %, 1990–2000 and 2000–2010)		-0.3	-1.1
Freshwater use (% of internal resources)	..	20.6	20.6
Access to improved water source (% total pop.)	73	79	88
Access to improved sanitation facilities (% total pop.)	91	91	92
Energy use per capita (kilograms of oil equivalent)	1,705	473	562
Carbon dioxide emissions per capita (metric tons)	2.4	0.9	1.2
Electricity use per capita (kilowatt-hours)	2,331	1,696	1,642
Economy			
GDP ($ billions)	2.7	1.4	6.5
GDP growth (annual %)	5.7	5.4	-0.9
GDP implicit price deflator (annual % growth)	7.9	27.2	7.4
Value added in agriculture (% of GDP)	34	37	20
Value added in industry (% of GDP)	35	31	26
Value added in services (% of GDP)	31	32	54
Exports of goods and services (% of GDP)	29	42	49
Imports of goods and services (% of GDP)	50	48	100
Gross capital formation (% of GDP)	24	20	32
Central government revenue (% of GDP)	15.5	14.2	23.6
Central government cash surplus/deficit (% of GDP)	..	-2.9	-6.6
States and markets			
Starting a business (days)	..	21	8
Stock market capitalization (% of GDP)	..	0.3	2.5
Military expenditures (% of GDP)	1.6	2.9	3.7
Mobile cellular subscriptions (per 100 people)	0.0	0.2	124.2
Individuals using the Internet (% of population)	0.0	1.0	21.7
Paved roads (% of total)	90.0	91.0	..
High-technology exports (% of manufactured exports)	..	15	5
Global links			
Merchandise trade (% of GDP)	..	77	112
Net barter terms of trade index (2000 = 100)	..	100	108
Total external debt stocks ($ billions)	0.0	1.9	6.0
Total debt service (% of exports)	0.4	30.2	10.9
Net migration (thousands)	-272	-242	-175
Personal remittances received ($ millions)	2	9	2,031
Foreign direct investment, net inflows ($ millions)	10	-2	372
Net official development assistance received ($ millions)	21	215	473

Lao PDR

East Asia & Pacific   **Lower middle income**

Population (millions)	6.6	Population growth (%)	1.9
Surface area (1,000 sq. km)	237	Population living below $1.25 a day (%)	33.9
GNI, Atlas ($ billions)	8.4	GNI per capita, Atlas ($)	1,270
GNI, PPP ($ billions)	17.9	GNI per capita, PPP ($)	2,690

	1990	2000	2012
People			
Share of poorest 20% in nat'l consumption/income (%)	9.3	8.6	7.6
Life expectancy at birth (years)	54	62	68
Total fertility rate (births per woman)	6.2	4.2	3.1
Adolescent fertility rate (births per 1,000 women 15-19)	107	77	65
Contraceptive prevalence (% of married women 15-49)	19	32	50
Births attended by skilled health staff (% of total)	..	19	42
Under-five mortality rate (per 1,000 live births)	163	120	72
Child malnutrition, underweight (% of under age 5)	39.8	36.4	31.6
Child immunization, measles (% of ages 12-23 mos.)	32	42	72
Primary completion rate, total (% of relevant age group)	43	67	95
Gross secondary enrollment, total (% of relevant age group)	23	34	47
Ratio of girls to boys in primary & secondary school (%)	77	81	92
HIV prevalence rate (% population of ages 15-49)	0.1	0.1	0.3
Environment			
Forests (1,000 sq. km)	173	165	157
Deforestation (avg. annual %, 1990-2000 and 2000-2010)		0.5	0.5
Freshwater use (% of internal resources)	..	..	2.2
Access to improved water source (% total pop.)	..	45	72
Access to improved sanitation facilities (% total pop.)	..	28	65
Energy use per capita (kilograms of oil equivalent)	..	..	..
Carbon dioxide emissions per capita (metric tons)	0.06	0.18	0.29
Electricity use per capita (kilowatt-hours)	..	..	..
Economy			
GDP ($ billions)	0.9	1.7	9.4
GDP growth (annual %)	6.7	5.8	8.2
GDP implicit price deflator (annual % growth)	37.9	24.8	4.4
Value added in agriculture (% of GDP)	61	45	28
Value added in industry (% of GDP)	15	17	36
Value added in services (% of GDP)	24	38	36
Exports of goods and services (% of GDP)	11	30	36
Imports of goods and services (% of GDP)	25	44	48
Gross capital formation (% of GDP)	14	14	32
Central government revenue (% of GDP)	..	..	16.5
Central government cash surplus/deficit (% of GDP)	..	..	-0.8
States and markets			
Starting a business (days)	..	153	92
Stock market capitalization (% of GDP)	..	..	..
Military expenditures (% of GDP)	9.0	0.8	0.2
Mobile cellular subscriptions (per 100 people)	0.0	0.2	64.7
Individuals using the Internet (% of population)	0.0	0.1	10.7
Paved roads (% of total)	24.0	14.1	13.7
High-technology exports (% of manufactured exports)	..	..	..
Global links			
Merchandise trade (% of GDP)	31	50	54
Net barter terms of trade index (2000 = 100)	..	100	109
Total external debt stocks ($ billions)	1.8	2.5	6.4
Total debt service (% of exports)	8.5	8.0	8.2
Net migration (thousands)	-45	-173	-75
Personal remittances received ($ millions)	10.9	0.7	58.5
Foreign direct investment, net inflows ($ millions)	6	34	294
Net official development assistance received ($ millions)	149	281	409

Latvia

Population (millions)	2.0	Population growth (%)	-1.2
Surface area (1,000 sq. km)	64	Population living below $1.25 a day (%)	<2
GNI, Atlas ($ billions)	28.6	GNI per capita, Atlas ($)	14,060
GNI, PPP ($ billions)	44.4	GNI per capita, PPP ($)	21,820

	1990	2000	2012
People			
Share of poorest 20% in nat'l consumption/income (%)	9.6	6.9	7.0
Life expectancy at birth (years)	69	70	74
Total fertility rate (births per woman)	2.0	1.2	1.4
Adolescent fertility rate (births per 1,000 women 15-19)	44	19	14
Contraceptive prevalence (% of married women 15-49)	..	..	..
Births attended by skilled health staff (% of total)	100	100	100
Under-five mortality rate (per 1,000 live births)	20	17	9
Child malnutrition, underweight (% of under age 5)	..	..	..
Child immunization, measles (% of ages 12-23 mos.)	95	97	90
Primary completion rate, total (% of relevant age group)	..	96	99
Gross secondary enrollment, total (% of relevant age group)	95	91	99
Ratio of girls to boys in primary & secondary school (%)	101	101	98
HIV prevalence rate (% population of ages 15-49)	..	..	..
Environment			
Forests (1,000 sq. km)	32	32	34
Deforestation (avg. annual %, 1990-2000 and 2000-2010)		-0.2	-0.3
Freshwater use (% of internal resources)	..	2.5	2.5
Access to improved water source (% total pop.)	98	98	98
Access to improved sanitation facilities (% total pop.)	..	79	..
Energy use per capita (kilograms of oil equivalent)	2,949	1,618	2,122
Carbon dioxide emissions per capita (metric tons)	5.2	2.6	3.6
Electricity use per capita (kilowatt-hours)	3,397	2,082	3,264
Economy			
GDP ($ billions)	7.4	7.8	28.4
GDP growth (annual %)	-7.9	6.9	5.0
GDP implicit price deflator (annual % growth)	24.1	4.2	3.5
Value added in agriculture (% of GDP)	22	5	4
Value added in industry (% of GDP)	46	24	22
Value added in services (% of GDP)	32	72	74
Exports of goods and services (% of GDP)	48	42	59
Imports of goods and services (% of GDP)	49	49	63
Gross capital formation (% of GDP)	40	24	26
Central government revenue (% of GDP)	..	26.1	24.8
Central government cash surplus/deficit (% of GDP)	..	-2.2	-2.8
States and markets			
Starting a business (days)	..	16	13
Stock market capitalization (% of GDP)	..	7.2	3.9
Military expenditures (% of GDP)	0.8	0.9	0.9
Mobile cellular subscriptions (per 100 people)	0.0	16.9	112.1
Individuals using the Internet (% of population)	0.0	6.3	74.0
Paved roads (% of total)	..	..	..
High-technology exports (% of manufactured exports)	..	4	10
Global links			
Merchandise trade (% of GDP)	..	65	109
Net barter terms of trade index (2000 = 100)	..	100	103
Total external debt stocks ($ millions)	..	..	..
Total debt service (% of exports)	..	..	..
Net migration (thousands)	-136	-83	-10
Personal remittances received ($ millions)	..	72	730
Foreign direct investment, net inflows ($ millions)	29	413	1,076
Net official development assistance received ($ millions)	..	..	..

Lebanon

Middle East & North Africa		Upper middle income	
Population (millions)	4.4	Population growth (%)	1.0
Surface area (1,000 sq. km)	10	Population living below $1.25 a day (%)	..
GNI, Atlas ($ billions)	40.7	GNI per capita, Atlas ($)	9,190
GNI, PPP ($ billions)	62.7	GNI per capita, PPP ($)	14,160

	1990	2000	2012
People			
Share of poorest 20% in nat'l consumption/income (%)	..	..	..
Life expectancy at birth (years)	70	74	80
Total fertility rate (births per woman)	3.0	2.2	1.5
Adolescent fertility rate (births per 1,000 women 15-19)	44	23	12
Contraceptive prevalence (% of married women 15-49)	..	63	54
Births attended by skilled health staff (% of total)	..	98	..
Under-five mortality rate (per 1,000 live births)	33	20	9
Child malnutrition, underweight (% of under age 5)	..	4.2	..
Child immunization, measles (% of ages 12-23 mos.)	61	71	80
Primary completion rate, total (% of relevant age group)	..	115	86
Gross secondary enrollment, total (% of relevant age group)	69	93	74
Ratio of girls to boys in primary & secondary school (%)	105	104	95
HIV prevalence rate (% population of ages 15-49)	..	..	..
Environment			
Forests (1,000 sq. km)	1.3	1.3	1.4
Deforestation (avg. annual %, 1990-2000 and 2000-2010)		0.0	-0.4
Freshwater use (% of internal resources)	..	29.9	27.3
Access to improved water source (% total pop.)	100	100	100
Access to improved sanitation facilities (% total pop.)	..	98	..
Energy use per capita (kilograms of oil equivalent)	723	1,517	1,449
Carbon dioxide emissions per capita (metric tons)	3.4	4.7	4.7
Electricity use per capita (kilowatt-hours)	518	3,019	3,499
Economy			
GDP ($ billions)	2.8	17.3	42.9
GDP growth (annual %)	26.5	1.3	1.4
GDP implicit price deflator (annual % growth)	15.5	-2.1	5.6
Value added in agriculture (% of GDP)	..	7	6
Value added in industry (% of GDP)	..	23	20
Value added in services (% of GDP)	..	70	73
Exports of goods and services (% of GDP)	18	14	29
Imports of goods and services (% of GDP)	100	36	49
Gross capital formation (% of GDP)	18	20	29
Central government revenue (% of GDP)	..	16.0	20.4
Central government cash surplus/deficit (% of GDP)	..	-18.4	-8.8
States and markets			
Starting a business (days)	..	46	9
Stock market capitalization (% of GDP)	..	9.2	24.0
Military expenditures (% of GDP)	7.6	5.4	4.0
Mobile cellular subscriptions (per 100 people)	0.0	23.0	80.8
Individuals using the Internet (% of population)	0.0	8.0	61.2
Paved roads (% of total)	95.0	84.9	..
High-technology exports (% of manufactured exports)	..	2	2
Global links			
Merchandise trade (% of GDP)	107	40	64
Net barter terms of trade index (2000 = 100)	..	100	98
Total external debt stocks ($ billions)	1.8	10.2	28.9
Total debt service (% of exports)	..	35.6	14.2
Net migration (thousands)	90	550	500
Personal remittances received ($ millions)	..	2,544	6,918
Foreign direct investment, net inflows ($ millions)	..	1,336	3,678
Net official development assistance received ($ millions)	286	200	710

Lesotho

Sub-Saharan Africa		Lower middle income	
Population (millions)	2.1	Population growth (%)	1.1
Surface area (1,000 sq. km)	30	Population living below $1.25 a day (%)	43.4
GNI, Atlas ($ billions)	2.8	GNI per capita, Atlas ($)	1,380
GNI, PPP ($ billions)	4.5	GNI per capita, PPP ($)	2,170

	1990	2000	2012
People			
Share of poorest 20% in nat'l consumption/income (%)	2.6	3.0	..
Life expectancy at birth (years)	59	47	49
Total fertility rate (births per woman)	4.9	4.1	3.1
Adolescent fertility rate (births per 1,000 women 15–19)	83	91	89
Contraceptive prevalence (% of married women 15–49)	23	30	47
Births attended by skilled health staff (% of total)	61	60	62
Under-five mortality rate (per 1,000 live births)	85	114	100
Child malnutrition, underweight (% of under age 5)	13.8	15.0	13.5
Child immunization, measles (% of ages 12–23 mos.)	80	74	85
Primary completion rate, total (% of relevant age group)	60	64	72
Gross secondary enrollment, total (% of relevant age group)	25	32	53
Ratio of girls to boys in primary & secondary school (%)	129	110	107
HIV prevalence rate (% population of ages 15–49)	0.8	22.9	23.1
Environment			
Forests (sq. km)	400	420	442
Deforestation (avg. annual %, 1990–2000 and 2000–2010)		-0.5	-0.5
Freshwater use (% of internal resources)	..	1.0	1.0
Access to improved water source (% total pop.)	78	79	81
Access to improved sanitation facilities (% total pop.)	..	24	30
Energy use per capita (kilograms of oil equivalent)	..	..	..
Carbon dioxide emissions per capita (metric tons)	..	..	0.01
Electricity use per capita (kilowatt-hours)	..	..	..
Economy			
GDP ($ millions)	545	771	2,448
GDP growth (annual %)	5.6	5.1	4.0
GDP implicit price deflator (annual % growth)	12.6	3.9	5.4
Value added in agriculture (% of GDP)	25	12	7
Value added in industry (% of GDP)	34	30	35
Value added in services (% of GDP)	41	58	58
Exports of goods and services (% of GDP)	18	35	47
Imports of goods and services (% of GDP)	122	135	108
Gross capital formation (% of GDP)	56	41	32
Central government revenue (% of GDP)	44.5	49.0	..
Central government cash surplus/deficit (% of GDP)	-0.6	-2.8	..
States and markets			
Starting a business (days)	..	93	29
Stock market capitalization (% of GDP)	..	..	..
Military expenditures (% of GDP)	5.1	4.0	1.9
Mobile cellular subscriptions (per 100 people)	0.0	1.2	75.3
Individuals using the Internet (% of population)	0.0	0.2	4.6
Paved roads (% of total)	18.0	18.0	..
High-technology exports (% of manufactured exports)	..	0	0
Global links			
Merchandise trade (% of GDP)	135	133	151
Net barter terms of trade index (2000 = 100)	100	100	78
Total external debt stocks ($ millions)	396	677	860
Total debt service (% of exports)	4.2	7.5	2.3
Net migration (thousands)	-46.3	-34.5	-20.0
Personal remittances received ($ millions)	428	478	554
Foreign direct investment, net inflows ($ millions)	17	32	198
Net official development assistance received ($ millions)	139	37	283

Liberia

Population (millions)	4.2	Population growth (%)	2.7
Surface area (1,000 sq. km)	111	Population living below $1.25 a day (%)	83.8
GNI, Atlas ($ billions)	1.5	GNI per capita, Atlas ($)	370
GNI, PPP ($ billions)	2.4	GNI per capita, PPP ($)	580

	1990	2000	2012
People			
Share of poorest 20% in nat'l consumption/income (%)	..	..	6.4
Life expectancy at birth (years)	47	52	60
Total fertility rate (births per woman)	6.5	5.9	4.9
Adolescent fertility rate (births per 1,000 women 15–19)	170	149	117
Contraceptive prevalence (% of married women 15–49)	..	10	11
Births attended by skilled health staff (% of total)	..	51	46
Under-five mortality rate (per 1,000 live births)	248	176	75
Child malnutrition, underweight (% of under age 5)	..	22.8	20.4
Child immunization, measles (% of ages 12-23 mos.)	0	63	80
Primary completion rate, total (% of relevant age group)	..	..	65
Gross secondary enrollment, total (% of relevant age group)	..	35	45
Ratio of girls to boys in primary & secondary school (%)	..	73	89
HIV prevalence rate (% population of ages 15–49)	0.3	2.2	0.9
Environment			
Forests (1,000 sq. km)	49	46	43
Deforestation (avg. annual %, 1990–2000 and 2000–2010)		0.6	0.7
Freshwater use (% of internal resources)	..	0.1	0.1
Access to improved water source (% total pop.)	..	61	75
Access to improved sanitation facilities (% total pop.)	..	14	17
Energy use per capita (kilograms of oil equivalent)	..	..	..
Carbon dioxide emissions per capita (metric tons)	0.2	0.2	0.2
Electricity use per capita (kilowatt-hours)	..	..	..
Economy			
GDP ($ millions)	384	529	1,734
GDP growth (annual %)	-51.0	25.7	10.2
GDP implicit price deflator (annual % growth)	-0.2	-6.9	4.1
Value added in agriculture (% of GDP)	54	76	39
Value added in industry (% of GDP)	17	4	16
Value added in services (% of GDP)	29	20	45
Exports of goods and services (% of GDP)	..	26	32
Imports of goods and services (% of GDP)	..	27	90
Gross capital formation (% of GDP)	..	8	25
Central government revenue (% of GDP)	..	..	24.8
Central government cash surplus/deficit (% of GDP)	..	..	-2.6
States and markets			
Starting a business (days)	..	..	5
Stock market capitalization (% of GDP)	..	..	..
Military expenditures (% of GDP)	3.7	0.2	0.8
Mobile cellular subscriptions (per 100 people)	0.0	0.1	57.1
Individuals using the Internet (% of population)	0.0	0.0	3.8
Paved roads (% of total)	5.5	6.0	..
High-technology exports (% of manufactured exports)	..	..	..
Global links			
Merchandise trade (% of GDP)	374	188	88
Net barter terms of trade index (2000 = 100)	..	100	139
Total external debt stocks ($ billions)	2.1	2.8	0.5
Total debt service (% of exports)	..	..	0.2
Net migration (thousands)	-300	-50	-20
Personal remittances received ($ millions)	..	..	360
Foreign direct investment, net inflows ($ millions)	225	21	1,354
Net official development assistance received ($ millions)	114	67	571

Libya

Middle East & North Africa				Upper middle income

Population (millions)	6.2	Population growth (%)		0.8
Surface area (1,000 sq. km)	1,760	Population living below $1.25 a day (%)		..
GNI, Atlas ($ billions)	77.1	GNI per capita, Atlas ($)		12,930
GNI, PPP ($ billions)	103.9	GNI per capita, PPP ($)		17,430

	1990	2000	2012
People			
Share of poorest 20% in nat'l consumption/income (%)	..	..	..
Life expectancy at birth (years)	69	72	75
Total fertility rate (births per woman)	5.0	3.1	2.4
Adolescent fertility rate (births per 1,000 women 15-19)	9	4	3
Contraceptive prevalence (% of married women 15-49)	..	..	..
Births attended by skilled health staff (% of total)	..	99	100
Under-five mortality rate (per 1,000 live births)	43	28	15
Child malnutrition, underweight (% of under age 5)	..	..	5.6
Child immunization, measles (% of ages 12-23 mos.)	89	93	98
Primary completion rate, total (% of relevant age group)	..	..	..
Gross secondary enrollment, total (% of relevant age group)	..	113	..
Ratio of girls to boys in primary & secondary school (%)	..	103	..
HIV prevalence rate (% population of ages 15-49)	..	..	..
Environment			
Forests (1,000 sq. km)	2.2	2.2	2.2
Deforestation (avg. annual %, 1990-2000 and 2000-2010)		0.0	0.0
Freshwater use (% of internal resources)	680.0	618.0	618.0
Access to improved water source (% total pop.)	54	54	..
Access to improved sanitation facilities (% total pop.)	97	97	97
Energy use per capita (kilograms of oil equivalent)	2,622	3,072	2,186
Carbon dioxide emissions per capita (metric tons)	8.6	9.1	9.8
Electricity use per capita (kilowatt-hours)	1,642	2,300	3,926
Economy			
GDP ($ billions)	28.9	33.9	62.4
GDP growth (annual %)	..	3.7	2.1
GDP implicit price deflator (annual % growth)	..	18.4	-32.8
Value added in agriculture (% of GDP)	..	5	..
Value added in industry (% of GDP)	..	66	..
Value added in services (% of GDP)	..	29	..
Exports of goods and services (% of GDP)	40	36	..
Imports of goods and services (% of GDP)	31	15	..
Gross capital formation (% of GDP)	19	13	..
Central government revenue (% of GDP)	..	..	..
Central government cash surplus/deficit (% of GDP)	..	..	..
States and markets			
Starting a business (days)	..	..	35
Stock market capitalization (% of GDP)	..	..	..
Military expenditures (% of GDP)	..	3.2	..
Mobile cellular subscriptions (per 100 people)	0.0	0.8	155.8
Individuals using the Internet (% of population)	0.0	0.2	14.0
Paved roads (% of total)	51.7	57.0	..
High-technology exports (% of manufactured exports)	..	..	..
Global links			
Merchandise trade (% of GDP)	64	50	80
Net barter terms of trade index (2000 = 100)	..	100	201
Total external debt stocks ($ millions)	..	..	..
Total debt service (% of exports)	..	..	..
Net migration (thousands)	4	-75	-239
Personal remittances received ($ millions)	..	9.0	..
Foreign direct investment, net inflows ($ millions)	159	141	1,784
Net official development assistance received ($ millions)	8.3	4.7	87.1

Liechtenstein

Population (thousands)	37	Population growth (%)	0.7
Surface area (sq. km)	160	Population living below $1.25 a day (%)	..
GNI, Atlas ($ billions)	4.9	GNI per capita, Atlas ($)	136,770
GNI, PPP ($ millions)	..	GNI per capita, PPP ($)	..

	1990	2000	2012
People			
Share of poorest 20% in nat'l consumption/income (%)	..	..	..
Life expectancy at birth (years)	..	77	82
Total fertility rate (births per woman)	..	1.6	1.5
Adolescent fertility rate (births per 1,000 women 15-19)	..	..	..
Contraceptive prevalence (% of married women 15-49)	..	..	..
Births attended by skilled health staff (% of total)	..	..	..
Under-five mortality rate (per 1,000 live births)	..	..	..
Child malnutrition, underweight (% of under age 5)	..	..	..
Child immunization, measles (% of ages 12-23 mos.)	..	..	..
Primary completion rate, total (% of relevant age group)	..	90	101
Gross secondary enrollment, total (% of relevant age group)	..	112	111
Ratio of girls to boys in primary & secondary school (%)	..	92	89
HIV prevalence rate (% population of ages 15-49)	..	..	..
Environment			
Forests (sq. km)	65	69	69
Deforestation (avg. annual %, 1990-2000 and 2000-2010)		-0.6	0.0
Freshwater use (% of internal resources)	..	..	..
Access to improved water source (% total pop.)	..	..	..
Access to improved sanitation facilities (% total pop.)	..	..	..
Energy use per capita (kilograms of oil equivalent)	..	..	..
Carbon dioxide emissions per capita (metric tons)	..	..	..
Electricity use per capita (kilowatt-hours)	..	..	..
Economy			
GDP ($ billions)	1.4	2.5	4.8
GDP growth (annual %)	2.3	3.2	-1.2
GDP implicit price deflator (annual % growth)	5.4	1.6	-0.5
Value added in agriculture (% of GDP)	..	..	..
Value added in industry (% of GDP)	..	..	..
Value added in services (% of GDP)	..	..	..
Exports of goods and services (% of GDP)	..	..	..
Imports of goods and services (% of GDP)	..	..	..
Gross capital formation (% of GDP)	..	..	..
Central government revenue (% of GDP)	..	..	..
Central government cash surplus/deficit (% of GDP)	..	..	..
States and markets			
Starting a business (days)	..	..	..
Stock market capitalization (% of GDP)	..	..	..
Military expenditures (% of GDP)	..	..	..
Mobile cellular subscriptions (per 100 people)	0.0	30.2	97.4
Individuals using the Internet (% of population)	0.0	36.5	89.4
Paved roads (% of total)	..	..	..
High-technology exports (% of manufactured exports)	..	..	..
Global links			
Merchandise trade (% of GDP)		..	..
Net barter terms of trade index (2000 = 100)		..	..
Total external debt stocks ($ millions)		..	..
Total debt service (% of exports)		..	..
Net migration (thousands)		..	..
Personal remittances received ($ millions)		..	..
Foreign direct investment, net inflows ($ millions)		..	..
Net official development assistance received ($ millions)		..	..

Lithuania

High income

Population (millions)	3.0	Population growth (%)	-1.3
Surface area (1,000 sq. km)	65	Population living below $1.25 a day (%)	<2
GNI, Atlas ($ billions)	41.3	GNI per capita, Atlas ($)	13,820
GNI, PPP ($ billions)	70.3	GNI per capita, PPP ($)	23,540

	1990	2000	2012
People			
Share of poorest 20% in nat'l consumption/income (%)	8.0	7.9	6.6
Life expectancy at birth (years)	71	72	74
Total fertility rate (births per woman)	2.0	1.4	1.6
Adolescent fertility rate (births per 1,000 women 15-19)	39	25	11
Contraceptive prevalence (% of married women 15-49)	..	..	..
Births attended by skilled health staff (% of total)	100	100	100
Under-five mortality rate (per 1,000 live births)	17	12	5
Child malnutrition, underweight (% of under age 5)	..	..	..
Child immunization, measles (% of ages 12-23 mos.)	89	97	93
Primary completion rate, total (% of relevant age group)	..	98	101
Gross secondary enrollment, total (% of relevant age group)	95	97	107
Ratio of girls to boys in primary & secondary school (%)	96	99	97
HIV prevalence rate (% population of ages 15-49)	..	..	..
Environment			
Forests (1,000 sq. km)	19	20	22
Deforestation (avg. annual %, 1990-2000 and 2000-2010)		-0.4	-0.7
Freshwater use (% of internal resources)	..	17.7	15.3
Access to improved water source (% total pop.)	87	91	96
Access to improved sanitation facilities (% total pop.)	84	89	94
Energy use per capita (kilograms of oil equivalent)	4,344	2,038	2,406
Carbon dioxide emissions per capita (metric tons)	6.0	3.5	4.4
Electricity use per capita (kilowatt-hours)	4,023	2,517	3,530
Economy			
GDP ($ billions)	10.5	11.4	42.3
GDP growth (annual %)	-5.7	3.3	3.7
GDP implicit price deflator (annual % growth)	228.3	0.9	3.1
Value added in agriculture (% of GDP)	27	6	4
Value added in industry (% of GDP)	31	30	28
Value added in services (% of GDP)	42	64	68
Exports of goods and services (% of GDP)	52	45	78
Imports of goods and services (% of GDP)	61	51	79
Gross capital formation (% of GDP)	33	19	19
Central government revenue (% of GDP)	..	25.9	26.3
Central government cash surplus/deficit (% of GDP)	..	-3.9	-5.1
States and markets			
Starting a business (days)	..	26	7
Stock market capitalization (% of GDP)	..	13.9	9.4
Military expenditures (% of GDP)	0.8	1.7	1.0
Mobile cellular subscriptions (per 100 people)	0.0	15.0	165.1
Individuals using the Internet (% of population)	0.0	6.4	68.0
Paved roads (% of total)	..	28.0	30.1
High-technology exports (% of manufactured exports)	0	4	10
Global links			
Merchandise trade (% of GDP)	..	81	146
Net barter terms of trade index (2000 = 100)	..	100	93
Total external debt stocks ($ millions)	..	..	..
Total debt service (% of exports)	..	..	..
Net migration (thousands)	-100	-155	-28
Personal remittances received ($ millions)	0	50	1,508
Foreign direct investment, net inflows ($ millions)	30	379	574
Net official development assistance received ($ millions)	..	..	..

Luxembourg

High income

Population (thousands)	531	Population growth (%)		2.4
Surface area (1,000 sq. km)	2.6	Population living below $1.25 a day (%)		..
GNI, Atlas ($ billions)	38.0	GNI per capita, Atlas ($)		71,640
GNI, PPP ($ billions)	32.4	GNI per capita, PPP ($)		60,950

	1990	2000	2012
People			
Share of poorest 20% in nat'l consumption/income (%)	..	8.4	..
Life expectancy at birth (years)	75	78	81
Total fertility rate (births per woman)	1.6	1.8	1.6
Adolescent fertility rate (births per 1,000 women 15-19)	12	11	8
Contraceptive prevalence (% of married women 15-49)	..	..	..
Births attended by skilled health staff (% of total)	..	100	..
Under-five mortality rate (per 1,000 live births)	9	5	2
Child malnutrition, underweight (% of under age 5)	..	..	..
Child immunization, measles (% of ages 12-23 mos.)	80	91	96
Primary completion rate, total (% of relevant age group)	..	..	84
Gross secondary enrollment, total (% of relevant age group)	69	97	101
Ratio of girls to boys in primary & secondary school (%)	102	103	103
HIV prevalence rate (% population of ages 15-49)	..	..	..
Environment			
Forests (sq. km)	860	868	868
Deforestation (avg. annual %, 1990-2000 and 2000-2010)		-0.1	0.0
Freshwater use (% of internal resources)	5.9	6.0	6.0
Access to improved water source (% total pop.)	100	100	100
Access to improved sanitation facilities (% total pop.)	100	100	100
Energy use per capita (kilograms of oil equivalent)	8,874	7,644	7,684
Carbon dioxide emissions per capita (metric tons)	26.2	18.9	21.4
Electricity use per capita (kilowatt-hours)	13,668	15,668	15,530
Economy			
GDP ($ billions)	12.7	20.3	55.2
GDP growth (annual %)	5.3	8.4	-0.2
GDP implicit price deflator (annual % growth)	2.5	2.0	3.0
Value added in agriculture (% of GDP)	1	1	0
Value added in industry (% of GDP)	27	19	13
Value added in services (% of GDP)	71	80	87
Exports of goods and services (% of GDP)	102	150	177
Imports of goods and services (% of GDP)	88	129	148
Gross capital formation (% of GDP)	24	23	21
Central government revenue (% of GDP)	..	39.8	39.5
Central government cash surplus/deficit (% of GDP)	..	5.5	-0.4
States and markets			
Starting a business (days)	..	..	19
Stock market capitalization (% of GDP)	82.9	167.8	127.5
Military expenditures (% of GDP)	0.8	0.6	0.6
Mobile cellular subscriptions (per 100 people)	0.2	69.5	145.4
Individuals using the Internet (% of population)	0.0	22.9	92.0
Paved roads (% of total)	99.1	100.0	..
High-technology exports (% of manufactured exports)	..	17	8
Global links			
Merchandise trade (% of GDP)	..	97	85
Net barter terms of trade index (2000 = 100)	..	100	76
Total external debt stocks ($ millions)	..	..	..
Total debt service (% of exports)	..	..	..
Net migration (thousands)	20.0	14.5	25.6
Personal remittances received ($ millions)	..	579	1,681
Foreign direct investment, net inflows ($ billions)	..	4.1	27.9
Net official development assistance received ($ millions)	..	..	..

Macao SAR, China

Population (thousands)	557	Population growth (%)		1.9
Surface area (sq. km)	28	Population living below $1.25 a day (%)		..
GNI, Atlas ($ billions)	*30.4*	GNI per capita, Atlas ($)		*55,720*
GNI, PPP ($ billions)	*37.1*	GNI per capita, PPP ($)		*68,000*

	1990	2000	2012
People			
Share of poorest 20% in nat'l consumption/income (%)	..	..	..
Life expectancy at birth (years)	75	78	80
Total fertility rate (births per woman)	1.7	0.9	1.1
Adolescent fertility rate (births per 1,000 women 15–19)	7	5	4
Contraceptive prevalence (% of married women 15–49)	..	..	..
Births attended by skilled health staff (% of total)	..	*100*	..
Under-five mortality rate (per 1,000 live births)	..	..	..
Child malnutrition, underweight (% of under age 5)	..	..	..
Child immunization, measles (% of ages 12–23 mos.)	..	..	..
Primary completion rate, total (% of relevant age group)	97	99	..
Gross secondary enrollment, total (% of relevant age group)	61	83	96
Ratio of girls to boys in primary & secondary school (%)	99	101	..
HIV prevalence rate (% population of ages 15–49)	..	..	..
Environment			
Forests (sq. km)	..	..	..
Deforestation (avg. annual %, 1990–2000 and 2000–2010)		..	..
Freshwater use (% of internal resources)	..	..	..
Access to improved water source (% total pop.)	..	..	..
Access to improved sanitation facilities (% total pop.)	..	..	..
Energy use per capita (kilograms of oil equivalent)	..	..	..
Carbon dioxide emissions per capita (metric tons)	2.9	3.8	*1.9*
Electricity use per capita (kilowatt-hours)	..	..	..
Economy			
GDP ($ billions)	3.0	6.1	43.6
GDP growth (annual %)	8.0	5.7	9.9
GDP implicit price deflator (annual % growth)	11.5	-2.0	7.3
Value added in agriculture (% of GDP)	*0*	0	*0*
Value added in industry (% of GDP)	*21*	15	*6*
Value added in services (% of GDP)	79	85	*94*
Exports of goods and services (% of GDP)	110	100	108
Imports of goods and services (% of GDP)	84	65	50
Gross capital formation (% of GDP)	25	12	15
Central government revenue (% of GDP)	..	19.9	38.6
Central government cash surplus/deficit (% of GDP)	..	1.6	23.8
States and markets			
Starting a business (days)	..	..	..
Stock market capitalization (% of GDP)	..	..	..
Military expenditures (% of GDP)	..	..	..
Mobile cellular subscriptions (per 100 people)	0.6	32.7	289.8
Individuals using the Internet (% of population)	0.0	13.6	64.3
Paved roads (% of total)	100.0	100.0	*100.0*
High-technology exports (% of manufactured exports)	2	1	*0*
Global links			
Merchandise trade (% of GDP)	108	85	23
Net barter terms of trade index (2000 = 100)	..	100	93
Total external debt stocks ($ millions)	..	..	..
Total debt service (% of exports)	..	..	..
Net migration (thousands)	*18.8*	29.9	35.0
Personal remittances received ($ millions)	..	*208*	46
Foreign direct investment, net inflows ($ millions)	0	-1	4,261
Net official development assistance received ($ millions)	0.2	0.3	..

Macedonia, FYR

Europe & Central Asia		Upper middle income	
Population (millions)	2.1	Population growth (%)	0.1
Surface area (1,000 sq. km)	26	Population living below $1.25 a day (%)	<2
GNI, Atlas ($ billions)	9.7	GNI per capita, Atlas ($)	4,620
GNI, PPP ($ billions)	24.3	GNI per capita, PPP ($)	11,540

	1990	2000	2012
People			
Share of poorest 20% in nat'l consumption/income (%)	..	6.5	4.9
Life expectancy at birth (years)	71	73	75
Total fertility rate (births per woman)	2.2	1.7	1.4
Adolescent fertility rate (births per 1,000 women 15-19)	41	29	18
Contraceptive prevalence (% of married women 15-49)	..	..	40
Births attended by skilled health staff (% of total)	89	98	98
Under-five mortality rate (per 1,000 live births)	37	16	7
Child malnutrition, underweight (% of under age 5)	..	1.9	2.1
Child immunization, measles (% of ages 12-23 mos.)	98	97	97
Primary completion rate, total (% of relevant age group)	96	95	94
Gross secondary enrollment, total (% of relevant age group)	74	83	82
Ratio of girls to boys in primary & secondary school (%)	98	97	99
HIV prevalence rate (% population of ages 15-49)	..	..	..
Environment			
Forests (1,000 sq. km)	9	10	10
Deforestation (avg. annual %, 1990-2000 and 2000-2010)		-0.5	-0.4
Freshwater use (% of internal resources)	..	12.9	19.0
Access to improved water source (% total pop.)	99	99	99
Access to improved sanitation facilities (% total pop.)	..	90	91
Energy use per capita (kilograms of oil equivalent)	1,233	1,300	1,484
Carbon dioxide emissions per capita (metric tons)	5.4	5.9	5.2
Electricity use per capita (kilowatt-hours)	2,650	2,871	3,881
Economy			
GDP ($ billions)	4.5	3.6	9.6
GDP growth (annual %)	-6.2	4.5	-0.3
GDP implicit price deflator (annual % growth)	93.7	8.2	0.0
Value added in agriculture (% of GDP)	9	12	11
Value added in industry (% of GDP)	44	34	26
Value added in services (% of GDP)	47	54	63
Exports of goods and services (% of GDP)	26	49	53
Imports of goods and services (% of GDP)	36	64	76
Gross capital formation (% of GDP)	19	22	29
Central government revenue (% of GDP)	..	..	28.2
Central government cash surplus/deficit (% of GDP)	..	..	-4.0
States and markets			
Starting a business (days)	..	48	2
Stock market capitalization (% of GDP)	..	0.2	5.8
Military expenditures (% of GDP)	..	1.9	1.4
Mobile cellular subscriptions (per 100 people)	0.0	5.6	106.2
Individuals using the Internet (% of population)	0.0	2.5	63.1
Paved roads (% of total)	58.9	58.0	58.3
High-technology exports (% of manufactured exports)	..	1	4
Global links			
Merchandise trade (% of GDP)	104	95	109
Net barter terms of trade index (2000 = 100)	..	100	89
Total external debt stocks ($ billions)	1.0	1.5	6.7
Total debt service (% of exports)	..	8.3	15.1
Net migration (thousands)	-130	4	-5
Personal remittances received ($ millions)	..	81	394
Foreign direct investment, net inflows ($ millions)	..	215	283
Net official development assistance received ($ millions)	3	250	149

Madagascar

<table>
<tr><td>Sub-Saharan Africa</td><td></td><td colspan="2" style="text-align:right">Low income</td></tr>
<tr><td>Population (millions)</td><td>22.3</td><td>Population growth (%)</td><td>2.8</td></tr>
<tr><td>Surface area (1,000 sq. km)</td><td>587</td><td>Population living below $1.25 a day (%)</td><td>81.3</td></tr>
<tr><td>GNI, Atlas ($ billions)</td><td>9.7</td><td>GNI per capita, Atlas ($)</td><td>430</td></tr>
<tr><td>GNI, PPP ($ billions)</td><td>20.8</td><td>GNI per capita, PPP ($)</td><td>930</td></tr>
</table>

	1990	2000	2012
People			
Share of poorest 20% in nat'l consumption/income (%)	5.1	4.9	5.4
Life expectancy at birth (years)	51	58	64
Total fertility rate (births per woman)	6.3	5.5	4.5
Adolescent fertility rate (births per 1,000 women 15–19)	150	152	123
Contraceptive prevalence (% of married women 15–49)	17	19	40
Births attended by skilled health staff (% of total)	57	46	44
Under-five mortality rate (per 1,000 live births)	159	109	58
Child malnutrition, underweight (% of under age 5)	35.5	36.8	..
Child immunization, measles (% of ages 12–23 mos.)	47	57	69
Primary completion rate, total (% of relevant age group)	35	36	70
Gross secondary enrollment, total (% of relevant age group)	18	..	38
Ratio of girls to boys in primary & secondary school (%)	96	..	98
HIV prevalence rate (% population of ages 15–49)	0.2	0.7	0.5
Environment			
Forests (1,000 sq. km)	137	131	125
Deforestation (avg. annual %, 1990–2000 and 2000–2010)		0.4	0.4
Freshwater use (% of internal resources)	..	4.4	4.4
Access to improved water source (% total pop.)	29	38	50
Access to improved sanitation facilities (% total pop.)	8	11	14
Energy use per capita (kilograms of oil equivalent)	..	..	..
Carbon dioxide emissions per capita (metric tons)	0.09	0.12	0.10
Electricity use per capita (kilowatt-hours)	..	..	..
Economy			
GDP ($ billions)	3.1	3.9	10.0
GDP growth (annual %)	3.1	4.8	3.1
GDP implicit price deflator (annual % growth)	11.5	7.2	5.8
Value added in agriculture (% of GDP)	29	29	29
Value added in industry (% of GDP)	13	14	16
Value added in services (% of GDP)	59	57	55
Exports of goods and services (% of GDP)	17	31	26
Imports of goods and services (% of GDP)	28	38	37
Gross capital formation (% of GDP)	17	15	33
Central government revenue (% of GDP)	..	11.7	10.3
Central government cash surplus/deficit (% of GDP)	..	-2.0	-1.7
States and markets			
Starting a business (days)	..	67	8
Stock market capitalization (% of GDP)	..	..	..
Military expenditures (% of GDP)	1.2	1.2	0.7
Mobile cellular subscriptions (per 100 people)	0.0	0.4	39.4
Individuals using the Internet (% of population)	0.0	0.2	2.1
Paved roads (% of total)	15.4	12.0	16.3
High-technology exports (% of manufactured exports)	8	1	0
Global links			
Merchandise trade (% of GDP)	31	50	46
Net barter terms of trade index (2000 = 100)	81	100	80
Total external debt stocks ($ billions)	3.7	4.7	2.9
Total debt service (% of exports)	45.9	9.7	2.1
Net migration (thousands)	-7.0	-5.0	-5.0
Personal remittances received ($ millions)	7.9	11.3	..
Foreign direct investment, net inflows ($ millions)	22	83	895
Net official development assistance received ($ millions)	397	320	379

Malawi

Sub-Saharan Africa		Low income

Population (millions)	15.9	Population growth (%)	2.9
Surface area (1,000 sq. km)	118	Population living below $1.25 a day (%)	61.6
GNI, Atlas ($ billions)	5.0	GNI per capita, Atlas ($)	320
GNI, PPP ($ billions)	11.6	GNI per capita, PPP ($)	730

	1990	2000	2012
People			
Share of poorest 20% in nat'l consumption/income (%)	..	7.0	5.6
Life expectancy at birth (years)	47	46	55
Total fertility rate (births per woman)	7.0	6.3	5.5
Adolescent fertility rate (births per 1,000 women 15-19)	156	161	145
Contraceptive prevalence (% of married women 15-49)	13	31	46
Births attended by skilled health staff (% of total)	55	56	71
Under-five mortality rate (per 1,000 live births)	244	174	71
Child malnutrition, underweight (% of under age 5)	24.4	21.5	13.8
Child immunization, measles (% of ages 12-23 mos.)	81	73	90
Primary completion rate, total (% of relevant age group)	28	65	74
Gross secondary enrollment, total (% of relevant age group)	16	32	34
Ratio of girls to boys in primary & secondary school (%)	81	93	101
HIV prevalence rate (% population of ages 15-49)	11.6	15.8	10.8
Environment			
Forests (1,000 sq. km)	39	36	32
Deforestation (avg. annual %, 1990-2000 and 2000-2010)		0.9	1.0
Freshwater use (% of internal resources)	..	6.0	6.0
Access to improved water source (% total pop.)	42	62	85
Access to improved sanitation facilities (% total pop.)	10	10	10
Energy use per capita (kilograms of oil equivalent)	..	..	..
Carbon dioxide emissions per capita (metric tons)	0.06	0.08	0.08
Electricity use per capita (kilowatt-hours)	..	..	..
Economy			
GDP ($ millions)	1,881	1,744	4,264
GDP growth (annual %)	5.7	1.6	1.9
GDP implicit price deflator (annual % growth)	10.7	30.5	18.5
Value added in agriculture (% of GDP)	45	40	30
Value added in industry (% of GDP)	29	18	19
Value added in services (% of GDP)	26	43	50
Exports of goods and services (% of GDP)	24	26	30
Imports of goods and services (% of GDP)	33	35	39
Gross capital formation (% of GDP)	23	14	16
Central government revenue (% of GDP)	..	..	..
Central government cash surplus/deficit (% of GDP)	..	..	..
States and markets			
Starting a business (days)	..	45	40
Stock market capitalization (% of GDP)	..	3.6	17.7
Military expenditures (% of GDP)	1.3	0.7	0.9
Mobile cellular subscriptions (per 100 people)	0.0	0.4	29.2
Individuals using the Internet (% of population)	0.0	0.1	4.4
Paved roads (% of total)	..	45.0	..
High-technology exports (% of manufactured exports)	0	2	3
Global links			
Merchandise trade (% of GDP)	53	52	86
Net barter terms of trade index (2000 = 100)	148	100	96
Total external debt stocks ($ billions)	1.6	2.7	1.3
Total debt service (% of exports)	29.3	13.5	2.0
Net migration (thousands)	-933	-22	0
Personal remittances received ($ millions)	..	0.7	28.3
Foreign direct investment, net inflows ($ millions)	23	26	129
Net official development assistance received ($ millions)	500	446	1,175

Malaysia

East Asia & Pacific		Upper middle income	
Population (millions)	29.2	Population growth (%)	1.7
Surface area (1,000 sq. km)	331	Population living below $1.25 a day (%)	<2
GNI, Atlas ($ billions)	287.0	GNI per capita, Atlas ($)	9,820
GNI, PPP ($ billions)	475.8	GNI per capita, PPP ($)	16,270

	1990	2000	2012
People			
Share of poorest 20% in nat'l consumption/income (%)	5.1	6.5	4.5
Life expectancy at birth (years)	71	73	75
Total fertility rate (births per woman)	3.5	2.8	2.0
Adolescent fertility rate (births per 1,000 women 15-19)	19	14	6
Contraceptive prevalence (% of married women 15-49)	50	49	..
Births attended by skilled health staff (% of total)	93	97	99
Under-five mortality rate (per 1,000 live births)	17	10	9
Child malnutrition, underweight (% of under age 5)	22.1	16.7	12.9
Child immunization, measles (% of ages 12-23 mos.)	70	88	95
Primary completion rate, total (% of relevant age group)	88	95	..
Gross secondary enrollment, total (% of relevant age group)	55	66	67
Ratio of girls to boys in primary & secondary school (%)	102	104	..
HIV prevalence rate (% population of ages 15-49)	0.1	0.4	0.4
Environment			
Forests (1,000 sq. km)	224	216	204
Deforestation (avg. annual %, 1990-2000 and 2000-2010)		0.4	0.5
Freshwater use (% of internal resources)	1.7	1.3	2.3
Access to improved water source (% total pop.)	88	96	100
Access to improved sanitation facilities (% total pop.)	84	92	96
Energy use per capita (kilograms of oil equivalent)	1,183	2,011	2,639
Carbon dioxide emissions per capita (metric tons)	3.1	5.4	7.7
Electricity use per capita (kilowatt-hours)	1,146	2,720	4,246
Economy			
GDP ($ billions)	44	94	305
GDP growth (annual %)	9.0	8.9	5.6
GDP implicit price deflator (annual % growth)	3.8	8.9	0.7
Value added in agriculture (% of GDP)	15	9	10
Value added in industry (% of GDP)	42	48	41
Value added in services (% of GDP)	43	43	49
Exports of goods and services (% of GDP)	74	120	87
Imports of goods and services (% of GDP)	72	101	75
Gross capital formation (% of GDP)	32	27	26
Central government revenue (% of GDP)	..	17.5	22.1
Central government cash surplus/deficit (% of GDP)	..	-4.1	-4.5
States and markets			
Starting a business (days)	..	37	6
Stock market capitalization (% of GDP)	110.4	124.7	156.2
Military expenditures (% of GDP)	2.6	1.6	1.5
Mobile cellular subscriptions (per 100 people)	0.5	21.9	141.3
Individuals using the Internet (% of population)	0.0	21.4	65.8
Paved roads (% of total)	70.0	76.0	80.9
High-technology exports (% of manufactured exports)	38	60	44
Global links			
Merchandise trade (% of GDP)	133	192	139
Net barter terms of trade index (2000 = 100)	103	100	101
Total external debt stocks ($ billions)	15	42	104
Total debt service (% of exports)	12.6	5.6	3.5
Net migration (thousands)	299	491	450
Personal remittances received ($ millions)	185	342	1,320
Foreign direct investment, net inflows ($ billions)	2.3	3.8	9.7
Net official development assistance received ($ millions)	468	46	15

Maldives

South Asia   **Upper middle income**

Population (thousands)	338	Population growth (%)	1.9
Surface area (sq. km)	300	Population living below $1.25 a day (%)	<2
GNI, Atlas ($ billions)	1.9	GNI per capita, Atlas ($)	5,750
GNI, PPP ($ billions)	2.6	GNI per capita, PPP ($)	7,560

	1990	2000	2012
People			
Share of poorest 20% in nat'l consumption/income (%)	..	6.5	..
Life expectancy at birth (years)	61	69	78
Total fertility rate (births per woman)	6.1	3.3	2.3
Adolescent fertility rate (births per 1,000 women 15-19)	136	38	4
Contraceptive prevalence (% of married women 15-49)	29	42	35
Births attended by skilled health staff (% of total)	..	70	95
Under-five mortality rate (per 1,000 live births)	94	45	11
Child malnutrition, underweight (% of under age 5)	..	25.7	17.8
Child immunization, measles (% of ages 12-23 mos.)	96	99	98
Primary completion rate, total (% of relevant age group)	..	184	110
Gross secondary enrollment, total (% of relevant age group)	..	54	..
Ratio of girls to boys in primary & secondary school (%)	..	101	..
HIV prevalence rate (% population of ages 15-49)	0.1	0.1	0.1
Environment			
Forests (sq. km)	9.0	9.0	9.0
Deforestation (avg. annual %, 1990-2000 and 2000-2010)		0.0	0.0
Freshwater use (% of internal resources)	..	11.3	19.7
Access to improved water source (% total pop.)	93	95	99
Access to improved sanitation facilities (% total pop.)	68	79	99
Energy use per capita (kilograms of oil equivalent)	236	..	..
Carbon dioxide emissions per capita (metric tons)	0.7	1.8	3.3
Electricity use per capita (kilowatt-hours)	..	..	..
Economy			
GDP ($ millions)	215	624	2,222
GDP growth (annual %)	..	6.1	3.4
GDP implicit price deflator (annual % growth)	..	1.7	5.0
Value added in agriculture (% of GDP)	..	9	4
Value added in industry (% of GDP)	..	15	21
Value added in services (% of GDP)	..	76	75
Exports of goods and services (% of GDP)	85	89	106
Imports of goods and services (% of GDP)	83	72	107
Gross capital formation (% of GDP)	..	26	..
Central government revenue (% of GDP)	22.1	30.0	27.5
Central government cash surplus/deficit (% of GDP)	-7.5	-5.0	-8.8
States and markets			
Starting a business (days)	..	13	9
Stock market capitalization (% of GDP)	..	..	..
Military expenditures (% of GDP)	..	..	..
Mobile cellular subscriptions (per 100 people)	0.0	2.8	165.6
Individuals using the Internet (% of population)	0.0	2.2	38.9
Paved roads (% of total)	..	..	..
High-technology exports (% of manufactured exports)	..	..	..
Global links			
Merchandise trade (% of GDP)	100	80	84
Net barter terms of trade index (2000 = 100)	..	100	102
Total external debt stocks ($ millions)	78	206	1,027
Total debt service (% of exports)	4.8	4.2	3.8
Net migration (thousands)	-3.1	-0.1	-0.1
Personal remittances received ($ millions)	1.7	2.2	3.1
Foreign direct investment, net inflows ($ millions)	6	22	284
Net official development assistance received ($ millions)	20.9	19.2	58.0

Mali

Population (millions)	14.9	Population growth (%)	3.0
Surface area (1,000 sq. km)	1,240	Population living below $1.25 a day (%)	50.4
GNI, Atlas ($ billions)	9.8	GNI per capita, Atlas ($)	660
GNI, PPP ($ billions)	16.9	GNI per capita, PPP ($)	1,140

	1990	2000	2012
People			
Share of poorest 20% in nat'l consumption/income (%)	..	6.1	8.0
Life expectancy at birth (years)	46	49	55
Total fertility rate (births per woman)	7.1	6.8	6.9
Adolescent fertility rate (births per 1,000 women 15–19)	193	187	176
Contraceptive prevalence (% of married women 15–49)	..	8	10
Births attended by skilled health staff (% of total)	..	41	56
Under-five mortality rate (per 1,000 live births)	253	220	128
Child malnutrition, underweight (% of under age 5)	..	30.1	27.9
Child immunization, measles (% of ages 12–23 mos.)	43	49	59
Primary completion rate, total (% of relevant age group)	10	33	59
Gross secondary enrollment, total (% of relevant age group)	7	19	51
Ratio of girls to boys in primary & secondary school (%)	59	71	83
HIV prevalence rate (% population of ages 15–49)	0.5	1.6	0.9
Environment			
Forests (1,000 sq. km)	141	133	124
Deforestation (avg. annual %, 1990–2000 and 2000–2010)		0.6	0.6
Freshwater use (% of internal resources)	..	10.9	10.9
Access to improved water source (% total pop.)	28	45	67
Access to improved sanitation facilities (% total pop.)	15	18	22
Energy use per capita (kilograms of oil equivalent)	..	..	..
Carbon dioxide emissions per capita (metric tons)	0.05	0.05	0.04
Electricity use per capita (kilowatt-hours)	..	..	..
Economy			
GDP ($ billions)	2.4	2.4	10.4
GDP growth (annual %)	-1.9	3.2	-0.4
GDP implicit price deflator (annual % growth)	4.9	5.6	5.7
Value added in agriculture (% of GDP)	46	42	42
Value added in industry (% of GDP)	16	21	23
Value added in services (% of GDP)	39	38	35
Exports of goods and services (% of GDP)	17	27	31
Imports of goods and services (% of GDP)	34	39	38
Gross capital formation (% of GDP)	23	25	16
Central government revenue (% of GDP)	..	13.4	17.3
Central government cash surplus/deficit (% of GDP)	..	-3.4	-2.5
States and markets			
Starting a business (days)	..	41	11
Stock market capitalization (% of GDP)	..	..	..
Military expenditures (% of GDP)	2.2	1.8	1.4
Mobile cellular subscriptions (per 100 people)	0.0	0.1	98.4
Individuals using the Internet (% of population)	0.0	0.1	2.2
Paved roads (% of total)	10.9	12.0	24.6
High-technology exports (% of manufactured exports)	..	15	1
Global links			
Merchandise trade (% of GDP)	40	56	49
Net barter terms of trade index (2000 = 100)	135	100	172
Total external debt stocks ($ billions)	2.5	3.0	3.1
Total debt service (% of exports)	15.3	14.1	2.4
Net migration (thousands)	-173	-67	-302
Personal remittances received ($ millions)	107	73	473
Foreign direct investment, net inflows ($ millions)	6	82	310
Net official development assistance received ($ millions)	479	288	1,001

Malta

Population (thousands)	419	Population growth (%)	0.8
Surface area (sq. km)	320	Population living below $1.25 a day (%)	..
GNI, Atlas ($ billions)	8.3	GNI per capita, Atlas ($)	19,710
GNI, PPP ($ billions)	11.3	GNI per capita, PPP ($)	26,930

	1990	2000	2012
People			
Share of poorest 20% in nat'l consumption/income (%)	..	..	..
Life expectancy at birth (years)	75	78	81
Total fertility rate (births per woman)	2.0	1.7	1.4
Adolescent fertility rate (births per 1,000 women 15-19)	12	16	18
Contraceptive prevalence (% of married women 15-49)	86	..	..
Births attended by skilled health staff (% of total)	98	..	100
Under-five mortality rate (per 1,000 live births)	11	8	7
Child malnutrition, underweight (% of under age 5)	..	..	..
Child immunization, measles (% of ages 12-23 mos.)	80	74	93
Primary completion rate, total (% of relevant age group)	94	94	92
Gross secondary enrollment, total (% of relevant age group)	82	80	95
Ratio of girls to boys in primary & secondary school (%)	95	100	100
HIV prevalence rate (% population of ages 15-49)	..	..	..
Environment			
Forests (sq. km)	3.0	3.0	3.0
Deforestation (avg. annual %, 1990-2000 and 2000-2010)		0.0	0.0
Freshwater use (% of internal resources)	..	106.7	106.7
Access to improved water source (% total pop.)	100	100	100
Access to improved sanitation facilities (% total pop.)	100	100	100
Energy use per capita (kilograms of oil equivalent)	1,963	1,773	2,060
Carbon dioxide emissions per capita (metric tons)	6.2	5.4	6.2
Electricity use per capita (kilowatt-hours)	2,824	4,410	4,689
Economy			
GDP ($ billions)	2.5	4.0	8.7
GDP growth (annual %)	6.3	6.8	1.0
GDP implicit price deflator (annual % growth)	3.2	4.2	2.3
Value added in agriculture (% of GDP)	3	2	2
Value added in industry (% of GDP)	56	51	33
Value added in services (% of GDP)	41	47	65
Exports of goods and services (% of GDP)	76	91	95
Imports of goods and services (% of GDP)	89	98	90
Gross capital formation (% of GDP)	31	25	12
Central government revenue (% of GDP)	..	84.7	37.2
Central government cash surplus/deficit (% of GDP)	..	-22.3	-2.7
States and markets			
Starting a business (days)	..	..	40
Stock market capitalization (% of GDP)	..	51.7	41.6
Military expenditures (% of GDP)	0.8	0.6	0.6
Mobile cellular subscriptions (per 100 people)	0.0	28.1	127.0
Individuals using the Internet (% of population)	0.0	13.1	70.0
Paved roads (% of total)	..	88.0	87.5
High-technology exports (% of manufactured exports)	45	72	46
Global links			
Merchandise trade (% of GDP)	122	148	116
Net barter terms of trade index (2000 = 100)	..	100	126
Total external debt stocks ($ millions)	..	..	..
Total debt service (% of exports)	..	..	..
Net migration (thousands)	5.8	3.5	4.5
Personal remittances received ($ millions)	58.2	20.0	33.5
Foreign direct investment, net inflows ($ millions)	46	601	599
Net official development assistance received ($ millions)	5.3	21.2	..

Marshall Islands

East Asia & Pacific		Upper middle income	
Population (thousands)	53	Population growth (%)	0.1
Surface area (sq. km)	180	Population living below $1.25 a day (%)	..
GNI, Atlas ($ millions)	212.4	GNI per capita, Atlas ($)	4,040
GNI, PPP ($ millions)	..	GNI per capita, PPP ($)	..

	1990	2000	2012
People			
Share of poorest 20% in nat'l consumption/income (%)	..	1.1	..
Life expectancy at birth (years)	..	65	..
Total fertility rate (births per woman)	..	5.7	..
Adolescent fertility rate (births per 1,000 women 15-19)	..	..	..
Contraceptive prevalence (% of married women 15-49)	..	34	45
Births attended by skilled health staff (% of total)	..	95	99
Under-five mortality rate (per 1,000 live births)	49	41	38
Child malnutrition, underweight (% of under age 5)	..	..	..
Child immunization, measles (% of ages 12-23 mos.)	52	94	78
Primary completion rate, total (% of relevant age group)	..	93	100
Gross secondary enrollment, total (% of relevant age group)	..	68	103
Ratio of girls to boys in primary & secondary school (%)	..	102	101
HIV prevalence rate (% population of ages 15-49)	..	..	..
Environment			
Forests (sq. km)	130	126	126
Deforestation (avg. annual %, 1990-2000 and 2000-2010)		0.0	0.0
Freshwater use (% of internal resources)	..	..	..
Access to improved water source (% total pop.)	92	93	95
Access to improved sanitation facilities (% total pop.)	65	70	76
Energy use per capita (kilograms of oil equivalent)	..	..	..
Carbon dioxide emissions per capita (metric tons)	1.0	1.5	2.0
Electricity use per capita (kilowatt-hours)	..	..	..
Economy			
GDP ($ millions)	78.5	110.9	182.4
GDP growth (annual %)	2.7	5.9	1.9
GDP implicit price deflator (annual % growth)	5.0	-3.0	4.9
Value added in agriculture (% of GDP)	..	..	..
Value added in industry (% of GDP)	..	..	..
Value added in services (% of GDP)	..	..	..
Exports of goods and services (% of GDP)	..	..	..
Imports of goods and services (% of GDP)	..	..	..
Gross capital formation (% of GDP)	..	..	..
Central government revenue (% of GDP)	..	..	..
Central government cash surplus/deficit (% of GDP)	..	..	..
States and markets			
Starting a business (days)	..	17	17
Stock market capitalization (% of GDP)	..	..	..
Military expenditures (% of GDP)	..	..	..
Mobile cellular subscriptions (per 100 people)	0.0	0.9	..
Individuals using the Internet (% of population)	0.0	1.5	10.0
Paved roads (% of total)	..	..	..
High-technology exports (% of manufactured exports)	..	..	..
Global links			
Merchandise trade (% of GDP)	..	58	96
Net barter terms of trade index (2000 = 100)	..	100	106
Total external debt stocks ($ millions)	..	..	..
Total debt service (% of exports)	..	..	..
Net migration (thousands)	..	..	..
Personal remittances received ($ millions)	..	..	..
Foreign direct investment, net inflows ($ millions)	1	126	38
Net official development assistance received ($ millions)	0.3	57.2	76.0

Mauritania

Sub-Saharan Africa   **Lower middle income**

Population (millions)	3.8	Population growth (%)	2.5
Surface area (1,000 sq. km)	1,031	Population living below $1.25 a day (%)	23.4
GNI, Atlas ($ billions)	4.2	GNI per capita, Atlas ($)	1,110
GNI, PPP ($ billions)	9.4	GNI per capita, PPP ($)	2,480

	1990	2000	2012
People			
Share of poorest 20% in nat'l consumption/income (%)	5.2	6.2	6.0
Life expectancy at birth (years)	58	60	61
Total fertility rate (births per woman)	6.0	5.4	4.7
Adolescent fertility rate (births per 1,000 women 15–19)	109	96	73
Contraceptive prevalence (% of married women 15–49)	4	8	9
Births attended by skilled health staff (% of total)	40	57	65
Under-five mortality rate (per 1,000 live births)	128	111	84
Child malnutrition, underweight (% of under age 5)	43.3	30.4	19.5
Child immunization, measles (% of ages 12–23 mos.)	38	46	75
Primary completion rate, total (% of relevant age group)	29	45	69
Gross secondary enrollment, total (% of relevant age group)	13	18	27
Ratio of girls to boys in primary & secondary school (%)	67	93	101
HIV prevalence rate (% population of ages 15–49)	0.1	0.6	0.4
Environment			
Forests (1,000 sq. km)	4.2	3.2	2.4
Deforestation (avg. annual %, 1990-2000 and 2000-2010)		2.7	2.7
Freshwater use (% of internal resources)	..	400.3	400.3
Access to improved water source (% total pop.)	30	40	50
Access to improved sanitation facilities (% total pop.)	16	21	27
Energy use per capita (kilograms of oil equivalent)	..	..	..
Carbon dioxide emissions per capita (metric tons)	1.3	0.5	0.6
Electricity use per capita (kilowatt-hours)	..	..	..
Economy			
GDP ($ millions)	1,020	1,294	4,199
GDP growth (annual %)	-1.8	-0.4	7.6
GDP implicit price deflator (annual % growth)	2.6	5.4	-3.6
Value added in agriculture (% of GDP)	30	37	17
Value added in industry (% of GDP)	29	28	46
Value added in services (% of GDP)	42	35	37
Exports of goods and services (% of GDP)	46	30	58
Imports of goods and services (% of GDP)	61	45	94
Gross capital formation (% of GDP)	20	21	37
Central government revenue (% of GDP)	..	..	..
Central government cash surplus/deficit (% of GDP)	..	..	..
States and markets			
Starting a business (days)	..	82	19
Stock market capitalization (% of GDP)	..	..	..
Military expenditures (% of GDP)	3.9	2.9	3.8
Mobile cellular subscriptions (per 100 people)	0.0	0.6	106.0
Individuals using the Internet (% of population)	0.0	0.2	5.4
Paved roads (% of total)	..	29.0	34.6
High-technology exports (% of manufactured exports)	..	..	..
Global links			
Merchandise trade (% of GDP)	84	63	126
Net barter terms of trade index (2000 = 100)	97	100	153
Total external debt stocks ($ billions)	2.1	2.4	3.3
Total debt service (% of exports)	30.7	27.8	4.9
Net migration (thousands)	-14.7	30.0	-20.0
Personal remittances received ($ millions)	13.7	2.2	..
Foreign direct investment, net inflows ($ millions)	7	40	1,204
Net official development assistance received ($ millions)	236	223	408

Mauritius

Sub-Saharan Africa		Upper middle income	
Population (millions)	1.3	Population growth (%)	0.4
Surface area (1,000 sq. km)	2.0	Population living below $1.25 a day (%)	..
GNI, Atlas ($ billions)	11.1	GNI per capita, Atlas ($)	8,570
GNI, PPP ($ billions)	19.5	GNI per capita, PPP ($)	15,060

	1990	2000	2012
People			
Share of poorest 20% in nat'l consumption/income (%)	..	..	..
Life expectancy at birth (years)	69	72	74
Total fertility rate (births per woman)	2.3	2.0	1.4
Adolescent fertility rate (births per 1,000 women 15-19)	43	36	31
Contraceptive prevalence (% of married women 15-49)	75	76	..
Births attended by skilled health staff (% of total)	91	99	..
Under-five mortality rate (per 1,000 live births)	23	19	15
Child malnutrition, underweight (% of under age 5)	..	..	..
Child immunization, measles (% of ages 12-23 mos.)	76	84	99
Primary completion rate, total (% of relevant age group)	114	103	99
Gross secondary enrollment, total (% of relevant age group)	52	77	96
Ratio of girls to boys in primary & secondary school (%)	100	98	102
HIV prevalence rate (% population of ages 15-49)	0.1	0.9	1.2
Environment			
Forests (sq. km)	388	387	350
Deforestation (avg. annual %, 1990-2000 and 2000-2010)		0.0	1.0
Freshwater use (% of internal resources)	20.6	22.2	26.4
Access to improved water source (% total pop.)	99	99	100
Access to improved sanitation facilities (% total pop.)	89	89	91
Energy use per capita (kilograms of oil equivalent)	453	..	..
Carbon dioxide emissions per capita (metric tons)	1.4	2.3	3.2
Electricity use per capita (kilowatt-hours)	..	..	..
Economy			
GDP ($ billions)	2.7	4.6	10.5
GDP growth (annual %)	7.2	9.0	3.2
GDP implicit price deflator (annual % growth)	10.1	2.1	3.2
Value added in agriculture (% of GDP)	13	7	3
Value added in industry (% of GDP)	33	31	25
Value added in services (% of GDP)	54	62	72
Exports of goods and services (% of GDP)	65	61	55
Imports of goods and services (% of GDP)	72	62	67
Gross capital formation (% of GDP)	30	26	25
Central government revenue (% of GDP)	..	..	22.4
Central government cash surplus/deficit (% of GDP)	..	..	-1.1
States and markets			
Starting a business (days)	..	..	6
Stock market capitalization (% of GDP)	10.1	29.0	67.6
Military expenditures (% of GDP)	0.3	0.2	0.2
Mobile cellular subscriptions (per 100 people)	0.2	15.2	119.9
Individuals using the Internet (% of population)	0.0	7.3	41.4
Paved roads (% of total)	93.0	97.0	98.1
High-technology exports (% of manufactured exports)	1	1	1
Global links			
Merchandise trade (% of GDP)	106	80	75
Net barter terms of trade index (2000 = 100)	93	100	71
Total external debt stocks ($ millions)	932	967	4,459
Total debt service (% of exports)	8.5	17.0	2.4
Net migration (thousands)	-5.6	-28.6	0.0
Personal remittances received ($ millions)	..	177	1
Foreign direct investment, net inflows ($ millions)	41	266	361
Net official development assistance received ($ millions)	88	20	178

Mexico

Latin America & Caribbean   **Upper middle income**

Population (millions)	120.8	Population growth (%)	1.2
Surface area (1,000 sq. km)	1,964	Population living below $1.25 a day (%)	<2
GNI, Atlas ($ billions)	1,165.1	GNI per capita, Atlas ($)	9,640
GNI, PPP ($ billions)	1,951.1	GNI per capita, PPP ($)	16,140

	1990	2000	2012
People			
Share of poorest 20% in nat'l consumption/income (%)	6.4	4.0	4.9
Life expectancy at birth (years)	71	74	77
Total fertility rate (births per woman)	3.4	2.7	2.2
Adolescent fertility rate (births per 1,000 women 15–19)	81	77	63
Contraceptive prevalence (% of married women 15–49)	63	70	73
Births attended by skilled health staff (% of total)	84	95	96
Under-five mortality rate (per 1,000 live births)	46	25	16
Child malnutrition, underweight (% of under age 5)	13.9	6.0	2.8
Child immunization, measles (% of ages 12–23 mos.)	75	96	99
Primary completion rate, total (% of relevant age group)	87	95	93
Gross secondary enrollment, total (% of relevant age group)	53	70	84
Ratio of girls to boys in primary & secondary school (%)	97	97	103
HIV prevalence rate (% population of ages 15–49)	0.4	0.4	0.2
Environment			
Forests (1,000 sq. km)	703	668	646
Deforestation (avg. annual %, 1990–2000 and 2000–2010)		0.5	0.3
Freshwater use (% of internal resources)	..	17.8	19.5
Access to improved water source (% total pop.)	82	89	95
Access to improved sanitation facilities (% total pop.)	66	75	85
Energy use per capita (kilograms of oil equivalent)	1,423	1,400	1,588
Carbon dioxide emissions per capita (metric tons)	3.7	3.7	3.8
Electricity use per capita (kilowatt-hours)	1,156	1,700	2,092
Economy			
GDP ($ billions)	263	692	1,178
GDP growth (annual %)	5.1	5.3	3.8
GDP implicit price deflator (annual % growth)	28.1	10.8	3.6
Value added in agriculture (% of GDP)	8	3	4
Value added in industry (% of GDP)	28	36	36
Value added in services (% of GDP)	64	61	61
Exports of goods and services (% of GDP)	19	26	33
Imports of goods and services (% of GDP)	20	27	34
Gross capital formation (% of GDP)	23	22	23
Central government revenue (% of GDP)	15.3	12.4	..
Central government cash surplus/deficit (% of GDP)	-2.5	-1.0	..
States and markets			
Starting a business (days)	..	58	6
Stock market capitalization (% of GDP)	12.4	18.1	44.6
Military expenditures (% of GDP)	0.5	0.5	0.6
Mobile cellular subscriptions (per 100 people)	0.1	13.6	83.4
Individuals using the Internet (% of population)	0.0	5.1	38.4
Paved roads (% of total)	35.1	34.0	37.8
High-technology exports (% of manufactured exports)	8	22	16
Global links			
Merchandise trade (% of GDP)	32	50	64
Net barter terms of trade index (2000 = 100)	102	100	109
Total external debt stocks ($ billions)	105	152	355
Total debt service (% of exports)	21.8	31.6	17.7
Net migration (thousands)	-796	-2,929	-1,200
Personal remittances received ($ billions)	3.1	7.5	23.4
Foreign direct investment, net inflows ($ billions)	2.5	18.1	15.5
Net official development assistance received ($ millions)	156	-58	418

Micronesia, Fed. Sts.

East Asia & Pacific		**Lower middle income**	
Population (thousands)	103	Population growth (%)	0.0
Surface area (sq. km)	700	Population living below $1.25 a day (%)	31.2
GNI, Atlas ($ millions)	333.6	GNI per capita, Atlas ($)	3,230
GNI, PPP ($ millions)	405.6	GNI per capita, PPP ($)	3,920

	1990	2000	2012
People			
Share of poorest 20% in nat'l consumption/income (%)	..	1.6	..
Life expectancy at birth (years)	66	67	69
Total fertility rate (births per woman)	5.0	4.3	3.3
Adolescent fertility rate (births per 1,000 women 15-19)	50	38	19
Contraceptive prevalence (% of married women 15-49)	..	23	55
Births attended by skilled health staff (% of total)	..	88	100
Under-five mortality rate (per 1,000 live births)	55	54	39
Child malnutrition, underweight (% of under age 5)	..	..	..
Child immunization, measles (% of ages 12-23 mos.)	81	85	91
Primary completion rate, total (% of relevant age group)	..	..	..
Gross secondary enrollment, total (% of relevant age group)	..	..	..
Ratio of girls to boys in primary & secondary school (%)	..	..	..
HIV prevalence rate (% population of ages 15-49)	..	..	..
Environment			
Forests (sq. km)	..	639	642
Deforestation (avg. annual %, 1990-2000 and 2000-2010)		0.0	0.0
Freshwater use (% of internal resources)	..	..	..
Access to improved water source (% total pop.)	91	90	89
Access to improved sanitation facilities (% total pop.)	19	34	57
Energy use per capita (kilograms of oil equivalent)	..	..	..
Carbon dioxide emissions per capita (metric tons)	..	1.3	1.0
Electricity use per capita (kilowatt-hours)	..	..	..
Economy			
GDP ($ millions)	147	233	326
GDP growth (annual %)	3.7	4.6	0.4
GDP implicit price deflator (annual % growth)	4.9	1.1	4.7
Value added in agriculture (% of GDP)	..	26	28
Value added in industry (% of GDP)	..	9	9
Value added in services (% of GDP)	..	65	63
Exports of goods and services (% of GDP)	..	..	..
Imports of goods and services (% of GDP)	..	..	..
Gross capital formation (% of GDP)	..	..	..
Central government revenue (% of GDP)	..	..	..
Central government cash surplus/deficit (% of GDP)	..	..	..
States and markets			
Starting a business (days)	..	16	16
Stock market capitalization (% of GDP)	..	..	..
Military expenditures (% of GDP)	..	..	..
Mobile cellular subscriptions (per 100 people)	0.0	0.0	30.2
Individuals using the Internet (% of population)	0.0	3.7	26.0
Paved roads (% of total)	15.9	18.0	..
High-technology exports (% of manufactured exports)	..	..	..
Global links			
Merchandise trade (% of GDP)	..	55	75
Net barter terms of trade index (2000 = 100)	..	100	98
Total external debt stocks ($ millions)	..	..	..
Total debt service (% of exports)	..	..	..
Net migration (thousands)	-2.2	-12.9	-8.2
Personal remittances received ($ millions)	..	..	..
Foreign direct investment, net inflows ($ millions)	..	-0.2	0.8
Net official development assistance received ($ millions)	0	102	115

Moldova

Population (millions)	3.6	Population growth (%)		0.0
Surface area (1,000 sq. km)	34	Population living below $1.25 a day (%)		<2
GNI, Atlas ($ billions)	7.4	GNI per capita, Atlas ($)		2,070
GNI, PPP ($ billions)	12.9	GNI per capita, PPP ($)		3,630

	1990	2000	2012
People			
Share of poorest 20% in nat'l consumption/income (%)	6.9	6.7	7.8
Life expectancy at birth (years)	67	67	69
Total fertility rate (births per woman)	2.4	1.6	1.5
Adolescent fertility rate (births per 1,000 women 15-19)	57	46	29
Contraceptive prevalence (% of married women 15-49)	..	62	..
Births attended by skilled health staff (% of total)	100	98	99
Under-five mortality rate (per 1,000 live births)	32	30	18
Child malnutrition, underweight (% of under age 5)	..	..	..
Child immunization, measles (% of ages 12-23 mos.)	73	89	91
Primary completion rate, total (% of relevant age group)	..	98	90
Gross secondary enrollment, total (% of relevant age group)	94	82	75
Ratio of girls to boys in primary & secondary school (%)	105	101	101
HIV prevalence rate (% population of ages 15-49)	0.1	0.5	0.7
Environment			
Forests (1,000 sq. km)	3.2	3.2	3.9
Deforestation (avg. annual %, 1990-2000 and 2000-2010)		-0.2	-1.8
Freshwater use (% of internal resources)	296.3	191.5	191.5
Access to improved water source (% total pop.)	..	93	97
Access to improved sanitation facilities (% total pop.)	..	79	87
Energy use per capita (kilograms of oil equivalent)	2,677	792	936
Carbon dioxide emissions per capita (metric tons)	5.7	1.0	1.4
Electricity use per capita (kilowatt-hours)	3,235	1,638	1,470
Economy			
GDP ($ billions)	3.6	1.3	7.3
GDP growth (annual %)	-2.4	2.1	-0.8
GDP implicit price deflator (annual % growth)	13.5	27.3	7.5
Value added in agriculture (% of GDP)	36	29	13
Value added in industry (% of GDP)	37	22	17
Value added in services (% of GDP)	27	49	70
Exports of goods and services (% of GDP)	48	50	44
Imports of goods and services (% of GDP)	51	75	84
Gross capital formation (% of GDP)	25	24	23
Central government revenue (% of GDP)	..	24.5	30.7
Central government cash surplus/deficit (% of GDP)	..	-1.5	-1.8
States and markets			
Starting a business (days)	..	42	7
Stock market capitalization (% of GDP)	..	3.2	..
Military expenditures (% of GDP)	0.5	0.4	0.3
Mobile cellular subscriptions (per 100 people)	0.0	3.4	102.0
Individuals using the Internet (% of population)	0.0	1.3	43.4
Paved roads (% of total)	87.1	86.0	86.2
High-technology exports (% of manufactured exports)	..	3	5
Global links			
Merchandise trade (% of GDP)	..	97	102
Net barter terms of trade index (2000 = 100)	..	100	101
Total external debt stocks ($ billions)	0.0	1.8	6.1
Total debt service (% of exports)	..	20.0	15.1
Net migration (thousands)	-132	-317	-103
Personal remittances received ($ millions)	..	179	1,786
Foreign direct investment, net inflows ($ millions)	17	128	185
Net official development assistance received ($ millions)	..	123	473

Monaco

High income

Population (thousands)	38	Population growth (%)	0.8
Surface area (sq. km)	2.0	Population living below $1.25 a day (%)	..
GNI, Atlas ($ billions)	..	GNI per capita, Atlas ($)	..
GNI, PPP ($ millions)	..	GNI per capita, PPP ($)	..

	1990	2000	2012
People			
Share of poorest 20% in nat'l consumption/income (%)	..	..	..
Life expectancy at birth (years)	..	..	..
Total fertility rate (births per woman)	..	..	..
Adolescent fertility rate (births per 1,000 women 15-19)	..	..	..
Contraceptive prevalence (% of married women 15-49)	..	..	..
Births attended by skilled health staff (% of total)	..	..	..
Under-five mortality rate (per 1,000 live births)	8	5	4
Child malnutrition, underweight (% of under age 5)	..	..	..
Child immunization, measles (% of ages 12-23 mos.)	99	99	99
Primary completion rate, total (% of relevant age group)	..	..	..
Gross secondary enrollment, total (% of relevant age group)	..	..	..
Ratio of girls to boys in primary & secondary school (%)	..	..	..
HIV prevalence rate (% population of ages 15-49)	..	..	..
Environment			
Forests (sq. km)	0.0	0.0	0.0
Deforestation (avg. annual %, 1990-2000 and 2000-2010)		0.0	0.0
Freshwater use (% of internal resources)	..	..	..
Access to improved water source (% total pop.)	100	100	100
Access to improved sanitation facilities (% total pop.)	100	100	100
Energy use per capita (kilograms of oil equivalent)	..	..	..
Carbon dioxide emissions per capita (metric tons)	..	..	..
Electricity use per capita (kilowatt-hours)	..	..	..
Economy			
GDP ($ billions)	2.5	2.6	6.1
GDP growth (annual %)	2.6	3.9	..
GDP implicit price deflator (annual % growth)	2.6	1.4	..
Value added in agriculture (% of GDP)	..	..	..
Value added in industry (% of GDP)	..	..	..
Value added in services (% of GDP)	..	..	..
Exports of goods and services (% of GDP)	..	..	..
Imports of goods and services (% of GDP)	..	..	..
Gross capital formation (% of GDP)	..	..	..
Central government revenue (% of GDP)	..	..	..
Central government cash surplus/deficit (% of GDP)	..	..	..
States and markets			
Starting a business (days)	..	..	..
Stock market capitalization (% of GDP)	..	..	..
Military expenditures (% of GDP)	..	..	..
Mobile cellular subscriptions (per 100 people)	0.0	43.4	88.3
Individuals using the Internet (% of population)	0.0	42.2	87.0
Paved roads (% of total)	100.0	100.0	100.0
High-technology exports (% of manufactured exports)	..	..	..
Global links			
Merchandise trade (% of GDP)	..	..	..
Net barter terms of trade index (2000 = 100)	..	..	..
Total external debt stocks ($ millions)	..	..	..
Total debt service (% of exports)	..	..	..
Net migration (thousands)	..	..	..
Personal remittances received ($ millions)	..	..	..
Foreign direct investment, net inflows ($ millions)	..	..	..
Net official development assistance received ($ millions)	..	..	..

Mongolia

Lower middle income

Population (millions)	2.8	Population growth (%)	1.5
Surface area (1,000 sq. km)	1,564	Population living below $1.25 a day (%)	..
GNI, Atlas ($ billions)	8.8	GNI per capita, Atlas ($)	3,160
GNI, PPP ($ billions)	14.0	GNI per capita, PPP ($)	5,020

	1990	2000	2012
People			
Share of poorest 20% in nat'l consumption/income (%)	..	7.5	7.1
Life expectancy at birth (years)	60	63	67
Total fertility rate (births per woman)	4.1	2.1	2.4
Adolescent fertility rate (births per 1,000 women 15-19)	37	26	19
Contraceptive prevalence (% of married women 15-49)	..	67	55
Births attended by skilled health staff (% of total)	..	97	99
Under-five mortality rate (per 1,000 live births)	107	63	28
Child malnutrition, underweight (% of under age 5)	10.8	11.6	..
Child immunization, measles (% of ages 12-23 mos.)	92	92	99
Primary completion rate, total (% of relevant age group)	..	87	130
Gross secondary enrollment, total (% of relevant age group)	89	65	103
Ratio of girls to boys in primary & secondary school (%)	106	112	100
HIV prevalence rate (% population of ages 15-49)	0.1	0.1	0.1
Environment			
Forests (1,000 sq. km)	125	117	108
Deforestation (avg. annual %, 1990-2000 and 2000-2010)		0.7	0.7
Freshwater use (% of internal resources)	..	1.2	1.2
Access to improved water source (% total pop.)	62	68	85
Access to improved sanitation facilities (% total pop.)	..	49	56
Energy use per capita (kilograms of oil equivalent)	1,560	1,000	1,310
Carbon dioxide emissions per capita (metric tons)	4.6	3.1	4.2
Electricity use per capita (kilowatt-hours)	1,546	1,076	1,577
Economy			
GDP ($ billions)	2.6	1.1	10.3
GDP growth (annual %)	-3.2	1.1	12.3
GDP implicit price deflator (annual % growth)	23.2	12.0	12.0
Value added in agriculture (% of GDP)	13	31	17
Value added in industry (% of GDP)	42	25	33
Value added in services (% of GDP)	45	44	50
Exports of goods and services (% of GDP)	18	54	51
Imports of goods and services (% of GDP)	40	68	77
Gross capital formation (% of GDP)	29	29	63
Central government revenue (% of GDP)	15.4	24.4	30.7
Central government cash surplus/deficit (% of GDP)	-0.5	0.2	-8.5
States and markets			
Starting a business (days)	..	20	11
Stock market capitalization (% of GDP)	..	3.2	12.6
Military expenditures (% of GDP)	4.6	2.1	1.1
Mobile cellular subscriptions (per 100 people)	0.0	6.4	120.7
Individuals using the Internet (% of population)	0.0	1.3	16.4
Paved roads (% of total)	..	4.0	..
High-technology exports (% of manufactured exports)	..	0	..
Global links			
Merchandise trade (% of GDP)	62	101	108
Net barter terms of trade index (2000 = 100)	..	100	206
Total external debt stocks ($ millions)	355	960	5,080
Total debt service (% of exports)	17.3	6.6	4.5
Net migration (thousands)	-88.4	-15.0	-15.0
Personal remittances received ($ millions)	..	12	320
Foreign direct investment, net inflows ($ millions)	11	54	4,452
Net official development assistance received ($ millions)	13	217	449

Montenegro

Europe & Central Asia		Upper middle income	
Population (thousands)	621	Population growth (%)	0.1
Surface area (1,000 sq. km)	14	Population living below $1.25 a day (%)	<2
GNI, Atlas ($ billions)	4.5	GNI per capita, Atlas ($)	7,220
GNI, PPP ($ billions)	9.1	GNI per capita, PPP ($)	14,590

	1990	2000	2012
People			
Share of poorest 20% in nat'l consumption/income (%)	..	..	8.8
Life expectancy at birth (years)	74	74	75
Total fertility rate (births per woman)	1.9	1.8	1.7
Adolescent fertility rate (births per 1,000 women 15-19)	26	22	15
Contraceptive prevalence (% of married women 15-49)	..	53	39
Births attended by skilled health staff (% of total)	..	99	100
Under-five mortality rate (per 1,000 live births)	17	14	6
Child malnutrition, underweight (% of under age 5)	..	..	..
Child immunization, measles (% of ages 12-23 mos.)	..	..	90
Primary completion rate, total (% of relevant age group)	..	..	101
Gross secondary enrollment, total (% of relevant age group)	..	93	91
Ratio of girls to boys in primary & secondary school (%)	..	100	101
HIV prevalence rate (% population of ages 15-49)	..	..	..
Environment			
Forests (1,000 sq. km)	5.4	5.4	5.4
Deforestation (avg. annual %, 1990-2000 and 2000-2010)		0.0	0.0
Freshwater use (% of internal resources)	..	..	..
Access to improved water source (% total pop.)	97	98	98
Access to improved sanitation facilities (% total pop.)	..	90	90
Energy use per capita (kilograms of oil equivalent)	..	..	1,900
Carbon dioxide emissions per capita (metric tons)	..	..	4.2
Electricity use per capita (kilowatt-hours)	..	..	5,747
Economy			
GDP ($ millions)	..	984	4,373
GDP growth (annual %)	..	3.1	-0.5
GDP implicit price deflator (annual % growth)	..	20.2	1.9
Value added in agriculture (% of GDP)	..	12	10
Value added in industry (% of GDP)	..	23	20
Value added in services (% of GDP)	..	64	70
Exports of goods and services (% of GDP)	..	37	42
Imports of goods and services (% of GDP)	..	51	66
Gross capital formation (% of GDP)	..	22	18
Central government revenue (% of GDP)	..	..	..
Central government cash surplus/deficit (% of GDP)	..	..	..
States and markets			
Starting a business (days)	..	..	10
Stock market capitalization (% of GDP)	..	..	87.5
Military expenditures (% of GDP)	..	..	1.9
Mobile cellular subscriptions (per 100 people)	..	..	181.3
Individuals using the Internet (% of population)	..	..	56.8
Paved roads (% of total)	..	63.0	70.4
High-technology exports (% of manufactured exports)	..	..	
Global links			
Merchandise trade (% of GDP)	..	..	64
Net barter terms of trade index (2000 = 100)	..	..	..
Total external debt stocks ($ millions)	..	..	2,833
Total debt service (% of exports)	..	..	13.6
Net migration (thousands)	-19.4	-5.6	-2.5
Personal remittances received ($ millions)	..	..	333
Foreign direct investment, net inflows ($ millions)	..	..	618
Net official development assistance received ($ millions)	..	8	103

Morocco

Population (millions)	32.5	Population growth (%)	1.4
Surface area (1,000 sq. km)	447	Population living below $1.25 a day (%)	2.5
GNI, Atlas ($ billions)	97.9	GNI per capita, Atlas ($)	2,960
GNI, PPP ($ billions)	167.4	GNI per capita, PPP ($)	5,060

	1990	2000	2012
People			
Share of poorest 20% in nat'l consumption/income (%)	6.6	6.5	6.5
Life expectancy at birth (years)	65	68	71
Total fertility rate (births per woman)	4.1	2.7	2.7
Adolescent fertility rate (births per 1,000 women 15-19)	55	38	36
Contraceptive prevalence (% of married women 15-49)	42	63	67
Births attended by skilled health staff (% of total)	31	63	74
Under-five mortality rate (per 1,000 live births)	80	50	31
Child malnutrition, underweight (% of under age 5)	8.1	9.9	3.1
Child immunization, measles (% of ages 12-23 mos.)	79	93	99
Primary completion rate, total (% of relevant age group)	50	58	99
Gross secondary enrollment, total (% of relevant age group)	37	38	69
Ratio of girls to boys in primary & secondary school (%)	69	83	91
HIV prevalence rate (% population of ages 15-49)	0.1	0.1	0.1
Environment			
Forests (1,000 sq. km)	50	50	51
Deforestation (avg. annual %, 1990-2000 and 2000-2010)		0.1	-0.2
Freshwater use (% of internal resources)	38.1	43.5	43.5
Access to improved water source (% total pop.)	73	78	84
Access to improved sanitation facilities (% total pop.)	52	64	75
Energy use per capita (kilograms of oil equivalent)	281	357	539
Carbon dioxide emissions per capita (metric tons)	1.0	1.2	1.6
Electricity use per capita (kilowatt-hours)	361	491	826
Economy			
GDP ($ billions)	25.8	37.0	96.0
GDP growth (annual %)	4.0	1.6	4.2
GDP implicit price deflator (annual % growth)	5.5	-0.6	-1.0
Value added in agriculture (% of GDP)	18	15	15
Value added in industry (% of GDP)	33	29	30
Value added in services (% of GDP)	48	56	56
Exports of goods and services (% of GDP)	26	28	36
Imports of goods and services (% of GDP)	32	33	50
Gross capital formation (% of GDP)	25	26	35
Central government revenue (% of GDP)	..	30.0	33.4
Central government cash surplus/deficit (% of GDP)	..	-3.1	-4.2
States and markets			
Starting a business (days)	..	36	11
Stock market capitalization (% of GDP)	3.7	29.4	54.8
Military expenditures (% of GDP)	4.1	2.3	3.5
Mobile cellular subscriptions (per 100 people)	0.0	8.2	120.0
Individuals using the Internet (% of population)	0.0	0.7	55.0
Paved roads (% of total)	49.1	56.0	70.6
High-technology exports (% of manufactured exports)	3	11	6
Global links			
Merchandise trade (% of GDP)	43	51	68
Net barter terms of trade index (2000 = 100)	85	100	145
Total external debt stocks ($ billions)	25.0	20.8	33.8
Total debt service (% of exports)	28.4	25.3	11.2
Net migration (thousands)	-611	-755	-450
Personal remittances received ($ billions)	2.0	2.2	6.5
Foreign direct investment, net inflows ($ millions)	165	221	2,842
Net official development assistance received ($ billions)	1.2	0.4	1.5

Mozambique

Sub-Saharan Africa				Low income
Population (millions)	25.2	Population growth (%)		2.5
Surface area (1,000 sq. km)	799	Population living below $1.25 a day (%)		59.6
GNI, Atlas ($ billions)	12.8	GNI per capita, Atlas ($)		510
GNI, PPP ($ billions)	25.3	GNI per capita, PPP ($)		1,000

	1990	2000	2012
People			
Share of poorest 20% in nat'l consumption/income (%)	..	5.4	5.2
Life expectancy at birth (years)	44	47	50
Total fertility rate (births per woman)	6.2	5.8	5.3
Adolescent fertility rate (births per 1,000 women 15-19)	116	157	138
Contraceptive prevalence (% of married women 15-49)	..	17	12
Births attended by skilled health staff (% of total)	..	48	54
Under-five mortality rate (per 1,000 live births)	233	166	90
Child malnutrition, underweight (% of under age 5)	..	23.0	15.6
Child immunization, measles (% of ages 12-23 mos.)	59	71	82
Primary completion rate, total (% of relevant age group)	26	16	52
Gross secondary enrollment, total (% of relevant age group)	7	6	26
Ratio of girls to boys in primary & secondary school (%)	73	75	90
HIV prevalence rate (% population of ages 15-49)	0.6	8.0	11.1
Environment			
Forests (1,000 sq. km)	434	412	388
Deforestation (avg. annual %, 1990-2000 and 2000-2010)		0.5	0.5
Freshwater use (% of internal resources)	0.6	0.7	0.7
Access to improved water source (% total pop.)	34	41	49
Access to improved sanitation facilities (% total pop.)	8	14	21
Energy use per capita (kilograms of oil equivalent)	436	392	415
Carbon dioxide emissions per capita (metric tons)	0.07	0.07	0.12
Electricity use per capita (kilowatt-hours)	40	122	447
Economy			
GDP ($ billions)	2.5	4.3	14.2
GDP growth (annual %)	1.0	1.1	7.4
GDP implicit price deflator (annual % growth)	34.1	12.0	3.0
Value added in agriculture (% of GDP)	37	24	30
Value added in industry (% of GDP)	18	25	23
Value added in services (% of GDP)	44	51	47
Exports of goods and services (% of GDP)	8	16	30
Imports of goods and services (% of GDP)	36	37	71
Gross capital formation (% of GDP)	22	31	48
Central government revenue (% of GDP)	..	..	24.0
Central government cash surplus/deficit (% of GDP)	..	..	-2.8
States and markets			
Starting a business (days)	..	153	13
Stock market capitalization (% of GDP)	..	..	..
Military expenditures (% of GDP)	3.4	1.3	0.9
Mobile cellular subscriptions (per 100 people)	0.0	0.3	36.2
Individuals using the Internet (% of population)	0.0	0.1	4.8
Paved roads (% of total)	16.8	19.0	20.8
High-technology exports (% of manufactured exports)	..	9	25
Global links			
Merchandise trade (% of GDP)	40	35	77
Net barter terms of trade index (2000 = 100)	175	100	100
Total external debt stocks ($ billions)	4.6	7.3	4.8
Total debt service (% of exports)	26.2	13.4	1.6
Net migration (thousands)	650	-20	-25
Personal remittances received ($ millions)	70	37	220
Foreign direct investment, net inflows ($ millions)	9	139	5,238
Net official development assistance received ($ millions)	998	906	2,097

Myanmar

East Asia & Pacific		**Low income**

Population (millions)	52.8	Population growth (%)	0.8
Surface area (1,000 sq. km)	677	Population living below $1.25 a day (%)	..
GNI, Atlas ($ millions)	..	GNI per capita, Atlas ($)	..
GNI, PPP ($ millions)	..	GNI per capita, PPP ($)	..

	1990	2000	2012
People			
Share of poorest 20% in nat'l consumption/income (%)	..	..	..
Life expectancy at birth (years)	59	62	65
Total fertility rate (births per woman)	3.4	2.4	2.0
Adolescent fertility rate (births per 1,000 women 15-19)	36	21	12
Contraceptive prevalence (% of married women 15-49)	17	37	46
Births attended by skilled health staff (% of total)	46	57	71
Under-five mortality rate (per 1,000 live births)	106	79	52
Child malnutrition, underweight (% of under age 5)	28.8	30.1	22.6
Child immunization, measles (% of ages 12-23 mos.)	68	84	84
Primary completion rate, total (% of relevant age group)	..	76	95
Gross secondary enrollment, total (% of relevant age group)	19	36	50
Ratio of girls to boys in primary & secondary school (%)	92	100	101
HIV prevalence rate (% population of ages 15-49)	0.2	0.8	0.6
Environment			
Forests (1,000 sq. km)	392	349	315
Deforestation (avg. annual %, 1990-2000 and 2000-2010)		1.2	0.9
Freshwater use (% of internal resources)	..	3.3	3.3
Access to improved water source (% total pop.)	56	67	86
Access to improved sanitation facilities (% total pop.)	..	61	77
Energy use per capita (kilograms of oil equivalent)	254	265	268
Carbon dioxide emissions per capita (metric tons)	0.1	0.2	0.2
Electricity use per capita (kilowatt-hours)	43	73	110
Economy			
GDP ($ millions)	..	..	..
GDP growth (annual %)	2.8	13.7	..
GDP implicit price deflator (annual % growth)	18.5	2.5	..
Value added in agriculture (% of GDP)	57	57	..
Value added in industry (% of GDP)	11	10	..
Value added in services (% of GDP)	32	33	..
Exports of goods and services (% of GDP)	2	0	..
Imports of goods and services (% of GDP)	4	1	..
Gross capital formation (% of GDP)	13	12	..
Central government revenue (% of GDP)	10.5	5.3	..
Central government cash surplus/deficit (% of GDP)	..	-2.7	..
States and markets			
Starting a business (days)	..	..	72
Stock market capitalization (% of GDP)	..	..	..
Military expenditures (% of GDP)	3.4	2.3	..
Mobile cellular subscriptions (per 100 people)	0.0	0.0	10.3
Individuals using the Internet (% of population)	0.0	0.0	1.1
Paved roads (% of total)	10.9	11.4	45.7
High-technology exports (% of manufactured exports)	0	..	0
Global links			
Merchandise trade (% of GDP)	..	..	..
Net barter terms of trade index (2000 = 100)	252	100	113
Total external debt stocks ($ billions)	4.7	5.8	2.6
Total debt service (% of exports)	18.2	1.2	0.1
Net migration (thousands)	-126	-1,000	-100
Personal remittances received ($ millions)	6	104	· 127
Foreign direct investment, net inflows ($ millions)	163	258	2,243
Net official development assistance received ($ millions)	161	106	504

Namibia

Sub-Saharan Africa		Upper middle income
Population (millions)	2.3	Population growth (%)	1.9
Surface area (1,000 sq. km)	824	Population living below $1.25 a day (%)	31.9
GNI, Atlas ($ billions)	12.7	GNI per capita, Atlas ($)	5,610
GNI, PPP ($ billions)	16.4	GNI per capita, PPP ($)	7,240

	1990	2000	2012
People			
Share of poorest 20% in nat'l consumption/income (%)	1.5	3.2	..
Life expectancy at birth (years)	61	55	64
Total fertility rate (births per woman)	5.2	4.0	3.1
Adolescent fertility rate (births per 1,000 women 15-19)	109	85	55
Contraceptive prevalence (% of married women 15-49)	41	44	55
Births attended by skilled health staff (% of total)	68	76	81
Under-five mortality rate (per 1,000 live births)	73	73	39
Child malnutrition, underweight (% of under age 5)	21.5	20.3	17.5
Child immunization, measles (% of ages 12-23 mos.)	76	69	76
Primary completion rate, total (% of relevant age group)	74	91	85
Gross secondary enrollment, total (% of relevant age group)	38	60	..
Ratio of girls to boys in primary & secondary school (%)	111	103	..
HIV prevalence rate (% population of ages 15-49)	1.1	14.2	13.3
Environment			
Forests (1,000 sq. km)	88	80	72
Deforestation (avg. annual %, 1990-2000 and 2000-2010)		0.9	1.0
Freshwater use (% of internal resources)	4.0	4.9	4.9
Access to improved water source (% total pop.)	67	79	92
Access to improved sanitation facilities (% total pop.)	24	28	32
Energy use per capita (kilograms of oil equivalent)	426	515	717
Carbon dioxide emissions per capita (metric tons)	0.02	0.87	1.46
Electricity use per capita (kilowatt-hours)	1,050	1,178	1,549
Economy			
GDP ($ billions)	2.4	3.9	13.1
GDP growth (annual %)	2.5	3.5	5.0
GDP implicit price deflator (annual % growth)	4.3	26.7	11.5
Value added in agriculture (% of GDP)	12	12	10
Value added in industry (% of GDP)	38	28	31
Value added in services (% of GDP)	50	60	59
Exports of goods and services (% of GDP)	52	41	43
Imports of goods and services (% of GDP)	67	45	52
Gross capital formation (% of GDP)	34	17	23
Central government revenue (% of GDP)	31.3	30.1	..
Central government cash surplus/deficit (% of GDP)	-2.6	-1.6	..
States and markets			
Starting a business (days)	..	85	66
Stock market capitalization (% of GDP)	0.7	8.0	10.0
Military expenditures (% of GDP)	8.4	2.4	3.1
Mobile cellular subscriptions (per 100 people)	0.0	4.3	95.0
Individuals using the Internet (% of population)	0.0	1.6	12.9
Paved roads (% of total)	10.8	13.6	14.5
High-technology exports (% of manufactured exports)	..	2	5
Global links			
Merchandise trade (% of GDP)	96	73	83
Net barter terms of trade index (2000 = 100)	93	100	123
Total external debt stocks ($ millions)	..	..	..
Total debt service (% of exports)	..	..	..
Net migration (thousands)	23.5	-50.0	-3.3
Personal remittances received ($ millions)	13.5	9.5	15.5
Foreign direct investment, net inflows ($ millions)	30	119	357
Net official development assistance received ($ millions)	120	152	265

Nepal

South Asia Low income

Population (millions)	27.5	Population growth (%)	1.2
Surface area (1,000 sq. km)	147	Population living below $1.25 a day (%)	24.8
GNI, Atlas ($ billions)	19.2	GNI per capita, Atlas ($)	700
GNI, PPP ($ billions)	40.4	GNI per capita, PPP ($)	1,470

	1990	2000	2012
People			
Share of poorest 20% in nat'l consumption/income (%)	..	6.5	8.3
Life expectancy at birth (years)	55	62	68
Total fertility rate (births per woman)	5.2	4.1	2.4
Adolescent fertility rate (births per 1,000 women 15-19)	135	120	74
Contraceptive prevalence (% of married women 15-49)	24	37	50
Births attended by skilled health staff (% of total)	7	12	36
Under-five mortality rate (per 1,000 live births)	142	82	42
Child malnutrition, underweight (% of under age 5)	..	43.0	29.1
Child immunization, measles (% of ages 12-23 mos.)	57	71	86
Primary completion rate, total (% of relevant age group)	55	70	100
Gross secondary enrollment, total (% of relevant age group)	35	37	67
Ratio of girls to boys in primary & secondary school (%)	55	74	106
HIV prevalence rate (% population of ages 15-49)	0.1	0.4	0.3
Environment			
Forests (1,000 sq. km)	48	39	36
Deforestation (avg. annual %, 1990-2000 and 2000-2010)		2.1	0.7
Freshwater use (% of internal resources)	..	5.0	4.9
Access to improved water source (% total pop.)	66	77	88
Access to improved sanitation facilities (% total pop.)	6	21	37
Energy use per capita (kilograms of oil equivalent)	320	350	383
Carbon dioxide emissions per capita (metric tons)	0.04	0.14	0.14
Electricity use per capita (kilowatt-hours)	37	61	106
Economy			
GDP ($ billions)	3.6	5.5	19.0
GDP growth (annual %)	4.6	6.2	4.9
GDP implicit price deflator (annual % growth)	10.7	4.5	6.5
Value added in agriculture (% of GDP)	52	41	37
Value added in industry (% of GDP)	16	22	15
Value added in services (% of GDP)	32	37	48
Exports of goods and services (% of GDP)	11	23	10
Imports of goods and services (% of GDP)	22	32	33
Gross capital formation (% of GDP)	18	24	35
Central government revenue (% of GDP)	8.4	10.6	15.9
Central government cash surplus/deficit (% of GDP)	..	..	-0.6
States and markets			
Starting a business (days)	..	31	17
Stock market capitalization (% of GDP)	..	14.4	21.9
Military expenditures (% of GDP)	1.1	1.0	1.4
Mobile cellular subscriptions (per 100 people)	0.0	0.0	59.6
Individuals using the Internet (% of population)	0.0	0.2	11.1
Paved roads (% of total)	37.5	31.0	53.9
High-technology exports (% of manufactured exports)	..	0	0
Global links			
Merchandise trade (% of GDP)	24	43	39
Net barter terms of trade index (2000 = 100)		100	78
Total external debt stocks ($ billions)	1.6	2.9	3.8
Total debt service (% of exports)	15.2	7.5	10.3
Net migration (thousands)	48	-638	-401
Personal remittances received ($ millions)	55	111	4,793
Foreign direct investment, net inflows ($ millions)	5.9	-0.5	92.0
Net official development assistance received ($ millions)	423	386	770

Netherlands

Population (millions)	16.8	Population growth (%)		0.4
Surface area (1,000 sq. km)	42	Population living below $1.25 a day (%)		..
GNI, Atlas ($ billions)	804.3	GNI per capita, Atlas ($)		48,000
GNI, PPP ($ billions)	733.0	GNI per capita, PPP ($)		43,750

	1990	2000	2012
People			
Share of poorest 20% in nat'l consumption/income (%)	..	7.6	..
Life expectancy at birth (years)	77	78	81
Total fertility rate (births per woman)	1.6	1.7	1.7
Adolescent fertility rate (births per 1,000 women 15-19)	7	7	6
Contraceptive prevalence (% of married women 15-49)	79	67	69
Births attended by skilled health staff (% of total)	..	100	..
Under-five mortality rate (per 1,000 live births)	8	6	4
Child malnutrition, underweight (% of under age 5)	..	..	..
Child immunization, measles (% of ages 12-23 mos.)	94	96	96
Primary completion rate, total (% of relevant age group)	..	98	..
Gross secondary enrollment, total (% of relevant age group)	116	123	128
Ratio of girls to boys in primary & secondary school (%)	97	97	99
HIV prevalence rate (% population of ages 15-49)	..	..	..
Environment			
Forests (1,000 sq. km)	3.5	3.6	3.7
Deforestation (avg. annual %, 1990-2000 and 2000-2010)		-0.4	-0.1
Freshwater use (% of internal resources)	72.6	81.3	96.5
Access to improved water source (% total pop.)	100	100	100
Access to improved sanitation facilities (% total pop.)	100	100	100
Energy use per capita (kilograms of oil equivalent)	4,393	4,598	4,668
Carbon dioxide emissions per capita (metric tons)	10.9	10.4	11.0
Electricity use per capita (kilowatt-hours)	5,218	6,560	7,036
Economy			
GDP ($ billions)	295	385	771
GDP growth (annual %)	4.2	3.9	-1.2
GDP implicit price deflator (annual % growth)	1.6	4.1	1.3
Value added in agriculture (% of GDP)	4	3	2
Value added in industry (% of GDP)	29	25	24
Value added in services (% of GDP)	67	73	74
Exports of goods and services (% of GDP)	56	70	88
Imports of goods and services (% of GDP)	53	65	80
Gross capital formation (% of GDP)	23	22	18
Central government revenue (% of GDP)	..	40.7	40.8
Central government cash surplus/deficit (% of GDP)	..	2.0	-3.9
States and markets			
Starting a business (days)	..	9	4
Stock market capitalization (% of GDP)	40.7	166.3	84.5
Military expenditures (% of GDP)	2.5	1.6	1.3
Mobile cellular subscriptions (per 100 people)	0.5	67.8	118.0
Individuals using the Internet (% of population)	0.3	44.0	93.0
Paved roads (% of total)	88.0	90.0	..
High-technology exports (% of manufactured exports)	16	36	20
Global links			
Merchandise trade (% of GDP)	87	117	162
Net barter terms of trade index (2000 = 100)	..	100	93
Total external debt stocks ($ millions)	..	..	..
Total debt service (% of exports)	..	..	..
Net migration (thousands)	220	145	50
Personal remittances received ($ billions)	0.7	1.2	1.6
Foreign direct investment, net inflows ($ billions)	10.7	63.1	6.7
Net official development assistance received ($ millions)	..	..	..

New Caledonia

High income

Population (thousands)	258	Population growth (%)	1.6
Surface area (1,000 sq. km)	19	Population living below $1.25 a day (%)	..
GNI, Atlas ($ billions)	..	GNI per capita, Atlas ($)	..
GNI, PPP ($ millions)	..	GNI per capita, PPP ($)	..

	1990	2000	2012
People			
Share of poorest 20% in nat'l consumption/income (%)	..	..	..
Life expectancy at birth (years)	70	75	76
Total fertility rate (births per woman)	3.2	2.6	2.1
Adolescent fertility rate (births per 1,000 women 15-19)	39	18	21
Contraceptive prevalence (% of married women 15-49)	..	..	..
Births attended by skilled health staff (% of total)	..	..	..
Under-five mortality rate (per 1,000 live births)	..	..	..
Child malnutrition, underweight (% of under age 5)	..	..	..
Child immunization, measles (% of ages 12-23 mos.)	..	..	..
Primary completion rate, total (% of relevant age group)	..	..	..
Gross secondary enrollment, total (% of relevant age group)	..	..	..
Ratio of girls to boys in primary & secondary school (%)	..	..	..
HIV prevalence rate (% population of ages 15-49)	..	..	..
Environment			
Forests (1,000 sq. km)	8.4	8.4	8.4
Deforestation (avg. annual %, 1990-2000 and 2000-2010)		0.0	0.0
Freshwater use (% of internal resources)	..		
Access to improved water source (% total pop.)	..	94	98
Access to improved sanitation facilities (% total pop.)	100	100	100
Energy use per capita (kilograms of oil equivalent)	..	..	..
Carbon dioxide emissions per capita (metric tons)	9.7	10.8	15.7
Electricity use per capita (kilowatt-hours)	..	..	..
Economy			
GDP ($ billions)	2.5	2.7	..
GDP growth (annual %)	3.6	2.1	..
GDP implicit price deflator (annual % growth)	-4.6	-0.6	..
Value added in agriculture (% of GDP)	4	..	..
Value added in industry (% of GDP)	23	..	..
Value added in services (% of GDP)	73	..	..
Exports of goods and services (% of GDP)	18	13	..
Imports of goods and services (% of GDP)	35	33	..
Gross capital formation (% of GDP)	31	..	..
Central government revenue (% of GDP)	..	..	..
Central government cash surplus/deficit (% of GDP)	..	..	..
States and markets			
Starting a business (days)	..	..	..
Stock market capitalization (% of GDP)	..	..	..
Military expenditures (% of GDP)	..	..	..
Mobile cellular subscriptions (per 100 people)	0.0	23.8	91.2
Individuals using the Internet (% of population)	0.0	13.9	58.0
Paved roads (% of total)	..	..	..
High-technology exports (% of manufactured exports)	..	1	11
Global links			
Merchandise trade (% of GDP)	53	57	..
Net barter terms of trade index (2000 = 100)	..	100	196
Total external debt stocks ($ millions)	..	..	..
Total debt service (% of exports)	..	..	..
Net migration (thousands)	4.8	4.8	5.7
Personal remittances received ($ millions)	..	333	519
Foreign direct investment, net inflows ($ millions)	31	-41	1,588
Net official development assistance received ($ millions)	302	315	..

New Zealand

High income

Population (millions)	4.4
Surface area (1,000 sq. km)	268
GNI, Atlas ($ billions)	163.6
GNI, PPP ($ billions)	144.6

Population growth (%)	0.6
Population living below $1.25 a day (%)	..
GNI per capita, Atlas ($)	36,900
GNI per capita, PPP ($)	32,620

	1990	2000	2012
People			
Share of poorest 20% in nat'l consumption/income (%)	..	..	..
Life expectancy at birth (years)	75	79	81
Total fertility rate (births per woman)	2.2	2.0	2.1
Adolescent fertility rate (births per 1,000 women 15-19)	33	28	25
Contraceptive prevalence (% of married women 15-49)	..	..	..
Births attended by skilled health staff (% of total)	..	97	..
Under-five mortality rate (per 1,000 live births)	11	7	6
Child malnutrition, underweight (% of under age 5)	..	..	..
Child immunization, measles (% of ages 12-23 mos.)	90	85	92
Primary completion rate, total (% of relevant age group)	..	..	..
Gross secondary enrollment, total (% of relevant age group)	89	111	120
Ratio of girls to boys in primary & secondary school (%)	99	103	103
HIV prevalence rate (% population of ages 15-49)	..	..	..
Environment			
Forests (1,000 sq. km)	77	83	83
Deforestation (avg. annual %, 1990-2000 and 2000-2010)		-0.7	0.0
Freshwater use (% of internal resources)	..	1.5	1.5
Access to improved water source (% total pop.)	100	100	100
Access to improved sanitation facilities (% total pop.)	..	..	..
Energy use per capita (kilograms of oil equivalent)	3,865	4,421	4,188
Carbon dioxide emissions per capita (metric tons)	7.1	8.5	7.2
Electricity use per capita (kilowatt-hours)	8,973	9,384	9,399
Economy			
GDP ($ billions)	45.0	52.0	171.3
GDP growth (annual %)	0.3	2.4	3.2
GDP implicit price deflator (annual % growth)	2.2	3.2	-0.8
Value added in agriculture (% of GDP)	7	8	7
Value added in industry (% of GDP)	29	25	24
Value added in services (% of GDP)	65	66	69
Exports of goods and services (% of GDP)	26	35	29
Imports of goods and services (% of GDP)	26	33	29
Gross capital formation (% of GDP)	20	21	20
Central government revenue (% of GDP)	..	33.5	34.9
Central government cash surplus/deficit (% of GDP)	..	1.7	-7.2
States and markets			
Starting a business (days)	..	12	1
Stock market capitalization (% of GDP)	19.6	36.3	46.6
Military expenditures (% of GDP)	1.8	1.2	1.1
Mobile cellular subscriptions (per 100 people)	1.6	40.0	110.4
Individuals using the Internet (% of population)	0.0	47.4	89.5
Paved roads (% of total)	57.0	63.0	66.2
High-technology exports (% of manufactured exports)	4	10	10
Global links			
Merchandise trade (% of GDP)	42	52	44
Net barter terms of trade index (2000 = 100)	..	100	129
Total external debt stocks ($ millions)	..	..	..
Total debt service (% of exports)	..	..	..
Net migration (thousands)	118	135	75
Personal remittances received ($ millions)	762	236	875
Foreign direct investment, net inflows ($ billions)	1.7	3.8	2.2
Net official development assistance received ($ millions)	..	..	..

Nicaragua

Latin America & Caribbean		Lower middle income	
Population (millions)	6.0	Population growth (%)	1.5
Surface area (1,000 sq. km)	130	Population living below $1.25 a day (%)	11.9
GNI, Atlas ($ billions)	9.9	GNI per capita, Atlas ($)	1,650
GNI, PPP ($ billions)	23.3	GNI per capita, PPP ($)	3,890

	1990	2000	2012
People			
Share of poorest 20% in nat'l consumption/income (%)	4.2	5.6	..
Life expectancy at birth (years)	64	70	74
Total fertility rate (births per woman)	4.8	3.3	2.5
Adolescent fertility rate (births per 1,000 women 15-19)	158	125	101
Contraceptive prevalence (% of married women 15-49)	49	69	72
Births attended by skilled health staff (% of total)	61	67	74
Under-five mortality rate (per 1,000 live births)	66	40	24
Child malnutrition, underweight (% of under age 5)	9.6	7.8	5.7
Child immunization, measles (% of ages 12-23 mos.)	82	86	99
Primary completion rate, total (% of relevant age group)	39	66	80
Gross secondary enrollment, total (% of relevant age group)	37	53	69
Ratio of girls to boys in primary & secondary school (%)	119	105	102
HIV prevalence rate (% population of ages 15-49)	0.1	0.1	0.3
Environment			
Forests (1,000 sq. km)	45	38	30
Deforestation (avg. annual %, 1990-2000 and 2000-2010)		1.7	2.0
Freshwater use (% of internal resources)	..	0.7	0.7
Access to improved water source (% total pop.)	74	80	85
Access to improved sanitation facilities (% total pop.)	43	48	52
Energy use per capita (kilograms of oil equivalent)	489	494	515
Carbon dioxide emissions per capita (metric tons)	0.6	0.7	0.8
Electricity use per capita (kilowatt-hours)	309	343	522
Economy			
GDP ($ billions)	1.0	5.1	10.5
GDP growth (annual %)	-0.1	4.1	5.2
GDP implicit price deflator (annual % growth)	5,018.1	8.6	8.8
Value added in agriculture (% of GDP)	..	19	20
Value added in industry (% of GDP)	..	22	27
Value added in services (% of GDP)	..	58	53
Exports of goods and services (% of GDP)	25	20	44
Imports of goods and services (% of GDP)	46	41	62
Gross capital formation (% of GDP)	19	30	25
Central government revenue (% of GDP)	30.0	11.6	16.5
Central government cash surplus/deficit (% of GDP)	-34.2	-2.8	0.5
States and markets			
Starting a business (days)	..	46	36
Stock market capitalization (% of GDP)	..	..	..
Military expenditures (% of GDP)	4.0	0.6	0.6
Mobile cellular subscriptions (per 100 people)	0.0	1.8	86.1
Individuals using the Internet (% of population)	0.0	1.0	13.5
Paved roads (% of total)	10.5	11.0	13.3
High-technology exports (% of manufactured exports)	6	5	5
Global links			
Merchandise trade (% of GDP)	96	48	81
Net barter terms of trade index (2000 = 100)	155	100	82
Total external debt stocks ($ billions)	10.8	6.8	8.9
Total debt service (% of exports)	5.0	25.6	12.3
Net migration (thousands)	-114	-206	-120
Personal remittances received ($ millions)	10	320	1,016
Foreign direct investment, net inflows ($ millions)	1	267	805
Net official development assistance received ($ millions)	330	560	532

Niger

Sub-Saharan Africa			Low income
Population (millions)	17.2	Population growth (%)	3.8
Surface area (1,000 sq. km)	1,267	Population living below $1.25 a day (%)	43.6
GNI, Atlas ($ billions)	6.7	GNI per capita, Atlas ($)	390
GNI, PPP ($ billions)	13.0	GNI per capita, PPP ($)	760

	1990	2000	2012
People			
Share of poorest 20% in nat'l consumption/income (%)	7.5	..	8.1
Life expectancy at birth (years)	44	51	58
Total fertility rate (births per woman)	7.8	7.7	7.6
Adolescent fertility rate (births per 1,000 women 15-19)	224	219	205
Contraceptive prevalence (% of married women 15-49)	4	14	14
Births attended by skilled health staff (% of total)	15	16	29
Under-five mortality rate (per 1,000 live births)	326	227	114
Child malnutrition, underweight (% of under age 5)	41.0	43.6	39.9
Child immunization, measles (% of ages 12-23 mos.)	25	37	73
Primary completion rate, total (% of relevant age group)	17	19	49
Gross secondary enrollment, total (% of relevant age group)	6	7	16
Ratio of girls to boys in primary & secondary school (%)	52	64	80
HIV prevalence rate (% population of ages 15-49)	0.2	1.0	0.5
Environment			
Forests (1,000 sq. km)	19	13	12
Deforestation (avg. annual %, 1990-2000 and 2000-2010)		3.7	1.0
Freshwater use (% of internal resources)	14.3	67.5	67.5
Access to improved water source (% total pop.)	34	42	52
Access to improved sanitation facilities (% total pop.)	5	7	9
Energy use per capita (kilograms of oil equivalent)	..	..	..
Carbon dioxide emissions per capita (metric tons)	0.11	0.07	0.09
Electricity use per capita (kilowatt-hours)	..	..	..
Economy			
GDP ($ billions)	2.5	1.8	6.8
GDP growth (annual %)	-1.3	-1.4	10.8
GDP implicit price deflator (annual % growth)	-1.6	4.5	3.1
Value added in agriculture (% of GDP)	35	38	38
Value added in industry (% of GDP)	16	18	20
Value added in services (% of GDP)	49	44	41
Exports of goods and services (% of GDP)	15	18	25
Imports of goods and services (% of GDP)	22	26	44
Gross capital formation (% of GDP)	11	11	34
Central government revenue (% of GDP)	..	..	..
Central government cash surplus/deficit (% of GDP)	..	..	..
States and markets			
Starting a business (days)	..	35	17
Stock market capitalization (% of GDP)	..	..	..
Military expenditures (% of GDP)	..	1.1	1.0
Mobile cellular subscriptions (per 100 people)	0.0	0.0	31.4
Individuals using the Internet (% of population)	0.0	0.0	1.4
Paved roads (% of total)	29.0	26.0	20.7
High-technology exports (% of manufactured exports)	..	6	6
Global links			
Merchandise trade (% of GDP)	27	38	65
Net barter terms of trade index (2000 = 100)	165	100	169
Total external debt stocks ($ billions)	1.8	1.7	2.3
Total debt service (% of exports)	17.8	8.0	2.0
Net migration (thousands)	-2.7	-28.5	-28.5
Personal remittances received ($ millions)	14	14	134
Foreign direct investment, net inflows ($ millions)	41	8	793
Net official development assistance received ($ millions)	388	209	902

Nigeria

Sub-Saharan Africa		Lower middle income	
Population (millions)	168.8	Population growth (%)	2.8
Surface area (1,000 sq. km)	924	Population living below $1.25 a day (%)	68.0
GNI, Atlas ($ billions)	242.7	GNI per capita, Atlas ($)	1,440
GNI, PPP ($ billions)	404.8	GNI per capita, PPP ($)	2,400

	1990	2000	2012
People			
Share of poorest 20% in nat'l consumption/income (%)	4.0	5.1	4.4
Life expectancy at birth (years)	46	47	52
Total fertility rate (births per woman)	6.5	6.1	6.0
Adolescent fertility rate (births per 1,000 women 15-19)	148	133	120
Contraceptive prevalence (% of married women 15-49)	6	15	18
Births attended by skilled health staff (% of total)	31	42	49
Under-five mortality rate (per 1,000 live births)	213	188	124
Child malnutrition, underweight (% of under age 5)	35.1	27.3	24.4
Child immunization, measles (% of ages 12-23 mos.)	54	33	42
Primary completion rate, total (% of relevant age group)	..	..	76
Gross secondary enrollment, total (% of relevant age group)	25	24	44
Ratio of girls to boys in primary & secondary school (%)	79	82	91
HIV prevalence rate (% population of ages 15-49)	0.8	3.3	3.1
Environment			
Forests (1,000 sq. km)	172	131	86
Deforestation (avg. annual %, 1990-2000 and 2000-2010)		2.7	3.7
Freshwater use (% of internal resources)	..	4.7	4.7
Access to improved water source (% total pop.)	46	55	64
Access to improved sanitation facilities (% total pop.)	37	32	28
Energy use per capita (kilograms of oil equivalent)	738	737	721
Carbon dioxide emissions per capita (metric tons)	0.5	0.6	0.5
Electricity use per capita (kilowatt-hours)	87	74	149
Economy			
GDP ($ billions)	31	46	263
GDP growth (annual %)	8.2	5.4	6.5
GDP implicit price deflator (annual % growth)	13.9	35.1	1.7
Value added in agriculture (% of GDP)	32	26	33
Value added in industry (% of GDP)	45	52	41
Value added in services (% of GDP)	23	22	26
Exports of goods and services (% of GDP)	35	52	55
Imports of goods and services (% of GDP)	18	20	23
Gross capital formation (% of GDP)	14	7	8
Central government revenue (% of GDP)	..	..	..
Central government cash surplus/deficit (% of GDP)	..	..	..
States and markets			
Starting a business (days)	..	36	28
Stock market capitalization (% of GDP)	4.5	9.1	21.5
Military expenditures (% of GDP)	0.8	0.8	0.9
Mobile cellular subscriptions (per 100 people)	0.0	0.0	66.8
Individuals using the Internet (% of population)	0.0	0.1	32.9
Paved roads (% of total)	..	15.0	..
High-technology exports (% of manufactured exports)	..	1	2
Global links			
Merchandise trade (% of GDP)	62	64	63
Net barter terms of trade index (2000 = 100)	89	100	222
Total external debt stocks ($ billions)	33.4	31.6	10.1
Total debt service (% of exports)	22.6	8.8	0.3
Net migration (thousands)	-96	-170	-300
Personal remittances received ($ billions)	0.0	1.4	20.6
Foreign direct investment, net inflows ($ billions)	0.6	1.1	7.1
Net official development assistance received ($ millions)	255	174	1,916

Northern Mariana Islands

High income

Population (thousands)	53	Population growth (%)	0.1
Surface area (sq. km)	460	Population living below $1.25 a day (%)	..
GNI, Atlas ($ millions)	..	GNI per capita, Atlas ($)	..
GNI, PPP ($ millions)	..	GNI per capita, PPP ($)	..

	1990	2000	2012
People			
Share of poorest 20% in nat'l consumption/income (%)	..	..	..
Life expectancy at birth (years)	..	..	..
Total fertility rate (births per woman)	..	..	..
Adolescent fertility rate (births per 1,000 women 15-19)	..	..	..
Contraceptive prevalence (% of married women 15-49)	..	..	..
Births attended by skilled health staff (% of total)	..	100	..
Under-five mortality rate (per 1,000 live births)	..	..	..
Child malnutrition, underweight (% of under age 5)	..	..	..
Child immunization, measles (% of ages 12-23 mos.)	..	..	..
Primary completion rate, total (% of relevant age group)	..	..	..
Gross secondary enrollment, total (% of relevant age group)	..	..	..
Ratio of girls to boys in primary & secondary school (%)	..	..	..
HIV prevalence rate (% population of ages 15-49)	..	..	..
Environment			
Forests (sq. km)	340	320	302
Deforestation (avg. annual %, 1990-2000 and 2000-2010)		0.5	0.5
Freshwater use (% of internal resources)	..	..	..
Access to improved water source (% total pop.)	94	96	98
Access to improved sanitation facilities (% total pop.)	69	74	80
Energy use per capita (kilograms of oil equivalent)	..	..	..
Carbon dioxide emissions per capita (metric tons)	..	..	..
Electricity use per capita (kilowatt-hours)	..	..	..
Economy			
GDP ($ millions)	..	..	..
GDP growth (annual %)	..	..	..
GDP implicit price deflator (annual % growth)	..	..	..
Value added in agriculture (% of GDP)	..	..	..
Value added in industry (% of GDP)	..	..	..
Value added in services (% of GDP)	..	..	..
Exports of goods and services (% of GDP)	..	..	..
Imports of goods and services (% of GDP)	..	..	..
Gross capital formation (% of GDP)	..	..	..
Central government revenue (% of GDP)	..	..	..
Central government cash surplus/deficit (% of GDP)	..	..	..
States and markets			
Starting a business (days)	..	..	..
Stock market capitalization (% of GDP)	..	..	..
Military expenditures (% of GDP)	..	..	..
Mobile cellular subscriptions (per 100 people)	0.0	4.4	..
Individuals using the Internet (% of population)	0.0	..	..
Paved roads (% of total)	..	..	..
High-technology exports (% of manufactured exports)	..	..	..
Global links			
Merchandise trade (% of GDP)	..	..	..
Net barter terms of trade index (2000 = 100)	..	100	85
Total external debt stocks ($ millions)	..	..	..
Total debt service (% of exports)	..	..	..
Net migration (thousands)	..	..	..
Personal remittances received ($ millions)	..	..	..
Foreign direct investment, net inflows ($ millions)	6.6	1.5	4.6
Net official development assistance received ($ millions)	63.1	0.1	..

Norway

Population (millions)	5.0	Population growth (%)	1.3
Surface area (1,000 sq. km)	324	Population living below $1.25 a day (%)	..
GNI, Atlas ($ billions)	495.7	GNI per capita, Atlas ($)	98,780
GNI, PPP ($ billions)	338.5	GNI per capita, PPP ($)	67,450

	1990	2000	2012
People			
Share of poorest 20% in nat'l consumption/income (%)	..	9.6	..
Life expectancy at birth (years)	77	79	81
Total fertility rate (births per woman)	1.9	1.9	1.9
Adolescent fertility rate (births per 1,000 women 15-19)	17	11	8
Contraceptive prevalence (% of married women 15-49)	74	87	..
Births attended by skilled health staff (% of total)	100	..	..
Under-five mortality rate (per 1,000 live births)	9	5	3
Child malnutrition, underweight (% of under age 5)	..	..	..
Child immunization, measles (% of ages 12-23 mos.)	87	88	94
Primary completion rate, total (% of relevant age group)	95	98	98
Gross secondary enrollment, total (% of relevant age group)	101	116	113
Ratio of girls to boys in primary & secondary school (%)	102	101	100
HIV prevalence rate (% population of ages 15-49)	..	..	..
Environment			
Forests (1,000 sq. km)	91	93	101
Deforestation (avg. annual %, 1990-2000 and 2000-2010)		-0.2	-0.8
Freshwater use (% of internal resources)	..	0.6	0.8
Access to improved water source (% total pop.)	100	100	100
Access to improved sanitation facilities (% total pop.)	100	100	100
Energy use per capita (kilograms of oil equivalent)	4,952	5,810	5,942
Carbon dioxide emissions per capita (metric tons)	7.4	8.6	11.7
Electricity use per capita (kilowatt-hours)	23,354	24,994	23,174
Economy			
GDP ($ billions)	118	168	500
GDP growth (annual %)	1.9	3.3	2.9
GDP implicit price deflator (annual % growth)	3.8	15.7	2.8
Value added in agriculture (% of GDP)	3	2	1
Value added in industry (% of GDP)	33	42	42
Value added in services (% of GDP)	63	56	57
Exports of goods and services (% of GDP)	40	47	41
Imports of goods and services (% of GDP)	34	29	28
Gross capital formation (% of GDP)	23	20	25
Central government revenue (% of GDP)	..	48.4	49.1
Central government cash surplus/deficit (% of GDP)	..	15.7	14.6
States and markets			
Starting a business (days)	..	18	7
Stock market capitalization (% of GDP)	22.2	38.6	50.6
Military expenditures (% of GDP)	2.9	1.7	1.4
Mobile cellular subscriptions (per 100 people)	4.6	71.8	116.7
Individuals using the Internet (% of population)	0.7	52.0	95.0
Paved roads (% of total)	69.0	76.0	80.7
High-technology exports (% of manufactured exports)	11	17	19
Global links			
Merchandise trade (% of GDP)	52	56	49
Net barter terms of trade index (2000 = 100)	..	100	162
Total external debt stocks ($ millions)	..	..	..
Total debt service (% of exports)	..	..	..
Net migration (thousands)	47	67	150
Personal remittances received ($ millions)	158	270	767
Foreign direct investment, net inflows ($ billions)	1.0	7.0	23.0
Net official development assistance received ($ millions)	..	..	..

Oman

High income

Population (millions)	3.3	Population growth (%)	9.1
Surface area (1,000 sq. km)	310	Population living below $1.25 a day (%)	..
GNI, Atlas ($ billions)	58.8	GNI per capita, Atlas ($)	19,450
GNI, PPP ($ billions)	71.0	GNI per capita, PPP ($)	25,330

	1990	2000	2012
People			
Share of poorest 20% in nat'l consumption/income (%)	..	..	..
Life expectancy at birth (years)	67	72	77
Total fertility rate (births per woman)	7.2	3.7	2.9
Adolescent fertility rate (births per 1,000 women 15-19)	81	30	11
Contraceptive prevalence (% of married women 15-49)	9	32	24
Births attended by skilled health staff (% of total)	..	95	99
Under-five mortality rate (per 1,000 live births)	39	17	12
Child malnutrition, underweight (% of under age 5)	21.4	11.3	8.6
Child immunization, measles (% of ages 12-23 mos.)	98	99	99
Primary completion rate, total (% of relevant age group)	65	83	104
Gross secondary enrollment, total (% of relevant age group)	42	80	94
Ratio of girls to boys in primary & secondary school (%)	85	97	105
HIV prevalence rate (% population of ages 15-49)	..	..	..
Environment			
Forests (sq. km)	20	20	20
Deforestation (avg. annual %, 1990-2000 and 2000-2010)		0.0	0.0
Freshwater use (% of internal resources)	87.4	97.1	94.4
Access to improved water source (% total pop.)	79	84	93
Access to improved sanitation facilities (% total pop.)	82	89	97
Energy use per capita (kilograms of oil equivalent)	2,330	3,687	8,356
Carbon dioxide emissions per capita (metric tons)	6.3	10.0	20.4
Electricity use per capita (kilowatt-hours)	2,189	3,312	6,292
Economy			
GDP ($ billions)	11.7	19.9	78.1
GDP growth (annual %)	-0.1	5.4	5.0
GDP implicit price deflator (annual % growth)	24.8	20.0	6.3
Value added in agriculture (% of GDP)	3	2	..
Value added in industry (% of GDP)	54	57	..
Value added in services (% of GDP)	43	41	..
Exports of goods and services (% of GDP)	47	59	62
Imports of goods and services (% of GDP)	28	31	32
Gross capital formation (% of GDP)	12	12	..
Central government revenue (% of GDP)	35.0	29.4	46.5
Central government cash surplus/deficit (% of GDP)	-0.3	-5.2	10.6
States and markets			
Starting a business (days)	..	35	8
Stock market capitalization (% of GDP)	8.5	17.4	25.7
Military expenditures (% of GDP)	16.5	10.6	8.6
Mobile cellular subscriptions (per 100 people)	0.2	7.4	159.3
Individuals using the Internet (% of population)	0.0	3.5	60.0
Paved roads (% of total)	21.0	25.0	49.3
High-technology exports (% of manufactured exports)	15	3	3
Global links			
Merchandise trade (% of GDP)	71	83	104
Net barter terms of trade index (2000 = 100)	..	100	244
Total external debt stocks ($ millions)	..	..	..
Total debt service (% of exports)	..	..	..
Net migration (thousands)	66	107	1,030
Personal remittances received ($ millions)	39.0	39.0	39.0
Foreign direct investment, net inflows ($ millions)	142	82	1,514
Net official development assistance received ($ millions)	68.2	79.7	-40.3

Pakistan

South Asia		Lower middle income
Population (millions)	179.2	Population growth (%)	1.7
Surface area (1,000 sq. km)	796	Population living below $1.25 a day (%)	21.0
GNI, Atlas ($ billions)	225.1	GNI per capita, Atlas ($)	1,260
GNI, PPP ($ billions)	516.5	GNI per capita, PPP ($)	2,880

	1990	2000	2012
People			
Share of poorest 20% in nat'l consumption/income (%)	8.1	8.7	9.6
Life expectancy at birth (years)	61	64	66
Total fertility rate (births per woman)	6.0	4.5	3.3
Adolescent fertility rate (births per 1,000 women 15-19)	83	48	27
Contraceptive prevalence (% of married women 15-49)	15	28	29
Births attended by skilled health staff (% of total)	19	23	49
Under-five mortality rate (per 1,000 live births)	138	112	86
Child malnutrition, underweight (% of under age 5)	39.0	31.3	30.9
Child immunization, measles (% of ages 12-23 mos.)	50	59	83
Primary completion rate, total (% of relevant age group)	..	..	72
Gross secondary enrollment, total (% of relevant age group)	21	28	37
Ratio of girls to boys in primary & secondary school (%)	50	75	82
HIV prevalence rate (% population of ages 15-49)	0.1	0.1	0.1
Environment			
Forests (1,000 sq. km)	25	21	16
Deforestation (avg. annual %, 1990-2000 and 2000-2010)		1.8	2.2
Freshwater use (% of internal resources)	282.9	313.8	333.6
Access to improved water source (% total pop.)	85	88	91
Access to improved sanitation facilities (% total pop.)	27	37	48
Energy use per capita (kilograms of oil equivalent)	386	445	482
Carbon dioxide emissions per capita (metric tons)	0.6	0.7	0.9
Electricity use per capita (kilowatt-hours)	269	359	449
Economy			
GDP ($ billions)	40	74	225
GDP growth (annual %)	4.5	4.3	4.0
GDP implicit price deflator (annual % growth)	6.5	24.9	5.6
Value added in agriculture (% of GDP)	26	26	24
Value added in industry (% of GDP)	25	23	22
Value added in services (% of GDP)	49	51	54
Exports of goods and services (% of GDP)	16	13	12
Imports of goods and services (% of GDP)	23	15	20
Gross capital formation (% of GDP)	19	17	15
Central government revenue (% of GDP)	19.1	13.9	12.6
Central government cash surplus/deficit (% of GDP)	-2.5	-4.1	-8.0
States and markets			
Starting a business (days)	..	24	21
Stock market capitalization (% of GDP)	7.1	8.9	19.4
Military expenditures (% of GDP)	6.8	4.0	3.1
Mobile cellular subscriptions (per 100 people)	0.0	0.2	67.1
Individuals using the Internet (% of population)	0.0	1.3	10.0
Paved roads (% of total)	54.0	56.0	72.6
High-technology exports (% of manufactured exports)	0	0	2
Global links			
Merchandise trade (% of GDP)	33	27	31
Net barter terms of trade index (2000 = 100)	109	100	54
Total external debt stocks ($ billions)	20.6	33.0	61.9
Total debt service (% of exports)	27.4	28.0	14.9
Net migration (thousands)	-1,400	-1,754	-1,634
Personal remittances received ($ billions)	2.0	1.1	14.0
Foreign direct investment, net inflows ($ millions)	245	308	854
Net official development assistance received ($ billions)	1.1	0.7	2.0

Palau

East Asia & Pacific		Upper middle income
Population (thousands)	21	Population growth (%)	0.7
Surface area (sq. km)	460	Population living below $1.25 a day (%)	..
GNI, Atlas ($ millions)	204.7	GNI per capita, Atlas ($)	9,860
GNI, PPP ($ millions)	350.1	GNI per capita, PPP ($)	16,870

	1990	2000	2012
People			
Share of poorest 20% in nat'l consumption/income (%)	..	..	..
Life expectancy at birth (years)	69	70	..
Total fertility rate (births per woman)	2.8	1.5	..
Adolescent fertility rate (births per 1,000 women 15-19)	..	..	..
Contraceptive prevalence (% of married women 15-49)	..	17	22
Births attended by skilled health staff (% of total)	99	100	100
Under-five mortality rate (per 1,000 live births)	34	28	21
Child malnutrition, underweight (% of under age 5)	..	..	..
Child immunization, measles (% of ages 12-23 mos.)	98	83	91
Primary completion rate, total (% of relevant age group)	..	99	..
Gross secondary enrollment, total (% of relevant age group)	..	86	..
Ratio of girls to boys in primary & secondary school (%)	..	100	..
HIV prevalence rate (% population of ages 15-49)	..	..	..
Environment			
Forests (sq. km)	380	396	403
Deforestation (avg. annual %, 1990-2000 and 2000-2010)		-0.4	-0.2
Freshwater use (% of internal resources)	..	..	..
Access to improved water source (% total pop.)	90	92	95
Access to improved sanitation facilities (% total pop.)	46	81	100
Energy use per capita (kilograms of oil equivalent)	4,869	..	..
Carbon dioxide emissions per capita (metric tons)	15.6	6.1	10.6
Electricity use per capita (kilowatt-hours)	..	..	..
Economy			
GDP ($ millions)	77	158	228
GDP growth (annual %)	-6.4	0.3	5.3
GDP implicit price deflator (annual % growth)	5.0	39.2	1.9
Value added in agriculture (% of GDP)	19	7	6
Value added in industry (% of GDP)	13	14	9
Value added in services (% of GDP)	69	79	86
Exports of goods and services (% of GDP)	20	7	70
Imports of goods and services (% of GDP)	39	80	77
Gross capital formation (% of GDP)	..	..	..
Central government revenue (% of GDP)	..	..	..
Central government cash surplus/deficit (% of GDP)	..	..	..
States and markets			
Starting a business (days)	..	24	28
Stock market capitalization (% of GDP)	..	..	..
Military expenditures (% of GDP)	..	..	..
Mobile cellular subscriptions (per 100 people)	..	12.6	82.6
Individuals using the Internet (% of population)	0.0	20.2	..
Paved roads (% of total)	..	..	..
High-technology exports (% of manufactured exports)	..	..	..
Global links			
Merchandise trade (% of GDP)	..	85	64
Net barter terms of trade index (2000 = 100)	..	100	105
Total external debt stocks ($ millions)	..	..	..
Total debt service (% of exports)	..	..	..
Net migration (thousands)	..	..	..
Personal remittances received ($ millions)	..	..	..
Foreign direct investment, net inflows ($ millions)	1.0	14.9	4.6
Net official development assistance received ($ millions)	0.0	39.1	15.0

Panama

Latin America & Caribbean		Upper middle income	
Population (millions)	3.8	Population growth (%)	1.6
Surface area (1,000 sq. km)	75	Population living below $1.25 a day (%)	6.6
GNI, Atlas ($ billions)	32.4	GNI per capita, Atlas ($)	8,510
GNI, PPP ($ billions)	57.6	GNI per capita, PPP ($)	15,150

	1990	2000	2012
People			
Share of poorest 20% in nat'l consumption/income (%)	1.2	1.9	3.3
Life expectancy at birth (years)	73	75	77
Total fertility rate (births per woman)	3.1	2.8	2.5
Adolescent fertility rate (births per 1,000 women 15-19)	97	93	79
Contraceptive prevalence (% of married women 15-49)	..	..	52
Births attended by skilled health staff (% of total)	86	93	89
Under-five mortality rate (per 1,000 live births)	32	26	19
Child malnutrition, underweight (% of under age 5)	..	5.1	3.9
Child immunization, measles (% of ages 12-23 mos.)	73	97	98
Primary completion rate, total (% of relevant age group)	80	91	98
Gross secondary enrollment, total (% of relevant age group)	59	65	84
Ratio of girls to boys in primary & secondary school (%)	100	101	101
HIV prevalence rate (% population of ages 15-49)	1.1	1.3	0.7
Environment			
Forests (1,000 sq. km)	38	34	32
Deforestation (avg. annual %, 1990-2000 and 2000-2010)		1.2	0.4
Freshwater use (% of internal resources)	1.1	0.3	0.3
Access to improved water source (% total pop.)	84	90	94
Access to improved sanitation facilities (% total pop.)	60	67	73
Energy use per capita (kilograms of oil equivalent)	600	841	1,085
Carbon dioxide emissions per capita (metric tons)	1.1	1.9	2.6
Electricity use per capita (kilowatt-hours)	828	1,256	1,829
Economy			
GDP ($ billions)	5.3	11.6	36.3
GDP growth (annual %)	8.1	2.7	10.7
GDP implicit price deflator (annual % growth)	0.6	-1.2	4.6
Value added in agriculture (% of GDP)	10	7	4
Value added in industry (% of GDP)	15	19	18
Value added in services (% of GDP)	75	74	78
Exports of goods and services (% of GDP)	87	73	84
Imports of goods and services (% of GDP)	79	70	78
Gross capital formation (% of GDP)	17	24	29
Central government revenue (% of GDP)	25.6	23.1	..
Central government cash surplus/deficit (% of GDP)	2.0	-0.8	..
States and markets			
Starting a business (days)	..	18	6
Stock market capitalization (% of GDP)	3.4	24.0	34.6
Military expenditures (% of GDP)	1.4	1.0	..
Mobile cellular subscriptions (per 100 people)	0.0	13.4	178.0
Individuals using the Internet (% of population)	0.0	6.6	45.2
Paved roads (% of total)	32.0	36.0	41.8
High-technology exports (% of manufactured exports)	..	1	35
Global links			
Merchandise trade (% of GDP)	35	36	109
Net barter terms of trade index (2000 = 100)	69	100	86
Total external debt stocks ($ billions)	6.5	6.6	12.3
Total debt service (% of exports)	6.2	9.4	8.7
Net migration (thousands)	0.4	16.9	28.6
Personal remittances received ($ millions)	110	16	402
Foreign direct investment, net inflows ($ millions)	136	624	3,383
Net official development assistance received ($ millions)	99.3	15.4	50.8

Papua New Guinea

East Asia & Pacific		Lower middle income	
Population (millions)	7.2	Population growth (%)	2.2
Surface area (1,000 sq. km)	463	Population living below $1.25 a day (%)	35.8
GNI, Atlas ($ billions)	12.8	GNI per capita, Atlas ($)	1,790
GNI, PPP ($ billions)	19.6	GNI per capita, PPP ($)	2,740

	1990	2000	2012
People			
Share of poorest 20% in nat'l consumption/income (%)	..	..	..
Life expectancy at birth (years)	56	59	62
Total fertility rate (births per woman)	4.8	4.5	3.8
Adolescent fertility rate (births per 1,000 women 15-19)	73	73	62
Contraceptive prevalence (% of married women 15-49)	..	..	32
Births attended by skilled health staff (% of total)	..	41	53
Under-five mortality rate (per 1,000 live births)	89	79	63
Child malnutrition, underweight (% of under age 5)	..	..	..
Child immunization, measles (% of ages 12-23 mos.)	67	62	67
Primary completion rate, total (% of relevant age group)	45	55	..
Gross secondary enrollment, total (% of relevant age group)	11	19	..
Ratio of girls to boys in primary & secondary school (%)	82	84	..
HIV prevalence rate (% population of ages 15-49)	0.1	0.7	0.5
Environment			
Forests (1,000 sq. km)	315	301	286
Deforestation (avg. annual %, 1990-2000 and 2000-2010)		0.5	0.5
Freshwater use (% of internal resources)	..	0.0	0.0
Access to improved water source (% total pop.)	34	35	40
Access to improved sanitation facilities (% total pop.)	20	19	19
Energy use per capita (kilograms of oil equivalent)	..	..	..
Carbon dioxide emissions per capita (metric tons)	0.5	0.5	0.5
Electricity use per capita (kilowatt-hours)	..	..	..
Economy			
GDP ($ billions)	3.2	3.5	15.7
GDP growth (annual %)	-3.0	-2.5	8.0
GDP implicit price deflator (annual % growth)	4.1	13.1	2.8
Value added in agriculture (% of GDP)	31	36	..
Value added in industry (% of GDP)	32	41	..
Value added in services (% of GDP)	37	23	..
Exports of goods and services (% of GDP)	41	66	..
Imports of goods and services (% of GDP)	49	49	..
Gross capital formation (% of GDP)	24	22	..
Central government revenue (% of GDP)	25.2	24.2	..
Central government cash surplus/deficit (% of GDP)	-2.2	-1.9	..
States and markets			
Starting a business (days)	..	51	53
Stock market capitalization (% of GDP)	..	49.3	68.4
Military expenditures (% of GDP)	2.1	0.9	0.5
Mobile cellular subscriptions (per 100 people)	0.0	0.2	37.8
Individuals using the Internet (% of population)	0.0	0.8	2.3
Paved roads (% of total)	3.2	4.0	..
High-technology exports (% of manufactured exports)	..	19	3
Global links			
Merchandise trade (% of GDP)	74	92	77
Net barter terms of trade index (2000 = 100)	..	100	193
Total external debt stocks ($ billions)	2.6	2.3	23.1
Total debt service (% of exports)	37.2	12.9	13.3
Net migration (thousands)	0.0	0.0	0.0
Personal remittances received ($ millions)	5.4	7.2	3.5
Foreign direct investment, net inflows ($ millions)	155	96	29
Net official development assistance received ($ millions)	412	275	665

Paraguay

Latin America & Caribbean				Lower middle income	

Population (millions)	6.7	Population growth (%)		1.7
Surface area (1,000 sq. km)	407	Population living below $1.25 a day (%)		7.2
GNI, Atlas ($ billions)	22.8	GNI per capita, Atlas ($)		3,400
GNI, PPP ($ billions)	38.2	GNI per capita, PPP ($)		5,720

	1990	2000	2012
People			
Share of poorest 20% in nat'l consumption/income (%)	5.8	2.7	3.3
Life expectancy at birth (years)	68	70	72
Total fertility rate (births per woman)	4.5	3.7	2.9
Adolescent fertility rate (births per 1,000 women 15-19)	92	86	67
Contraceptive prevalence (% of married women 15-49)	48	73	79
Births attended by skilled health staff (% of total)	66	77	82
Under-five mortality rate (per 1,000 live births)	46	33	22
Child malnutrition, underweight (% of under age 5)	2.8	..	..
Child immunization, measles (% of ages 12-23 mos.)	69	92	91
Primary completion rate, total (% of relevant age group)	65	92	86
Gross secondary enrollment, total (% of relevant age group)	31	61	70
Ratio of girls to boys in primary & secondary school (%)	98	98	100
HIV prevalence rate (% population of ages 15-49)	0.1	0.1	0.3
Environment			
Forests (1,000 sq. km)	212	194	174
Deforestation (avg. annual %, 1990-2000 and 2000-2010)		0.9	1.0
Freshwater use (% of internal resources)	..	0.5	0.5
Access to improved water source (% total pop.)	53	73	94
Access to improved sanitation facilities (% total pop.)	37	58	80
Energy use per capita (kilograms of oil equivalent)	723	720	739
Carbon dioxide emissions per capita (metric tons)	0.5	0.7	0.8
Electricity use per capita (kilowatt-hours)	501	880	1,228
Economy			
GDP ($ billions)	5.7	8.2	25.5
GDP growth (annual %)	4.1	-2.3	-1.2
GDP implicit price deflator (annual % growth)	38.5	11.7	4.6
Value added in agriculture (% of GDP)	17	16	17
Value added in industry (% of GDP)	39	36	28
Value added in services (% of GDP)	44	49	55
Exports of goods and services (% of GDP)	51	46	47
Imports of goods and services (% of GDP)	38	38	47
Gross capital formation (% of GDP)	19	16	15
Central government revenue (% of GDP)	..	..	20.2
Central government cash surplus/deficit (% of GDP)	..	..	1.6
States and markets			
Starting a business (days)	..	74	35
Stock market capitalization (% of GDP)	0.3	2.9	3.8
Military expenditures (% of GDP)	1.6	1.4	1.7
Mobile cellular subscriptions (per 100 people)	0.0	15.3	101.6
Individuals using the Internet (% of population)	0.0	0.7	27.1
Paved roads (% of total)	..	12.0	15.6
High-technology exports (% of manufactured exports)	0	3	7
Global links			
Merchandise trade (% of GDP)	41	37	74
Net barter terms of trade index (2000 = 100)	103	100	111
Total external debt stocks ($ billions)	2.2	3.1	6.3
Total debt service (% of exports)	8.4	11.2	6.3
Net migration (thousands)	-30.4	-44.6	-40.0
Personal remittances received ($ millions)	34	278	634
Foreign direct investment, net inflows ($ millions)	77	104	363
Net official development assistance received ($ millions)	57	82	104

Peru

Latin America & Caribbean		Upper middle income	
Population (millions)	30.0	Population growth (%)	1.3
Surface area (1,000 sq. km)	1,285	Population living below $1.25 a day (%)	4.9
GNI, Atlas ($ billions)	181.8	GNI per capita, Atlas ($)	6,060
GNI, PPP ($ billions)	302.7	GNI per capita, PPP ($)	10,090

	1990	2000	2012
People			
Share of poorest 20% in nat'l consumption/income (%)	..	3.4	3.9
Life expectancy at birth (years)	66	71	75
Total fertility rate (births per woman)	3.8	2.9	2.4
Adolescent fertility rate (births per 1,000 women 15-19)	71	65	51
Contraceptive prevalence (% of married women 15-49)	59	69	76
Births attended by skilled health staff (% of total)	53	59	87
Under-five mortality rate (per 1,000 live births)	79	40	18
Child malnutrition, underweight (% of under age 5)	8.8	5.2	4.5
Child immunization, measles (% of ages 12-23 mos.)	64	97	94
Primary completion rate, total (% of relevant age group)	88	102	91
Gross secondary enrollment, total (% of relevant age group)	67	85	86
Ratio of girls to boys in primary & secondary school (%)	96	97	98
HIV prevalence rate (% population of ages 15-49)	0.6	0.7	0.4
Environment			
Forests (1,000 sq. km)	702	692	678
Deforestation (avg. annual %, 1990-2000 and 2000-2010)		0.1	0.2
Freshwater use (% of internal resources)	1.2	1.2	1.2
Access to improved water source (% total pop.)	74	81	87
Access to improved sanitation facilities (% total pop.)	54	63	73
Energy use per capita (kilograms of oil equivalent)	447	470	695
Carbon dioxide emissions per capita (metric tons)	1.0	1.2	2.0
Electricity use per capita (kilowatt-hours)	548	678	1,248
Economy			
GDP ($ billions)	26	53	204
GDP growth (annual %)	-5.1	3.0	6.3
GDP implicit price deflator (annual % growth)	6,836.9	3.7	1.6
Value added in agriculture (% of GDP)	9	8	7
Value added in industry (% of GDP)	27	30	35
Value added in services (% of GDP)	64	62	58
Exports of goods and services (% of GDP)	16	16	26
Imports of goods and services (% of GDP)	14	18	24
Gross capital formation (% of GDP)	16	20	28
Central government revenue (% of GDP)	12.5	17.4	19.5
Central government cash surplus/deficit (% of GDP)	-8.1	-2.1	1.2
States and markets			
Starting a business (days)	..	98	25
Stock market capitalization (% of GDP)	3.1	19.8	47.5
Military expenditures (% of GDP)	1.2	1.8	1.3
Mobile cellular subscriptions (per 100 people)	0.0	4.9	98.0
Individuals using the Internet (% of population)	0.0	3.1	38.2
Paved roads (% of total)	9.9	14.0	13.3
High-technology exports (% of manufactured exports)	1	4	3
Global links			
Merchandise trade (% of GDP)	22	27	43
Net barter terms of trade index (2000 = 100)	114	100	164
Total external debt stocks ($ billions)	20.2	28.8	54.1
Total debt service (% of exports)	11.1	27.9	12.5
Net migration (thousands)	-300	-625	-300
Personal remittances received ($ millions)	87	718	2,788
Foreign direct investment, net inflows ($ billions)	0.0	0.8	12.2
Net official development assistance received ($ millions)	397	397	394

Philippines

East Asia & Pacific   **Lower middle income**

Population (millions)	96.7	Population growth (%)	1.7
Surface area (1,000 sq. km)	300	Population living below $1.25 a day (%)	18.4
GNI, Atlas ($ billions)	241.7	GNI per capita, Atlas ($)	2,500
GNI, PPP ($ billions)	423.6	GNI per capita, PPP ($)	4,380

	1990	2000	2012
People			
Share of poorest 20% in nat'l consumption/income (%)	5.9	5.4	6.0
Life expectancy at birth (years)	65	67	69
Total fertility rate (births per woman)	4.3	3.8	3.1
Adolescent fertility rate (births per 1,000 women 15-19)	51	52	47
Contraceptive prevalence (% of married women 15-49)	40	47	49
Births attended by skilled health staff (% of total)	53	58	72
Under-five mortality rate (per 1,000 live births)	59	40	30
Child malnutrition, underweight (% of under age 5)	29.9	20.7	20.2
Child immunization, measles (% of ages 12-23 mos.)	85	78	85
Primary completion rate, total (% of relevant age group)	89	100	91
Gross secondary enrollment, total (% of relevant age group)	72	75	85
Ratio of girls to boys in primary & secondary school (%)	100	103	101
HIV prevalence rate (% population of ages 15-49)	0.1	0.1	0.1
Environment			
Forests (1,000 sq. km)	66	71	77
Deforestation (avg. annual %, 1990-2000 and 2000-2010)		-0.8	-0.7
Freshwater use (% of internal resources)	..	..	17.0
Access to improved water source (% total pop.)	84	88	92
Access to improved sanitation facilities (% total pop.)	57	66	74
Energy use per capita (kilograms of oil equivalent)	462	513	426
Carbon dioxide emissions per capita (metric tons)	0.7	0.9	0.9
Electricity use per capita (kilowatt-hours)	361	502	647
Economy			
GDP ($ billions)	44	81	250
GDP growth (annual %)	3.0	4.4	6.8
GDP implicit price deflator (annual % growth)	13.0	5.7	1.9
Value added in agriculture (% of GDP)	22	14	12
Value added in industry (% of GDP)	34	34	31
Value added in services (% of GDP)	44	52	57
Exports of goods and services (% of GDP)	28	51	31
Imports of goods and services (% of GDP)	33	53	34
Gross capital formation (% of GDP)	24	18	18
Central government revenue (% of GDP)	16.2	14.2	14.5
Central government cash surplus/deficit (% of GDP)	-2.8	-3.7	-1.9
States and markets			
Starting a business (days)	..	49	35
Stock market capitalization (% of GDP)	13.4	32.0	105.6
Military expenditures (% of GDP)	2.1	1.6	1.2
Mobile cellular subscriptions (per 100 people)	0.0	8.3	106.5
Individuals using the Internet (% of population)	0.0	2.0	36.2
Paved roads (% of total)	..	20.0	..
High-technology exports (% of manufactured exports)	32	73	49
Global links			
Merchandise trade (% of GDP)	48	95	47
Net barter terms of trade index (2000 = 100)	87	100	66
Total external debt stocks ($ billions)	30.6	58.5	61.4
Total debt service (% of exports)	27.6	16.0	8.0
Net migration (thousands)	-695	-1,128	-700
Personal remittances received ($ billions)	1.5	7.0	24.6
Foreign direct investment, net inflows ($ billions)	0.5	2.2	2.8
Net official development assistance received ($ millions)	1,271	572	5

Poland

Population (millions)	38.5	Population growth (%)		0.0
Surface area (1,000 sq. km)	313	Population living below $1.25 a day (%)		<2
GNI, Atlas ($ billions)	488.0	GNI per capita, Atlas ($)		12,660
GNI, PPP ($ billions)	838.6	GNI per capita, PPP ($)		21,760

	1990	2000	2012
People			
Share of poorest 20% in nat'l consumption/income (%)	9.2	7.8	7.9
Life expectancy at birth (years)	71	74	77
Total fertility rate (births per woman)	2.1	1.4	1.3
Adolescent fertility rate (births per 1,000 women 15-19)	31	17	12
Contraceptive prevalence (% of married women 15-49)	73	..	..
Births attended by skilled health staff (% of total)	100	100	..
Under-five mortality rate (per 1,000 live births)	17	9	5
Child malnutrition, underweight (% of under age 5)	..	..	..
Child immunization, measles (% of ages 12-23 mos.)	95	97	98
Primary completion rate, total (% of relevant age group)	97	95	95
Gross secondary enrollment, total (% of relevant age group)	87	100	98
Ratio of girls to boys in primary & secondary school (%)	101	98	99
HIV prevalence rate (% population of ages 15-49)	..	..	..
Environment			
Forests (1,000 sq. km)	89	91	94
Deforestation (avg. annual %, 1990-2000 and 2000-2010)		-0.2	-0.3
Freshwater use (% of internal resources)	28.3	23.9	22.3
Access to improved water source (% total pop.)	..	..	..
Access to improved sanitation facilities (% total pop.)	..	89	..
Energy use per capita (kilograms of oil equivalent)	2,705	2,317	2,505
Carbon dioxide emissions per capita (metric tons)	9.6	7.8	8.3
Electricity use per capita (kilowatt-hours)	3,272	3,240	3,832
Economy			
GDP ($ billions)	65	171	490
GDP growth (annual %)	-7.0	4.3	1.8
GDP implicit price deflator (annual % growth)	55.3	7.3	2.5
Value added in agriculture (% of GDP)	8	5	4
Value added in industry (% of GDP)	50	32	32
Value added in services (% of GDP)	42	63	65
Exports of goods and services (% of GDP)	26	27	46
Imports of goods and services (% of GDP)	20	34	46
Gross capital formation (% of GDP)	24	25	21
Central government revenue (% of GDP)	..	31.5	30.5
Central government cash surplus/deficit (% of GDP)	..	-2.8	-4.3
States and markets			
Starting a business (days)	..	31	30
Stock market capitalization (% of GDP)	0.2	18.3	36.3
Military expenditures (% of GDP)	2.4	1.8	1.9
Mobile cellular subscriptions (per 100 people)	0.0	17.6	140.3
Individuals using the Internet (% of population)	0.0	7.3	65.0
Paved roads (% of total)	61.6	67.0	68.0
High-technology exports (% of manufactured exports)	3	3	7
Global links			
Merchandise trade (% of GDP)	40	47	77
Net barter terms of trade index (2000 = 100)	..	100	97
Total external debt stocks ($ millions)	..	..	..
Total debt service (% of exports)	..	..	..
Net migration (thousands)	-222	-115	-38
Personal remittances received ($ billions)	..	1.5	6.9
Foreign direct investment, net inflows ($ billions)	0.1	9.3	6.7
Net official development assistance received ($ millions)	..	..	..

Portugal

Population (millions)	10.5	Population growth (%)	-0.4
Surface area (1,000 sq. km)	92	Population living below $1.25 a day (%)	..
GNI, Atlas ($ billions)	217.0	GNI per capita, Atlas ($)	20,640
GNI, PPP ($ billions)	266.3	GNI per capita, PPP ($)	25,330

	1990	2000	2012
People			
Share of poorest 20% in nat'l consumption/income (%)	..	..	..
Life expectancy at birth (years)	74	76	80
Total fertility rate (births per woman)	1.6	1.6	1.3
Adolescent fertility rate (births per 1,000 women 15-19)	25	20	13
Contraceptive prevalence (% of married women 15-49)	..	..	67
Births attended by skilled health staff (% of total)	98	100	..
Under-five mortality rate (per 1,000 live births)	15	7	4
Child malnutrition, underweight (% of under age 5)	..	..	..
Child immunization, measles (% of ages 12-23 mos.)	85	87	97
Primary completion rate, total (% of relevant age group)	..	..	..
Gross secondary enrollment, total (% of relevant age group)	60	105	110
Ratio of girls to boys in primary & secondary school (%)	97	101	100
HIV prevalence rate (% population of ages 15-49)	..	..	..
Environment			
Forests (1,000 sq. km)	33	34	35
Deforestation (avg. annual %, 1990-2000 and 2000-2010)		-0.3	-0.1
Freshwater use (% of internal resources)	..	22.3	22.3
Access to improved water source (% total pop.)	96	98	100
Access to improved sanitation facilities (% total pop.)	94	98	100
Energy use per capita (kilograms of oil equivalent)	1,677	2,398	2,087
Carbon dioxide emissions per capita (metric tons)	4.2	6.1	5.0
Electricity use per capita (kilowatt-hours)	2,542	3,989	4,848
Economy			
GDP ($ billions)	78	117	212
GDP growth (annual %)	4.0	3.9	-3.2
GDP implicit price deflator (annual % growth)	13.1	3.3	-0.3
Value added in agriculture (% of GDP)	9	4	2
Value added in industry (% of GDP)	29	28	24
Value added in services (% of GDP)	63	68	74
Exports of goods and services (% of GDP)	30	29	39
Imports of goods and services (% of GDP)	37	40	39
Gross capital formation (% of GDP)	27	28	17
Central government revenue (% of GDP)	..	34.6	39.9
Central government cash surplus/deficit (% of GDP)	..	-2.6	-4.0
States and markets			
Starting a business (days)	..	78	3
Stock market capitalization (% of GDP)	11.8	51.7	30.9
Military expenditures (% of GDP)	2.4	1.9	1.8
Mobile cellular subscriptions (per 100 people)	0.1	64.7	116.1
Individuals using the Internet (% of population)	0.0	16.4	64.0
Paved roads (% of total)	..	86.0	..
High-technology exports (% of manufactured exports)	4	6	4
Global links			
Merchandise trade (% of GDP)	54	55	61
Net barter terms of trade index (2000 = 100)	..	100	91
Total external debt stocks ($ millions)	..	..	..
Total debt service (% of exports)	..	..	..
Net migration (thousands)	149	180	100
Personal remittances received ($ billions)	4.5	3.5	3.9
Foreign direct investment, net inflows ($ billions)	2.6	6.7	13.4
Net official development assistance received ($ millions)	..	..	..

Puerto Rico

Population (millions)	3.7	Population growth (%)		-0.7
Surface area (1,000 sq. km)	8.9	Population living below $1.25 a day (%)		..
GNI, Atlas ($ billions)	66.0	GNI per capita, Atlas ($)		18,000
GNI, PPP ($ millions)	..	GNI per capita, PPP ($)		..

	1990	2000	2012
People			
Share of poorest 20% in nat'l consumption/income (%)	..	..	..
Life expectancy at birth (years)	74	77	79
Total fertility rate (births per woman)	2.2	2.0	1.6
Adolescent fertility rate (births per 1,000 women 15-19)	70	68	47
Contraceptive prevalence (% of married women 15-49)	..	84	..
Births attended by skilled health staff (% of total)	..	100	..
Under-five mortality rate (per 1,000 live births)	..	..	..
Child malnutrition, underweight (% of under age 5)	..	..	..
Child immunization, measles (% of ages 12-23 mos.)	..	..	..
Primary completion rate, total (% of relevant age group)	..	..	..
Gross secondary enrollment, total (% of relevant age group)	..	..	78
Ratio of girls to boys in primary & secondary school (%)	..	..	104
HIV prevalence rate (% population of ages 15-49)	..	..	..
Environment			
Forests (1,000 sq. km)	2.9	4.6	5.6
Deforestation (avg. annual %, 1990-2000 and 2000-2010)		-4.9	-1.8
Freshwater use (% of internal resources)	11.2	12.1	14.0
Access to improved water source (% total pop.)	94	94	..
Access to improved sanitation facilities (% total pop.)	99	99	99
Energy use per capita (kilograms of oil equivalent)	..	..	..
Carbon dioxide emissions per capita (metric tons)	..	..	..
Electricity use per capita (kilowatt-hours)	..	..	..
Economy			
GDP ($ billions)	30.6	61.7	101.5
GDP growth (annual %)	3.8	6.3	0.5
GDP implicit price deflator (annual % growth)	4.3	0.3	2.2
Value added in agriculture (% of GDP)	2	1	1
Value added in industry (% of GDP)	43	43	50
Value added in services (% of GDP)	55	56	49
Exports of goods and services (% of GDP)	76	72	79
Imports of goods and services (% of GDP)	72	62	59
Gross capital formation (% of GDP)	17	20	10
Central government revenue (% of GDP)	..	..	..
Central government cash surplus/deficit (% of GDP)	..	..	..
States and markets			
Starting a business (days)	..	7	6
Stock market capitalization (% of GDP)	..	..	..
Military expenditures (% of GDP)	..	..	..
Mobile cellular subscriptions (per 100 people)	0.6	34.7	82.6
Individuals using the Internet (% of population)	0.0	10.5	51.4
Paved roads (% of total)	..	94.0	..
High-technology exports (% of manufactured exports)	..	..	..
Global links			
Merchandise trade (% of GDP)	..	..	..
Net barter terms of trade index (2000 = 100)	..	..	..
Total external debt stocks ($ millions)	..	..	..
Total debt service (% of exports)	..	..	..
Net migration (thousands)	0	-146	-104
Personal remittances received ($ millions)	..	..	..
Foreign direct investment, net inflows ($ millions)	..	..	..
Net official development assistance received ($ millions)	..	..	..

Qatar

Population (millions)	2.1	Population growth (%)		7.1
Surface area (1,000 sq. km)	12	Population living below $1.25 a day (%)		..
GNI, Atlas ($ billions)	142.6	GNI per capita, Atlas ($)		74,600
GNI, PPP ($ billions)	168.8	GNI per capita, PPP ($)		88,350

	1990	2000	2012
People			
Share of poorest 20% in nat'l consumption/income (%)	..	..	3.9
Life expectancy at birth (years)	75	77	78
Total fertility rate (births per woman)	4.0	3.2	2.0
Adolescent fertility rate (births per 1,000 women 15-19)	49	21	10
Contraceptive prevalence (% of married women 15-49)	..	43	..
Births attended by skilled health staff (% of total)	..	100	100
Under-five mortality rate (per 1,000 live births)	21	12	7
Child malnutrition, underweight (% of under age 5)	..	..	..
Child immunization, measles (% of ages 12-23 mos.)	79	91	97
Primary completion rate, total (% of relevant age group)	73	92	..
Gross secondary enrollment, total (% of relevant age group)	80	86	112
Ratio of girls to boys in primary & secondary school (%)	106	110	..
HIV prevalence rate (% population of ages 15-49)	..	..	..
Environment			
Forests (sq. km)	0.0	0.0	0.0
Deforestation (avg. annual %, 1990-2000 and 2000-2010)		0.0	0.0
Freshwater use (% of internal resources)	..	524.8	792.9
Access to improved water source (% total pop.)	100	100	100
Access to improved sanitation facilities (% total pop.)	100	100	100
Energy use per capita (kilograms of oil equivalent)	13,696	18,320	17,419
Carbon dioxide emissions per capita (metric tons)	24.7	58.5	40.3
Electricity use per capita (kilowatt-hours)	9,586	14,319	15,755
Economy			
GDP ($ billions)	7.4	17.8	192.4
GDP growth (annual %)		3.3	6.2
GDP implicit price deflator (annual % growth)	..	-4.4	4.4
Value added in agriculture (% of GDP)	..	..	..
Value added in industry (% of GDP)	..	..	..
Value added in services (% of GDP)	..	..	..
Exports of goods and services (% of GDP)	..	67	75
Imports of goods and services (% of GDP)	..	22	28
Gross capital formation (% of GDP)	..	20	28
Central government revenue (% of GDP)	..	..	34.2
Central government cash surplus/deficit (% of GDP)	..	..	2.9
States and markets			
Starting a business (days)	..	..	9
Stock market capitalization (% of GDP)	..	29.0	65.7
Military expenditures (% of GDP)	..	3.9	1.5
Mobile cellular subscriptions (per 100 people)	0.8	20.4	126.9
Individuals using the Internet (% of population)	0.0	4.9	88.1
Paved roads (% of total)	85.6	90.0	..
High-technology exports (% of manufactured exports)	0	0	0
Global links			
Merchandise trade (% of GDP)	76	84	86
Net barter terms of trade index (2000 = 100)	..	100	218
Total external debt stocks ($ millions)	..	..	..
Total debt service (% of exports)	..	..	..
Net migration (thousands)	-22	170	500
Personal remittances received ($ millions)	..	..	803
Foreign direct investment, net inflows ($ millions)	5	252	327
Net official development assistance received ($ millions)	3.0	..	..

Romania

Population (millions)	20.1	Population growth (%)	-0.4
Surface area (1,000 sq. km)	238	Population living below $1.25 a day (%)	<2
GNI, Atlas ($ billions)	171.9	GNI per capita, Atlas ($)	8,560
GNI, PPP ($ billions)	354.3	GNI per capita, PPP ($)	17,650

	1990	2000	2012
People			
Share of poorest 20% in nat'l consumption/income (%)	9.9	8.2	8.8
Life expectancy at birth (years)	70	71	75
Total fertility rate (births per woman)	1.8	1.3	1.5
Adolescent fertility rate (births per 1,000 women 15-19)	52	33	31
Contraceptive prevalence (% of married women 15-49)	57	64	..
Births attended by skilled health staff (% of total)	100	99	99
Under-five mortality rate (per 1,000 live births)	38	27	12
Child malnutrition, underweight (% of under age 5)	5.0	3.7	..
Child immunization, measles (% of ages 12-23 mos.)	92	98	94
Primary completion rate, total (% of relevant age group)	88	90	97
Gross secondary enrollment, total (% of relevant age group)	102	81	96
Ratio of girls to boys in primary & secondary school (%)	98	101	98
HIV prevalence rate (% population of ages 15-49)	..	..	..
Environment			
Forests (1,000 sq. km)	64	64	66
Deforestation (avg. annual %, 1990-2000 and 2000-2010)		0.0	-0.3
Freshwater use (% of internal resources)	48.3	21.2	16.3
Access to improved water source (% total pop.)	75	84	..
Access to improved sanitation facilities (% total pop.)	71	72	..
Energy use per capita (kilograms of oil equivalent)	2,683	1,614	1,778
Carbon dioxide emissions per capita (metric tons)	6.8	4.0	3.9
Electricity use per capita (kilowatt-hours)	2,925	1,988	2,639
Economy			
GDP ($ billions)	38.3	37.3	169.4
GDP growth (annual %)	-5.6	2.1	0.4
GDP implicit price deflator (annual % growth)	13.6	45.3	5.2
Value added in agriculture (% of GDP)	24	12	6
Value added in industry (% of GDP)	50	33	42
Value added in services (% of GDP)	26	55	52
Exports of goods and services (% of GDP)	17	33	40
Imports of goods and services (% of GDP)	26	38	45
Gross capital formation (% of GDP)	30	19	27
Central government revenue (% of GDP)	..	25.7	30.1
Central government cash surplus/deficit (% of GDP)	..	-2.0	-5.1
States and markets			
Starting a business (days)	..	29	9
Stock market capitalization (% of GDP)	..	2.9	9.4
Military expenditures (% of GDP)	4.5	2.5	1.3
Mobile cellular subscriptions (per 100 people)	0.0	11.2	105.0
Individuals using the Internet (% of population)	0.0	3.6	50.0
Paved roads (% of total)	51.0	53.0	..
High-technology exports (% of manufactured exports)	3	6	6
Global links			
Merchandise trade (% of GDP)	33	63	75
Net barter terms of trade index (2000 = 100)	..	100	111
Total external debt stocks ($ billions)	1	11	132
Total debt service (% of exports)	0.3	20.1	34.2
Net migration (thousands)	-411	-52	-45
Personal remittances received ($ millions)	..	96	3,674
Foreign direct investment, net inflows ($ billions)	0.0	1.0	2.0
Net official development assistance received ($ millions)	..	..	..

Russian Federation

High income

Population (millions)	143.5	Population growth (%)		0.4
Surface area (1,000 sq. km)	17,098	Population living below $1.25 a day (%)		<2
GNI, Atlas ($ billions)	1,822.7	GNI per capita, Atlas ($)		12,700
GNI, PPP ($ billions)	3,272.9	GNI per capita, PPP ($)		22,800

	1990	2000	2012
People			
Share of poorest 20% in nat'l consumption/income (%)	*4.4*	*6.1*	*6.5*
Life expectancy at birth (years)	69	65	70
Total fertility rate (births per woman)	1.9	1.2	1.6
Adolescent fertility rate (births per 1,000 women 15-19)	51	31	26
Contraceptive prevalence (% of married women 15-49)	*63*	*84*	80
Births attended by skilled health staff (% of total)	99	99	100
Under-five mortality rate (per 1,000 live births)	26	23	10
Child malnutrition, underweight (% of under age 5)	..	..	..
Child immunization, measles (% of ages 12-23 mos.)	*83*	97	98
Primary completion rate, total (% of relevant age group)	..	91	98
Gross secondary enrollment, total (% of relevant age group)	96	*92*	85
Ratio of girls to boys in primary & secondary school (%)	..	*100*	98
HIV prevalence rate (% population of ages 15-49)	..	..	..
Environment			
Forests (1,000 sq. km)	8,090	8,093	*8,092*
Deforestation (avg. annual %, 1990-2000 and 2000-2010)		0.0	*0.0*
Freshwater use (% of internal resources)	..	1.5	*1.5*
Access to improved water source (% total pop.)	93	95	97
Access to improved sanitation facilities (% total pop.)	74	72	70
Energy use per capita (kilograms of oil equivalent)	5,929	4,233	*5,113*
Carbon dioxide emissions per capita (metric tons)	*14.4*	10.6	*12.2*
Electricity use per capita (kilowatt-hours)	6,673	5,209	*6,486*
Economy			
GDP ($ billions)	517	260	2,015
GDP growth (annual %)	-3.0	10.0	3.4
GDP implicit price deflator (annual % growth)	15.9	37.7	8.5
Value added in agriculture (% of GDP)	17	6	4
Value added in industry (% of GDP)	48	38	36
Value added in services (% of GDP)	35	56	60
Exports of goods and services (% of GDP)	18	44	29
Imports of goods and services (% of GDP)	18	24	22
Gross capital formation (% of GDP)	30	19	26
Central government revenue (% of GDP)	..	31.8	31.4
Central government cash surplus/deficit (% of GDP)	..	7.0	3.3
States and markets			
Starting a business (days)	..	*43*	15
Stock market capitalization (% of GDP)	*0.0*	15.0	43.4
Military expenditures (% of GDP)	19.1	3.7	4.5
Mobile cellular subscriptions (per 100 people)	0.0	2.2	182.9
Individuals using the Internet (% of population)	0.0	2.0	53.3
Paved roads (% of total)	74.2	*67.4*	..
High-technology exports (% of manufactured exports)		16	8
Global links			
Merchandise trade (% of GDP)	..	58	43
Net barter terms of trade index (2000 = 100)	..	100	249
Total external debt stocks ($ millions)	..	..	..
Total debt service (% of exports)	..	..	..
Net migration (thousands)	2,220	1,635	1,100
Personal remittances received ($ billions)	..	1.3	5.8
Foreign direct investment, net inflows ($ billions)	*1.2*	2.7	50.7
Net official development assistance received ($ millions)	..	..	..

Rwanda

Sub-Saharan Africa				Low income

Population (millions)	11.5	Population growth (%)		2.8
Surface area (1,000 sq. km)	26	Population living below $1.25 a day (%)		63.2
GNI, Atlas ($ billions)	6.9	GNI per capita, Atlas ($)		600
GNI, PPP ($ billions)	15.1	GNI per capita, PPP ($)		1,320

	1990	2000	2012
People			
Share of poorest 20% in nat'l consumption/income (%)	..	4.8	5.2
Life expectancy at birth (years)	33	48	63
Total fertility rate (births per woman)	7.3	5.9	4.6
Adolescent fertility rate (births per 1,000 women 15-19)	64	49	34
Contraceptive prevalence (% of married women 15-49)	21	13	52
Births attended by skilled health staff (% of total)	26	31	69
Under-five mortality rate (per 1,000 live births)	151	182	55
Child malnutrition, underweight (% of under age 5)	24.3	20.3	11.7
Child immunization, measles (% of ages 12-23 mos.)	83	74	97
Primary completion rate, total (% of relevant age group)	43	23	58
Gross secondary enrollment, total (% of relevant age group)	16	11	32
Ratio of girls to boys in primary & secondary school (%)	95	93	102
HIV prevalence rate (% population of ages 15-49)	5.3	4.7	2.9
Environment			
Forests (1,000 sq. km)	3.2	3.4	4.5
Deforestation (avg. annual %, 1990-2000 and 2000-2010)		-0.8	-2.4
Freshwater use (% of internal resources)	..	1.6	1.6
Access to improved water source (% total pop.)	60	66	71
Access to improved sanitation facilities (% total pop.)	30	47	64
Energy use per capita (kilograms of oil equivalent)	..	..	..
Carbon dioxide emissions per capita (metric tons)	0.09	0.08	0.05
Electricity use per capita (kilowatt-hours)	..	..	..
Economy			
GDP ($ billions)	2.6	1.7	7.1
GDP growth (annual %)	-2.4	8.3	8.0
GDP implicit price deflator (annual % growth)	13.5	2.8	5.9
Value added in agriculture (% of GDP)	33	37	33
Value added in industry (% of GDP)	25	14	16
Value added in services (% of GDP)	43	49	51
Exports of goods and services (% of GDP)	6	6	13
Imports of goods and services (% of GDP)	14	25	34
Gross capital formation (% of GDP)	15	13	23
Central government revenue (% of GDP)	9.8	..	15.0
Central government cash surplus/deficit (% of GDP)	-8.8	..	-0.9
States and markets			
Starting a business (days)	..	18	2
Stock market capitalization (% of GDP)	..	..	..
Military expenditures (% of GDP)	3.7	3.5	1.1
Mobile cellular subscriptions (per 100 people)	0.0	0.5	49.7
Individuals using the Internet (% of population)	0.0	0.1	8.0
Paved roads (% of total)	9.0	8.0	..
High-technology exports (% of manufactured exports)	..	2	2
Global links			
Merchandise trade (% of GDP)	16	15	35
Net barter terms of trade index (2000 = 100)	40	100	215
Total external debt stocks ($ billions)	0.7	1.3	1.3
Total debt service (% of exports)	14.3	25.7	2.2
Net migration (thousands)	-1,533	-64	-45
Personal remittances received ($ millions)	3	7	182
Foreign direct investment, net inflows ($ millions)	8	8	160
Net official development assistance received ($ millions)	288	321	879

Samoa

East Asia & Pacific   **Lower middle income**

Population (thousands)	189	Population growth (%)	0.8
Surface area (1,000 sq. km)	2.8	Population living below $1.25 a day (%)	..
GNI, Atlas ($ millions)	615.0	GNI per capita, Atlas ($)	3,260
GNI, PPP ($ millions)	803.2	GNI per capita, PPP ($)	4,250

	1990	2000	2012
People			
Share of poorest 20% in nat'l consumption/income (%)	..	..	..
Life expectancy at birth (years)	65	69	73
Total fertility rate (births per woman)	5.1	4.5	4.2
Adolescent fertility rate (births per 1,000 women 15-19)	36	40	28
Contraceptive prevalence (% of married women 15-49)	..	25	29
Births attended by skilled health staff (% of total)	76	100	81
Under-five mortality rate (per 1,000 live births)	30	22	18
Child malnutrition, underweight (% of under age 5)	..	1.7	..
Child immunization, measles (% of ages 12-23 mos.)	89	93	85
Primary completion rate, total (% of relevant age group)	..	94	102
Gross secondary enrollment, total (% of relevant age group)	..	78	86
Ratio of girls to boys in primary & secondary school (%)	..	107	105
HIV prevalence rate (% population of ages 15-49)	..	..	..
Environment			
Forests (1,000 sq. km)	1.3	1.7	1.7
Deforestation (avg. annual %, 1990-2000 and 2000-2010)		-2.8	0.0
Freshwater use (% of internal resources)	..	..	..
Access to improved water source (% total pop.)	89	93	99
Access to improved sanitation facilities (% total pop.)	93	92	92
Energy use per capita (kilograms of oil equivalent)	265	..	..
Carbon dioxide emissions per capita (metric tons)	0.8	0.8	0.9
Electricity use per capita (kilowatt-hours)	..	..	..
Economy			
GDP ($ millions)	112	240	684
GDP growth (annual %)	-4.4	7.0	2.9
GDP implicit price deflator (annual % growth)	9.0	2.8	1.6
Value added in agriculture (% of GDP)	..	17	10
Value added in industry (% of GDP)	..	26	27
Value added in services (% of GDP)	..	57	63
Exports of goods and services (% of GDP)	..	34	32
Imports of goods and services (% of GDP)	..	57	61
Gross capital formation (% of GDP)	..	..	..
Central government revenue (% of GDP)	..	..	0.0
Central government cash surplus/deficit (% of GDP)	..	..	0.0
States and markets			
Starting a business (days)	..	42	9
Stock market capitalization (% of GDP)	..	..	..
Military expenditures (% of GDP)	..	..	..
Mobile cellular subscriptions (per 100 people)	0.0	1.4	..
Individuals using the Internet (% of population)	0.0	0.6	12.9
Paved roads (% of total)	..	14.0	..
High-technology exports (% of manufactured exports)	..	1	0
Global links			
Merchandise trade (% of GDP)	80	71	62
Net barter terms of trade index (2000 = 100)	..	100	81
Total external debt stocks ($ millions)	92	139	423
Total debt service (% of exports)	10.6	5.7	5.3
Net migration (thousands)	-13.7	-15.7	-12.7
Personal remittances received ($ millions)	43	45	159
Foreign direct investment, net inflows ($ millions)	6.6	-1.5	23.5
Net official development assistance received ($ millions)	48	27	121

San Marino

High income

Population (thousands)	31	Population growth (%)	0.6
Surface area (sq. km)	60	Population living below $1.25 a day (%)	..
GNI, Atlas ($ billions)	..	GNI per capita, Atlas ($)	..
GNI, PPP ($ millions)	..	GNI per capita, PPP ($)	..

	1990	2000	2012
People			
Share of poorest 20% in nat'l consumption/income (%)	..	..	..
Life expectancy at birth (years)	..	81	83
Total fertility rate (births per woman)	..	..	1.3
Adolescent fertility rate (births per 1,000 women 15-19)	..	..	..
Contraceptive prevalence (% of married women 15-49)	..	..	..
Births attended by skilled health staff (% of total)	..	..	..
Under-five mortality rate (per 1,000 live births)	11	6	3
Child malnutrition, underweight (% of under age 5)	..	..	..
Child immunization, measles (% of ages 12-23 mos.)	0	74	87
Primary completion rate, total (% of relevant age group)	..	..	93
Gross secondary enrollment, total (% of relevant age group)	..	..	95
Ratio of girls to boys in primary & secondary school (%)	..	..	100
HIV prevalence rate (% population of ages 15-49)	..	..	..
Environment			
Forests (sq. km)	0.0	0.0	0.0
Deforestation (avg. annual %, 1990-2000 and 2000-2010)		0.0	0.0
Freshwater use (% of internal resources)	..	..	..
Access to improved water source (% total pop.)	..	..	..
Access to improved sanitation facilities (% total pop.)	..	..	..
Energy use per capita (kilograms of oil equivalent)	..	..	..
Carbon dioxide emissions per capita (metric tons)	..	..	..
Electricity use per capita (kilowatt-hours)	..	..	..
Economy			
GDP ($ millions)	..	774	..
GDP growth (annual %)	2.1	2.2	..
GDP implicit price deflator (annual % growth)	8.4	2.6	..
Value added in agriculture (% of GDP)	..	..	..
Value added in industry (% of GDP)	..	..	..
Value added in services (% of GDP)	..	..	..
Exports of goods and services (% of GDP)	..	..	..
Imports of goods and services (% of GDP)	..	..	..
Gross capital formation (% of GDP)	..	..	..
Central government revenue (% of GDP)	..	46.4	..
Central government cash surplus/deficit (% of GDP)	..	1.3	..
States and markets			
Starting a business (days)	..	..	40
Stock market capitalization (% of GDP)	..	..	..
Military expenditures (% of GDP)	..	..	..
Mobile cellular subscriptions (per 100 people)	0.0	53.8	115.2
Individuals using the Internet (% of population)	0.0	48.8	50.9
Paved roads (% of total)	..	..	..
High-technology exports (% of manufactured exports)	..	..	..
Global links			
Merchandise trade (% of GDP)	..	..	..
Net barter terms of trade index (2000 = 100)	..	..	..
Total external debt stocks ($ millions)	..	..	..
Total debt service (% of exports)	..	..	..
Net migration (thousands)	..	..	..
Personal remittances received ($ millions)	..	..	..
Foreign direct investment, net inflows ($ millions)	..	..	..
Net official development assistance received ($ millions)	..	..	..

São Tomé and Príncipe

Sub-Saharan Africa		Lower middle income	
Population (thousands)	188	Population growth (%)	2.7
Surface area (sq. km)	960	Population living below $1.25 a day (%)	28.2
GNI, Atlas ($ millions)	246.6	GNI per capita, Atlas ($)	1,310
GNI, PPP ($ millions)	339.8	GNI per capita, PPP ($)	1,810

	1990	2000	2012
People			
Share of poorest 20% in nat'l consumption/income (%)	..	5.2	..
Life expectancy at birth (years)	62	63	66
Total fertility rate (births per woman)	5.4	4.7	4.1
Adolescent fertility rate (births per 1,000 women 15-19)	113	89	65
Contraceptive prevalence (% of married women 15-49)	..	29	38
Births attended by skilled health staff (% of total)	..	79	82
Under-five mortality rate (per 1,000 live births)	104	87	53
Child malnutrition, underweight (% of under age 5)	..	10.1	14.4
Child immunization, measles (% of ages 12-23 mos.)	71	69	92
Primary completion rate, total (% of relevant age group)	77	43	104
Gross secondary enrollment, total (% of relevant age group)	34	36	80
Ratio of girls to boys in primary & secondary school (%)	95	100	102
HIV prevalence rate (% population of ages 15-49)	0.1	0.9	1.0
Environment			
Forests (sq. km)	270	270	270
Deforestation (avg. annual %, 1990-2000 and 2000-2010)		0.0	0.0
Freshwater use (% of internal resources)	..	0.3	0.3
Access to improved water source (% total pop.)	..	78	97
Access to improved sanitation facilities (% total pop.)	..	21	34
Energy use per capita (kilograms of oil equivalent)	200	..	..
Carbon dioxide emissions per capita (metric tons)	0.4	0.3	0.6
Electricity use per capita (kilowatt-hours)	..	..	..
Economy			
GDP ($ millions)	..	77	263
GDP growth (annual %)	..	2.0	4.0
GDP implicit price deflator (annual % growth)	..	19.6	10.4
Value added in agriculture (% of GDP)	..	12	..
Value added in industry (% of GDP)	..	10	..
Value added in services (% of GDP)	..	77	..
Exports of goods and services (% of GDP)	..	21	11
Imports of goods and services (% of GDP)	..	57	53
Gross capital formation (% of GDP)	..	..	..
Central government revenue (% of GDP)	..	13.8	18.0
Central government cash surplus/deficit (% of GDP)	..	-16.4	-12.6
States and markets			
Starting a business (days)	..	..	5
Stock market capitalization (% of GDP)	..	..	..
Military expenditures (% of GDP)	..	..	..
Mobile cellular subscriptions (per 100 people)	0.0	0.0	65.0
Individuals using the Internet (% of population)	0.0	4.6	21.6
Paved roads (% of total)	61.6	68.0	..
High-technology exports (% of manufactured exports)	..	1	14
Global links			
Merchandise trade (% of GDP)	..	43	57
Net barter terms of trade index (2000 = 100)	101	100	107
Total external debt stocks ($ millions)	150	304	202
Total debt service (% of exports)	34.8	25.4	6.9
Net migration (thousands)	-3.7	-6.0	-1.5
Personal remittances received ($ millions)	0.3	0.5	6.4
Foreign direct investment, net inflows ($ millions)	-0.1	3.8	22.5
Net official development assistance received ($ millions)	54.1	34.9	48.8

Saudi Arabia

High income

Population (millions)	28.3	Population growth (%)		1.9
Surface area (1,000 sq. km)	2,150	Population living below $1.25 a day (%)		..
GNI, Atlas ($ billions)	687.8	GNI per capita, Atlas ($)		24,310
GNI, PPP ($ billions)	837.4	GNI per capita, PPP ($)		30,160

	1990	2000	2012
People			
Share of poorest 20% in nat'l consumption/income (%)	..	..	..
Life expectancy at birth (years)	69	73	75
Total fertility rate (births per woman)	5.8	4.0	2.7
Adolescent fertility rate (births per 1,000 women 15-19)	69	27	10
Contraceptive prevalence (% of married women 15-49)	..	21	24
Births attended by skilled health staff (% of total)	..	96	97
Under-five mortality rate (per 1,000 live births)	47	22	9
Child malnutrition, underweight (% of under age 5)	..	..	..
Child immunization, measles (% of ages 12-23 mos.)	88	94	98
Primary completion rate, total (% of relevant age group)	..	..	106
Gross secondary enrollment, total (% of relevant age group)	..	..	114
Ratio of girls to boys in primary & secondary school (%)	..	..	102
HIV prevalence rate (% population of ages 15-49)	..	..	..
Environment			
Forests (1,000 sq. km)	9.8	9.8	9.8
Deforestation (avg. annual %, 1990-2000 and 2000-2010)		0.0	0.0
Freshwater use (% of internal resources)	709.2	709.2	986.3
Access to improved water source (% total pop.)	92	95	97
Access to improved sanitation facilities (% total pop.)	92	97	100
Energy use per capita (kilograms of oil equivalent)	3,687	5,030	6,738
Carbon dioxide emissions per capita (metric tons)	13.4	14.7	17.0
Electricity use per capita (kilowatt-hours)	4,025	5,811	8,161
Economy			
GDP ($ billions)	117	188	711
GDP growth (annual %)	8.3	4.9	5.1
GDP implicit price deflator (annual % growth)	13.1	11.6	1.0
Value added in agriculture (% of GDP)	6	5	2
Value added in industry (% of GDP)	49	54	63
Value added in services (% of GDP)	45	41	35
Exports of goods and services (% of GDP)	41	44	56
Imports of goods and services (% of GDP)	32	25	30
Gross capital formation (% of GDP)	15	19	26
Central government revenue (% of GDP)	..	..	..
Central government cash surplus/deficit (% of GDP)	..	..	..
States and markets			
Starting a business (days)	..	74	21
Stock market capitalization (% of GDP)	36.7	35.6	52.5
Military expenditures (% of GDP)	14.0	10.6	8.0
Mobile cellular subscriptions (per 100 people)	0.1	6.8	187.4
Individuals using the Internet (% of population)	0.0	2.2	54.0
Paved roads (% of total)	40.6	30.0	..
High-technology exports (% of manufactured exports)	0	0	1
Global links			
Merchandise trade (% of GDP)	59	57	75
Net barter terms of trade index (2000 = 100)	..	100	216
Total external debt stocks ($ millions)	..	..	..
Total debt service (% of exports)	..	..	..
Net migration (thousands)	-122	2,198	300
Personal remittances received ($ millions)	..	..	246
Foreign direct investment, net inflows ($ billions)	1.9	-1.9	12.2
Net official development assistance received ($ millions)	14.7	22.0	..

Senegal

Sub-Saharan Africa		Lower middle income	
Population (millions)	13.7	Population growth (%)	2.9
Surface area (1,000 sq. km)	197	Population living below $1.25 a day (%)	29.6
GNI, Atlas ($ billions)	14.2	GNI per capita, Atlas ($)	1,030
GNI, PPP ($ billions)	25.8	GNI per capita, PPP ($)	1,880

	1990	2000	2012
People			
Share of poorest 20% in nat'l consumption/income (%)	3.5	6.6	6.1
Life expectancy at birth (years)	57	58	63
Total fertility rate (births per woman)	6.6	5.6	5.0
Adolescent fertility rate (births per 1,000 women 15-19)	134	107	94
Contraceptive prevalence (% of married women 15-49)	7	11	13
Births attended by skilled health staff (% of total)	47	58	65
Under-five mortality rate (per 1,000 live births)	142	139	60
Child malnutrition, underweight (% of under age 5)	19.0	20.3	14.4
Child immunization, measles (% of ages 12-23 mos.)	51	48	84
Primary completion rate, total (% of relevant age group)	42	39	60
Gross secondary enrollment, total (% of relevant age group)	15	16	41
Ratio of girls to boys in primary & secondary school (%)	68	82	101
HIV prevalence rate (% population of ages 15-49)	0.1	0.5	0.5
Environment			
Forests (1,000 sq. km)	93	89	84
Deforestation (avg. annual %, 1990-2000 and 2000-2010)		0.5	0.5
Freshwater use (% of internal resources)	..	8.6	8.6
Access to improved water source (% total pop.)	60	66	74
Access to improved sanitation facilities (% total pop.)	35	43	52
Energy use per capita (kilograms of oil equivalent)	224	243	264
Carbon dioxide emissions per capita (metric tons)	0.4	0.4	0.5
Electricity use per capita (kilowatt-hours)	104	102	187
Economy			
GDP ($ billions)	5.7	4.7	14.0
GDP growth (annual %)	-0.7	3.2	3.5
GDP implicit price deflator (annual % growth)	0.0	1.9	1.7
Value added in agriculture (% of GDP)	20	19	17
Value added in industry (% of GDP)	22	23	24
Value added in services (% of GDP)	58	58	59
Exports of goods and services (% of GDP)	25	28	24
Imports of goods and services (% of GDP)	32	37	42
Gross capital formation (% of GDP)	9	20	28
Central government revenue (% of GDP)	..	..	20.2
Central government cash surplus/deficit (% of GDP)	..	..	-6.2
States and markets			
Starting a business (days)	..	59	6
Stock market capitalization (% of GDP)	..	..	..
Military expenditures (% of GDP)	2.0	1.3	1.5
Mobile cellular subscriptions (per 100 people)	0.0	2.5	83.6
Individuals using the Internet (% of population)	0.0	0.4	19.2
Paved roads (% of total)	27.2	29.0	35.5
High-technology exports (% of manufactured exports)	..	7	1
Global links			
Merchandise trade (% of GDP)	35	52	64
Net barter terms of trade index (2000 = 100)	172	100	109
Total external debt stocks ($ billions)	3.8	3.7	4.9
Total debt service (% of exports)	21.1	16.3	9.0
Net migration (thousands)	-70	-151	-100
Personal remittances received ($ millions)	142	233	1,478
Foreign direct investment, net inflows ($ millions)	57	63	338
Net official development assistance received ($ millions)	812	431	1,080

Serbia

Europe & Central Asia		Upper middle income	

Population (millions)	7.2	Population growth (%)	-0.5
Surface area (1,000 sq. km)	88	Population living below $1.25 a day (%)	<2
GNI, Atlas ($ billions)	38.1	GNI per capita, Atlas ($)	5,280
GNI, PPP ($ billions)	82.6	GNI per capita, PPP ($)	11,430

	1990	2000	2012
People			
Share of poorest 20% in nat'l consumption/income (%)	..	8.0	8.4
Life expectancy at birth (years)	71	72	75
Total fertility rate (births per woman)	1.8	1.5	1.3
Adolescent fertility rate (births per 1,000 women 15-19)	39	25	17
Contraceptive prevalence (% of married women 15-49)	..	59	61
Births attended by skilled health staff (% of total)	..	98	100
Under-five mortality rate (per 1,000 live births)	28	13	7
Child malnutrition, underweight (% of under age 5)	..	..	1.6
Child immunization, measles (% of ages 12-23 mos.)	82	89	87
Primary completion rate, total (% of relevant age group)	..	..	93
Gross secondary enrollment, total (% of relevant age group)	..	91	92
Ratio of girls to boys in primary & secondary school (%)	..	101	101
HIV prevalence rate (% population of ages 15-49)	..	..	..
Environment			
Forests (1,000 sq. km)	23	25	28
Deforestation (avg. annual %, 1990-2000 and 2000-2010)		-0.6	-1.0
Freshwater use (% of internal resources)	..	..	49.0
Access to improved water source (% total pop.)	99	100	99
Access to improved sanitation facilities (% total pop.)	96	96	97
Energy use per capita (kilograms of oil equivalent)	2,599	1,826	2,230
Carbon dioxide emissions per capita (metric tons)	..	..	6.3
Electricity use per capita (kilowatt-hours)	4,629	4,199	4,474
Economy			
GDP ($ billions)	..	6.1	37.5
GDP growth (annual %)	-8.0	5.3	-1.7
GDP implicit price deflator (annual % growth)	..	77.4	5.5
Value added in agriculture (% of GDP)	..	20	9
Value added in industry (% of GDP)	..	30	27
Value added in services (% of GDP)	..	50	64
Exports of goods and services (% of GDP)	..	24	38
Imports of goods and services (% of GDP)	..	40	54
Gross capital formation (% of GDP)	..	9	26
Central government revenue (% of GDP)	..	..	37.6
Central government cash surplus/deficit (% of GDP)	..	..	-4.5
States and markets			
Starting a business (days)	..	56	12
Stock market capitalization (% of GDP)	..	4.9	19.9
Military expenditures (% of GDP)	..	5.5	2.2
Mobile cellular subscriptions (per 100 people)	..	..	117.8
Individuals using the Internet (% of population)	..	..	48.1
Paved roads (% of total)	..	63.0	63.5
High-technology exports (% of manufactured exports)	..	..	..
Global links			
Merchandise trade (% of GDP)	..	..	81
Net barter terms of trade index (2000 = 100)	..	..	104
Total external debt stocks ($ billions)	17.8[f]	11.6[f]	34.4
Total debt service (% of exports)	..	..	36.7
Net migration (thousands)	428	-324	-100
Personal remittances received ($ millions)	..	..	2,763
Foreign direct investment, net inflows ($ millions)	126[f]	52[f]	355
Net official development assistance received ($ billions)	..	1.1[f]	1.1

Seychelles

Sub-Saharan Africa		Upper middle income	
Population (thousands)	88	Population growth (%)	1.0
Surface area (sq. km)	460	Population living below $1.25 a day (%)	<2
GNI, Atlas ($ billions)	1.1	GNI per capita, Atlas ($)	12,180
GNI, PPP ($ billions)	2.3	GNI per capita, PPP ($)	25,580

	1990	2000	2012
People			
Share of poorest 20% in nat'l consumption/income (%)	..	5.7	3.7
Life expectancy at birth (years)	71	73	73
Total fertility rate (births per woman)	2.7	2.1	2.4
Adolescent fertility rate (births per 1,000 women 15-19)	68	58	56
Contraceptive prevalence (% of married women 15-49)	..	..	..
Births attended by skilled health staff (% of total)	..	..	..
Under-five mortality rate (per 1,000 live births)	17	14	13
Child malnutrition, underweight (% of under age 5)	5.0	..	..
Child immunization, measles (% of ages 12-23 mos.)	86	97	98
Primary completion rate, total (% of relevant age group)	107	102	105
Gross secondary enrollment, total (% of relevant age group)	121	100	101
Ratio of girls to boys in primary & secondary school (%)	100	104	107
HIV prevalence rate (% population of ages 15-49)	..	..	..
Environment			
Forests (sq. km)	407	407	407
Deforestation (avg. annual %, 1990-2000 and 2000-2010)		0.0	0.0
Freshwater use (% of internal resources)	..	..	..
Access to improved water source (% total pop.)	96	96	96
Access to improved sanitation facilities (% total pop.)	97	97	97
Energy use per capita (kilograms of oil equivalent)	537	..	..
Carbon dioxide emissions per capita (metric tons)	1.6	7.0	7.8
Electricity use per capita (kilowatt-hours)	..	..	..
Economy			
GDP ($ millions)	369	615	1,129
GDP growth (annual %)	7.5	4.2	2.8
GDP implicit price deflator (annual % growth)	6.4	1.3	13.1
Value added in agriculture (% of GDP)	5	3	2
Value added in industry (% of GDP)	16	29	14
Value added in services (% of GDP)	79	68	84
Exports of goods and services (% of GDP)	15	32	45
Imports of goods and services (% of GDP)	51	55	98
Gross capital formation (% of GDP)	..	..	..
Central government revenue (% of GDP)	51.6	38.7	34.3
Central government cash surplus/deficit (% of GDP)	-4.9	-13.9	4.8
States and markets			
Starting a business (days)	..	..	39
Stock market capitalization (% of GDP)	..	..	..
Military expenditures (% of GDP)	4.0	1.7	0.8
Mobile cellular subscriptions (per 100 people)	0.0	32.5	147.8
Individuals using the Internet (% of population)	0.0	7.4	47.1
Paved roads (% of total)	56.9	96.1	96.5
High-technology exports (% of manufactured exports)	1	2	..
Global links			
Merchandise trade (% of GDP)	66	87	115
Net barter terms of trade index (2000 = 100)	78	100	78
Total external debt stocks ($ millions)	185	304	2,024
Total debt service (% of exports)	9.1	4.2	64.3
Net migration (thousands)	0.6	2.5	-1.6
Personal remittances received ($ millions)	7.5	3.2	1.3
Foreign direct investment, net inflows ($ millions)	20.2	24.3	11.6
Net official development assistance received ($ millions)	35.6	23.1	35.3

Sierra Leone

Low income

Population (millions)	6.0	Population growth (%)	1.9
Surface area (1,000 sq. km)	72	Population living below $1.25 a day (%)	51.7
GNI, Atlas ($ billions)	3.5	GNI per capita, Atlas ($)	580
GNI, PPP ($ billions)	8.0	GNI per capita, PPP ($)	1,340

	1990	2000	2012
People			
Share of poorest 20% in nat'l consumption/income (%)	..	6.1	7.8
Life expectancy at birth (years)	37	38	45
Total fertility rate (births per woman)	6.5	5.9	4.8
Adolescent fertility rate (births per 1,000 women 15-19)	139	128	101
Contraceptive prevalence (% of married women 15-49)	3	4	11
Births attended by skilled health staff (% of total)	..	42	63
Under-five mortality rate (per 1,000 live births)	257	234	182
Child malnutrition, underweight (% of under age 5)	25.4	24.7	21.1
Child immunization, measles (% of ages 12-23 mos.)	0	37	80
Primary completion rate, total (% of relevant age group)	..	..	72
Gross secondary enrollment, total (% of relevant age group)	16	26	..
Ratio of girls to boys in primary & secondary school (%)	64	70	..
HIV prevalence rate (% population of ages 15-49)	0.1	0.9	1.5
Environment			
Forests (1,000 sq. km)	31	29	27
Deforestation (avg. annual %, 1990-2000 and 2000-2010)		0.7	0.7
Freshwater use (% of internal resources)	..	0.3	0.3
Access to improved water source (% total pop.)	37	47	60
Access to improved sanitation facilities (% total pop.)	11	12	13
Energy use per capita (kilograms of oil equivalent)	..	..	..
Carbon dioxide emissions per capita (metric tons)	0.10	0.10	0.12
Electricity use per capita (kilowatt-hours)	..	..	..
Economy			
GDP ($ millions)	650	636	3,796
GDP growth (annual %)	3.3	6.7	15.2
GDP implicit price deflator (annual % growth)	70.6	3.3	12.0
Value added in agriculture (% of GDP)	47	58	57
Value added in industry (% of GDP)	19	28	8
Value added in services (% of GDP)	34	13	35
Exports of goods and services (% of GDP)	35	18	16
Imports of goods and services (% of GDP)	34	39	54
Gross capital formation (% of GDP)	13	1	40
Central government revenue (% of GDP)	5.6	11.4	11.4
Central government cash surplus/deficit (% of GDP)	..	-9.3	-5.2
States and markets			
Starting a business (days)	..	26	12
Stock market capitalization (% of GDP)	..	..	..
Military expenditures (% of GDP)	1.4	3.7	0.7
Mobile cellular subscriptions (per 100 people)	0.0	0.3	37.0
Individuals using the Internet (% of population)	0.0	0.1	1.3
Paved roads (% of total)	10.6	8.0	..
High-technology exports (% of manufactured exports)	..	28	..
Global links			
Merchandise trade (% of GDP)	44	25	63
Net barter terms of trade index (2000 = 100)	..	100	58
Total external debt stocks ($ billions)	1.2	1.2	1.1
Total debt service (% of exports)	10.0	76.4	1.5
Net migration (thousands)	-450	500	-21
Personal remittances received ($ millions)	0.0	7.1	61.0
Foreign direct investment, net inflows ($ millions)	32	39	548
Net official development assistance received ($ millions)	59	181	443

Singapore

Population (millions)	5.3	Population growth (%)		2.5
Surface area (sq. km)	710	Population living below $1.25 a day (%)		..
GNI, Atlas ($ billions)	250.8	GNI per capita, Atlas ($)		47,210
GNI, PPP ($ billions)	319.3	GNI per capita, PPP ($)		60,110

	1990	2000	2012
People			
Share of poorest 20% in nat'l consumption/income (%)	..	5.0	..
Life expectancy at birth (years)	76	78	82
Total fertility rate (births per woman)	1.9	1.4	1.3
Adolescent fertility rate (births per 1,000 women 15-19)	8	8	6
Contraceptive prevalence (% of married women 15-49)	65	..	..
Births attended by skilled health staff (% of total)	..	100	..
Under-five mortality rate (per 1,000 live births)	8	4	3
Child malnutrition, underweight (% of under age 5)	..	3.3	..
Child immunization, measles (% of ages 12-23 mos.)	84	96	95
Primary completion rate, total (% of relevant age group)	..	..	..
Gross secondary enrollment, total (% of relevant age group)	..	..	..
Ratio of girls to boys in primary & secondary school (%)	..	..	..
HIV prevalence rate (% population of ages 15-49)	..	..	..
Environment			
Forests (sq. km)	23	23	23
Deforestation (avg. annual %, 1990-2000 and 2000-2010)		0.0	0.0
Freshwater use (% of internal resources)	..	31.7	31.7
Access to improved water source (% total pop.)	100	100	100
Access to improved sanitation facilities (% total pop.)	99	100	100
Energy use per capita (kilograms of oil equivalent)	3,779	4,641	6,452
Carbon dioxide emissions per capita (metric tons)	15.4	12.2	2.7
Electricity use per capita (kilowatt-hours)	4,983	7,575	8,404
Economy			
GDP ($ billions)	36	96	275
GDP growth (annual %)	10.1	9.0	1.3
GDP implicit price deflator (annual % growth)	4.4	3.6	2.1
Value added in agriculture (% of GDP)	0	0	0
Value added in industry (% of GDP)	32	35	27
Value added in services (% of GDP)	68	65	73
Exports of goods and services (% of GDP)	177	192	201
Imports of goods and services (% of GDP)	167	179	178
Gross capital formation (% of GDP)	35	33	27
Central government revenue (% of GDP)	25.4	26.2	18.7
Central government cash surplus/deficit (% of GDP)	10.5	11.2	9.0
States and markets			
Starting a business (days)	..	8	3
Stock market capitalization (% of GDP)	95.0	159.3	150.8
Military expenditures (% of GDP)	4.6	4.6	3.5
Mobile cellular subscriptions (per 100 people)	1.7	70.1	152.1
Individuals using the Internet (% of population)	0.0	36.0	74.2
Paved roads (% of total)	97.1	100.0	100.0
High-technology exports (% of manufactured exports)	40	63	45
Global links			
Merchandise trade (% of GDP)	314	284	287
Net barter terms of trade index (2000 = 100)	116	100	81
Total external debt stocks ($ millions)	..	..	..
Total debt service (% of exports)	..	..	..
Net migration (thousands)	249	436	400
Personal remittances received ($ millions)	..	..	..
Foreign direct investment, net inflows ($ billions)	5.6	16.5	56.7
Net official development assistance received ($ millions)	-3.1	..	..

Sint Maarten (Dutch part)

High income

Population (thousands)	39	Population growth (%)		1.6
Surface area (sq. km)	34	Population living below $1.25 a day (%)		..
GNI, Atlas ($ millions)	..	GNI per capita, Atlas ($)		..
GNI, PPP ($ millions)	..	GNI per capita, PPP ($)		..

	1990	2000	2012
People			
Share of poorest 20% in nat'l consumption/income (%)	..	..	..
Life expectancy at birth (years)	..	..	76
Total fertility rate (births per woman)	..	..	1.7
Adolescent fertility rate (births per 1,000 women 15-19)	..	..	..
Contraceptive prevalence (% of married women 15-49)	..	..	..
Births attended by skilled health staff (% of total)	..	..	..
Under-five mortality rate (per 1,000 live births)	..	..	..
Child malnutrition, underweight (% of under age 5)	..	..	..
Child immunization, measles (% of ages 12-23 mos.)	..	..	..
Primary completion rate, total (% of relevant age group)	..	..	..
Gross secondary enrollment, total (% of relevant age group)	..	..	..
Ratio of girls to boys in primary & secondary school (%)	..	..	..
HIV prevalence rate (% population of ages 15-49)	..	..	..
Environment			
Forests (sq. km)	..	..	..
Deforestation (avg. annual %, 1990-2000 and 2000-2010)		..	..
Freshwater use (% of internal resources)	..	..	..
Access to improved water source (% total pop.)	..	..	..
Access to improved sanitation facilities (% total pop.)	..	..	..
Energy use per capita (kilograms of oil equivalent)	..	..	..
Carbon dioxide emissions per capita (metric tons)	..	..	..
Electricity use per capita (kilowatt-hours)	..	..	..
Economy			
GDP ($ millions)	..	..	..
GDP growth (annual %)	..	..	..
GDP implicit price deflator (annual % growth)	..	..	..
Value added in agriculture (% of GDP)	..	..	..
Value added in industry (% of GDP)	..	..	..
Value added in services (% of GDP)	..	..	..
Exports of goods and services (% of GDP)	..	..	..
Imports of goods and services (% of GDP)	..	..	..
Gross capital formation (% of GDP)	..	..	..
Central government revenue (% of GDP)	..	..	..
Central government cash surplus/deficit (% of GDP)	..	..	..
States and markets			
Starting a business (days)	..	..	..
Stock market capitalization (% of GDP)	..	..	..
Military expenditures (% of GDP)	..	..	..
Mobile cellular subscriptions (per 100 people)	..	..	..
Individuals using the Internet (% of population)	..	..	..
Paved roads (% of total)	..	..	..
High-technology exports (% of manufactured exports)	..	..	..
Global links			
Merchandise trade (% of GDP)	..	..	..
Net barter terms of trade index (2000 = 100)	..	..	..
Total external debt stocks ($ millions)	..	..	..
Total debt service (% of exports)	..	..	..
Net migration (thousands)	..	..	..
Personal remittances received ($ millions)	..	..	12.5
Foreign direct investment, net inflows ($ millions)	..	..	13.5
Net official development assistance received ($ millions)	..	..	..

Slovak Republic

High income

Population (millions)	5.4	Population growth (%)	0.2
Surface area (1,000 sq. km)	49	Population living below $1.25 a day (%)	<2
GNI, Atlas ($ billions)	93.0	GNI per capita, Atlas ($)	17,190
GNI, PPP ($ billions)	137.5	GNI per capita, PPP ($)	25,430

	1990	2000	2012
People			
Share of poorest 20% in nat'l consumption/income (%)	11.9	9.2	10.1
Life expectancy at birth (years)	71	73	76
Total fertility rate (births per woman)	2.1	1.3	1.3
Adolescent fertility rate (births per 1,000 women 15-19)	48	23	16
Contraceptive prevalence (% of married women 15-49)	74	..	..
Births attended by skilled health staff (% of total)	100	100	99
Under-five mortality rate (per 1,000 live births)	18	12	8
Child malnutrition, underweight (% of under age 5)	..	..	..
Child immunization, measles (% of ages 12-23 mos.)	0	98	99
Primary completion rate, total (% of relevant age group)	96	97	95
Gross secondary enrollment, total (% of relevant age group)	87	86	94
Ratio of girls to boys in primary & secondary school (%)	102	101	100
HIV prevalence rate (% population of ages 15-49)	..	..	..
Environment			
Forests (1,000 sq. km)	19	19	19
Deforestation (avg. annual %, 1990-2000 and 2000-2010)		0.0	-0.1
Freshwater use (% of internal resources)	..	9.3	5.5
Access to improved water source (% total pop.)	100	100	100
Access to improved sanitation facilities (% total pop.)	100	100	100
Energy use per capita (kilograms of oil equivalent)	4,025	3,293	3,084
Carbon dioxide emissions per capita (metric tons)	8.5	6.9	6.7
Electricity use per capita (kilowatt-hours)	5,542	4,956	5,348
Economy			
GDP ($ billions)	11.7	28.7	91.1
GDP growth (annual %)	-2.7	1.4	1.8
GDP implicit price deflator (annual % growth)	6.9	9.4	1.3
Value added in agriculture (% of GDP)	7	4	4
Value added in industry (% of GDP)	59	36	35
Value added in services (% of GDP)	33	59	61
Exports of goods and services (% of GDP)	27	70	89
Imports of goods and services (% of GDP)	36	73	87
Gross capital formation (% of GDP)	33	26	22
Central government revenue (% of GDP)	..	35.3	28.4
Central government cash surplus/deficit (% of GDP)	..	-3.2	-4.9
States and markets			
Starting a business (days)	..	103	19
Stock market capitalization (% of GDP)	..	4.2	5.1
Military expenditures (% of GDP)	2.0	1.7	1.1
Mobile cellular subscriptions (per 100 people)	0.0	23.1	111.9
Individuals using the Internet (% of population)	0.0	9.4	80.0
Paved roads (% of total)	..	87.0	100.0
High-technology exports (% of manufactured exports)	..	4	9
Global links			
Merchandise trade (% of GDP)	91	86	175
Net barter terms of trade index (2000 = 100)	..	100	92
Total external debt stocks ($ millions)	..	..	..
Total debt service (% of exports)	..	..	..
Net migration (thousands)	-15.1	5.8	15.0
Personal remittances received ($ millions)	79	18	1,928
Foreign direct investment, net inflows ($ billions)	0.2	2.1	1.5
Net official development assistance received ($ millions)	..	..	..

Slovenia

High income

Population (millions)	2.1	Population growth (%)	0.2
Surface area (1,000 sq. km)	20	Population living below $1.25 a day (%)	<2
GNI, Atlas ($ billions)	46.9	GNI per capita, Atlas ($)	22,810
GNI, PPP ($ billions)	58.1	GNI per capita, PPP ($)	28,240

	1990	2000	2012
People			
Share of poorest 20% in nat'l consumption/income (%)	9.3	8.7	..
Life expectancy at birth (years)	73	75	80
Total fertility rate (births per woman)	1.5	1.3	1.6
Adolescent fertility rate (births per 1,000 women 15-19)	18	6	1
Contraceptive prevalence (% of married women 15-49)	..	..	..
Births attended by skilled health staff (% of total)	100	100	100
Under-five mortality rate (per 1,000 live births)	10	6	3
Child malnutrition, underweight (% of under age 5)	..	..	..
Child immunization, measles (% of ages 12-23 mos.)	90	95	95
Primary completion rate, total (% of relevant age group)	93	96	101
Gross secondary enrollment, total (% of relevant age group)	87	99	98
Ratio of girls to boys in primary & secondary school (%)	102	103	100
HIV prevalence rate (% population of ages 15-49)	..	..	..
Environment			
Forests (1,000 sq. km)	12	12	13
Deforestation (avg. annual %, 1990-2000 and 2000-2010)		-0.4	-0.2
Freshwater use (% of internal resources)	..	..	5.0
Access to improved water source (% total pop.)	100	100	100
Access to improved sanitation facilities (% total pop.)	100	100	100
Energy use per capita (kilograms of oil equivalent)	2,858	3,224	3,472
Carbon dioxide emissions per capita (metric tons)	6.3	7.2	7.5
Electricity use per capita (kilowatt-hours)	5,335	5,778	6,806
Economy			
GDP ($ billions)	17.4	20.0	45.3
GDP growth (annual %)	-8.9	4.3	-2.5
GDP implicit price deflator (annual % growth)	94.9	5.2	0.2
Value added in agriculture (% of GDP)	6	3	2
Value added in industry (% of GDP)	42	36	32
Value added in services (% of GDP)	52	61	66
Exports of goods and services (% of GDP)	91	54	71
Imports of goods and services (% of GDP)	79	57	70
Gross capital formation (% of GDP)	17	27	21
Central government revenue (% of GDP)	39.8	38.9	36.9
Central government cash surplus/deficit (% of GDP)	3.2	-1.1	-5.9
States and markets			
Starting a business (days)	..	60	6
Stock market capitalization (% of GDP)	..	12.7	14.3
Military expenditures (% of GDP)	2.2	1.1	1.2
Mobile cellular subscriptions (per 100 people)	0.0	61.1	108.6
Individuals using the Internet (% of population)	0.0	15.1	70.0
Paved roads (% of total)	72.0	100.0	100.0
High-technology exports (% of manufactured exports)	3	5	6
Global links			
Merchandise trade (% of GDP)	102	95	141
Net barter terms of trade index (2000 = 100)	..	100	94
Total external debt stocks ($ millions)	..	..	..
Total debt service (% of exports)	..	..	..
Net migration (thousands)	-16.5	16.8	22.0
Personal remittances received ($ millions)	38	205	644
Foreign direct investment, net inflows ($ millions)	111	136	-227
Net official development assistance received ($ millions)	7.1	60.8	..

Solomon Islands

Population (thousands)	550	Population growth (%)	2.1
Surface area (1,000 sq. km)	29	Population living below $1.25 a day (%)	..
GNI, Atlas ($ millions)	620.1	GNI per capita, Atlas ($)	1,130
GNI, PPP ($ millions)	1,172.6	GNI per capita, PPP ($)	2,130

	1990	2000	2012
People			
Share of poorest 20% in nat'l consumption/income (%)	..	..	..
Life expectancy at birth (years)	57	63	68
Total fertility rate (births per woman)	5.9	4.7	4.1
Adolescent fertility rate (births per 1,000 women 15-19)	90	71	65
Contraceptive prevalence (% of married women 15-49)	..	7	35
Births attended by skilled health staff (% of total)	..	85	86
Under-five mortality rate (per 1,000 live births)	39	35	31
Child malnutrition, underweight (% of under age 5)	16.3	..	11.5
Child immunization, measles (% of ages 12-23 mos.)	70	85	85
Primary completion rate, total (% of relevant age group)	60	..	85
Gross secondary enrollment, total (% of relevant age group)	14	21	48
Ratio of girls to boys in primary & secondary school (%)	82	89	98
HIV prevalence rate (% population of ages 15-49)	..	..	..
Environment			
Forests (1,000 sq. km)	23	23	22
Deforestation (avg. annual %, 1990-2000 and 2000-2010)		0.2	0.2
Freshwater use (% of internal resources)	..	..	..
Access to improved water source (% total pop.)	..	80	81
Access to improved sanitation facilities (% total pop.)	..	25	29
Energy use per capita (kilograms of oil equivalent)	171	..	..
Carbon dioxide emissions per capita (metric tons)	0.5	0.4	0.4
Electricity use per capita (kilowatt-hours)	..	..	..
Economy			
GDP ($ millions)	303	435	1,008
GDP growth (annual %)	6.0	-14.3	3.9
GDP implicit price deflator (annual % growth)	7.2	10.7	7.8
Value added in agriculture (% of GDP)	29	35	39
Value added in industry (% of GDP)	5	13	6
Value added in services (% of GDP)	66	53	55
Exports of goods and services (% of GDP)	30	24	26
Imports of goods and services (% of GDP)	65	39	43
Gross capital formation (% of GDP)	20	7	..
Central government revenue (% of GDP)	..	..	..
Central government cash surplus/deficit (% of GDP)	..	..	..
States and markets			
Starting a business (days)	..	56	9
Stock market capitalization (% of GDP)	..	..	..
Military expenditures (% of GDP)	..	..	..
Mobile cellular subscriptions (per 100 people)	0.0	0.3	55.0
Individuals using the Internet (% of population)	0.0	0.5	7.0
Paved roads (% of total)	2.1	2.0	..
High-technology exports (% of manufactured exports)	..	..	87
Global links			
Merchandise trade (% of GDP)	53	37	96
Net barter terms of trade index (2000 = 100)	85	100	90
Total external debt stocks ($ millions)	120	156	228
Total debt service (% of exports)	11.8	7.1	4.5
Net migration (thousands)	-1.0	-4.9	-11.9
Personal remittances received ($ millions)	..	4.3	17.2
Foreign direct investment, net inflows ($ millions)	10.4	13.0	68.3
Net official development assistance received ($ millions)	46	68	305

Somalia

Sub-Saharan Africa			Low income
Population (millions)	10.2	Population growth (%)	2.9
Surface area (1,000 sq. km)	638	Population living below $1.25 a day (%)	..
GNI, Atlas ($ millions)	..	GNI per capita, Atlas ($)	..
GNI, PPP ($ millions)	..	GNI per capita, PPP ($)	..

	1990	2000	2012
People			
Share of poorest 20% in nat'l consumption/income (%)	..	..	..
Life expectancy at birth (years)	45	51	55
Total fertility rate (births per woman)	7.4	7.6	6.7
Adolescent fertility rate (births per 1,000 women 15-19)	92	127	110
Contraceptive prevalence (% of married women 15-49)	..	8	15
Births attended by skilled health staff (% of total)	..	34	33
Under-five mortality rate (per 1,000 live births)	177	171	147
Child malnutrition, underweight (% of under age 5)	..	22.8	32.8
Child immunization, measles (% of ages 12-23 mos.)	30	24	46
Primary completion rate, total (% of relevant age group)	..	..	..
Gross secondary enrollment, total (% of relevant age group)	..	..	..
Ratio of girls to boys in primary & secondary school (%)	..	..	..
HIV prevalence rate (% population of ages 15-49)	0.1	0.7	0.5
Environment			
Forests (1,000 sq. km)	83	75	67
Deforestation (avg. annual %, 1990-2000 and 2000-2010)		1.0	1.1
Freshwater use (% of internal resources)	..	54.8	55.0
Access to improved water source (% total pop.)	..	23	31
Access to improved sanitation facilities (% total pop.)	..	22	23
Energy use per capita (kilograms of oil equivalent)	..	..	..
Carbon dioxide emissions per capita (metric tons)	0.00	0.07	0.06
Electricity use per capita (kilowatt-hours)	..	..	..
Economy			
GDP ($ millions)	917	..	..
GDP growth (annual %)	-1.5	..	..
GDP implicit price deflator (annual % growth)	215.5	..	..
Value added in agriculture (% of GDP)	65	..	..
Value added in industry (% of GDP)	..	..	..
Value added in services (% of GDP)	..	..	..
Exports of goods and services (% of GDP)	10	..	..
Imports of goods and services (% of GDP)	38	..	..
Gross capital formation (% of GDP)	16	..	..
Central government revenue (% of GDP)	..	..	..
Central government cash surplus/deficit (% of GDP)	..	..	..
States and markets			
Starting a business (days)	..	..	..
Stock market capitalization (% of GDP)	..	..	..
Military expenditures (% of GDP)	..	..	..
Mobile cellular subscriptions (per 100 people)	0.0	1.1	22.6
Individuals using the Internet (% of population)	0.0	0.0	1.4
Paved roads (% of total)	11.1	12.0	..
High-technology exports (% of manufactured exports)	..	..	..
Global links			
Merchandise trade (% of GDP)	..	..	..
Net barter terms of trade index (2000 = 100)	..	100	108
Total external debt stocks ($ billions)	2.4	2.6	3.1
Total debt service (% of exports)	47.6	..	..
Net migration (thousands)	-893	-200	-150
Personal remittances received ($ millions)	..	..	..
Foreign direct investment, net inflows ($ millions)	6	0	107
Net official development assistance received ($ millions)	515	102	999

South Africa

Sub-Saharan Africa   **Upper middle income**

Population (millions)	52.3	
Surface area (1,000 sq. km)	1,219	
GNI, Atlas ($ billions)	389.8	
GNI, PPP ($ billions)	563.3	

Population growth (%)	1.3
Population living below $1.25 a day (%)	13.8
GNI per capita, Atlas ($)	7,460
GNI per capita, PPP ($)	10,780

	1990	2000	2012
People			
Share of poorest 20% in nat'l consumption/income (%)	3.0	3.1	2.7
Life expectancy at birth (years)	62	56	56
Total fertility rate (births per woman)	3.7	2.9	2.4
Adolescent fertility rate (births per 1,000 women 15-19)	93	75	51
Contraceptive prevalence (% of married women 15-49)	57	60	..
Births attended by skilled health staff (% of total)	..	91	..
Under-five mortality rate (per 1,000 live births)	61	74	45
Child malnutrition, underweight (% of under age 5)	..	10.1	8.7
Child immunization, measles (% of ages 12-23 mos.)	79	72	79
Primary completion rate, total (% of relevant age group)	76	87	..
Gross secondary enrollment, total (% of relevant age group)	66	84	102
Ratio of girls to boys in primary & secondary school (%)	103	100	98
HIV prevalence rate (% population of ages 15-49)	0.2	14.1	17.9
Environment			
Forests (1,000 sq. km)	92	92	92
Deforestation (avg. annual %, 1990-2000 and 2000-2010)		0.0	0.0
Freshwater use (% of internal resources)	29.7	27.9	27.9
Access to improved water source (% total pop.)	81	87	95
Access to improved sanitation facilities (% total pop.)	58	65	74
Energy use per capita (kilograms of oil equivalent)	2,584	2,483	2,741
Carbon dioxide emissions per capita (metric tons)	9.5	8.4	9.0
Electricity use per capita (kilowatt-hours)	4,431	4,681	4,604
Economy			
GDP ($ billions)	112	133	384
GDP growth (annual %)	-0.3	4.2	2.5
GDP implicit price deflator (annual % growth)	15.5	8.8	5.5
Value added in agriculture (% of GDP)	5	3	3
Value added in industry (% of GDP)	40	32	28
Value added in services (% of GDP)	55	65	69
Exports of goods and services (% of GDP)	24	28	28
Imports of goods and services (% of GDP)	19	25	31
Gross capital formation (% of GDP)	18	16	19
Central government revenue (% of GDP)	..	26.3	29.0
Central government cash surplus/deficit (% of GDP)	..	-2.0	-4.4
States and markets			
Starting a business (days)	..	38	19
Stock market capitalization (% of GDP)	123.2	154.2	159.3
Military expenditures (% of GDP)	3.9	1.4	1.2
Mobile cellular subscriptions (per 100 people)	0.0	18.6	130.6
Individuals using the Internet (% of population)	0.0	5.3	41.0
Paved roads (% of total)	..	20.0	..
High-technology exports (% of manufactured exports)	7	7	6
Global links			
Merchandise trade (% of GDP)	37	45	55
Net barter terms of trade index (2000 = 100)	104	100	145
Total external debt stocks ($ billions)	..	25	138
Total debt service (% of exports)	..	9.9	7.9
Net migration (thousands)	805	1,072	-100
Personal remittances received ($ millions)	136	344	1,085
Foreign direct investment, net inflows ($ millions)	-76	969	4,644
Net official development assistance received ($ millions)	270	486	1,067

South Sudan

Sub-Saharan Africa			Low income
Population (millions)	10.8	Population growth (%)	4.3
Surface area (1,000 sq. km)	644	Population living below $1.25 a day (%)	..
GNI, Atlas ($ billions)	8.6	GNI per capita, Atlas ($)	790
GNI, PPP ($ millions)	..	GNI per capita, PPP ($)	..

	1990	2000	2012
People			
Share of poorest 20% in nat'l consumption/income (%)	..	..	..
Life expectancy at birth (years)	44	49	55
Total fertility rate (births per woman)	6.8	6.1	5.0
Adolescent fertility rate (births per 1,000 women 15-19)	138	122	75
Contraceptive prevalence (% of married women 15-49)	..	..	4
Births attended by skilled health staff (% of total)	..	..	19
Under-five mortality rate (per 1,000 live births)	251	181	104
Child malnutrition, underweight (% of under age 5)	..	..	32.5
Child immunization, measles (% of ages 12-23 mos.)	..	..	62
Primary completion rate, total (% of relevant age group)	..	..	..
Gross secondary enrollment, total (% of relevant age group)	..	..	..
Ratio of girls to boys in primary & secondary school (%)	..	..	..
HIV prevalence rate (% population of ages 15-49)	0.1	3.0	2.7
Environment			
Forests (1,000 sq. km)	..	..	148
Deforestation (avg. annual %, 1990-2000 and 2000-2010)		..	..
Freshwater use (% of internal resources)	..	..	..
Access to improved water source (% total pop.)	..	..	57
Access to improved sanitation facilities (% total pop.)	..	..	9
Energy use per capita (kilograms of oil equivalent)	..	..	..
Carbon dioxide emissions per capita (metric tons)	..	..	..
Electricity use per capita (kilowatt-hours)	..	..	..
Economy			
GDP ($ billions)	..	..	10.2
GDP growth (annual %)	..	..	-47.6
GDP implicit price deflator (annual % growth)	..	..	6.1
Value added in agriculture (% of GDP)	..	..	..
Value added in industry (% of GDP)	..	..	..
Value added in services (% of GDP)	..	..	..
Exports of goods and services (% of GDP)	..	..	10
Imports of goods and services (% of GDP)	..	..	43
Gross capital formation (% of GDP)	..	..	12
Central government revenue (% of GDP)	..	..	..
Central government cash surplus/deficit (% of GDP)	..	..	..
States and markets			
Starting a business (days)	..	..	17
Stock market capitalization (% of GDP)	..	..	..
Military expenditures (% of GDP)	..	..	9.4
Mobile cellular subscriptions (per 100 people)	..	..	21.2
Individuals using the Internet (% of population)	..	..	..
Paved roads (% of total)	..	..	..
High-technology exports (% of manufactured exports)	..	..	..
Global links			
Merchandise trade (% of GDP)	..	..	..
Net barter terms of trade index (2000 = 100)	..	..	..
Total external debt stocks ($ millions)	..	..	..
Total debt service (% of exports)	..	..	..
Net migration (thousands)	-1,095	432	865
Personal remittances received ($ millions)	..	..	..
Foreign direct investment, net inflows ($ millions)	..	..	..
Net official development assistance received ($ millions)	..	..	1,578

Spain

Population (millions)	46.8	Population growth (%)	0.0
Surface area (1,000 sq. km)	506	Population living below $1.25 a day (%)	..
GNI, Atlas ($ billions)	1,368.8	GNI per capita, Atlas ($)	29,270
GNI, PPP ($ billions)	1,485.1	GNI per capita, PPP ($)	31,760

	1990	2000	2012
People			
Share of poorest 20% in nat'l consumption/income (%)	..	7.0	..
Life expectancy at birth (years)	77	79	82
Total fertility rate (births per woman)	1.4	1.2	1.3
Adolescent fertility rate (births per 1,000 women 15-19)	12	9	11
Contraceptive prevalence (% of married women 15-49)	..	72	66
Births attended by skilled health staff (% of total)	..	..	..
Under-five mortality rate (per 1,000 live births)	11	7	5
Child malnutrition, underweight (% of under age 5)	..	..	..
Child immunization, measles (% of ages 12-23 mos.)	99	94	97
Primary completion rate, total (% of relevant age group)	101	..	102
Gross secondary enrollment, total (% of relevant age group)	102	111	131
Ratio of girls to boys in primary & secondary school (%)	103	103	100
HIV prevalence rate (% population of ages 15-49)	..	..	..
Environment			
Forests (1,000 sq. km)	138	170	183
Deforestation (avg. annual %, 1990-2000 and 2000-2010)		-2.1	-0.7
Freshwater use (% of internal resources)	33.2	33.0	29.2
Access to improved water source (% total pop.)	100	100	100
Access to improved sanitation facilities (% total pop.)	100	100	100
Energy use per capita (kilograms of oil equivalent)	2,319	3,026	2,666
Carbon dioxide emissions per capita (metric tons)	5.6	7.3	5.8
Electricity use per capita (kilowatt-hours)	3,538	5,207	5,530
Economy			
GDP ($ billions)	520	580	1,323
GDP growth (annual %)	3.8	5.0	-1.6
GDP implicit price deflator (annual % growth)	7.3	3.4	0.0
Value added in agriculture (% of GDP)	6	4	2
Value added in industry (% of GDP)	34	31	26
Value added in services (% of GDP)	61	65	72
Exports of goods and services (% of GDP)	16	29	33
Imports of goods and services (% of GDP)	19	32	32
Gross capital formation (% of GDP)	26	26	20
Central government revenue (% of GDP)	..	31.1	23.6
Central government cash surplus/deficit (% of GDP)	..	-0.5	-3.6
States and markets			
Starting a business (days)	..	114	23
Stock market capitalization (% of GDP)	21.3	86.9	75.2
Military expenditures (% of GDP)	1.7	1.2	0.9
Mobile cellular subscriptions (per 100 people)	0.1	60.2	108.4
Individuals using the Internet (% of population)	0.0	13.6	72.0
Paved roads (% of total)	99.0	99.0	..
High-technology exports (% of manufactured exports)	7	8	7
Global links			
Merchandise trade (% of GDP)	28	47	47
Net barter terms of trade index (2000 = 100)	..	100	89
Total external debt stocks ($ millions)	..	..	..
Total debt service (% of exports)	..	..	..
Net migration (thousands)	319	2,829	600
Personal remittances received ($ billions)	2.2	4.9	9.6
Foreign direct investment, net inflows ($ billions)	14.0	38.8	36.2
Net official development assistance received ($ millions)	..	..	..

Sri Lanka

South Asia			Lower middle income

Population (millions)	20.3	Population growth (%)	1.0
Surface area (1,000 sq. km)	66	Population living below $1.25 a day (%)	4.1
GNI, Atlas ($ billions)	59.3	GNI per capita, Atlas ($)	2,920
GNI, PPP ($ billions)	122.5	GNI per capita, PPP ($)	6,030

	1990	2000	2012
People			
Share of poorest 20% in nat'l consumption/income (%)	8.7	6.8	7.7
Life expectancy at birth (years)	70	71	74
Total fertility rate (births per woman)	2.5	2.2	2.3
Adolescent fertility rate (births per 1,000 women 15-19)	31	28	17
Contraceptive prevalence (% of married women 15-49)	66	70	68
Births attended by skilled health staff (% of total)	94	96	99
Under-five mortality rate (per 1,000 live births)	21	17	10
Child malnutrition, underweight (% of under age 5)	33.8	22.8	21.6
Child immunization, measles (% of ages 12-23 mos.)	80	99	99
Primary completion rate, total (% of relevant age group)	97	106	97
Gross secondary enrollment, total (% of relevant age group)	72	..	99
Ratio of girls to boys in primary & secondary school (%)	102	..	103
HIV prevalence rate (% population of ages 15-49)	0.1	0.1	0.1
Environment			
Forests (1,000 sq. km)	24	21	18
Deforestation (avg. annual %, 1990-2000 and 2000-2010)		1.2	1.1
Freshwater use (% of internal resources)	18.5	24.6	24.5
Access to improved water source (% total pop.)	68	79	94
Access to improved sanitation facilities (% total pop.)	68	79	92
Energy use per capita (kilograms of oil equivalent)	324	436	499
Carbon dioxide emissions per capita (metric tons)	0.2	0.5	0.6
Electricity use per capita (kilowatt-hours)	154	290	490
Economy			
GDP ($ billions)	8.0	16.3	59.4
GDP growth (annual %)	6.4	6.0	6.4
GDP implicit price deflator (annual % growth)	20.1	7.3	8.9
Value added in agriculture (% of GDP)	26	20	11
Value added in industry (% of GDP)	26	27	31
Value added in services (% of GDP)	48	53	57
Exports of goods and services (% of GDP)	30	39	23
Imports of goods and services (% of GDP)	38	50	36
Gross capital formation (% of GDP)	22	28	30
Central government revenue (% of GDP)	21.0	16.8	13.9
Central government cash surplus/deficit (% of GDP)	-5.2	-8.4	-6.1
States and markets			
Starting a business (days)	..	58	8
Stock market capitalization (% of GDP)	11.4	6.6	28.7
Military expenditures (% of GDP)	2.3	5.0	2.4
Mobile cellular subscriptions (per 100 people)	0.0	2.3	91.6
Individuals using the Internet (% of population)	0.0	0.6	18.3
Paved roads (% of total)	..	85.8	14.9
High-technology exports (% of manufactured exports)	1	3	1
Global links			
Merchandise trade (% of GDP)	57	77	48
Net barter terms of trade index (2000 = 100)	82	100	75
Total external debt stocks ($ billions)	5.9	9.2	25.4
Total debt service (% of exports)	16.1	12.1	13.3
Net migration (thousands)	-256	-100	-317
Personal remittances received ($ billions)	0.4	1.2	6.0
Foreign direct investment, net inflows ($ millions)	43	173	898
Net official development assistance received ($ millions)	728	275	488

St. Kitts and Nevis

High income

Population (thousands)	54	Population growth (%)	1.2
Surface area (sq. km)	260	Population living below $1.25 a day (%)	..
GNI, Atlas ($ millions)	729.5	GNI per capita, Atlas ($)	13,610
GNI, PPP ($ millions)	944.9	GNI per capita, PPP ($)	17,630

	1990	2000	2012
People			
Share of poorest 20% in nat'l consumption/income (%)	..	..	..
Life expectancy at birth (years)	68	71	..
Total fertility rate (births per woman)	2.6	2.1	..
Adolescent fertility rate (births per 1,000 women 15-19)	..	..	..
Contraceptive prevalence (% of married women 15-49)	..	..	54
Births attended by skilled health staff (% of total)	..	99	100
Under-five mortality rate (per 1,000 live births)	29	18	9
Child malnutrition, underweight (% of under age 5)	..	..	..
Child immunization, measles (% of ages 12-23 mos.)	99	99	95
Primary completion rate, total (% of relevant age group)	118	103	93
Gross secondary enrollment, total (% of relevant age group)	78	105	79
Ratio of girls to boys in primary & secondary school (%)	101	106	103
HIV prevalence rate (% population of ages 15-49)	..	..	..
Environment			
Forests (sq. km)	110	110	110
Deforestation (avg. annual %, 1990-2000 and 2000-2010)		0.0	0.0
Freshwater use (% of internal resources)	..	..	..
Access to improved water source (% total pop.)	98	98	98
Access to improved sanitation facilities (% total pop.)	..	87	..
Energy use per capita (kilograms of oil equivalent)	529	..	..
Carbon dioxide emissions per capita (metric tons)	1.6	2.3	4.8
Electricity use per capita (kilowatt-hours)	..	..	..
Economy			
GDP ($ millions)	159	417	767
GDP growth (annual %)	2.3	0.7	6.9
GDP implicit price deflator (annual % growth)	8.7	35.7	2.6
Value added in agriculture (% of GDP)	6	2	2
Value added in industry (% of GDP)	29	31	24
Value added in services (% of GDP)	65	68	75
Exports of goods and services (% of GDP)	52	36	33
Imports of goods and services (% of GDP)	83	60	44
Gross capital formation (% of GDP)	55	43	28
Central government revenue (% of GDP)	24.2	22.6	31.1
Central government cash surplus/deficit (% of GDP)	-1.5	-11.3	10.7
States and markets			
Starting a business (days)	..	..	19
Stock market capitalization (% of GDP)	..	53.1	85.6
Military expenditures (% of GDP)	..	..	..
Mobile cellular subscriptions (per 100 people)	0.0	2.6	156.8
Individuals using the Internet (% of population)	0.0	5.9	79.3
Paved roads (% of total)	38.5	42.5	..
High-technology exports (% of manufactured exports)	5	1	0
Global links			
Merchandise trade (% of GDP)	87	55	36
Net barter terms of trade index (2000 = 100)	..	100	71
Total external debt stocks ($ millions)	..	..	..
Total debt service (% of exports)	..	..	..
Net migration (thousands)	..	..	..
Personal remittances received ($ millions)	19.3	27.1	45.1
Foreign direct investment, net inflows ($ millions)	49	96	100
Net official development assistance received ($ millions)	8.1	3.9	21.9

St. Lucia

Latin America & Caribbean		Upper middle income	
Population (thousands)	181	Population growth (%)	0.9
Surface area (sq. km)	620	Population living below $1.25 a day (%)	20.9
GNI, Atlas ($ billions)	1.2	GNI per capita, Atlas ($)	6,890
GNI, PPP ($ billions)	2.0	GNI per capita, PPP ($)	11,300

	1990	2000	2012
People			
Share of poorest 20% in nat'l consumption/income (%)	..	..	..
Life expectancy at birth (years)	71	71	75
Total fertility rate (births per woman)	3.4	2.3	1.9
Adolescent fertility rate (births per 1,000 women 15-19)	105	65	56
Contraceptive prevalence (% of married women 15-49)	47	47	..
Births attended by skilled health staff (% of total)	..	100	100
Under-five mortality rate (per 1,000 live births)	22	18	18
Child malnutrition, underweight (% of under age 5)	..	..	..
Child immunization, measles (% of ages 12-23 mos.)	82	88	99
Primary completion rate, total (% of relevant age group)	124	105	92
Gross secondary enrollment, total (% of relevant age group)	49	74	91
Ratio of girls to boys in primary & secondary school (%)	103	106	98
HIV prevalence rate (% population of ages 15-49)	..	..	..
Environment			
Forests (sq. km)	438	467	470
Deforestation (avg. annual %, 1990-2000 and 2000-2010)		-0.6	-0.1
Freshwater use (% of internal resources)	..	..	..
Access to improved water source (% total pop.)	93	94	94
Access to improved sanitation facilities (% total pop.)	58	62	65
Energy use per capita (kilograms of oil equivalent)	405	..	..
Carbon dioxide emissions per capita (metric tons)	1.2	2.1	2.3
Electricity use per capita (kilowatt-hours)	..	..	..
Economy			
GDP ($ millions)	397	764	1,239
GDP growth (annual %)	23.5	0.7	0.5
GDP implicit price deflator (annual % growth)	3.2	9.7	-2.1
Value added in agriculture (% of GDP)	15	6	4
Value added in industry (% of GDP)	18	18	16
Value added in services (% of GDP)	67	76	80
Exports of goods and services (% of GDP)	73	49	48
Imports of goods and services (% of GDP)	84	58	63
Gross capital formation (% of GDP)	26	27	28
Central government revenue (% of GDP)	..	23.6	24.2
Central government cash surplus/deficit (% of GDP)	..	-1.1	-6.8
States and markets			
Starting a business (days)	..	..	15
Stock market capitalization (% of GDP)	..	..	..
Military expenditures (% of GDP)	..	..	..
Mobile cellular subscriptions (per 100 people)	0.0	1.6	125.5
Individuals using the Internet (% of population)	0.0	5.1	48.6
Paved roads (% of total)	..	..	..
High-technology exports (% of manufactured exports)	1	6	..
Global links			
Merchandise trade (% of GDP)	100	52	72
Net barter terms of trade index (2000 = 100)	..	100	91
Total external debt stocks ($ millions)	79	222	473
Total debt service (% of exports)	2.2	7.9	6.9
Net migration (thousands)	-4.8	-0.2	0.0
Personal remittances received ($ millions)	16.1	26.4	29.8
Foreign direct investment, net inflows ($ millions)	45	54	109
Net official development assistance received ($ millions)	12.3	11.0	26.8

St. Martin (French part)

High income

Population (thousands)	31	Population growth (%)	1.1
Surface area (sq. km)	54	Population living below $1.25 a day (%)	..
GNI, Atlas ($ millions)	..	GNI per capita, Atlas ($)	..
GNI, PPP ($ millions)	..	GNI per capita, PPP ($)	..

	1990	2000	2012
People			
Share of poorest 20% in nat'l consumption/income (%)	..	..	..
Life expectancy at birth (years)	75	77	79
Total fertility rate (births per woman)	2.1	1.8	1.8
Adolescent fertility rate (births per 1,000 women 15-19)	..	..	..
Contraceptive prevalence (% of married women 15-49)	..	..	..
Births attended by skilled health staff (% of total)	..	..	..
Under-five mortality rate (per 1,000 live births)	..	..	..
Child malnutrition, underweight (% of under age 5)	..	..	..
Child immunization, measles (% of ages 12-23 mos.)	..	..	..
Primary completion rate, total (% of relevant age group)	..	..	..
Gross secondary enrollment, total (% of relevant age group)	..	..	..
Ratio of girls to boys in primary & secondary school (%)	..	..	..
HIV prevalence rate (% population of ages 15-49)	..	..	..
Environment			
Forests (sq. km)	..	..	..
Deforestation (avg. annual %, 1990-2000 and 2000-2010)		0.0	0.0
Freshwater use (% of internal resources)	..	..	..
Access to improved water source (% total pop.)	..	..	..
Access to improved sanitation facilities (% total pop.)	..	..	..
Energy use per capita (kilograms of oil equivalent)	..	..	..
Carbon dioxide emissions per capita (metric tons)	..	..	..
Electricity use per capita (kilowatt-hours)	..	..	..
Economy			
GDP ($ millions)	..	..	..
GDP growth (annual %)	..	..	..
GDP implicit price deflator (annual % growth)	..	..	..
Value added in agriculture (% of GDP)	..	..	..
Value added in industry (% of GDP)	..	..	..
Value added in services (% of GDP)	..	..	..
Exports of goods and services (% of GDP)	..	..	..
Imports of goods and services (% of GDP)	..	..	..
Gross capital formation (% of GDP)	..	..	..
Central government revenue (% of GDP)	..	..	..
Central government cash surplus/deficit (% of GDP)	..	..	..
States and markets			
Starting a business (days)	..	..	..
Stock market capitalization (% of GDP)	..	..	..
Military expenditures (% of GDP)	..	..	..
Mobile cellular subscriptions (per 100 people)	..	..	..
Individuals using the Internet (% of population)	..	..	..
Paved roads (% of total)	..	..	..
High-technology exports (% of manufactured exports)	..	..	..
Global links			
Merchandise trade (% of GDP)	..	..	..
Net barter terms of trade index (2000 = 100)	..	..	..
Total external debt stocks ($ millions)	..	..	..
Total debt service (% of exports)	..	..	..
Net migration (thousands)	..	..	..
Personal remittances received ($ millions)	..	..	..
Foreign direct investment, net inflows ($ millions)	..	..	..
Net official development assistance received ($ millions)	..	..	..

St. Vincent and the Grenadines

Latin America & Caribbean   **Upper middle income**

Population (thousands)	109	Population growth (%)	0.0
Surface area (sq. km)	390	Population living below $1.25 a day (%)	..
GNI, Atlas ($ millions)	699.9	GNI per capita, Atlas ($)	6,400
GNI, PPP ($ millions)	1,188.4	GNI per capita, PPP ($)	10,870

	1990	2000	2012
People			
Share of poorest 20% in nat'l consumption/income (%)	..	..	..
Life expectancy at birth (years)	70	71	72
Total fertility rate (births per woman)	3.0	2.4	2.0
Adolescent fertility rate (births per 1,000 women 15-19)	91	69	55
Contraceptive prevalence (% of married women 15-49)	58	58	48
Births attended by skilled health staff (% of total)	..	100	99
Under-five mortality rate (per 1,000 live births)	25	22	23
Child malnutrition, underweight (% of under age 5)	..	..	..
Child immunization, measles (% of ages 12-23 mos.)	96	96	94
Primary completion rate, total (% of relevant age group)	..	93	99
Gross secondary enrollment, total (% of relevant age group)	60	83	101
Ratio of girls to boys in primary & secondary school (%)	107	106	96
HIV prevalence rate (% population of ages 15-49)	..	..	..
Environment			
Forests (sq. km)	253	260	268
Deforestation (avg. annual %, 1990-2000 and 2000-2010)		-0.3	-0.3
Freshwater use (% of internal resources)	..		
Access to improved water source (% total pop.)	88	93	95
Access to improved sanitation facilities (% total pop.)	63	73	..
Energy use per capita (kilograms of oil equivalent)	274	..	..
Carbon dioxide emissions per capita (metric tons)	0.8	1.5	1.9
Electricity use per capita (kilowatt-hours)	..	..	..
Economy			
GDP ($ millions)	198	397	713
GDP growth (annual %)	5.0	-0.6	2.3
GDP implicit price deflator (annual % growth)	6.4	20.4	1.3
Value added in agriculture (% of GDP)	21	9	7
Value added in industry (% of GDP)	23	20	20
Value added in services (% of GDP)	56	72	73
Exports of goods and services (% of GDP)	66	45	27
Imports of goods and services (% of GDP)	77	50	57
Gross capital formation (% of GDP)	30	23	24
Central government revenue (% of GDP)	25.6	24.3	24.6
Central government cash surplus/deficit (% of GDP)	..	-0.4	-2.0
States and markets			
Starting a business (days)	..	..	10
Stock market capitalization (% of GDP)	..	..	..
Military expenditures (% of GDP)	..	..	..
Mobile cellular subscriptions (per 100 people)	0.0	2.2	123.9
Individuals using the Internet (% of population)	0.0	3.2	47.5
Paved roads (% of total)	..	68.0	..
High-technology exports (% of manufactured exports)	0	0	0
Global links			
Merchandise trade (% of GDP)	110	53	55
Net barter terms of trade index (2000 = 100)	..	100	107
Total external debt stocks ($ millions)	63	195	267
Total debt service (% of exports)	3.3	7.2	16.6
Net migration (thousands)	-8.7	-5.2	-5.0
Personal remittances received ($ millions)	15.6	22.5	29.7
Foreign direct investment, net inflows ($ millions)	8	38	125
Net official development assistance received ($ millions)	15.4	6.2	8.6

Sudan

Sub-Saharan Africa		Lower middle income	
Population (millions)	37.2ᵍ	Population growth (%)	2.1ᵍ
Surface area (1,000 sq. km)	1,879ᵍ	Population living below $1.25 a day (%)	19.8
GNI, Atlas ($ billions)	55.9ᵍ	GNI per capita, Atlas ($)	1,500ᵍ
GNI, PPP ($ billions)	77.1ᵍ	GNI per capita, PPP ($)	2,070ᵍ

	1990	2000	2012
People			
Share of poorest 20% in nat'l consumption/income (%)	..	..	6.8
Life expectancy at birth (years)	56ᵍ	58ᵍ	62ᵍ
Total fertility rate (births per woman)	6.2ᵍ	5.4ᵍ	4.5ᵍ
Adolescent fertility rate (births per 1,000 women 15-19)	105ᵍ	116ᵍ	84ᵍ
Contraceptive prevalence (% of married women 15-49)	9ᵍ	7ᵍ	9
Births attended by skilled health staff (% of total)	69	..	23
Under-five mortality rate (per 1,000 live births)	128ᵍ	106ᵍ	73ᵍ
Child malnutrition, underweight (% of under age 5)	31.8	38.4	27.0ᵍ
Child immunization, measles (% of ages 12-23 mos.)	57	58	85ᵍ
Primary completion rate, total (% of relevant age group)	..	..	..
Gross secondary enrollment, total (% of relevant age group)	..	..	..
Ratio of girls to boys in primary & secondary school (%)	..	..	..
HIV prevalence rate (% population of ages 15-49)	..	..	..
Environment			
Forests (1,000 sq. km)	764	705	551
Deforestation (avg. annual %, 1990-2000 and 2000-2010)		0.8	0.1
Freshwater use (% of internal resources)	51.7	123.8	123.8
Access to improved water source (% total pop.)	67	62	55ᵍ
Access to improved sanitation facilities (% total pop.)	27	25	24ᵍ
Energy use per capita (kilograms of oil equivalent)	412	388	355
Carbon dioxide emissions per capita (metric tons)	0.2	0.2	0.3
Electricity use per capita (kilowatt-hours)	50	63	143
Economy			
GDP ($ billions)	12.4	12.3	58.8ᵍ
GDP growth (annual %)	-5.5	6.3	-10.1ʰ
GDP implicit price deflator (annual % growth)	66.2	9.9	36.9ʰ
Value added in agriculture (% of GDP)	41	42	28ᵍ
Value added in industry (% of GDP)	15	21	31ᵍ
Value added in services (% of GDP)	44	37	41ᵍ
Exports of goods and services (% of GDP)	4	16	6ᵍ
Imports of goods and services (% of GDP)	7	13	18ᵍ
Gross capital formation (% of GDP)	11	25	24ᵍ
Central government revenue (% of GDP)	..	8.0	..
Central government cash surplus/deficit (% of GDP)	..	-0.4	..
States and markets			
Starting a business (days)	..	..	36
Stock market capitalization (% of GDP)	..	..	..
Military expenditures (% of GDP)	2.6	4.8	..
Mobile cellular subscriptions (per 100 people)	0.0	0.1	74.4
Individuals using the Internet (% of population)	0.0	0.0	21.0
Paved roads (% of total)	33.8	36.0	..
High-technology exports (% of manufactured exports)	..	4	1
Global links			
Merchandise trade (% of GDP)	8	27	21
Net barter terms of trade index (2000 = 100)	100	100	243
Total external debt stocks ($ billions)	14.8	16.1	21.8
Total debt service (% of exports)	9.7	13.5	8.9
Net migration (thousands)	1,200ᵍ	-430ᵍ	-800ᵍ
Personal remittances received ($ millions)	62	641	401
Foreign direct investment, net inflows ($ millions)	-31	392	2,488
Net official development assistance received ($ millions)	848	225	983ᵍ

Suriname

Latin America & Caribbean		Upper middle income	
Population (thousands)	535	Population growth (%)	0.9
Surface area (1,000 sq. km)	164	Population living below $1.25 a day (%)	15.5
GNI, Atlas ($ billions)	4.6	GNI per capita, Atlas ($)	8,680
GNI, PPP ($ billions)	4.5	GNI per capita, PPP ($)	8,380

	1990	2000	2012
People			
Share of poorest 20% in nat'l consumption/income (%)	..	3.2	..
Life expectancy at birth (years)	68	68	71
Total fertility rate (births per woman)	2.7	2.7	2.3
Adolescent fertility rate (births per 1,000 women 15-19)	54	47	35
Contraceptive prevalence (% of married women 15-49)	48	42	48
Births attended by skilled health staff (% of total)	..	85	91
Under-five mortality rate (per 1,000 live births)	51	33	21
Child malnutrition, underweight (% of under age 5)	..	11.4	5.8
Child immunization, measles (% of ages 12-23 mos.)	65	84	73
Primary completion rate, total (% of relevant age group)	88	..	88
Gross secondary enrollment, total (% of relevant age group)	56	73	85
Ratio of girls to boys in primary & secondary school (%)	116	107	110
HIV prevalence rate (% population of ages 15-49)	0.3	1.2	1.1
Environment			
Forests (1,000 sq. km)	148	148	148
Deforestation (avg. annual %, 1990-2000 and 2000-2010)		0.0	0.0
Freshwater use (% of internal resources)	..	0.8	0.8
Access to improved water source (% total pop.)	..	89	95
Access to improved sanitation facilities (% total pop.)	..	81	80
Energy use per capita (kilograms of oil equivalent)	1,367	..	..
Carbon dioxide emissions per capita (metric tons)	4.5	4.6	4.5
Electricity use per capita (kilowatt-hours)	..	..	..
Economy			
GDP ($ millions)	388	892	5,012
GDP growth (annual %)	-0.5	-0.1	3.9
GDP implicit price deflator (annual % growth)	43.8	54.8	11.7
Value added in agriculture (% of GDP)	9	11	9
Value added in industry (% of GDP)	24	25	39
Value added in services (% of GDP)	67	64	52
Exports of goods and services (% of GDP)	42	20	..
Imports of goods and services (% of GDP)	44	33	..
Gross capital formation (% of GDP)	11	12	6
Central government revenue (% of GDP)	..	34.1	25.2
Central government cash surplus/deficit (% of GDP)	..	1.1	-0.7
States and markets			
Starting a business (days)	..	..	208
Stock market capitalization (% of GDP)	..	..	..
Military expenditures (% of GDP)	..	..	..
Mobile cellular subscriptions (per 100 people)	0.0	8.8	106.5
Individuals using the Internet (% of population)	0.0	2.5	34.7
Paved roads (% of total)	24.0	26.0	..
High-technology exports (% of manufactured exports)	..	8	7
Global links			
Merchandise trade (% of GDP)	243	104	84
Net barter terms of trade index (2000 = 100)	..	100	135
Total external debt stocks ($ millions)	..	..	..
Total debt service (% of exports)	..	..	..
Net migration (thousands)	-3.3	0.0	-5.0
Personal remittances received ($ millions)	0.5	1.3	8.1
Foreign direct investment, net inflows ($ millions)	-77	-148	66
Net official development assistance received ($ millions)	61.1	34.3	39.6

Swaziland

Population (millions)	1.2	Population growth (%)	1.5
Surface area (1,000 sq. km)	17	Population living below $1.25 a day (%)	40.6
GNI, Atlas ($ billions)	3.5	GNI per capita, Atlas ($)	2,860
GNI, PPP ($ billions)	5.9	GNI per capita, PPP ($)	4,760

	1990	2000	2012
People			
Share of poorest 20% in nat'l consumption/income (%)	..	4.5	4.1
Life expectancy at birth (years)	59	49	49
Total fertility rate (births per woman)	5.7	4.2	3.4
Adolescent fertility rate (births per 1,000 women 15-19)	132	105	72
Contraceptive prevalence (% of married women 15-49)	20	28	65
Births attended by skilled health staff (% of total)	..	70	82
Under-five mortality rate (per 1,000 live births)	71	121	80
Child malnutrition, underweight (% of under age 5)	..	9.1	5.8
Child immunization, measles (% of ages 12-23 mos.)	85	92	88
Primary completion rate, total (% of relevant age group)	63	61	77
Gross secondary enrollment, total (% of relevant age group)	49	42	60
Ratio of girls to boys in primary & secondary school (%)	..	96	92
HIV prevalence rate (% population of ages 15-49)	0.8	24.3	26.5
Environment			
Forests (1,000 sq. km)	4.7	5.2	5.7
Deforestation (avg. annual %, 1990-2000 and 2000-2010)		-0.9	-0.8
Freshwater use (% of internal resources)	..	39.5	39.5
Access to improved water source (% total pop.)	39	52	74
Access to improved sanitation facilities (% total pop.)	49	52	57
Energy use per capita (kilograms of oil equivalent)	358	..	..
Carbon dioxide emissions per capita (metric tons)	0.5	1.1	0.9
Electricity use per capita (kilowatt-hours)	..	..	..
Economy			
GDP ($ millions)	1,115	1,524	3,744
GDP growth (annual %)	21.0	1.8	-1.5
GDP implicit price deflator (annual % growth)	30.4	9.9	8.3
Value added in agriculture (% of GDP)	10	12	7
Value added in industry (% of GDP)	43	44	48
Value added in services (% of GDP)	46	44	45
Exports of goods and services (% of GDP)	59	74	67
Imports of goods and services (% of GDP)	69	88	75
Gross capital formation (% of GDP)	15	18	10
Central government revenue (% of GDP)	..	27.3	..
Central government cash surplus/deficit (% of GDP)	..	-2.7	..
States and markets			
Starting a business (days)	..	..	38
Stock market capitalization (% of GDP)	1.5	4.8	..
Military expenditures (% of GDP)	1.3	1.6	3.2
Mobile cellular subscriptions (per 100 people)	0.0	3.1	65.4
Individuals using the Internet (% of population)	0.0	0.9	20.8
Paved roads (% of total)	..	30.0	..
High-technology exports (% of manufactured exports)	..	0	..
Global links			
Merchandise trade (% of GDP)	109	128	103
Net barter terms of trade index (2000 = 100)	100	100	110
Total external debt stocks ($ millions)	257	273	460
Total debt service (% of exports)	5.4	2.2	2.2
Net migration (thousands)	-38.2	-46.1	-6.0
Personal remittances received ($ millions)	113	57	31
Foreign direct investment, net inflows ($ millions)	30.1	90.7	89.7
Net official development assistance received ($ millions)	53.6	13.1	88.2

Sweden

Population (millions)	9.5	Population growth (%)	0.7
Surface area (1,000 sq. km)	450	Population living below $1.25 a day (%)	..
GNI, Atlas ($ billions)	534.3	GNI per capita, Atlas ($)	56,120
GNI, PPP ($ billions)	418.5	GNI per capita, PPP ($)	43,960

	1990	2000	2012
People			
Share of poorest 20% in nat'l consumption/income (%)	..	9.1	..
Life expectancy at birth (years)	78	80	82
Total fertility rate (births per woman)	2.1	1.5	1.9
Adolescent fertility rate (births per 1,000 women 15-19)	12	7	7
Contraceptive prevalence (% of married women 15-49)	..	..	..
Births attended by skilled health staff (% of total)	..	..	..
Under-five mortality rate (per 1,000 live births)	7	4	3
Child malnutrition, underweight (% of under age 5)	..	..	..
Child immunization, measles (% of ages 12-23 mos.)	96	91	97
Primary completion rate, total (% of relevant age group)	97	100	102
Gross secondary enrollment, total (% of relevant age group)	90	152	97
Ratio of girls to boys in primary & secondary school (%)	102	115	99
HIV prevalence rate (% population of ages 15-49)	..	..	..
Environment			
Forests (1,000 sq. km)	273	274	282
Deforestation (avg. annual %, 1990-2000 and 2000-2010)		0.0	-0.3
Freshwater use (% of internal resources)	1.7	1.6	1.5
Access to improved water source (% total pop.)	100	100	100
Access to improved sanitation facilities (% total pop.)	100	100	100
Energy use per capita (kilograms of oil equivalent)	5,515	5,360	5,134
Carbon dioxide emissions per capita (metric tons)	6.0	5.6	5.6
Electricity use per capita (kilowatt-hours)	15,836	15,682	14,030
Economy			
GDP ($ billions)	248	247	524
GDP growth (annual %)	0.8	4.5	0.9
GDP implicit price deflator (annual % growth)	9.5	1.4	1.0
Value added in agriculture (% of GDP)	4	2	2
Value added in industry (% of GDP)	30	28	25
Value added in services (% of GDP)	66	70	73
Exports of goods and services (% of GDP)	30	47	49
Imports of goods and services (% of GDP)	29	40	43
Gross capital formation (% of GDP)	24	19	19
Central government revenue (% of GDP)	..	39.6	31.9
Central government cash surplus/deficit (% of GDP)	..	3.5	-0.4
States and markets			
Starting a business (days)	..	16	16
Stock market capitalization (% of GDP)	39.4	132.8	107.0
Military expenditures (% of GDP)	2.5	2.0	1.2
Mobile cellular subscriptions (per 100 people)	5.4	71.8	124.6
Individuals using the Internet (% of population)	0.6	45.7	94.0
Paved roads (% of total)	..	31.2	23.2
High-technology exports (% of manufactured exports)	13	23	13
Global links			
Merchandise trade (% of GDP)	45	65	64
Net barter terms of trade index (2000 = 100)	..	100	92
Total external debt stocks ($ millions)	..	..	..
Total debt service (% of exports)	..	..	..
Net migration (thousands)	156	142	200
Personal remittances received ($ millions)	153	438	812
Foreign direct investment, net inflows ($ billions)	2.0	23.9	4.0
Net official development assistance received ($ millions)	..	..	..

Switzerland

Population (millions)	8.0	Population growth (%)	1.1
Surface area (1,000 sq. km)	41	Population living below $1.25 a day (%)	..
GNI, Atlas ($ billions)	647.5	GNI per capita, Atlas ($)	80,970
GNI, PPP ($ billions)	439.8	GNI per capita, PPP ($)	55,000

	1990	2000	2012
People			
Share of poorest 20% in nat'l consumption/income (%)	..	7.6	..
Life expectancy at birth (years)	77	80	83
Total fertility rate (births per woman)	1.6	1.5	1.5
Adolescent fertility rate (births per 1,000 women 15-19)	6	5	2
Contraceptive prevalence (% of married women 15-49)	..	..	..
Births attended by skilled health staff (% of total)	..	..	100
Under-five mortality rate (per 1,000 live births)	8	6	4
Child malnutrition, underweight (% of under age 5)	..	..	..
Child immunization, measles (% of ages 12-23 mos.)	90	81	92
Primary completion rate, total (% of relevant age group)	51	96	96
Gross secondary enrollment, total (% of relevant age group)	96	95	96
Ratio of girls to boys in primary & secondary school (%)	97	97	98
HIV prevalence rate (% population of ages 15-49)	..	..	..
Environment			
Forests (1,000 sq. km)	12	12	12
Deforestation (avg. annual %, 1990-2000 and 2000-2010)		-0.4	-0.4
Freshwater use (% of internal resources)	..	6.5	6.5
Access to improved water source (% total pop.)	100	100	100
Access to improved sanitation facilities (% total pop.)	100	100	100
Energy use per capita (kilograms of oil equivalent)	3,628	3,480	3,189
Carbon dioxide emissions per capita (metric tons)	6.4	5.4	5.0
Electricity use per capita (kilowatt-hours)	7,445	7,845	7,928
Economy			
GDP ($ billions)	244	256	631
GDP growth (annual %)	3.7	3.7	1.0
GDP implicit price deflator (annual % growth)	4.6	1.5	0.1
Value added in agriculture (% of GDP)	3	1	1
Value added in industry (% of GDP)	31	26	27
Value added in services (% of GDP)	66	72	73
Exports of goods and services (% of GDP)	36	45	52
Imports of goods and services (% of GDP)	35	40	42
Gross capital formation (% of GDP)	30	23	21
Central government revenue (% of GDP)	..	18.0	18.0
Central government cash surplus/deficit (% of GDP)	..	-0.2	0.6
States and markets			
Starting a business (days)	..	20	18
Stock market capitalization (% of GDP)	65.6	309.4	171.0
Military expenditures (% of GDP)	1.7	1.1	0.8
Mobile cellular subscriptions (per 100 people)	1.9	64.7	130.2
Individuals using the Internet (% of population)	0.6	47.1	85.2
Paved roads (% of total)	..	100.0	100.0
High-technology exports (% of manufactured exports)	16	23	26
Global links			
Merchandise trade (% of GDP)	55	64	67
Net barter terms of trade index (2000 = 100)	..	100	80
Total external debt stocks ($ millions)	..	..	..
Total debt service (% of exports)	..	..	..
Net migration (thousands)	247	186	320
Personal remittances received ($ billions)	0.9	1.1	3.0
Foreign direct investment, net inflows ($ billions)	5.5	19.8	2.7
Net official development assistance received ($ millions)	..	..	..

Syrian Arab Republic

Middle East & North Africa		Lower middle income

Population (millions)	22.4	Population growth (%)	2.0
Surface area (1,000 sq. km)	185	Population living below $1.25 a day (%)	<2
GNI, Atlas ($ billions)	..	GNI per capita, Atlas ($)	..
GNI, PPP ($ billions)	..	GNI per capita, PPP ($)	..

	1990	2000	2012
People			
Share of poorest 20% in nat'l consumption/income (%)	..	7.7	..
Life expectancy at birth (years)	70	73	75
Total fertility rate (births per woman)	5.3	4.0	3.0
Adolescent fertility rate (births per 1,000 women 15–19)	74	58	42
Contraceptive prevalence (% of married women 15–49)	40	45	54
Births attended by skilled health staff (% of total)	77	90	96
Under-five mortality rate (per 1,000 live births)	38	24	15
Child malnutrition, underweight (% of under age 5)	11.5	6.0	10.1
Child immunization, measles (% of ages 12–23 mos.)	87	84	61
Primary completion rate, total (% of relevant age group)	90	92	107
Gross secondary enrollment, total (% of relevant age group)	51	44	74
Ratio of girls to boys in primary & secondary school (%)	85	92	99
HIV prevalence rate (% population of ages 15–49)	..	..	..
Environment			
Forests (1,000 sq. km)	3.7	4.3	5.0
Deforestation (avg. annual %, 1990–2000 and 2000–2010)		-1.5	-1.3
Freshwater use (% of internal resources)	..	229.4	235.0
Access to improved water source (% total pop.)	86	88	90
Access to improved sanitation facilities (% total pop.)	85	89	96
Energy use per capita (kilograms of oil equivalent)	840	963	910
Carbon dioxide emissions per capita (metric tons)	3.0	3.1	2.9
Electricity use per capita (kilowatt-hours)	689	1,067	1,715
Economy			
GDP ($ billions)	12.3	19.3	..
GDP growth (annual %)	7.6	2.7	..
GDP implicit price deflator (annual % growth)	19.3	9.7	..
Value added in agriculture (% of GDP)	30	24	..
Value added in industry (% of GDP)	25	38	..
Value added in services (% of GDP)	45	38	..
Exports of goods and services (% of GDP)	28	35	..
Imports of goods and services (% of GDP)	28	29	..
Gross capital formation (% of GDP)	17	17	..
Central government revenue (% of GDP)	21.9	26.6	23.9
Central government cash surplus/deficit (% of GDP)	..	-1.1	-2.1
States and markets			
Starting a business (days)	..	43	13
Stock market capitalization (% of GDP)	..	..	..
Military expenditures (% of GDP)	6.4	5.3	3.9
Mobile cellular subscriptions (per 100 people)	0.0	0.2	59.3
Individuals using the Internet (% of population)	0.0	0.2	24.3
Paved roads (% of total)	..	72.0	64.9
High-technology exports (% of manufactured exports)	..	1	1
Global links			
Merchandise trade (% of GDP)	54	44	..
Net barter terms of trade index (2000 = 100)	..	100	147
Total external debt stocks ($ billions)	17.1	22.2	4.7
Total debt service (% of exports)	..	6.8	3.1
Net migration (thousands)	-70	-380	-1,500
Personal remittances received ($ millions)	385	180	1,623
Foreign direct investment, net inflows ($ millions)	40	270	1,469
Net official development assistance received ($ millions)	883	159	1,672

Tajikistan

Population (millions)	8.0	Population growth (%)	2.5
Surface area (1,000 sq. km)	143	Population living below $1.25 a day (%)	6.6
GNI, Atlas ($ billions)	7.1	GNI per capita, Atlas ($)	880
GNI, PPP ($ billions)	17.4	GNI per capita, PPP ($)	2,180

	1990	2000	2012
People			
Share of poorest 20% in nat'l consumption/income (%)	..	8.4	8.3
Life expectancy at birth (years)	63	64	67
Total fertility rate (births per woman)	5.2	4.0	3.8
Adolescent fertility rate (births per 1,000 women 15–19)	57	45	43
Contraceptive prevalence (% of married women 15–49)	..	34	28
Births attended by skilled health staff (% of total)	90	71	87
Under-five mortality rate (per 1,000 live births)	105	91	58
Child malnutrition, underweight (% of under age 5)	..	..	15.0
Child immunization, measles (% of ages 12–23 mos.)	68	88	94
Primary completion rate, total (% of relevant age group)	..	91	98
Gross secondary enrollment, total (% of relevant age group)	103	73	86
Ratio of girls to boys in primary & secondary school (%)	..	89	91
HIV prevalence rate (% population of ages 15–49)	0.1	0.1	0.3
Environment			
Forests (1,000 sq. km)	4.1	4.1	4.1
Deforestation (avg. annual %, 1990–2000 and 2000–2010)		-0.1	0.0
Freshwater use (% of internal resources)	..	18.8	18.1
Access to improved water source (% total pop.)	..	60	72
Access to improved sanitation facilities (% total pop.)	..	90	94
Energy use per capita (kilograms of oil equivalent)	1,002	347	306
Carbon dioxide emissions per capita (metric tons)	1.3	0.4	0.4
Electricity use per capita (kilowatt-hours)	3,350	2,172	1,714
Economy			
GDP ($ billions)	2.6	0.9	7.6
GDP growth (annual %)	-0.6	8.3	7.5
GDP implicit price deflator (annual % growth)	6.2	22.7	11.9
Value added in agriculture (% of GDP)	33	27	26
Value added in industry (% of GDP)	38	39	26
Value added in services (% of GDP)	29	34	48
Exports of goods and services (% of GDP)	28	99	18
Imports of goods and services (% of GDP)	35	101	64
Gross capital formation (% of GDP)	25	9	20
Central government revenue (% of GDP)	..	10.6	..
Central government cash surplus/deficit (% of GDP)	..	-0.8	..
States and markets			
Starting a business (days)	..	..	33
Stock market capitalization (% of GDP)	..	..	..
Military expenditures (% of GDP)	0.4	1.2	..
Mobile cellular subscriptions (per 100 people)	0.0	0.0	81.5
Individuals using the Internet (% of population)	0.0	0.0	14.5
Paved roads (% of total)	71.6	..	..
High-technology exports (% of manufactured exports)	..	42	..
Global links			
Merchandise trade (% of GDP)	..	170	67
Net barter terms of trade index (2000 = 100)	..	100	99
Total external debt stocks ($ billions)	0.0	1.1	3.6
Total debt service (% of exports)	..	12.7	25.5
Net migration (thousands)	-289	-97	-100
Personal remittances received ($ millions)	..	79	3,626
Foreign direct investment, net inflows ($ millions)	9	24	198
Net official development assistance received ($ millions)	12	124	394

Tanzania

Sub-Saharan Africa				Low income
Population (millions)	47.8	Population growth (%)		3.0
Surface area (1,000 sq. km)	947	Population living below $1.25 a day (%)		67.9
GNI, Atlas ($ billions)	26.7	GNI per capita, Atlas ($)		570
GNI, PPP ($ billions)	72.4	GNI per capita, PPP ($)		1,560

	1990	2000	2012
People			
Share of poorest 20% in nat'l consumption/income (%)	7.4	7.3	6.8
Life expectancy at birth (years)	50	50	61
Total fertility rate (births per woman)	6.2	5.7	5.3
Adolescent fertility rate (births per 1,000 women 15–19)	142	133	123
Contraceptive prevalence (% of married women 15–49)	10	25	34
Births attended by skilled health staff (% of total)	44	36	49
Under-five mortality rate (per 1,000 live births)	166	132	54
Child malnutrition, underweight (% of under age 5)	25.1	25.3	16.2
Child immunization, measles (% of ages 12–23 mos.)	80	78	97
Primary completion rate, total (% of relevant age group)	62	50	81
Gross secondary enrollment, total (% of relevant age group)	5	..	35
Ratio of girls to boys in primary & secondary school (%)	97	..	100
HIV prevalence rate (% population of ages 15–49)	5.0	7.8	5.1
Environment			
Forests (1,000 sq. km)	415	375	330
Deforestation (avg. annual %, 1990–2000 and 2000–2010)		1.0	1.1
Freshwater use (% of internal resources)	..	6.2	6.2
Access to improved water source (% total pop.)	55	54	53
Access to improved sanitation facilities (% total pop.)	7	9	12
Energy use per capita (kilograms of oil equivalent)	382	394	448
Carbon dioxide emissions per capita (metric tons)	0.09	0.08	0.15
Electricity use per capita (kilowatt-hours)	51	58	92
Economy			
GDP ($ billions)	4.3	10.2	28.2
GDP growth (annual %)	7.0	4.9	6.9
GDP implicit price deflator (annual % growth)	22.4	7.6	11.5
Value added in agriculture (% of GDP)	46	33	28
Value added in industry (% of GDP)	18	19	25
Value added in services (% of GDP)	36	47	47
Exports of goods and services (% of GDP)	13	13	30
Imports of goods and services (% of GDP)	37	20	47
Gross capital formation (% of GDP)	26	17	39
Central government revenue (% of GDP)	..	..	17.3
Central government cash surplus/deficit (% of GDP)	..	..	-7.2
States and markets			
Starting a business (days)	..	28	26
Stock market capitalization (% of GDP)	..	2.3	6.4
Military expenditures (% of GDP)	2.0	1.3	1.1
Mobile cellular subscriptions (per 100 people)	0.0	0.3	57.0
Individuals using the Internet (% of population)	0.0	0.1	4.0
Paved roads (% of total)	..	4.0	14.9
High-technology exports (% of manufactured exports)	..	1	10
Global links			
Merchandise trade (% of GDP)	32	22	59
Net barter terms of trade index (2000 = 100)	107	100	145
Total external debt stocks ($ billions)	6.4	7.2	11.6
Total debt service (% of exports)	32.9	11.9	1.9
Net migration (thousands)	591	-345	-150
Personal remittances received ($ millions)	..	8.0	67.4
Foreign direct investment, net inflows ($ millions)	0	463	1,707
Net official development assistance received ($ billions)	1.2	1.1	2.8

Thailand

East Asia & Pacific		Upper middle income	
Population (millions)	66.8	Population growth (%)	0.3
Surface area (1,000 sq. km)	513	Population living below $1.25 a day (%)	<2
GNI, Atlas ($ billions)	347.8	GNI per capita, Atlas ($)	5,210
GNI, PPP ($ billions)	619.5	GNI per capita, PPP ($)	9,280

	1990	2000	2012
People			
Share of poorest 20% in nat'l consumption/income (%)	5.9	6.2	6.8
Life expectancy at birth (years)	70	71	74
Total fertility rate (births per woman)	2.1	1.7	1.4
Adolescent fertility rate (births per 1,000 women 15–19)	51	43	41
Contraceptive prevalence (% of married women 15–49)	66	79	80
Births attended by skilled health staff (% of total)	..	99	100
Under-five mortality rate (per 1,000 live births)	38	23	13
Child malnutrition, underweight (% of under age 5)	16.3	..	7.0
Child immunization, measles (% of ages 12-23 mos.)	80	94	98
Primary completion rate, total (% of relevant age group)	..	85	..
Gross secondary enrollment, total (% of relevant age group)	29	63	87
Ratio of girls to boys in primary & secondary school (%)	97	98	102
HIV prevalence rate (% population of ages 15–49)	0.8	1.9	1.1
Environment			
Forests (1,000 sq. km)	195	190	190
Deforestation (avg. annual %, 1990-2000 and 2000-2010)		0.3	0.0
Freshwater use (% of internal resources)	..	..	25.5
Access to improved water source (% total pop.)	86	92	96
Access to improved sanitation facilities (% total pop.)	82	91	93
Energy use per capita (kilograms of oil equivalent)	741	1,159	1,790
Carbon dioxide emissions per capita (metric tons)	1.7	3.0	4.4
Electricity use per capita (kilowatt-hours)	709	1,462	2,316
Economy			
GDP ($ billions)	85	123	366
GDP growth (annual %)	11.2	4.8	6.5
GDP implicit price deflator (annual % growth)	5.8	1.3	1.3
Value added in agriculture (% of GDP)	12	9	12
Value added in industry (% of GDP)	37	42	44
Value added in services (% of GDP)	50	49	44
Exports of goods and services (% of GDP)	34	67	75
Imports of goods and services (% of GDP)	42	58	74
Gross capital formation (% of GDP)	41	23	30
Central government revenue (% of GDP)	..	19.5	21.3
Central government cash surplus/deficit (% of GDP)	..	1.5	-1.2
States and markets			
Starting a business (days)	..	33	28
Stock market capitalization (% of GDP)	28.0	24.0	104.7
Military expenditures (% of GDP)	2.7	1.5	1.5
Mobile cellular subscriptions (per 100 people)	0.1	4.9	127.3
Individuals using the Internet (% of population)	0.0	3.7	26.5
Paved roads (% of total)	88.4	97.5	..
High-technology exports (% of manufactured exports)	21	33	21
Global links			
Merchandise trade (% of GDP)	66	107	130
Net barter terms of trade index (2000 = 100)	119	100	93
Total external debt stocks ($ billions)	28	80	134
Total debt service (% of exports)	16.9	16.3	4.1
Net migration (thousands)	-1,108	1,103	100
Personal remittances received ($ billions)	1.0	1.7	4.7
Foreign direct investment, net inflows ($ billions)	2.4	3.4	10.7
Net official development assistance received ($ millions)	796	697	-135

Timor-Leste

East Asia & Pacific		Lower middle income
Population (millions)	1.2	Population growth (%)	2.9
Surface area (1,000 sq. km)	15	Population living below $1.25 a day (%)	..
GNI, Atlas ($ billions)	4.4	GNI per capita, Atlas ($)	3,620
GNI, PPP ($ billions)	7.5	GNI per capita, PPP ($)	6,230

	1990	2000	2012
People			
Share of poorest 20% in nat'l consumption/income (%)	..	..	..
Life expectancy at birth (years)	48	59	67
Total fertility rate (births per woman)	5.3	7.1	5.3
Adolescent fertility rate (births per 1,000 women 15-19)	57	71	52
Contraceptive prevalence (% of married women 15-49)	25	8	22
Births attended by skilled health staff (% of total)	..	24	29
Under-five mortality rate (per 1,000 live births)	171	106	57
Child malnutrition, underweight (% of under age 5)	..	40.6	45.3
Child immunization, measles (% of ages 12-23 mos.)	..	56	62
Primary completion rate, total (% of relevant age group)	..	..	71
Gross secondary enrollment, total (% of relevant age group)	..	36	57
Ratio of girls to boys in primary & secondary school (%)	..	..	97
HIV prevalence rate (% population of ages 15-49)	..	..	..
Environment			
Forests (1,000 sq. km)	9.7	8.5	7.3
Deforestation (avg. annual %, 1990-2000 and 2000-2010)		1.2	1.4
Freshwater use (% of internal resources)	..	..	14.3
Access to improved water source (% total pop.)	..	54	70
Access to improved sanitation facilities (% total pop.)	..	37	39
Energy use per capita (kilograms of oil equivalent)	..	..	..
Carbon dioxide emissions per capita (metric tons)	..	0.2	0.2
Electricity use per capita (kilowatt-hours)	..	..	..
Economy			
GDP ($ millions)	..	350	1,293
GDP growth (annual %)	..	13.7	0.6
GDP implicit price deflator (annual % growth)	..	5.5	13.9
Value added in agriculture (% of GDP)	..	30	17
Value added in industry (% of GDP)	..	17	26
Value added in services (% of GDP)	..	53	57
Exports of goods and services (% of GDP)	..	10	10
Imports of goods and services (% of GDP)	..	172	120
Gross capital formation (% of GDP)	..	37	65
Central government revenue (% of GDP)	..	..	..
Central government cash surplus/deficit (% of GDP)	..	..	..
States and markets			
Starting a business (days)	..	..	94
Stock market capitalization (% of GDP)	..	..	..
Military expenditures (% of GDP)	..	..	2.9
Mobile cellular subscriptions (per 100 people)	0.0	2.1	55.7
Individuals using the Internet (% of population)	0.0	0.0	0.9
Paved roads (% of total)	..	..	..
High-technology exports (% of manufactured exports)	..	..	..
Global links			
Merchandise trade (% of GDP)	..	32	30
Net barter terms of trade index (2000 = 100)	..	..	..
Total external debt stocks ($ millions)	..	..	..
Total debt service (% of exports)	..	..	..
Net migration (thousands)	-4.4	0.0	-75.0
Personal remittances received ($ millions)	..	..	114
Foreign direct investment, net inflows ($ millions)	..	4.5	18.9
Net official development assistance received ($ millions)	0	231	283

Togo

Sub-Saharan Africa   **Low income**

Population (millions)	6.6	Population growth (%)	2.6
Surface area (1,000 sq. km)	57	Population living below $1.25 a day (%)	28.2
GNI, Atlas ($ billions)	3.3	GNI per capita, Atlas ($)	500
GNI, PPP ($ billions)	6.0	GNI per capita, PPP ($)	900

	1990	2000	2012
People			
Share of poorest 20% in nat'l consumption/income (%)	..	..	6.0
Life expectancy at birth (years)	56	54	56
Total fertility rate (births per woman)	6.3	5.3	4.7
Adolescent fertility rate (births per 1,000 women 15-19)	117	93	92
Contraceptive prevalence (% of married women 15-49)	34	26	15
Births attended by skilled health staff (% of total)	31	49	59
Under-five mortality rate (per 1,000 live births)	143	122	96
Child malnutrition, underweight (% of under age 5)	21.2	23.2	16.5
Child immunization, measles (% of ages 12-23 mos.)	73	58	72
Primary completion rate, total (% of relevant age group)	36	65	74
Gross secondary enrollment, total (% of relevant age group)	22	32	55
Ratio of girls to boys in primary & secondary school (%)	58	69	..
HIV prevalence rate (% population of ages 15-49)	0.8	4.4	2.9
Environment			
Forests (1,000 sq. km)	6.9	4.9	2.7
Deforestation (avg. annual %, 1990-2000 and 2000-2010)		3.4	5.1
Freshwater use (% of internal resources)	..	1.5	1.5
Access to improved water source (% total pop.)	48	53	61
Access to improved sanitation facilities (% total pop.)	13	12	11
Energy use per capita (kilograms of oil equivalent)	334	434	427
Carbon dioxide emissions per capita (metric tons)	0.2	0.3	0.2
Electricity use per capita (kilowatt-hours)	91	96	..
Economy			
GDP ($ millions)	1,628	1,294	3,814
GDP growth (annual %)	-0.2	-0.8	5.6
GDP implicit price deflator (annual % growth)	3.0	-4.3	6.0
Value added in agriculture (% of GDP)	34	35	31
Value added in industry (% of GDP)	23	18	16
Value added in services (% of GDP)	44	47	53
Exports of goods and services (% of GDP)	33	34	40
Imports of goods and services (% of GDP)	45	48	57
Gross capital formation (% of GDP)	27	15	19
Central government revenue (% of GDP)	..	..	19.1
Central government cash surplus/deficit (% of GDP)	..	..	-6.3
States and markets			
Starting a business (days)	..	65	19
Stock market capitalization (% of GDP)	..	..	..
Military expenditures (% of GDP)	3.1	1.7	1.6
Mobile cellular subscriptions (per 100 people)	0.0	1.0	49.9
Individuals using the Internet (% of population)	0.0	0.8	4.0
Paved roads (% of total)	21.2	32.0	21.0
High-technology exports (% of manufactured exports)	1	1	0
Global links			
Merchandise trade (% of GDP)	52	71	73
Net barter terms of trade index (2000 = 100)	133	100	29
Total external debt stocks ($ billions)	1.3	1.4	0.8
Total debt service (% of exports)	12.3	6.6	2.6
Net migration (thousands)	-95.0	-10.0	-10.0
Personal remittances received ($ millions)	27	34	337
Foreign direct investment, net inflows ($ millions)	18	42	166
Net official development assistance received ($ millions)	258	70	241

Tonga

East Asia & Pacific		Upper middle income	
Population (thousands)	105	Population growth (%)	0.4
Surface area (sq. km)	750	Population living below $1.25 a day (%)	..
GNI, Atlas ($ millions)	442.5	GNI per capita, Atlas ($)	4,220
GNI, PPP ($ millions)	527.2	GNI per capita, PPP ($)	5,020

	1990	2000	2012
People			
Share of poorest 20% in nat'l consumption/income (%)	..	..	..
Life expectancy at birth (years)	70	71	72
Total fertility rate (births per woman)	4.6	4.3	3.8
Adolescent fertility rate (births per 1,000 women 15–19)	26	22	18
Contraceptive prevalence (% of married women 15–49)	..	33	32
Births attended by skilled health staff (% of total)	92	95	98
Under-five mortality rate (per 1,000 live births)	23	18	13
Child malnutrition, underweight (% of under age 5)	..	..	..
Child immunization, measles (% of ages 12–23 mos.)	86	95	95
Primary completion rate, total (% of relevant age group)	128	107	100
Gross secondary enrollment, total (% of relevant age group)	98	106	91
Ratio of girls to boys in primary & secondary school (%)	99	102	102
HIV prevalence rate (% population of ages 15–49)	..	..	..
Environment			
Forests (sq. km)	90	90	90
Deforestation (avg. annual %, 1990–2000 and 2000–2010)		0.0	0.0
Freshwater use (% of internal resources)	..	..	..
Access to improved water source (% total pop.)	99	99	99
Access to improved sanitation facilities (% total pop.)	95	94	91
Energy use per capita (kilograms of oil equivalent)	266	..	..
Carbon dioxide emissions per capita (metric tons)	0.8	1.2	1.5
Electricity use per capita (kilowatt-hours)	..	..	..
Economy			
GDP ($ millions)	114	189	472
GDP growth (annual %)	-2.0	3.4	0.8
GDP implicit price deflator (annual % growth)	12.2	3.1	2.3
Value added in agriculture (% of GDP)	36	23	19
Value added in industry (% of GDP)	14	21	21
Value added in services (% of GDP)	50	56	59
Exports of goods and services (% of GDP)	34	15	18
Imports of goods and services (% of GDP)	65	47	63
Gross capital formation (% of GDP)	18	22	33
Central government revenue (% of GDP)	..	..	..
Central government cash surplus/deficit (% of GDP)	..	..	..
States and markets			
Starting a business (days)	..	32	16
Stock market capitalization (% of GDP)	..	..	..
Military expenditures (% of GDP)	..	..	..
Mobile cellular subscriptions (per 100 people)	0.0	0.2	53.4
Individuals using the Internet (% of population)	0.0	2.4	34.9
Paved roads (% of total)	..	27.0	..
High-technology exports (% of manufactured exports)	..	0	7
Global links			
Merchandise trade (% of GDP)	64	42	48
Net barter terms of trade index (2000 = 100)	..	100	82
Total external debt stocks ($ millions)	44	74	197
Total debt service (% of exports)	3.5	8.9	7.8
Net migration (thousands)	-11.1	-8.1	-8.1
Personal remittances received ($ millions)	24.0	52.5	59.6
Foreign direct investment, net inflows ($ millions)	0.2	4.8	8.1
Net official development assistance received ($ millions)	29.8	18.8	78.3

Trinidad and Tobago

High income

Population (millions)	1.3	Population growth (%)		0.3
Surface area (1,000 sq. km)	5.1	Population living below $1.25 a day (%)		4.2
GNI, Atlas ($ billions)	19.7	GNI per capita, Atlas ($)		14,710
GNI, PPP ($ billions)	30.6	GNI per capita, PPP ($)		22,860

	1990	2000	2012
People			
Share of poorest 20% in nat'l consumption/income (%)	5.5	..	..
Life expectancy at birth (years)	68	69	70
Total fertility rate (births per woman)	2.5	1.8	1.8
Adolescent fertility rate (births per 1,000 women 15-19)	62	41	35
Contraceptive prevalence (% of married women 15-49)	..	38	43
Births attended by skilled health staff (% of total)	..	96	98
Under-five mortality rate (per 1,000 live births)	33	28	21
Child malnutrition, underweight (% of under age 5)	..	4.4	..
Child immunization, measles (% of ages 12-23 mos.)	70	90	85
Primary completion rate, total (% of relevant age group)	100	93	95
Gross secondary enrollment, total (% of relevant age group)	83	..	..
Ratio of girls to boys in primary & secondary school (%)	103	..	..
HIV prevalence rate (% population of ages 15-49)	0.4	1.2	1.6
Environment			
Forests (1,000 sq. km)	2.4	2.3	2.3
Deforestation (avg. annual %, 1990-2000 and 2000-2010)		0.3	0.3
Freshwater use (% of internal resources)	..	6.0	6.0
Access to improved water source (% total pop.)	90	92	94
Access to improved sanitation facilities (% total pop.)	93	92	92
Energy use per capita (kilograms of oil equivalent)	4,900	8,560	15,691
Carbon dioxide emissions per capita (metric tons)	13.9	19.3	38.2
Electricity use per capita (kilowatt-hours)	2,683	3,991	6,332
Economy			
GDP ($ billions)	5.1	8.2	23.3
GDP growth (annual %)	1.5	6.1	1.5
GDP implicit price deflator (annual % growth)	15.5	12.9	-2.5
Value added in agriculture (% of GDP)	3	1	1
Value added in industry (% of GDP)	47	49	57
Value added in services (% of GDP)	50	49	42
Exports of goods and services (% of GDP)	45	59	88
Imports of goods and services (% of GDP)	29	45	63
Gross capital formation (% of GDP)	13	20	..
Central government revenue (% of GDP)	28.1	27.1	35.5
Central government cash surplus/deficit (% of GDP)	-0.2	2.0	-1.6
States and markets			
Starting a business (days)	..	..	38
Stock market capitalization (% of GDP)	13.7	53.1	65.0
Military expenditures (% of GDP)	0.1	0.0	1.3
Mobile cellular subscriptions (per 100 people)	0.0	12.8	140.8
Individuals using the Internet (% of population)	0.0	7.7	59.5
Paved roads (% of total)	46.2	51.0	..
High-technology exports (% of manufactured exports)	0	1	0
Global links			
Merchandise trade (% of GDP)	61	93	96
Net barter terms of trade index (2000 = 100)	100	100	157
Total external debt stocks ($ millions)	..	..	..
Total debt service (% of exports)	..	..	..
Net migration (thousands)	-32.0	-13.2	-15.0
Personal remittances received ($ millions)	3	38	126
Foreign direct investment, net inflows ($ millions)	109	680	2,527
Net official development assistance received ($ millions)	17.8	-1.5	4.3

Tunisia

Middle East & North Africa		Upper middle income	
Population (millions)	10.8	Population growth (%)	1.0
Surface area (1,000 sq. km)	164	Population living below $1.25 a day (%)	<2
GNI, Atlas ($ billions)	44.8	GNI per capita, Atlas ($)	4,150
GNI, PPP ($ billions)	99.2	GNI per capita, PPP ($)	9,210

	1990	2000	2012
People			
Share of poorest 20% in nat'l consumption/income (%)	5.9	6.0	6.7
Life expectancy at birth (years)	70	73	75
Total fertility rate (births per woman)	3.5	2.1	2.2
Adolescent fertility rate (births per 1,000 women 15–19)	20	7	5
Contraceptive prevalence (% of married women 15–49)	50	66	63
Births attended by skilled health staff (% of total)	69	90	99
Under-five mortality rate (per 1,000 live births)	51	30	16
Child malnutrition, underweight (% of under age 5)	8.5	3.5	3.3
Child immunization, measles (% of ages 12–23 mos.)	93	95	96
Primary completion rate, total (% of relevant age group)	80	90	102
Gross secondary enrollment, total (% of relevant age group)	45	75	91
Ratio of girls to boys in primary & secondary school (%)	84	99	101
HIV prevalence rate (% population of ages 15–49)	0.1	0.1	0.1
Environment			
Forests (1,000 sq. km)	6	8	10
Deforestation (avg. annual %, 1990–2000 and 2000–2010)		-2.7	-1.9
Freshwater use (% of internal resources)	73.3	67.9	67.9
Access to improved water source (% total pop.)	82	89	97
Access to improved sanitation facilities (% total pop.)	73	82	90
Energy use per capita (kilograms of oil equivalent)	607	764	890
Carbon dioxide emissions per capita (metric tons)	1.6	2.1	2.5
Electricity use per capita (kilowatt-hours)	638	991	1,297
Economy			
GDP ($ billions)	12.3	21.5	45.7
GDP growth (annual %)	7.9	4.7	3.6
GDP implicit price deflator (annual % growth)	4.5	3.3	5.3
Value added in agriculture (% of GDP)	18	11	9
Value added in industry (% of GDP)	34	30	30
Value added in services (% of GDP)	49	58	61
Exports of goods and services (% of GDP)	44	40	48
Imports of goods and services (% of GDP)	51	43	59
Gross capital formation (% of GDP)	27	26	24
Central government revenue (% of GDP)	30.7	26.5	31.0
Central government cash surplus/deficit (% of GDP)	-3.2	-2.4	-5.0
States and markets			
Starting a business (days)	..	11	11
Stock market capitalization (% of GDP)	4.3	13.2	19.5
Military expenditures (% of GDP)	2.0	1.5	1.6
Mobile cellular subscriptions (per 100 people)	0.0	1.2	118.1
Individuals using the Internet (% of population)	0.0	2.8	41.4
Paved roads (% of total)	76.1	68.0	76.3
High-technology exports (% of manufactured exports)	2	3	6
Global links			
Merchandise trade (% of GDP)	74	67	91
Net barter terms of trade index (2000 = 100)	109	100	97
Total external debt stocks ($ billions)	7.7	11.4	25.5
Total debt service (% of exports)	27.0	21.9	11.5
Net migration (thousands)	43.9	-71.4	-32.9
Personal remittances received ($ millions)	551	796	2,266
Foreign direct investment, net inflows ($ millions)	76	752	1,554
Net official development assistance received ($ millions)	393	222	1,017

Turkey

Europe & Central Asia		Upper middle income	

Population (millions)	74.0	Population growth (%)	1.3
Surface area (1,000 sq. km)	784	Population living below $1.25 a day (%)	<2
GNI, Atlas ($ billions)	801.1	GNI per capita, Atlas ($)	10,830
GNI, PPP ($ billions)	1,360.6	GNI per capita, PPP ($)	18,390

	1990	2000	2012
People			
Share of poorest 20% in nat'l consumption/income (%)	..	5.6	5.5
Life expectancy at birth (years)	64	70	75
Total fertility rate (births per woman)	3.1	2.5	2.1
Adolescent fertility rate (births per 1,000 women 15–19)	65	48	31
Contraceptive prevalence (% of married women 15–49)	63	71	73
Births attended by skilled health staff (% of total)	76	83	95
Under-five mortality rate (per 1,000 live births)	74	37	14
Child malnutrition, underweight (% of under age 5)	8.7	3.5	..
Child immunization, measles (% of ages 12–23 mos.)	78	87	98
Primary completion rate, total (% of relevant age group)	93	..	103
Gross secondary enrollment, total (% of relevant age group)	50	73	89
Ratio of girls to boys in primary & secondary school (%)	78	82	95
HIV prevalence rate (% population of ages 15–49)	..	..	..
Environment			
Forests (1,000 sq. km)	97	101	115
Deforestation (avg. annual %, 1990-2000 and 2000-2010)		-0.5	-1.1
Freshwater use (% of internal resources)	13.9	18.5	17.7
Access to improved water source (% total pop.)	85	93	100
Access to improved sanitation facilities (% total pop.)	84	87	91
Energy use per capita (kilograms of oil equivalent)	977	1,209	1,564
Carbon dioxide emissions per capita (metric tons)	2.7	3.4	4.1
Electricity use per capita (kilowatt-hours)	928	1,654	2,709
Economy			
GDP ($ billions)	151	267	789
GDP growth (annual %)	9.3	6.8	2.2
GDP implicit price deflator (annual % growth)	58.2	49.2	6.8
Value added in agriculture (% of GDP)	18	11	9
Value added in industry (% of GDP)	32	31	27
Value added in services (% of GDP)	50	57	64
Exports of goods and services (% of GDP)	13	20	26
Imports of goods and services (% of GDP)	18	23	32
Gross capital formation (% of GDP)	25	21	20
Central government revenue (% of GDP)	..	..	33.0
Central government cash surplus/deficit (% of GDP)	..	..	-1.1
States and markets			
Starting a business (days)	..	38	6
Stock market capitalization (% of GDP)	12.7	26.1	39.1
Military expenditures (% of GDP)	3.5	3.7	2.3
Mobile cellular subscriptions (per 100 people)	0.1	25.5	91.5
Individuals using the Internet (% of population)	0.0	3.8	45.1
Paved roads (% of total)	..	34.0	89.4
High-technology exports (% of manufactured exports)	1	5	2
Global links			
Merchandise trade (% of GDP)	23	31	49
Net barter terms of trade index (2000 = 100)	109	100	87
Total external debt stocks ($ billions)	49	117	337
Total debt service (% of exports)	33.8	38.9	26.1
Net migration (thousands)	-200	-100	350
Personal remittances received ($ billions)	3.2	4.6	1.0
Foreign direct investment, net inflows ($ billions)	0.7	1.0	12.5
Net official development assistance received ($ billions)	1.3	0.3	3.0

Turkmenistan

Europe & Central Asia		Upper middle income	
Population (millions)	5.2	Population growth (%)	1.3
Surface area (1,000 sq. km)	488	Population living below $1.25 a day (%)	24.8
GNI, Atlas ($ billions)	28.0	GNI per capita, Atlas ($)	5,410
GNI, PPP ($ billions)	46.9	GNI per capita, PPP ($)	9,070

	1990	2000	2012
People			
Share of poorest 20% in nat'l consumption/income (%)	6.9	6.1	..
Life expectancy at birth (years)	63	64	65
Total fertility rate (births per woman)	4.3	2.8	2.4
Adolescent fertility rate (births per 1,000 women 15-19)	25	25	18
Contraceptive prevalence (% of married women 15-49)	..	62	48
Births attended by skilled health staff (% of total)	..	97	100
Under-five mortality rate (per 1,000 live births)	90	79	53
Child malnutrition, underweight (% of under age 5)	..	10.5	..
Child immunization, measles (% of ages 12-23 mos.)	76	96	99
Primary completion rate, total (% of relevant age group)	..	..	..
Gross secondary enrollment, total (% of relevant age group)	..	..	..
Ratio of girls to boys in primary & secondary school (%)	..	..	..
HIV prevalence rate (% population of ages 15-49)	..	..	..
Environment			
Forests (1,000 sq. km)	41	41	41
Deforestation (avg. annual %, 1990-2000 and 2000-2010)		0.0	0.0
Freshwater use (% of internal resources)	..	1,773.0	1,989.3
Access to improved water source (% total pop.)	..	83	71
Access to improved sanitation facilities (% total pop.)	98	98	99
Energy use per capita (kilograms of oil equivalent)	4,776	3,304	4,839
Carbon dioxide emissions per capita (metric tons)	7.2	7.9	10.5
Electricity use per capita (kilowatt-hours)	2,293	1,698	2,444
Economy			
GDP ($ billions)	3.2	2.9	35.2
GDP growth (annual %)	35.4	5.5	11.1
GDP implicit price deflator (annual % growth)	-20.9	23.5	8.3
Value added in agriculture (% of GDP)	32	24	15
Value added in industry (% of GDP)	30	44	48
Value added in services (% of GDP)	38	31	37
Exports of goods and services (% of GDP)	39	96	73
Imports of goods and services (% of GDP)	27	81	44
Gross capital formation (% of GDP)	40	35	47
Central government revenue (% of GDP)	..	..	..
Central government cash surplus/deficit (% of GDP)	..	..	..
States and markets			
Starting a business (days)	..	..	..
Stock market capitalization (% of GDP)	..	..	..
Military expenditures (% of GDP)	..	2.9	..
Mobile cellular subscriptions (per 100 people)	0.0	0.2	76.4
Individuals using the Internet (% of population)	0.0	0.1	7.2
Paved roads (% of total)	73.5	81.0	..
High-technology exports (% of manufactured exports)	..	5	..
Global links			
Merchandise trade (% of GDP)	..	148	73
Net barter terms of trade index (2000 = 100)	..	100	238
Total external debt stocks ($ millions)	276	2,609	492
Total debt service (% of exports)	..	..	..
Net migration (thousands)	44	-114	-25
Personal remittances received ($ millions)	..	..	..
Foreign direct investment, net inflows ($ millions)	79	131	3,159
Net official development assistance received ($ millions)	6.6	35.3	38.0

Turks and Caicos Islands

High income

Population (thousands)	32	Population growth (%)		2.2
Surface area (sq. km)	950	Population living below $1.25 a day (%)		..
GNI, Atlas ($ millions)	..	GNI per capita, Atlas ($)		..
GNI, PPP ($ millions)	..	GNI per capita, PPP ($)		..

	1990	2000	2012
People			
Share of poorest 20% in nat'l consumption/income (%)	..	..	..
Life expectancy at birth (years)	..	..	..
Total fertility rate (births per woman)	..	..	..
Adolescent fertility rate (births per 1,000 women 15-19)	..	..	..
Contraceptive prevalence (% of married women 15-49)	..	..	..
Births attended by skilled health staff (% of total)	..	88	100
Under-five mortality rate (per 1,000 live births)	..	..	..
Child malnutrition, underweight (% of under age 5)	..	..	..
Child immunization, measles (% of ages 12-23 mos.)	..	..	..
Primary completion rate, total (% of relevant age group)	..	84	..
Gross secondary enrollment, total (% of relevant age group)	..	95	..
Ratio of girls to boys in primary & secondary school (%)	..	98	..
HIV prevalence rate (% population of ages 15-49)	..	..	..
Environment			
Forests (sq. km)	344	344	344
Deforestation (avg. annual %, 1990-2000 and 2000-2010)		0.0	0.0
Freshwater use (% of internal resources)		..	..
Access to improved water source (% total pop.)	..	87	..
Access to improved sanitation facilities (% total pop.)	..	81	..
Energy use per capita (kilograms of oil equivalent)	..	..	..
Carbon dioxide emissions per capita (metric tons)	..	0.8	5.2
Electricity use per capita (kilowatt-hours)	..	..	..
Economy			
GDP ($ millions)	..	..	..
GDP growth (annual %)	..	..	..
GDP implicit price deflator (annual % growth)	..	..	..
Value added in agriculture (% of GDP)	..	..	..
Value added in industry (% of GDP)	..	..	..
Value added in services (% of GDP)	..	..	..
Exports of goods and services (% of GDP)	..	..	..
Imports of goods and services (% of GDP)	..	..	..
Gross capital formation (% of GDP)	..	..	..
Central government revenue (% of GDP)	..	..	..
Central government cash surplus/deficit (% of GDP)	..	..	..
States and markets			
Starting a business (days)	..	..	..
Stock market capitalization (% of GDP)	..	..	..
Military expenditures (% of GDP)	..	..	..
Mobile cellular subscriptions (per 100 people)	..	..	..
Individuals using the Internet (% of population)	..	..	..
Paved roads (% of total)	..	..	..
High-technology exports (% of manufactured exports)	..	20	2
Global links			
Merchandise trade (% of GDP)	..	..	..
Net barter terms of trade index (2000 = 100)	..	100	68
Total external debt stocks ($ millions)	..	..	..
Total debt service (% of exports)	..	..	..
Net migration (thousands)	..	..	..
Personal remittances received ($ millions)	..	..	..
Foreign direct investment, net inflows ($ millions)	..	..	..
Net official development assistance received ($ millions)	11.6	6.7	..

Tuvalu

East Asia & Pacific		Upper middle income	
Population (thousands)	10	Population growth (%)	0.2
Surface area (sq. km)	30	Population living below $1.25 a day (%)	..
GNI, Atlas ($ millions)	55.7	GNI per capita, Atlas ($)	5,650
GNI, PPP ($ millions)	..	GNI per capita, PPP ($)	..

	1990	2000	2012
People			
Share of poorest 20% in nat'l consumption/income (%)	..	..	..
Life expectancy at birth (years)	..	..	..
Total fertility rate (births per woman)	..	..	..
Adolescent fertility rate (births per 1,000 women 15-19)		..	..
Contraceptive prevalence (% of married women 15-49)	39	32	31
Births attended by skilled health staff (% of total)	100	100	98
Under-five mortality rate (per 1,000 live births)	58	42	30
Child malnutrition, underweight (% of under age 5)	..	..	1.6
Child immunization, measles (% of ages 12-23 mos.)	95	81	98
Primary completion rate, total (% of relevant age group)	..	102	..
Gross secondary enrollment, total (% of relevant age group)	..	80	..
Ratio of girls to boys in primary & secondary school (%)	..	112	..
HIV prevalence rate (% population of ages 15-49)	..	..	..
Environment			
Forests (sq. km)	10.0	10.0	10.0
Deforestation (avg. annual %, 1990-2000 and 2000-2010)		0.0	0.0
Freshwater use (% of internal resources)	..	..	..
Access to improved water source (% total pop.)	90	94	98
Access to improved sanitation facilities (% total pop.)	73	78	83
Energy use per capita (kilograms of oil equivalent)	..	..	..
Carbon dioxide emissions per capita (metric tons)	..	..	..
Electricity use per capita (kilowatt-hours)	..	..	..
Economy			
GDP ($ millions)	8.8	13.7	39.9
GDP growth (annual %)	3.6	-1.0	0.2
GDP implicit price deflator (annual % growth)	2.6	12.8	0.9
Value added in agriculture (% of GDP)	..	20	25
Value added in industry (% of GDP)	..	8	6
Value added in services (% of GDP)	..	72	69
Exports of goods and services (% of GDP)	..	..	..
Imports of goods and services (% of GDP)	..	..	..
Gross capital formation (% of GDP)	..	..	..
Central government revenue (% of GDP)	..	..	..
Central government cash surplus/deficit (% of GDP)	..	..	..
States and markets			
Starting a business (days)	..	..	..
Stock market capitalization (% of GDP)	..	..	..
Military expenditures (% of GDP)	..	..	..
Mobile cellular subscriptions (per 100 people)	0.0	0.0	28.4
Individuals using the Internet (% of population)	0.0	5.2	35.0
Paved roads (% of total)	..	..	..
High-technology exports (% of manufactured exports)	..	28	..
Global links			
Merchandise trade (% of GDP)	58	36	63
Net barter terms of trade index (2000 = 100)	..	..	..
Total external debt stocks ($ millions)	..	..	..
Total debt service (% of exports)	..	..	..
Net migration (thousands)	..	..	..
Personal remittances received ($ millions)	..	..	..
Foreign direct investment, net inflows ($ millions)	..	..	..
Net official development assistance received ($ millions)	5.1	4.0	24.5

Uganda

Population (millions)	36.3	Population growth (%) 3.4
Surface area (1,000 sq. km)	242	Population living below $1.25 a day (%) *38.0*
GNI, Atlas ($ billions)	17.6	GNI per capita, Atlas ($) 480
GNI, PPP ($ billions)	47.1	GNI per capita, PPP ($) 1,300

	1990	2000	2012
People			
Share of poorest 20% in nat'l consumption/income (%)	*4.9*	*5.9*	*5.8*
Life expectancy at birth (years)	48	48	59
Total fertility rate (births per woman)	7.1	6.9	6.0
Adolescent fertility rate (births per 1,000 women 15-19)	195	180	127
Contraceptive prevalence (% of married women 15-49)	5	23	30
Births attended by skilled health staff (% of total)	*38*	39	57
Under-five mortality rate (per 1,000 live births)	178	147	69
Child malnutrition, underweight (% of under age 5)	*19.7*	19.0	*14.1*
Child immunization, measles (% of ages 12-23 mos.)	52	57	82
Primary completion rate, total (% of relevant age group)	..	59	53
Gross secondary enrollment, total (% of relevant age group)	11	16	28
Ratio of girls to boys in primary & secondary school (%)	78	92	98
HIV prevalence rate (% population of ages 15-49)	12.3	7.2	7.2
Environment			
Forests (1,000 sq. km)	48	39	*29*
Deforestation (avg. annual %, 1990-2000 and 2000-2010)		2.0	*2.6*
Freshwater use (% of internal resources)	..	*0.8*	*0.8*
Access to improved water source (% total pop.)	42	56	75
Access to improved sanitation facilities (% total pop.)	26	30	34
Energy use per capita (kilograms of oil equivalent)	..	..	..
Carbon dioxide emissions per capita (metric tons)	0.05	0.06	*0.11*
Electricity use per capita (kilowatt-hours)	..	..	..
Economy			
GDP ($ billions)	4.3	6.2	20.0
GDP growth (annual %)	6.5	3.1	3.4
GDP implicit price deflator (annual % growth)	44.4	11.1	24.1
Value added in agriculture (% of GDP)	57	29	26
Value added in industry (% of GDP)	11	23	29
Value added in services (% of GDP)	32	48	45
Exports of goods and services (% of GDP)	7	11	23
Imports of goods and services (% of GDP)	19	22	39
Gross capital formation (% of GDP)	13	19	25
Central government revenue (% of GDP)	..	10.8	16.4
Central government cash surplus/deficit (% of GDP)	..	-1.9	-3.9
States and markets			
Starting a business (days)	..	*34*	32
Stock market capitalization (% of GDP)	..	0.6	36.4
Military expenditures (% of GDP)	3.3	2.5	1.4
Mobile cellular subscriptions (per 100 people)	0.0	0.5	45.0
Individuals using the Internet (% of population)	0.0	0.2	14.7
Paved roads (% of total)	..	*23.0*	..
High-technology exports (% of manufactured exports)	..	4	21
Global links			
Merchandise trade (% of GDP)	10	31	42
Net barter terms of trade index (2000 = 100)	146	100	110
Total external debt stocks ($ billions)	2.6	3.5	3.8
Total debt service (% of exports)	81.4	10.6	1.4
Net migration (thousands)	*120*	-5	-150
Personal remittances received ($ millions)	..	238	733
Foreign direct investment, net inflows ($ millions)	-6	161	1,721
Net official development assistance received ($ millions)	663	853	1,655

Ukraine

Europe & Central Asia		Lower middle income
Population (millions)	45.6	Population growth (%)	-0.2
Surface area (1,000 sq. km)	604	Population living below $1.25 a day (%)	<2
GNI, Atlas ($ billions)	159.6	GNI per capita, Atlas ($)	3,500
GNI, PPP ($ billions)	327.1	GNI per capita, PPP ($)	7,180

	1990	2000	2012
People			
Share of poorest 20% in nat'l consumption/income (%)	9.5	8.8	9.9
Life expectancy at birth (years)	70	68	71
Total fertility rate (births per woman)	1.8	1.1	1.5
Adolescent fertility rate (births per 1,000 women 15-19)	61	35	26
Contraceptive prevalence (% of married women 15-49)	..	72	67
Births attended by skilled health staff (% of total)	100	100	100
Under-five mortality rate (per 1,000 live births)	20	19	11
Child malnutrition, underweight (% of under age 5)	..	4.1	..
Child immunization, measles (% of ages 12-23 mos.)	90	99	79
Primary completion rate, total (% of relevant age group)	100	91	103
Gross secondary enrollment, total (% of relevant age group)	94	99	98
Ratio of girls to boys in primary & secondary school (%)	104	101	99
HIV prevalence rate (% population of ages 15-49)	0.1	0.8	0.9
Environment			
Forests (1,000 sq. km)	93	95	97
Deforestation (avg. annual %, 1990-2000 and 2000-2010)		-0.3	-0.2
Freshwater use (% of internal resources)	49.0	72.5	72.5
Access to improved water source (% total pop.)	..	97	98
Access to improved sanitation facilities (% total pop.)	..	95	94
Energy use per capita (kilograms of oil equivalent)	4,856	2,721	2,766
Carbon dioxide emissions per capita (metric tons)	12.3	6.5	6.6
Electricity use per capita (kilowatt-hours)	4,787	2,778	3,662
Economy			
GDP ($ billions)	81.5	31.3	176.3
GDP growth (annual %)	-6.3	5.9	0.2
GDP implicit price deflator (annual % growth)	16.3	23.1	8.0
Value added in agriculture (% of GDP)	26	17	9
Value added in industry (% of GDP)	45	36	30
Value added in services (% of GDP)	30	47	61
Exports of goods and services (% of GDP)	28	62	51
Imports of goods and services (% of GDP)	29	57	59
Gross capital formation (% of GDP)	27	20	18
Central government revenue (% of GDP)	..	26.8	36.3
Central government cash surplus/deficit (% of GDP)	..	-0.6	-2.3
States and markets			
Starting a business (days)	..	40	21
Stock market capitalization (% of GDP)	..	6.0	11.7
Military expenditures (% of GDP)	0.5	3.6	2.8
Mobile cellular subscriptions (per 100 people)	0.0	1.7	130.3
Individuals using the Internet (% of population)	0.0	0.7	33.7
Paved roads (% of total)	93.7	97.0	97.9
High-technology exports (% of manufactured exports)	..	5	6
Global links			
Merchandise trade (% of GDP)	..	91	87
Net barter terms of trade index (2000 = 100)	..	100	118
Total external debt stocks ($ billions)	1	14	135
Total debt service (% of exports)	..	18.4	31.5
Net migration (thousands)	74	-165	-40
Personal remittances received ($ millions)	..	33	8,449
Foreign direct investment, net inflows ($ millions)	200	595	7,833
Net official development assistance received ($ millions)	..	..	769

United Arab Emirates

High income

Population (millions)	9.2	Population growth (%)	3.1
Surface area (1,000 sq. km)	84	Population living below $1.25 a day (%)	..
GNI, Atlas ($ billions)	355.5	GNI per capita, Atlas ($)	38,620
GNI, PPP ($ billions)	381.4	GNI per capita, PPP ($)	41,430

	1990	2000	2012
People			
Share of poorest 20% in nat'l consumption/income (%)	..	..	..
Life expectancy at birth (years)	72	74	77
Total fertility rate (births per woman)	4.4	2.6	1.8
Adolescent fertility rate (births per 1,000 women 15-19)	55	26	28
Contraceptive prevalence (% of married women 15-49)	..	..	..
Births attended by skilled health staff (% of total)	..	100	100
Under-five mortality rate (per 1,000 live births)	17	11	8
Child malnutrition, underweight (% of under age 5)	..	..	..
Child immunization, measles (% of ages 12-23 mos.)	80	94	94
Primary completion rate, total (% of relevant age group)	92	89	111
Gross secondary enrollment, total (% of relevant age group)	62	84	..
Ratio of girls to boys in primary & secondary school (%)	106	103	..
HIV prevalence rate (% population of ages 15-49)	..	..	..
Environment			
Forests (1,000 sq. km)	2.5	3.1	3.2
Deforestation (avg. annual %, 1990-2000 and 2000-2010)		-2.4	-0.2
Freshwater use (% of internal resources)	..	1,936.0	2,665.3
Access to improved water source (% total pop.)	100	100	100
Access to improved sanitation facilities (% total pop.)	97	97	98
Energy use per capita (kilograms of oil equivalent)	11,306	11,216	7,407
Carbon dioxide emissions per capita (metric tons)	28.8	37.2	19.9
Electricity use per capita (kilowatt-hours)	8,604	12,752	9,389
Economy			
GDP ($ billions)	51	104	384
GDP growth (annual %)	18.3	10.9	4.4
GDP implicit price deflator (annual % growth)	3.3	11.5	5.5
Value added in agriculture (% of GDP)	1	2	1
Value added in industry (% of GDP)	59	49	60
Value added in services (% of GDP)	40	49	39
Exports of goods and services (% of GDP)	..	49	95
Imports of goods and services (% of GDP)	..	41	74
Gross capital formation (% of GDP)	..	22	23
Central government revenue (% of GDP)	..	..	3.4
Central government cash surplus/deficit (% of GDP)	..	..	0.1
States and markets			
Starting a business (days)	..	19	8
Stock market capitalization (% of GDP)	..	5.5	17.7
Military expenditures (% of GDP)	..	5.6	5.5
Mobile cellular subscriptions (per 100 people)	1.9	47.2	149.6
Individuals using the Internet (% of population)	0.0	23.6	85.0
Paved roads (% of total)	94.2	100.0	..
High-technology exports (% of manufactured exports)	0	1	..
Global links			
Merchandise trade (% of GDP)	69	81	135
Net barter terms of trade index (2000 = 100)	..	100	186
Total external debt stocks ($ millions)	..	..	..
Total debt service (% of exports)	..	..	..
Net migration (thousands)	328	864	514
Personal remittances received ($ millions)	..	..	..
Foreign direct investment, net inflows ($ billions)	-0.1	-0.5	9.6
Net official development assistance received ($ millions)	3.5	..	..

United Kingdom

Population (millions)	63.6	Population growth (%)	0.6
Surface area (1,000 sq. km)	244	Population living below $1.25 a day (%)	..
GNI, Atlas ($ billions)	2,448.8	GNI per capita, Atlas ($)	38,500
GNI, PPP ($ billions)	2,266.0	GNI per capita, PPP ($)	35,620

	1990	2000	2012
People			
Share of poorest 20% in nat'l consumption/income (%)	..	6.1	..
Life expectancy at birth (years)	76	78	82
Total fertility rate (births per woman)	1.8	1.6	1.9
Adolescent fertility rate (births per 1,000 women 15-19)	31	29	26
Contraceptive prevalence (% of married women 15-49)	70	76	84
Births attended by skilled health staff (% of total)	..	99	..
Under-five mortality rate (per 1,000 live births)	9	7	5
Child malnutrition, underweight (% of under age 5)	..	..	..
Child immunization, measles (% of ages 12-23 mos.)	87	88	93
Primary completion rate, total (% of relevant age group)	..	..	..
Gross secondary enrollment, total (% of relevant age group)	84	102	97
Ratio of girls to boys in primary & secondary school (%)	102	101	100
HIV prevalence rate (% population of ages 15-49)	..	..	..
Environment			
Forests (1,000 sq. km)	26	28	29
Deforestation (avg. annual %, 1990-2000 and 2000-2010)		-0.7	-0.3
Freshwater use (% of internal resources)	8.3	10.8	9.0
Access to improved water source (% total pop.)	100	100	100
Access to improved sanitation facilities (% total pop.)	100	100	100
Energy use per capita (kilograms of oil equivalent)	3,597	3,786	3,024
Carbon dioxide emissions per capita (metric tons)	10.0	9.2	7.9
Electricity use per capita (kilowatt-hours)	5,357	6,115	5,472
Economy			
GDP ($ billions)	1,019	1,494	2,476
GDP growth (annual %)	0.8	4.4	0.3
GDP implicit price deflator (annual % growth)	8.4	0.8	1.7
Value added in agriculture (% of GDP)	2	1	1
Value added in industry (% of GDP)	32	27	21
Value added in services (% of GDP)	67	72	79
Exports of goods and services (% of GDP)	24	27	32
Imports of goods and services (% of GDP)	26	29	34
Gross capital formation (% of GDP)	20	18	15
Central government revenue (% of GDP)	..	36.6	36.3
Central government cash surplus/deficit (% of GDP)	..	3.9	-7.6
States and markets			
Starting a business (days)	..	13	12
Stock market capitalization (% of GDP)	83.3	172.5	122.0
Military expenditures (% of GDP)	3.8	2.4	2.4
Mobile cellular subscriptions (per 100 people)	1.9	73.7	135.3
Individuals using the Internet (% of population)	0.1	26.8	87.0
Paved roads (% of total)	100.0	100.0	100.0
High-technology exports (% of manufactured exports)	24	32	22
Global links			
Merchandise trade (% of GDP)	40	42	46
Net barter terms of trade index (2000 = 100)	..	100	99
Total external debt stocks ($ millions)	..	..	..
Total debt service (% of exports)	..	..	..
Net migration (thousands)	205	968	900
Personal remittances received ($ billions)	2.1	3.6	1.8
Foreign direct investment, net inflows ($ billions)	34	122	56
Net official development assistance received ($ millions)	..	..	..

United States

High income

Population (millions)	313.9	Population growth (%)		0.7
Surface area (1,000 sq. km)	9,832	Population living below $1.25 a day (%)		..
GNI, Atlas ($ billions)	16,430.4	GNI per capita, Atlas ($)		52,340
GNI, PPP ($ billions)	16,514.5	GNI per capita, PPP ($)		52,610

	1990	2000	2012
People			
Share of poorest 20% in nat'l consumption/income (%)	..	5.4	..
Life expectancy at birth (years)	75	77	79
Total fertility rate (births per woman)	2.1	2.1	1.9
Adolescent fertility rate (births per 1,000 women 15-19)	57	46	31
Contraceptive prevalence (% of married women 15-49)	71	73	79
Births attended by skilled health staff (% of total)	99	99	..
Under-five mortality rate (per 1,000 live births)	11	8	7
Child malnutrition, underweight (% of under age 5)	0.9	1.1	..
Child immunization, measles (% of ages 12-23 mos.)	90	91	92
Primary completion rate, total (% of relevant age group)	..	99	98
Gross secondary enrollment, total (% of relevant age group)	91	92	94
Ratio of girls to boys in primary & secondary school (%)	100	100	99
HIV prevalence rate (% population of ages 15-49)	..	..	..
Environment			
Forests (1,000 sq. km)	2,963	3,002	3,044
Deforestation (avg. annual %, 1990-2000 and 2000-2010)		-0.1	-0.1
Freshwater use (% of internal resources)	16.4	16.8	17.0
Access to improved water source (% total pop.)	98	99	99
Access to improved sanitation facilities (% total pop.)	100	100	100
Energy use per capita (kilograms of oil equivalent)	7,672	8,057	6,793
Carbon dioxide emissions per capita (metric tons)	19.1	20.2	17.6
Electricity use per capita (kilowatt-hours)	11,713	13,671	13,246
Economy			
GDP ($ billions)	5,980	10,290	16,245
GDP growth (annual %)	1.9	4.1	2.8
GDP implicit price deflator (annual % growth)	3.7	2.3	1.7
Value added in agriculture (% of GDP)	2	1	1
Value added in industry (% of GDP)	28	23	20
Value added in services (% of GDP)	70	75	79
Exports of goods and services (% of GDP)	9	11	14
Imports of goods and services (% of GDP)	11	14	17
Gross capital formation (% of GDP)	21	24	19
Central government revenue (% of GDP)	..	17.3	16.5
Central government cash surplus/deficit (% of GDP)	..	-2.9	-7.5
States and markets			
Starting a business (days)	..	6	5
Stock market capitalization (% of GDP)	51.2	146.8	114.9
Military expenditures (% of GDP)	5.1	2.9	4.2
Mobile cellular subscriptions (per 100 people)	2.1	38.5	95.4
Individuals using the Internet (% of population)	0.8	43.1	81.0
Paved roads (% of total)	..	63.0	67.4
High-technology exports (% of manufactured exports)	33	34	18
Global links			
Merchandise trade (% of GDP)	15	20	24
Net barter terms of trade index (2000 = 100)	103	100	95
Total external debt stocks ($ millions)	..	..	..
Total debt service (% of exports)	..	..	..
Net migration (thousands)	4,455	5,322	5,000
Personal remittances received ($ billions)	1.2	4.4	6.3
Foreign direct investment, net inflows ($ billions)	48	321	204
Net official development assistance received ($ millions)	..	..	..

Uruguay

Population (millions)	3.4	Population growth (%)		0.3
Surface area (1,000 sq. km)	176	Population living below $1.25 a day (%)		<2
GNI, Atlas ($ billions)	46.1	GNI per capita, Atlas ($)		13,580
GNI, PPP ($ billions)	52.0	GNI per capita, PPP ($)		15,310

	1990	2000	2012
People			
Share of poorest 20% in nat'l consumption/income (%)	5.3	4.7	4.9
Life expectancy at birth (years)	73	75	77
Total fertility rate (births per woman)	2.5	2.2	2.1
Adolescent fertility rate (births per 1,000 women 15–19)	69	65	58
Contraceptive prevalence (% of married women 15–49)	..	77	..
Births attended by skilled health staff (% of total)	..	100	100
Under-five mortality rate (per 1,000 live births)	23	16	7
Child malnutrition, underweight (% of under age 5)	..	5.2	4.5
Child immunization, measles (% of ages 12-23 mos.)	97	89	96
Primary completion rate, total (% of relevant age group)	95	97	104
Gross secondary enrollment, total (% of relevant age group)	81	98	90
Ratio of girls to boys in primary & secondary school (%)	..	105	104
HIV prevalence rate (% population of ages 15–49)	0.1	0.4	0.7
Environment			
Forests (1,000 sq. km)	9	14	18
Deforestation (avg. annual %, 1990-2000 and 2000-2010)		-4.4	-2.1
Freshwater use (% of internal resources)	..	6.2	6.2
Access to improved water source (% total pop.)	95	97	99
Access to improved sanitation facilities (% total pop.)	92	94	96
Energy use per capita (kilograms of oil equivalent)	724	931	1,309
Carbon dioxide emissions per capita (metric tons)	1.3	1.6	2.0
Electricity use per capita (kilowatt-hours)	1,244	2,031	2,810
Economy			
GDP ($ billions)	9.3	22.8	49.9
GDP growth (annual %)	0.3	-1.9	3.9
GDP implicit price deflator (annual % growth)	106.8	3.5	8.8
Value added in agriculture (% of GDP)	9	7	8
Value added in industry (% of GDP)	35	25	25
Value added in services (% of GDP)	56	69	67
Exports of goods and services (% of GDP)	24	17	26
Imports of goods and services (% of GDP)	18	20	30
Gross capital formation (% of GDP)	12	14	21
Central government revenue (% of GDP)	23.8	24.7	30.8
Central government cash surplus/deficit (% of GDP)	0.5	-3.0	-2.1
States and markets			
Starting a business (days)	..	45	7
Stock market capitalization (% of GDP)	1.7	0.7	0.4
Military expenditures (% of GDP)	3.5	2.5	1.9
Mobile cellular subscriptions (per 100 people)	0.0	12.4	147.1
Individuals using the Internet (% of population)	0.0	10.5	55.1
Paved roads (% of total)	..	10.0	..
High-technology exports (% of manufactured exports)	3	2	9
Global links			
Merchandise trade (% of GDP)	33	25	41
Net barter terms of trade index (2000 = 100)	116	100	104
Total external debt stocks ($ millions)	..	..	..
Total debt service (% of exports)	..	..	..
Net migration (thousands)	-20	-104	-30
Personal remittances received ($ millions)	..	0.0	96.6
Foreign direct investment, net inflows ($ millions)	42	269	2,907
Net official development assistance received ($ millions)	52.4	17.4	19.3

Uzbekistan

Population (millions)	29.8	Population growth (%)		1.5
Surface area (1,000 sq. km)	447	Population living below $1.25 a day (%)		..
GNI, Atlas ($ billions)	51.2	GNI per capita, Atlas ($)		1,720
GNI, PPP ($ billions)	109.1	GNI per capita, PPP ($)		3,670

	1990	2000	2012
People			
Share of poorest 20% in nat'l consumption/income (%)	10.6	7.8	..
Life expectancy at birth (years)	67	67	68
Total fertility rate (births per woman)	4.1	2.6	2.5
Adolescent fertility rate (births per 1,000 women 15–19)	56	50	39
Contraceptive prevalence (% of married women 15–49)	..	67	65
Births attended by skilled health staff (% of total)	..	96	100
Under-five mortality rate (per 1,000 live births)	74	61	40
Child malnutrition, underweight (% of under age 5)	..	7.1	4.4
Child immunization, measles (% of ages 12–23 mos.)	84	99	99
Primary completion rate, total (% of relevant age group)	..	95	92
Gross secondary enrollment, total (% of relevant age group)	99	88	105
Ratio of girls to boys in primary & secondary school (%)	..	98	98
HIV prevalence rate (% population of ages 15–49)	0.1	0.2	0.1
Environment			
Forests (1,000 sq. km)	30	32	33
Deforestation (avg. annual %, 1990-2000 and 2000-2010)		-0.5	-0.2
Freshwater use (% of internal resources)	..	370.7	342.7
Access to improved water source (% total pop.)	90	89	87
Access to improved sanitation facilities (% total pop.)	84	91	100
Energy use per capita (kilograms of oil equivalent)	2,261	2,059	1,628
Carbon dioxide emissions per capita (metric tons)	5.3	4.9	3.7
Electricity use per capita (kilowatt-hours)	2,383	1,780	1,626
Economy			
GDP ($ billions)	13.4	13.8	51.1
GDP growth (annual %)	1.6	3.8	8.2
GDP implicit price deflator (annual % growth)	4.0	47.3	14.8
Value added in agriculture (% of GDP)	33	34	19
Value added in industry (% of GDP)	33	23	32
Value added in services (% of GDP)	34	43	49
Exports of goods and services (% of GDP)	29	25	28
Imports of goods and services (% of GDP)	48	22	30
Gross capital formation (% of GDP)	32	23	23
Central government revenue (% of GDP)	..	..	..
Central government cash surplus/deficit (% of GDP)	..	..	..
States and markets			
Starting a business (days)	..	29	9
Stock market capitalization (% of GDP)	..	0.2	..
Military expenditures (% of GDP)	..	1.2	..
Mobile cellular subscriptions (per 100 people)	0.0	0.2	71.0
Individuals using the Internet (% of population)	0.0	0.5	36.5
Paved roads (% of total)	79.0	87.0	..
High-technology exports (% of manufactured exports)	..	..	..
Global links			
Merchandise trade (% of GDP)	..	40	43
Net barter terms of trade index (2000 = 100)	..	100	172
Total external debt stocks ($ billions)	0.1	5.0	8.9
Total debt service (% of exports)	..	..	..
Net migration (thousands)	-275	-780	-200
Personal remittances received ($ millions)	..	..	..
Foreign direct investment, net inflows ($ millions)	9	75	1,094
Net official development assistance received ($ millions)	2	186	255

Vanuatu

East Asia & Pacific		Lower middle income	
Population (thousands)	247	Population growth (%)	2.2
Surface area (1,000 sq. km)	12	Population living below $1.25 a day (%)	..
GNI, Atlas ($ millions)	741.4	GNI per capita, Atlas ($)	3,000
GNI, PPP ($ millions)	1,062.9	GNI per capita, PPP ($)	4,300

	1990	2000	2012
People			
Share of poorest 20% in nat'l consumption/income (%)	..	..	..
Life expectancy at birth (years)	63	68	71
Total fertility rate (births per woman)	4.9	4.4	3.4
Adolescent fertility rate (births per 1,000 women 15-19)	73	58	45
Contraceptive prevalence (% of married women 15-49)	15	28	38
Births attended by skilled health staff (% of total)	..	88	74
Under-five mortality rate (per 1,000 live births)	35	24	18
Child malnutrition, underweight (% of under age 5)	..	..	11.7
Child immunization, measles (% of ages 12-23 mos.)	66	61	52
Primary completion rate, total (% of relevant age group)	84	92	84
Gross secondary enrollment, total (% of relevant age group)	18	35	60
Ratio of girls to boys in primary & secondary school (%)	93	101	98
HIV prevalence rate (% population of ages 15-49)	..	..	..
Environment			
Forests (1,000 sq. km)	4.4	4.4	4.4
Deforestation (avg. annual %, 1990-2000 and 2000-2010)		0.0	0.0
Freshwater use (% of internal resources)	..	..	..
Access to improved water source (% total pop.)	62	76	91
Access to improved sanitation facilities (% total pop.)	..	42	58
Energy use per capita (kilograms of oil equivalent)	159	..	..
Carbon dioxide emissions per capita (metric tons)	0.5	0.4	0.5
Electricity use per capita (kilowatt-hours)	..	..	..
Economy			
GDP ($ millions)	158	272	787
GDP growth (annual %)	11.7	5.9	2.3
GDP implicit price deflator (annual % growth)	-1.0	2.2	1.4
Value added in agriculture (% of GDP)	..	26	25
Value added in industry (% of GDP)	..	13	11
Value added in services (% of GDP)	..	61	64
Exports of goods and services (% of GDP)	47	39	48
Imports of goods and services (% of GDP)	73	48	51
Gross capital formation (% of GDP)	33	20	27
Central government revenue (% of GDP)	26.1	19.4	18.7
Central government cash surplus/deficit (% of GDP)	5.1	-0.1	-2.3
States and markets			
Starting a business (days)	..	39	35
Stock market capitalization (% of GDP)	..	..	..
Military expenditures (% of GDP)	..	..	..
Mobile cellular subscriptions (per 100 people)	0.0	0.2	59.1
Individuals using the Internet (% of population)	0.0	2.1	10.6
Paved roads (% of total)	21.6	24.0	..
High-technology exports (% of manufactured exports)	20	0	54
Global links			
Merchandise trade (% of GDP)	73	42	44
Net barter terms of trade index (2000 = 100)	..	100	88
Total external debt stocks ($ millions)	38	96	369
Total debt service (% of exports)	2.3	1.6	2.1
Net migration (thousands)	-0.3	-0.5	0.0
Personal remittances received ($ millions)	8.2	34.7	22.0
Foreign direct investment, net inflows ($ millions)	13.1	20.3	37.7
Net official development assistance received ($ millions)	50	46	101

Venezuela, RB

Latin America & Caribbean		Upper middle income	
Population (millions)	30.0	Population growth (%)	1.5
Surface area (1,000 sq. km)	912	Population living below $1.25 a day (%)	6.6
GNI, Atlas ($ billions)	373.3	GNI per capita, Atlas ($)	12,460
GNI, PPP ($ billions)	386.9	GNI per capita, PPP ($)	12,920

	1990	2000	2012
People			
Share of poorest 20% in nat'l consumption/income (%)	4.5	4.0	4.3
Life expectancy at birth (years)	71	72	74
Total fertility rate (births per woman)	3.4	2.8	2.4
Adolescent fertility rate (births per 1,000 women 15-19)	100	93	83
Contraceptive prevalence (% of married women 15-49)	58	70	..
Births attended by skilled health staff (% of total)	..	94	..
Under-five mortality rate (per 1,000 live births)	30	21	15
Child malnutrition, underweight (% of under age 5)	6.7	3.9	2.9
Child immunization, measles (% of ages 12-23 mos.)	61	84	87
Primary completion rate, total (% of relevant age group)	78	83	96
Gross secondary enrollment, total (% of relevant age group)	56	60	85
Ratio of girls to boys in primary & secondary school (%)	105	105	102
HIV prevalence rate (% population of ages 15-49)	0.4	0.6	0.6
Environment			
Forests (1,000 sq. km)	520	492	460
Deforestation (avg. annual %, 1990-2000 and 2000-2010)		0.6	0.6
Freshwater use (% of internal resources)	..	1.3	1.3
Access to improved water source (% total pop.)	90	92	..
Access to improved sanitation facilities (% total pop.)	82	89	..
Energy use per capita (kilograms of oil equivalent)	2,206	2,312	2,380
Carbon dioxide emissions per capita (metric tons)	6.2	6.2	6.9
Electricity use per capita (kilowatt-hours)	2,464	2,644	3,313
Economy			
GDP ($ billions)	47	117	381
GDP growth (annual %)	6.5	3.7	5.6
GDP implicit price deflator (annual % growth)	41.7	29.5	14.1
Value added in agriculture (% of GDP)	5	4	6
Value added in industry (% of GDP)	61	50	52
Value added in services (% of GDP)	34	46	42
Exports of goods and services (% of GDP)	39	30	26
Imports of goods and services (% of GDP)	20	18	24
Gross capital formation (% of GDP)	10	24	27
Central government revenue (% of GDP)	24.5	21.2	..
Central government cash surplus/deficit (% of GDP)	3.0	-1.2	..
States and markets			
Starting a business (days)	..	141	144
Stock market capitalization (% of GDP)	17.8	6.9	6.6
Military expenditures (% of GDP)	1.9	1.5	1.1
Mobile cellular subscriptions (per 100 people)	0.0	22.3	101.9
Individuals using the Internet (% of population)	0.0	3.4	44.0
Paved roads (% of total)	35.6	34.0	..
High-technology exports (% of manufactured exports)	4	3	2
Global links			
Merchandise trade (% of GDP)	53	42	41
Net barter terms of trade index (2000 = 100)	90	100	262
Total external debt stocks ($ billions)	33.2	42.8	72.1
Total debt service (% of exports)	23.3	16.9	5.6
Net migration (thousands)	40.0	40.0	40.0
Personal remittances received ($ millions)	1	17	118
Foreign direct investment, net inflows ($ billions)	0.5	4.7	2.2
Net official development assistance received ($ millions)	76.4	76.1	48.1

Vietnam

East Asia & Pacific		Lower middle income	
Population (millions)	88.8	Population growth (%)	1.1
Surface area (1,000 sq. km)	331	Population living below $1.25 a day (%)	16.9
GNI, Atlas ($ billions)	137.5	GNI per capita, Atlas ($)	1,550
GNI, PPP ($ billions)	321.4	GNI per capita, PPP ($)	3,620

	1990	2000	2012
People			
Share of poorest 20% in nat'l consumption/income (%)	7.8	7.5	7.4
Life expectancy at birth (years)	71	74	76
Total fertility rate (births per woman)	3.6	2.0	1.8
Adolescent fertility rate (births per 1,000 women 15–19)	31	29	29
Contraceptive prevalence (% of married women 15–49)	53	74	78
Births attended by skilled health staff (% of total)	..	70	93
Under-five mortality rate (per 1,000 live births)	51	32	23
Child malnutrition, underweight (% of under age 5)	36.9	26.7	12.0
Child immunization, measles (% of ages 12–23 mos.)	88	97	96
Primary completion rate, total (% of relevant age group)	..	98	101
Gross secondary enrollment, total (% of relevant age group)	34	57	..
Ratio of girls to boys in primary & secondary school (%)	..	93	..
HIV prevalence rate (% population of ages 15–49)	0.1	0.3	0.4
Environment			
Forests (1,000 sq. km)	94	117	139
Deforestation (avg. annual %, 1990–2000 and 2000–2010)		-2.3	-1.6
Freshwater use (% of internal resources)	..	12.6	22.8
Access to improved water source (% total pop.)	61	77	95
Access to improved sanitation facilities (% total pop.)	37	54	75
Energy use per capita (kilograms of oil equivalent)	271	370	697
Carbon dioxide emissions per capita (metric tons)	0.3	0.7	1.7
Electricity use per capita (kilowatt-hours)	98	295	1,073
Economy			
GDP ($ billions)	6.5	33.6	155.8
GDP growth (annual %)	5.1	6.8	5.2
GDP implicit price deflator (annual % growth)	42.1	11.6	10.9
Value added in agriculture (% of GDP)	39	23	20
Value added in industry (% of GDP)	23	34	39
Value added in services (% of GDP)	39	43	42
Exports of goods and services (% of GDP)	36	50	80
Imports of goods and services (% of GDP)	45	53	77
Gross capital formation (% of GDP)	13	27	27
Central government revenue (% of GDP)	..	..	..
Central government cash surplus/deficit (% of GDP)	..	..	..
States and markets			
Starting a business (days)	..	59	34
Stock market capitalization (% of GDP)	..	0.4	21.1
Military expenditures (% of GDP)	7.9	2.0	2.2
Mobile cellular subscriptions (per 100 people)	0.0	1.0	147.7
Individuals using the Internet (% of population)	0.0	0.3	39.5
Paved roads (% of total)	23.5	43.9	47.6
High-technology exports (% of manufactured exports)	..	11	14
Global links			
Merchandise trade (% of GDP)	80	90	147
Net barter terms of trade index (2000 = 100)	..	100	101
Total external debt stocks ($ billions)	23.3	12.9	59.1
Total debt service (% of exports)	..	7.5	4.4
Net migration (thousands)	-394	-772	-200
Personal remittances received ($ billions)	..	1.3	8.6
Foreign direct investment, net inflows ($ billions)	0.2	1.3	8.4
Net official development assistance received ($ billions)	0.2	1.7	4.1

Virgin Islands (U.S.)

High income

Population (thousands)	105	Population growth (%)	-0.5
Surface area (sq. km)	350	Population living below $1.25 a day (%)	..
GNI, Atlas ($ billions)	..	GNI per capita, Atlas ($)	..
GNI, PPP ($ millions)	..	GNI per capita, PPP ($)	..

	1990	2000	2012
People			
Share of poorest 20% in nat'l consumption/income (%)	..	..	..
Life expectancy at birth (years)	75	77	79
Total fertility rate (births per woman)	3.0	2.1	1.8
Adolescent fertility rate (births per 1,000 women 15-19)	79	55	51
Contraceptive prevalence (% of married women 15-49)	..	78	..
Births attended by skilled health staff (% of total)	..	98	..
Under-five mortality rate (per 1,000 live births)	..	..	..
Child malnutrition, underweight (% of under age 5)	..	..	..
Child immunization, measles (% of ages 12-23 mos.)	..	..	..
Primary completion rate, total (% of relevant age group)	..	..	..
Gross secondary enrollment, total (% of relevant age group)	105	..	..
Ratio of girls to boys in primary & secondary school (%)	93	..	..
HIV prevalence rate (% population of ages 15-49)	..	..	..
Environment			
Forests (sq. km)	236	219	201
Deforestation (avg. annual %, 1990-2000 and 2000-2010)		0.7	0.8
Freshwater use (% of internal resources)	..	..	..
Access to improved water source (% total pop.)	100	100	100
Access to improved sanitation facilities (% total pop.)	96	96	96
Energy use per capita (kilograms of oil equivalent)	..	..	..
Carbon dioxide emissions per capita (metric tons)	..	..	..
Electricity use per capita (kilowatt-hours)	..	..	..
Economy			
GDP ($ millions)	1,565	..	..
GDP growth (annual %)	7.1	..	..
GDP implicit price deflator (annual % growth)	4.1	..	..
Value added in agriculture (% of GDP)	..	..	..
Value added in industry (% of GDP)	..	..	..
Value added in services (% of GDP)	..	..	..
Exports of goods and services (% of GDP)	..	..	..
Imports of goods and services (% of GDP)	..	..	..
Gross capital formation (% of GDP)	..	..	..
Central government revenue (% of GDP)	..	..	..
Central government cash surplus/deficit (% of GDP)	..	..	..
States and markets			
Starting a business (days)	..	..	..
Stock market capitalization (% of GDP)	..	..	..
Military expenditures (% of GDP)	..	..	..
Mobile cellular subscriptions (per 100 people)	0.0	32.3	..
Individuals using the Internet (% of population)	0.0	13.8	40.5
Paved roads (% of total)	..	..	..
High-technology exports (% of manufactured exports)	..	..	..
Global links			
Merchandise trade (% of GDP)	..	..	..
Net barter terms of trade index (2000 = 100)	..	..	..
Total external debt stocks ($ millions)	..	..	..
Total debt service (% of exports)	..	..	..
Net migration (thousands)	-4.6	-5.3	-3.6
Personal remittances received ($ millions)	..	..	..
Foreign direct investment, net inflows ($ millions)	..	..	..
Net official development assistance received ($ millions)	..	..	..

West Bank and Gaza

Middle East & North Africa		Lower middle income	
Population (millions)	4.0	Population growth (%)	3.0
Surface area (1,000 sq. km)	6.0	Population living below $1.25 a day (%)	<2
GNI, Atlas ($ billions)	..	GNI per capita, Atlas ($)	..
GNI, PPP ($ billions)	..	GNI per capita, PPP ($)	..

	1990	2000	2012
People			
Share of poorest 20% in nat'l consumption/income (%)	..	..	7.4
Life expectancy at birth (years)	68	71	73
Total fertility rate (births per woman)	6.5	5.4	4.1
Adolescent fertility rate (births per 1,000 women 15-19)	104	82	46
Contraceptive prevalence (% of married women 15-49)	..	51	53
Births attended by skilled health staff (% of total)	..	97	99
Under-five mortality rate (per 1,000 live births)	43	30	23
Child malnutrition, underweight (% of under age 5)	..	..	2.2
Child immunization, measles (% of ages 12-23 mos.)	..	..	..
Primary completion rate, total (% of relevant age group)	..	98	90
Gross secondary enrollment, total (% of relevant age group)	..	81	83
Ratio of girls to boys in primary & secondary school (%)	..	102	105
HIV prevalence rate (% population of ages 15-49)	..	..	..
Environment			
Forests (sq. km)	91	91	92
Deforestation (avg. annual %, 1990-2000 and 2000-2010)		0.0	-0.1
Freshwater use (% of internal resources)	..	34.4	51.5
Access to improved water source (% total pop.)	..	92	82
Access to improved sanitation facilities (% total pop.)	..	90	94
Energy use per capita (kilograms of oil equivalent)	..	..	..
Carbon dioxide emissions per capita (metric tons)	..	0.3	0.6
Electricity use per capita (kilowatt-hours)	..	..	..
Economy			
GDP ($ billions)	..	4.1	..
GDP growth (annual %)	..	-5.6	..
GDP implicit price deflator (annual % growth)	..	2.9	..
Value added in agriculture (% of GDP)	..	..	..
Value added in industry (% of GDP)	..	..	..
Value added in services (% of GDP)	..	..	..
Exports of goods and services (% of GDP)	..	16	..
Imports of goods and services (% of GDP)	..	71	..
Gross capital formation (% of GDP)	..	33	..
Central government revenue (% of GDP)	..	..	..
Central government cash surplus/deficit (% of GDP)	..	..	..
States and markets			
Starting a business (days)	..	..	45
Stock market capitalization (% of GDP)	..	18.6	..
Military expenditures (% of GDP)	..	..	..
Mobile cellular subscriptions (per 100 people)	0.0	0.2	75.6
Individuals using the Internet (% of population)	0.0	1.1	41.1
Paved roads (% of total)	..	100.0	100.0
High-technology exports (% of manufactured exports)	..	..	..
Global links			
Merchandise trade (% of GDP)	..	..	..
Net barter terms of trade index (2000 = 100)	..	..	..
Total external debt stocks ($ millions)	..	..	..
Total debt service (% of exports)	..	..	..
Net migration (thousands)	35	-190	-44
Personal remittances received ($ billions)	..	1.0	1.7
Foreign direct investment, net inflows ($ millions)	..	62	235
Net official development assistance received ($ millions)	179	685	2,001

Yemen, Rep.

Middle East & North Africa		Lower middle income	
Population (millions)	23.9	Population growth (%)	2.3
Surface area (1,000 sq. km)	528	Population living below $1.25 a day (%)	17.5
GNI, Atlas ($ billions)	30.4	GNI per capita, Atlas ($)	1,270
GNI, PPP ($ billions)	55.1	GNI per capita, PPP ($)	2,310

	1990	2000	2012
People			
Share of poorest 20% in nat'l consumption/income (%)	..	7.4	..
Life expectancy at birth (years)	58	60	63
Total fertility rate (births per woman)	8.7	6.4	4.2
Adolescent fertility rate (births per 1,000 women 15-19)	150	96	47
Contraceptive prevalence (% of married women 15-49)	10	23	28
Births attended by skilled health staff (% of total)	16	27	36
Under-five mortality rate (per 1,000 live births)	125	97	60
Child malnutrition, underweight (% of under age 5)	29.6	43.1	..
Child immunization, measles (% of ages 12-23 mos.)	69	71	71
Primary completion rate, total (% of relevant age group)	..	59	70
Gross secondary enrollment, total (% of relevant age group)	..	46	47
Ratio of girls to boys in primary & secondary school (%)	..	55	77
HIV prevalence rate (% population of ages 15-49)	0.1	0.1	0.1
Environment			
Forests (1,000 sq. km)	5.5	5.5	5.5
Deforestation (avg. annual %, 1990-2000 and 2000-2010)		0.0	0.0
Freshwater use (% of internal resources)	139.6	161.9	169.8
Access to improved water source (% total pop.)	66	60	55
Access to improved sanitation facilities (% total pop.)	24	39	53
Energy use per capita (kilograms of oil equivalent)	213	271	312
Carbon dioxide emissions per capita (metric tons)	0.8	0.8	1.0
Electricity use per capita (kilowatt-hours)	125	141	193
Economy			
GDP ($ billions)	5.6	9.6	35.6
GDP growth (annual %)	6.3	6.2	0.1
GDP implicit price deflator (annual % growth)	12.0	23.3	6.0
Value added in agriculture (% of GDP)	24	14	8
Value added in industry (% of GDP)	34	46	29
Value added in services (% of GDP)	41	40	63
Exports of goods and services (% of GDP)	12	41	30
Imports of goods and services (% of GDP)	17	34	35
Gross capital formation (% of GDP)	12	19	12
Central government revenue (% of GDP)	16.2	23.4	..
Central government cash surplus/deficit (% of GDP)	-6.7	-2.3	..
States and markets			
Starting a business (days)	..	72	40
Stock market capitalization (% of GDP)	..	..	..
Military expenditures (% of GDP)	6.6	4.9	4.0
Mobile cellular subscriptions (per 100 people)	0.0	0.2	58.3
Individuals using the Internet (% of population)	0.0	0.1	17.4
Paved roads (% of total)	9.1	16.0	..
High-technology exports (% of manufactured exports)	..	0	0
Global links			
Merchandise trade (% of GDP)	40	66	58
Net barter terms of trade index (2000 = 100)	..	100	168
Total external debt stocks ($ billions)	6.4	5.2	7.6
Total debt service (% of exports)	11.1	5.9	2.8
Net migration (thousands)	673	-100	-135
Personal remittances received ($ billions)	1.5	1.3	1.4
Foreign direct investment, net inflows ($ millions)	-131	6	349
Net official development assistance received ($ millions)	450	311	709

Zambia

Sub-Saharan Africa		Lower middle income
Population (millions)	14.1	Population growth (%)	3.2
Surface area (1,000 sq. km)	753	Population living below $1.25 a day (%)	74.5
GNI, Atlas ($ billions)	19.0	GNI per capita, Atlas ($)	1,350
GNI, PPP ($ billions)	22.4	GNI per capita, PPP ($)	1,590

	1990	2000	2012
People			
Share of poorest 20% in nat'l consumption/income (%)	3.0	6.2	3.6
Life expectancy at birth (years)	44	42	57
Total fertility rate (births per woman)	6.5	6.1	5.7
Adolescent fertility rate (births per 1,000 women 15–19)	107	151	125
Contraceptive prevalence (% of married women 15–49)	15	22	41
Births attended by skilled health staff (% of total)	51	47	47
Under-five mortality rate (per 1,000 live births)	192	169	89
Child malnutrition, underweight (% of under age 5)	21.2	19.6	14.9
Child immunization, measles (% of ages 12–23 mos.)	90	85	83
Primary completion rate, total (% of relevant age group)	..	63	91
Gross secondary enrollment, total (% of relevant age group)	21	..	101
Ratio of girls to boys in primary & secondary school (%)	87	..	95
HIV prevalence rate (% population of ages 15–49)	10.4	15.3	12.7
Environment			
Forests (1,000 sq. km)	528	511	493
Deforestation (avg. annual %, 1990–2000 and 2000–2010)		0.3	0.3
Freshwater use (% of internal resources)	2.2	2.2	2.2
Access to improved water source (% total pop.)	49	53	63
Access to improved sanitation facilities (% total pop.)	41	41	43
Energy use per capita (kilograms of oil equivalent)	688	618	621
Carbon dioxide emissions per capita (metric tons)	0.3	0.2	0.2
Electricity use per capita (kilowatt-hours)	781	616	599
Economy			
GDP ($ billions)	3.3	3.3	20.6
GDP growth (annual %)	-0.5	3.5	7.2
GDP implicit price deflator (annual % growth)	106.4	30.8	5.9
Value added in agriculture (% of GDP)	21	22	20
Value added in industry (% of GDP)	51	25	38
Value added in services (% of GDP)	28	53	42
Exports of goods and services (% of GDP)	36	26	46
Imports of goods and services (% of GDP)	37	40	43
Gross capital formation (% of GDP)	17	17	25
Central government revenue (% of GDP)	20.4	19.6	21.4
Central government cash surplus/deficit (% of GDP)	..	1.8	5.0
States and markets			
Starting a business (days)	..	35	7
Stock market capitalization (% of GDP)	..	7.2	14.6
Military expenditures (% of GDP)	3,705.7	1,792.0	1,555.9
Mobile cellular subscriptions (per 100 people)	0.0	1.0	74.8
Individuals using the Internet (% of population)	0.0	0.2	13.5
Paved roads (% of total)	16.6	22.0	..
High-technology exports (% of manufactured exports)	2	0	25
Global links			
Merchandise trade (% of GDP)	77	55	80
Net barter terms of trade index (2000 = 100)	207	100	184
Total external debt stocks ($ billions)	6.9	5.8	5.4
Total debt service (% of exports)	14.7	21.2	2.2
Net migration (thousands)	-11.2	-81.7	-40.0
Personal remittances received ($ millions)	..	36.3	72.9
Foreign direct investment, net inflows ($ millions)	203	122	1,066
Net official development assistance received ($ millions)	475	795	958

Zimbabwe

Sub-Saharan Africa		**Low income**
Population (millions)	13.7	Population growth (%)	2.7
Surface area (1,000 sq. km)	391	Population living below $1.25 a day (%)	..
GNI, Atlas ($ billions)	8.9	GNI per capita, Atlas ($)	650
GNI, PPP ($ millions)	..	GNI per capita, PPP ($)	..

	1990	2000	2012
People			
Share of poorest 20% in nat'l consumption/income (%)	..	..	..
Life expectancy at birth (years)	59	44	58
Total fertility rate (births per woman)	5.2	4.1	3.6
Adolescent fertility rate (births per 1,000 women 15-19)	110	92	60
Contraceptive prevalence (% of married women 15-49)	43	54	59
Births attended by skilled health staff (% of total)	70	73	66
Under-five mortality rate (per 1,000 live births)	74	102	90
Child malnutrition, underweight (% of under age 5)	8.0	11.5	10.1
Child immunization, measles (% of ages 12-23 mos.)	87	75	90
Primary completion rate, total (% of relevant age group)	..	91	..
Gross secondary enrollment, total (% of relevant age group)	45	43	..
Ratio of girls to boys in primary & secondary school (%)	96	95	..
HIV prevalence rate (% population of ages 15-49)	10.7	25.7	14.7
Environment			
Forests (1,000 sq. km)	222	189	153
Deforestation (avg. annual %, 1990-2000 and 2000-2010)		1.6	1.9
Freshwater use (% of internal resources)	..	34.3	34.3
Access to improved water source (% total pop.)	79	80	80
Access to improved sanitation facilities (% total pop.)	41	40	40
Energy use per capita (kilograms of oil equivalent)	889	789	697
Carbon dioxide emissions per capita (metric tons)	1.5	1.1	0.7
Electricity use per capita (kilowatt-hours)	863	853	757
Economy			
GDP ($ billions)	8.8	6.7	9.8
GDP growth (annual %)	7.0	-3.1	4.4
GDP implicit price deflator (annual % growth)	-0.9	0.6	5.9
Value added in agriculture (% of GDP)	16	18	14
Value added in industry (% of GDP)	33	24	35
Value added in services (% of GDP)	50	57	51
Exports of goods and services (% of GDP)	23	38	44
Imports of goods and services (% of GDP)	23	36	76
Gross capital formation (% of GDP)	17	14	25
Central government revenue (% of GDP)	24.1	..	..
Central government cash surplus/deficit (% of GDP)	-2.6	..	..
States and markets			
Starting a business (days)	..	97	90
Stock market capitalization (% of GDP)	27.3	36.4	120.5
Military expenditures (% of GDP)	4.6	5.2	3.2
Mobile cellular subscriptions (per 100 people)	0.0	2.1	91.9
Individuals using the Internet (% of population)	0.0	0.4	17.1
Paved roads (% of total)	14.0	19.0	..
High-technology exports (% of manufactured exports)	1	2	6
Global links			
Merchandise trade (% of GDP)	41	57	84
Net barter terms of trade index (2000 = 100)	98	100	105
Total external debt stocks ($ billions)	3.3	3.8	7.7
Total debt service (% of exports)	23.1	..	..
Net migration (thousands)	-192	-700	400
Personal remittances received ($ millions)	0.8	..	..
Foreign direct investment, net inflows ($ millions)	-12	23	400
Net official development assistance received ($ millions)	334	176	1,001

Notes

a. Data series will be calculated upon finalization of the ongoing revisions to official statistics reported by the National Statistics and Censuses Institute of Argentina.

b. Data for Argentina are officially reported by the National Statistics and Censuses Institute of Argentina. The IMF has, however, issued a declaration of censure and called on Argentina to adopt remedial measures to address the quality of the official GDP and CPI data. Alternative data sources have shown significantly lower real growth and higher inflation than the official data since 2008. In this context, the World Bank is also using alternative data sources and estimates for the surveillance of macroeconomic developments in Argentina.

c. Includes Taiwan, China.

d. Estimates differ from statistics of the government of China, which has published the following estimates for military expenditure: 1.2 percent of GDP in 2000 and 1.3 percent in 2012 (see National Bureau of Statistics of China, www.stats.gov.cn).

e. Refers to area free from ice.

f. Includes Montenegro.

g. Excludes South Sudan.

h. Excludes South Sudan after July 9, 2011.

Glossary

Access to improved sanitation facilities refers to the percentage of the population using improved sanitation facilities. The improved sanitation facilities include flush/pour flush (to piped sewer system, septic tank, pit latrine), ventilated improved pit (VIP) latrine, pit latrine with slab, and composting toilet. (World Health Organization and United Nations Children's Fund)

Access to improved water source refers to the percentage of the population using an improved drinking water source. The improved drinking water source includes piped water on premises (piped household water connection located inside the user's dwelling, plot or yard), and other improved drinking water sources (public taps or standpipes, tube wells or boreholes, protected dug wells, protected springs, and rainwater collection). (World Health Organization and United Nations Children's Fund)

Adolescent fertility rate is the number of births per 1,000 women ages 15–19. (United Nations Population Division)

Births attended by skilled health staff are the percentage of deliveries attended by personnel trained to give the necessary supervision, care, and advice to women during pregnancy, labor, and the postpartum period; to conduct deliveries on their own; and to care for newborns. (United Nations Children's Fund, ChildInfo, and ICF International)

Carbon dioxide emissions per capita are emissions stemming from the burning of fossil fuels and the manufacture of cement divided by midyear population. They include carbon dioxide produced during consumption of solid, liquid, and gas fuels and gas flaring. (Carbon Dioxide Information Analysis Center)

Central government cash surplus/deficit is revenue (including grants) minus expense, minus net acquisition of nonfinancial assets. Before 2005 nonfinancial assets were included under revenue and expenditure in gross terms. The concept of cash surplus or deficit is close to the earlier overall budget balance (still missing is lending minus repayments, which is brought into the balance sheet as a financing item under net acquisition of financial assets). (International Monetary Fund)

Central government revenue is cash receipts from taxes, social contributions, and other revenues such as fines, fees, rent, and income from property or sales. Grants are also considered revenue but are excluded here. (International Monetary Fund)

Child immunization, measles, is the percentage of children ages 12–23 months at the time of the survey who received a dose of measles vaccine by age 12 months or at any time before the interview date. A child is considered adequately immunized against measles after receiving one dose of the vaccine. (World Health Organization and United Nations Children's Fund)

Child malnutrition, underweight, is the percentage of children under age 5 whose weight for age is more than two standard deviations below median for the international reference population ages 0–59 months. The data conform to the new Child Growth Standards released by the World Health Organization in 2006. (World Health Organization)

Glossary

Contraceptive prevalence is the percentage of women married or in-union ages 15–49 who are practicing, or whose sexual partners are practicing, any form of contraception. (United Nations Children's Fund and ICF International)

Deforestation is the permanent conversion of natural forest areas to other uses, including shifting cultivation, permanent agriculture, ranching, settlements, and infrastructure development. Deforested areas do not include areas logged but intended for regeneration or areas degraded by fuelwood gathering, acid precipitation, or forest fires. Negative numbers indicate an increase in forest area. (Food and Agriculture Organization)

Electricity use per capita is the production of power plants and combined heat and power plants less transmission, distribution, and transformation losses and own use by heat and power plants plus imports less exports divided by midyear population. (International Energy Agency)

Energy use per capita is the use of primary energy before transformation to other end-use fuels, which is equal to indigenous production plus imports and stock changes, minus exports and fuels supplied to ships and aircraft engaged in international transportation, divided by midyear population. (International Energy Agency)

Exports of goods and services are the value of all goods and other market services provided to the rest of the world, including the value of merchandise, freight, insurance, transport, travel, royalties, license fees, and other services. Compensation of employees, investment income (formerly called factor services), and transfer payments are excluded. (World Bank, Organisation for Economic Co-operation and Development, and United Nations)

Foreign direct investment, net inflows, are investments to acquire a lasting management interest in an enterprise operating in an economy other than that of the investor. They are the sum of inflows of equity capital, reinvestment of earnings, other long-term capital, and short-term capital as shown in the balance of payments. Net inflows refer to new investments made during the reporting period netted against disinvesments. (World Bank and International Monetary Fund)

Forests are land under natural or planted stands of trees, whether productive or not. (Food and Agriculture Organization)

Freshwater use is total freshwater withdrawals for domestic, industrial, and agricultural use, not counting evaporation losses from storage basins. Internal resources refer to internal renewable resources only (flows of rivers and groundwater from rainfall in the country). Withdrawals can exceed 100 percent of internal renewable resources because river flows from other countries are not included, because extraction from nonrenewable aquifers or desalination plants is considerable, or because there is significant water reuse. (Food and Agriculture Organization and World Resources Institute)

Glossary

GDP is gross domestic product at purchaser prices. It is the sum of gross value added by all resident producers in the economy plus any product taxes and minus any subsidies not included in the value of the products. It is calculated without deductions for depreciation of fabricated assets or for depletion and degradation of natural resources. (World Bank, Organisation for Economic Co-operation and Development, and United Nations)

GDP growth is the one-year rate of growth in real gross domestic product. (World Bank and Organisation for Economic Co-operation and Development)

GDP implicit price deflator is the one-year rate of price change in the economy as a whole. (World Bank, Organisation for Economic Co-operation and Development, and United Nations)

GNI is gross national income. It is calculated as gross domestic product (GDP) plus net receipts of primary income (employee compensation and investment income) from abroad. GDP is the sum of value added by all resident producers plus any product taxes (less subsidies) not included in the valuation of output. (World Bank)

GNI per capita is gross national income (GNI) converted to U.S. dollars using the World Bank Atlas method divided by midyear population. GNI is the sum of value added by all resident producers plus any product taxes (less subsidies) not included in the valuation of output plus net receipts of primary income (compensation of employees and property income) from abroad. GNI, calculated in national currency, is usually converted to U.S. dollars at official exchange rates for comparisons across economies. The World Bank Atlas method is used to smooth fluctuations in prices and exchange rates. It averages the exchange rate for a given year and the two preceding years, adjusted for differences in rates of inflation between the country and the Euro area, Japan, the United Kingdom, and the United States. (World Bank)

GNI, PPP, is gross national income (GNI) converted to international dollars using purchasing power parities (PPP). An international dollar has the same purchasing power over GNI that a U.S. dollar has in the United States. (World Bank)

GNI per capita, PPP, is gross national income (GNI) converted to international dollars using purchasing power parities (PPP), divided by midyear population. An international dollar has the same purchasing power over GNI that a U.S. dollar has in the United States. (World Bank)

Gross capital formation is outlays on additions to the fixed assets of the economy plus net changes in the level of inventories. Fixed assets include land improvements (fences, ditches, drains, and so on); plant, machinery, and equipment purchases; and the construction of roads, railways, and the like, including schools, offices, hospitals, private residential dwellings, and commercial and industrial buildings. Inventories are stocks of goods held by firms to meet temporary or unexpected fluctuations in production or sales and work in progress. According to the 1993 System of National Accounts, net acquisitions of valuables are also considered capital formation. (World Bank, Organisation for Economic Co-operation and Development, and United Nations)

Glossary

Gross secondary enrollment, total, is the ratio of total enrollment in secondary education, regardless of age, to the population of the age group that officially corresponds to secondary education. Secondary education completes the provision of basic education that begins at the primary level and aims at laying the foundations for lifelong learning and human development by offering more subject- or skill-oriented instruction using more specialized teachers. (United Nations Educational, Scientific and Cultural Organization Institute for Statistics)

High-technology exports are products with high research and development intensity, as in aerospace, computers, pharmaceuticals, scientific instruments and electrical machinery. (United Nations Statistics Division's Commodity Trade database)

HIV prevalence rate is the percentage of people ages 15–49 who are infected with HIV. (Joint United Nations Programme on HIV/AIDS and World Health Organization)

Imports of goods and services are the value of all goods and other market services received from the rest of the world, including the value of merchandise, freight, insurance, transport, travel, royalties, license fees and other services. Labor and property income (formerly called factor services) and transfer payments are excluded. (World Bank, Organisation for Economic Co-operation and Development, and United Nations)

Individuals using the Internet refers to the percentage of individuals who have used the Internet (from any location) in the last 12 months. Internet can be used via a computer, mobile phone, personal digital assistant, games machine, digital TV, etc. (International Telecommunication Union)

Life expectancy at birth is the number of years a newborn infant would live if prevailing patterns of mortality at the time of birth were to stay the same throughout life. (Eurostat, United Nations Population Division, and World Bank)

Merchandise trade is the sum of merchandise exports and imports measured in current U.S. dollars as a percentage of GDP. (World Trade Organization and World Bank)

Glossary

Military expenditures data from SIPRI are derived from the NATO definition, which includes all current and capital expenditures on the armed forces, including peacekeeping forces; defense ministries and other government agencies engaged in defense projects; paramilitary forces, if these are judged to be trained and equipped for military operations; and military space activities. Such expenditures include military and civil personnel, including retirement pensions of military personnel and social services for personnel; operation and maintenance; procurement; military research and development; and military aid (in the military expenditures of the donor country). Excluded are civil defense and current expenditures for previous military activities, such as for veterans' benefits, demobilization, conversion, and destruction of weapons. This definition cannot be applied for all countries, however, since that would require much more detailed information than is available about what is included in military budgets and off-budget military expenditure items. (For example, military budgets might or might not cover civil defense, reserves and auxiliary forces, police and paramilitary forces, dual-purpose forces such as military and civilian police, military grants in kind, pensions for military personnel, and social security contributions paid by one part of government to another.) (Stockholm International Peace Research Institute)

Mobile cellular subscriptions are subscriptions to a public mobile telephone service using cellular technology, which provide access to the public switched telephone network. Postpaid and prepaid subscriptions are included. (International Telecommunication Union)

Net barter terms of trade index is the ratio of the export unit value index to the corresponding import unit value index measured relative to the base year 2000. (United Nations Conference on Trade and Development and International Monetary Fund)

Net migration is the total number of immigrants less the total number of emigrants, including both citizens and noncitizens, during the period. Data are five-year estimates for 1985–90, 1995–2000, and 2005–10. (United Nations Population Division)

Net official development assistance received is official development assistance flows (net of repayment of principal) as defined by the Development Assistance Committee (DAC) that are made to countries and territories on the DAC list of aid recipients. (Organisation for Economic Co-operation and Development)

Paved roads are roads surfaced with crushed stone (macadam) and hydrocarbon binder or bituminized agents, with concrete, or with cobblestones, as a percentage of all the country's roads, measured in length. (International Road Federation)

Personal remittances received refers to personal transfers and compensation of employees. They comprise current transfers in cash or kind received by resident households from nonresident households and wages and salaries earned by nonresident workers or resident workers employed by nonresident entities. (International Monetary Fund and World Bank)

Glossary

Population is the midyear estimate of all residents regardless of legal status citizenship, except for refugees not permanently settled in the country of asylum who are generally considered part of the population of their country of origin. (Eurostat, United Nations Population Division, and World Bank)

Population below $1.25 a day is the percentage of the population living on less than $1.25 a day at 2005 international prices. Data are the most recent estimate since 2000. (World Bank)

Population growth is the exponential growth rate from the previous midyear population. (World Bank)

Primary completion rate, total, is the percentage of students completing the last year of primary school. It is calculated by dividing the total number of students in the last grade of primary school minus the number of repeaters in that grade by the total number of children of official completing age. Because of the change from the International Standard Classification of Education 1976 (ISCED76) to ISCED97, data for years before 1999 are not fully comparable with data for 1999 onward. (United Nations Educational, Scientific and Cultural Organization Institute for Statistics)

Ratio of girls to boys in primary and secondary school is the ratio of the female to male gross enrollment rate in primary and secondary school. (United Nations Educational, Scientific and Cultural Organization Institute for Statistics)

Share of poorest 20% in national consumption or income is the share of total national income or consumption that accrues to the poorest quintile. (World Bank)

Starting a business is the number of calendar days needed to complete the procedures to legally operate a business. If a procedure can be expedited at additional cost, the fastest procedure, independent of cost, is chosen. Data listed for 2012 are for June 2013. (World Bank)

Stock market capitalization is the share price times the number of shares outstanding. (Standard and Poor's)

Surface area is a country's total area, including areas under inland bodies of water and some coastal waterways. (Food and Agriculture Organization)

Total debt service is the sum of principal repayments and interest actually paid on long-term debt (public and publicly guaranteed and private nonguaranteed); interest paid on short-term debt; and repayments (repurchases and charges) to the International Monetary Fund, expressed as a percentage of exports of goods and services and primary income. Exports of goods and services and primary income are the total value of exports of goods and services, receipts of compensation of nonresident workers, and investment income from abroad. (World Bank and International Monetary Fund)

Glossary

Total external debt stocks are debt owed to nonresident creditors and repayable in foreign currencies, goods, or services by public and private entities in the country. They are the sum of long-term external debt, short-term debt, and use of International Monetary Fund credit. Debt repayable in domestic currency is excluded. (World Bank)

Total fertility rate is the number of children that would be born to a woman if she were to live to the end of her childbearing years and bear children in accordance with current age-specific fertility rates. (Eurostat, United Nations Population Division, and World Bank)

Under-five mortality rate is the probability that a newborn baby will die before age five if subject to current age-specific mortality rates. (United Nations Children's Fund, World Health Organization, World Bank, and United Nations Population Division)

Value added in agriculture is the net output of agriculture (International Standard Industrial Classification divisions 1–5 including forestry and fishing) after totaling outputs and subtracting intermediate outputs. (World Bank, Organisation for Economic Co-operation and Development, and United Nations)

Value added in industry is the net output of industry (International Standard Industrial Classification divisions 10–45, which includes mining, manufacturing, construction, electricity, water, and gas) after totaling outputs and subtracting intermediate inputs. (World Bank, Organisation for Economic Co-operation and Development, and United Nations)

Value added in services is the net output of services (International Standard Industrial Classification divisions 50–99) after totaling outputs and subtracting intermediate inputs. This sector is derived as a residual and may not properly reflect the sum of services outputs, including banking and financial services. (World Bank, Organisation for Economic Co-operation and Development, and United Nations)